# The Illustrated
# Reference Book of
# Ancient History

# Picture Credits

*The Illustrated Reference Book of Ancient History*
This edition published in 1982 by
**WINDWARD**
an imprint owned by W. H. Smith & Son Limited
Registered No. 237811 England Trading as WHS Distributors St John's House East Street Leicester LE1 6NE

© Mitchell Beazley Encyclopaedias Limited 1980, 1982

Pages 2–159 © Mitchell Beazley Encyclopaedias Limited 1976 and 1977

Artwork © Mitchell Beazley Publishers Limited 1970, 1971, 1972, 1973, 1974, 1975 and 1976
© International Visual Resource 1972
© Mitchell Beazley Encyclopaedias Limited 1976

ISBN 0 7112 0244 3

Phototypeset in Great Britain by Filmtype Services Limited, Scarborough
Printed in Yugoslavia by Mladinska Knjiga

The Joy of Knowledge
GENERAL EDITOR: JAMES MITCHELL

# The Illustrated Reference Book of Ancient History

**WINDWARD**

# Preface

## How to use this book

*Ancient History* is one complete section of *The Joy of Knowledge*. It contains all the general knowledge my editors and I think most interesting about the history of man from his earliest beginnings to the thirteenth century. It is intended to be an informative, easily understood guide through this fascinating field of study.

**The spread system**
Every topic in *The Joy of Knowledge* takes the form of an article that occupies two facing pages of text and pictures; what we call a "spread". Each two-page spread in the book is organized in the same way. It is the heart of our approach to explaining things.

The spread system is a strict discipline but once you get used to it we hope you'll find the structure to be systematic and reassuring. You should start to feel at home in all sorts of unlikely areas of knowledge with the spread system to guide you. It works like this.

Each two-page spread in *Ancient History,* as throughout *The Joy of Knowledge,* tells a self-contained story. It explains all the essential facts you need to know about its subject in as efficient a manner as possible. We believe that the discipline of having to get in all the essential and relevant facts in this comparatively small space actually makes for better results than a rambling essay could achieve – text that has to get straight to the point, pictures and diagrams that illustrate the salient points in a clear and comprehensible fashion, and captions that really work and explain the point of the pictures.

The spreads are, in a sense, the building blocks of knowledge. Like the various circuits and components that go to make up a computer, they are also systematically "programmed" to help the reader find out things more easily and remember them better. Each spread, for example, has a main article of about 850 words summarising the subject. This article is illustrated by an average of ten pictures and diagrams, the captions of which both complement and supplement the basic information in the main article. Each spread, too, has a "key" picture or diagram in the top right-hand corner. The purpose of this picture is twofold: it summarises the story of the spread visually and it is intended to act as a memory stimulator to help you recall all the integrated facts and pictures on a given subject.

**Where to start**
A good way to begin acquiring knowledge from this particular part of *The Joy of Knowledge* is initially to read the Introduction. The Introduction provides a useful framework for the information contained in the following pages. If, however, you prefer to plunge straight into the book (but don't have much basic general knowledge on the subject) I suggest you look first at the spreads "The tools of history" beginning on page 2, "The development of archaeology" on page 4, "Beginnings of agriculture" on page 6 and "Europe 1200–500 BC" on page 46. Once you have absorbed the information on these spreads you can build up a more comprehensive general knowledge by exploring the rest of the book.

*Ancient History* is an absorbing book about the lives and deeds of people who inhabited the earth before us and have undoubtedly influenced the way we live today. I hope you will find it both stimulating and helpful.

# Contents

# Editor's introduction

Many historical accounts written before the eighteenth century were either compilations of existing oral tradition, such as much of the Bible, or accounts of contemporary events, such as Julius Caesar's commentaries on those Gallic and civil wars in which he had himself played the leading part. There were backward-looking historians, but the studious and scientific investigation of the past is largely a modern development. Why should we, and our recent forebears, have become so interested in our antecedents?

Part of the answer lies in the effect that the Industrial Revolution of the late eighteenth and early nineteenth centuries had on our perception of the world. In the relatively static world of a predominantly rural, agrarian economy, the common man had no need to enquire in what way his life differed from that of previous generations. He knew what the answer was, namely, that in its essentials it did not differ. He tilled the ground, reaped the harvest, feared for the weather, and watched his family stricken down by disease in much the same way that his grandfather and his grandfather's grandfather had. In pre-industrial society, apart from a few cataclysmic events, such as the Black Death, most of the changes that did occur were spread so gradually over the centuries as to be barely perceptible. It required several thousand years for the completion of the first agricultural revolution, that decisive change in man's way of supporting himself. By comparison, the Industrial Revolution was a lightning affair. And whatever the character of the revolution which we are currently undergoing – whether "nuclear" or "electronic" – it promises to be even faster than the Industrial Revolution.

We see about us almost daily evidence that human society is constantly in a process of change. This leads to our asking "what did things use to be like?". We wish to understand the chain of past events in order to gain some notion of how we arrived at our present condition. Of course, if all things changed, so that the life of a society bore no resemblance to that of its predecessors, the study of history would be powerless to tell us anything about ourselves. The past would be an alien world, stubbornly withholding any clues to the progress of our development. But the changes that have taken place have done so against a backdrop of continuity. Historians are as eager to establish points of continuity as they are to discover moments of change. Such an approach is essential if we are to profit from their study because only by comparing the past with our age can we discover and avoid the pitfalls that beset our ancestors.

We use the word "history" in two senses. In everyday language the words "history" and "the past" are often taken to mean the same thing. In its proper use, the word "history" means the *recorded* past. The history of the eighth century is not the aggregate of all the things that happened during the century; on the contrary, it is merely the interpretation that historians have put upon the scattered fragments of evidence which survive from that period. We should remember, too, that much of the surviving evidence is simply not used by historians, either because it has not yet been discovered or, just as frequently, because it has not been deemed worthy of notice. The death of a miller in Chester in 1387 may be recorded and preserved in a parish register; but until some historian picks up that fact and uses it, it lies buried in the past, awaiting the day when it will be given historical significance. Moreover, the longer it stays undiscovered the more likely is the possibility that it will be lost forever.

The raw materials of history are, therefore, much to the frustration of historians, nothing more than small fragments. In addition, these often carry their own bias. Our picture of a past age often depends upon what men of the time considered important enough to be recorded. For instance, our view of the later Middle Ages as an age of faith, although undoubtedly not an entirely mistaken view, relies greatly upon the circumstance that almost the only literate men of those days were monks and clerics. It is hardly surprising that their annals should have a distinctly religious and ecclesiastical colouring.

The nature of historical evidence, then, leads us to accept the judgement of the late nineteenth-century American philosopher, William James, that history is the most difficult of the "sciences" because no historian can place confidence in a single statement that he makes.

This informative volume traces the history of man from his earliest hominid beginnings, through the rise and fall of early civilizations, to the faint, dawning rays of that intellectual and essentially urban revival which was to issue in the full sunlight of the Renaissance. Until the development of written language by the Sumerians, and indeed for some time beyond, historians are largely dependent upon the inferences that they are able to draw from archaeological evidence: fossil remains, cave drawings, traces of buildings and the like. Evidence of men's diet, and therefore of their social customs, can also be found by the examination of soil. In the past two decades or so, our "knowledge" of man's

prehistory has grown substantially and has become more refined. This results partly from the use of new scientific aids, such as radio-carbon dating and partly from the great increase in the number of scholars engaged in prehistorical research. We are now able to construct with some clarity the outlines, at least, of prehistoric man's economy, trade, housing, and political and social organization.

From the earliest centres of civilization in the Near East of the 3rd millennium BC – the three great early civilizations, the Egyptian on the Nile, the Mesopotamian on the Tigris and the Euphrates, and the civilization of the Indus valley were all founded on the banks of major river systems – the history of literate man spreads itself across Europe and Asia. That history has, what seems to us, its peaks and its troughs; and certain themes stand out in our imagination above others. Our interest naturally dwells on the splendid achievements of the Greeks and the Romans, whose legacy to the culture of Europe has been rich and enduring. But we should not forget that in other parts of the world, in China and Japan, and in South and Central America, highly sophisticated civilizations were also making their unique contributions to the development of human society. Of special concern to us is the growth of religion, not only the rise of medieval Western Christendom, with its ambition of a world united in one faith and one body politic in the Holy Roman Empire, ruled jointly by Pope and Emperor, but also the triumphant spread of Buddhism and Islam over the greater part of the Asian and Arabian world.

The spread of Christianity and the Barbarian invasions coincided with the disruption and finally the demise of the Roman

Empire. The centuries that followed used to be called the "Dark Ages". Historians nowadays shy away from such tendentious language. Of course, in one sense at least, those centuries were dark enough. The vigorous scientific tradition of the Greeks was allowed to wither; its revival awaited the restless curiosity which is the stamp of the Renaissance mental spirit, imbued with an impatient scepticism of the prevailing wisdom which held that all natural phenomena received an adequate description in religious language.

The outstanding feature of European social organization before the fourteenth century is the evolution of the feudal system, that system of land tenure and of social, political and military organization which, despite local variations, was remarkably uniform throughout western Europe. How the feudal system actually worked, and the conflicts between central, kingly authority and the local sway of powerful, land engrossing barons to which it gave rise, varied significantly from region to region. Nevertheless, the essential principles were the same everywhere. It is therefore appropriate that in this thoughtful book emphasis is laid upon the British example of the feudal system. To have given equal treatment to all parts of western Europe would have meant sacrificing depth of analysis to breadth. One other seeming omission is worthy of remark: the early civilizations of pre-Columbian America. It is reasonable to say that the American continents do not impinge upon European and Asian history until the great age of exploration, that is, until the fifteenth century, and their treatment should be postponed to *The Ages of Discovery,* the volume that follows this one, in which the history of the Americas is taken back to its beginnings.

# The tools of history

In his search for knowledge of the past, the historian uses various sources. The earliest historians relied largely on eye-witnesses, hearsay and word-of-mouth tradition. But England's first true historian, the Venerable Bede (673–735), also used written documents. Historians today extend their search even more widely. Government records for taxation and parish records tell about economic affairs. Art and poetry reveal cultural and spiritual life. Place-names show what diverse peoples have come to form a nation. Archaeology exposes many aspects of both rural and urban life that are described in no documents. And for the long prehistoric era leading up to the invention of writing, archaeology provides the only evidence.

## Written records of King Arthur

The historian of early times often has to learn to use documents compiled long after the events they describe, or which copy, perhaps inaccurately, records that were contemporary. Or he may find legends and traditions wrapped round a kernel of fact, so that he has to peel off later fictions from a central truth.

A good example of the many tools used by historians to decipher fact from the most obscure evidence is the search for a historical basis of the semi-legendary King Arthur. In the period after the collapse of the Roman Empire in the fifth century AD, Anglo-Saxons from the far side of the North Sea and Scots from Ireland seized much of Britain from the native Britons and Picts, and in doing so created the basic racial mix of the British people. Our primary source for the recording of these events, the sixth-century British monk Gildas, describes a wholesale slaughter of the Britons by the pagan Saxons.

Gildas also records a great British victory over the invaders at Mount Badon [8], a battle that came to be associated with the name of Arthur. Most people think of Arthur as the idealized chivalrous king described by Thomas Malory in *Le Morte d'Arthur* (1470), or *The Idylls of the King*, by Alfred, Lord Tennyson (1809–92), or in even later versions of these romantic tales. It is often assumed that such a figure must be mythical.

But by his study of the sources the historian can remove successive layers of romance to reach the historical truth. Arthur was first described as a great emperor in the twelfth century in the *History of the Kings of Britain* by Geoffrey of Monmouth (c. 1100–54). Three centuries earlier the British writer Nennius represented Arthur as the war-leader of the Britons against the Saxons [1]. In his own day, records kept in a Welsh monastery refer to the victory of Badon, (now thought to have been fought c. 490), and to Arthur's death along with Mordred's at the battle of Camlann.

This establishes Arthur as an historic personage – a great warrior, although not a king, who defended Britain against the Saxons. This is all the written documents can tell us. For further information we have to rely on the findings of the archaeologist.

## The techniques of archaeology

Archaeology studies the physical remains of the past, and so gains insight into the material culture and living conditions of the characters of history. If documents prove that Arthur was a great war leader, then archaeology can show the kind of base that he may have

---

**1 Medieval manuscripts** were handwritten, and errors or extraneous ideas might occur during later copying. This 9th-century account of the 12 battles that Arthur is said to have fought is by the Welsh monk Nennius, and is thought to have been a summary of an early Welsh poem of which no other record exists. None of the battle sites can be located with certainty, and the description of the battle at Mt Badon "in which 960 enemy fell in a single attack by Arthur" shows how the inflation of Arthur into a superhuman hero was under way by the time of Nennius. Arthur is called "leader of battles" for the British kings, a statement more likely to have been factual.

**2 Cadbury Castle, Somerset**, has been identified with Camelot, Arthur's court, since at least 1540. But in fact Camelot was simply the invention of 12th-century poets. Archaeological excavation, however, shows that Cadbury might instead have been the strong base or rallying point that Arthur needed to defend Britain against the Anglo-Saxons. The hill-fort had been first built c. 500 BC, but was refortified with a stone and timber rampart and gates that can be dated to AD 460–540, the years in which Arthur flourished. The fort was strategically situated to resist any westward drive of the Anglo-Saxons from Wessex towards the Bristol Channel.

---

**4 Tintagel Castle, Cornwall**, on a superbly defensible headland, was built in its present form in the 12th century. It has been linked with Arthurian legend since the work of Geoffrey of Monmouth, but probably was used in Arthur's day as a Celtic monastery. Mediterranean style pots of that period have been found there.

---

| | Key |
|---|---|
| | Late Saxon town wall |
| | Arthurian rampart AD 460–550 |
| | Roman period (site abandoned) |
| | Iron Age IV (ended AD 45–61) |
| | Iron Age III |
| | Iron Age II |
| | Iron Age I 500 BC |
| | Late Bronze Age |

**3 Stratification**, the overlaying of earlier buildings by later ones, provides the basic clues by which archaeologists unravel the story of the past, particularly for a complex defensive system such as at Cadbury Camelot. Illustrated here is a schematic representation of the side of a trench excavated through the innermost of the four banks of the hillfort. At the base is the ground surface where the first Iron Age defence was built c. 500 BC. Below this was found pottery of the late Bronze Age, c. 1000 BC. The Iron Age Rampart I had a frame of wood that soon decayed, making it necessary to build Rampart II. This also collapsed and was followed by two other ramparts. The last, Rampart IV, was destroyed by the Romans in AD 45–61. After being abandoned for a long time, a new bank rampart was built. This was overlaid by a Late Saxon town wall about AD 1010, so it must be earlier than that, but later than the Iron Age. Contemporary pots suggest the date 460–550, the period of Arthur.

fortified [2, 6], and the weapons, jewellery and equipment that his followers used.

A wide armoury of techniques is used to discover ancient sites, including walking the countryside, air-photography which gives a map-like view of sites [2, 4, 7], and geophysical prospecting to reveal ancient fireplaces, rubbish pits and other disturbances of the ground. Excavation is a precisely controlled process that seeks to recover the faintest traces of collapsed or decayed buildings [6].

For dating, the archaeologist traditionally relies on stratification [3], or layering, to reveal how later buildings lie on top of earlier ones; and typology [5] which compares developing types of the same class of object. The techniques of typology are familiar to anyone who can estimate the date and make of a motor car by its appearance.

### Dating archaeological finds

In historical periods, written references to sites, inscriptions, and dated coins, all help to establish chronology. Stratification and typology can only establish the relative age of sites and objects; not how old they are in absolute years. For this several scientific techniques have been developed. Some of these depend on radioactive decay, measuring the extent of the decay of the radioactive carbon present in all living things.

Another practice, that of tree-ring dating or dendrochronology, studies the annual growth rings of trees. The width of the rings varies from year to year in a distinctive rhythm. Counting back from the present, it is possible to match early phases of the rhythm on living trees with that on timber beams in ancient buildings. The tree-ring count may be extended backwards for thousands of years.

These techniques are most useful in prehistory, but they can also be applied to historic times. A clear example of this is the dating of the Winchester Round Table [Key]. Typological study of the carpentry suggests a date in the mid-fourteenth century. Radiocarbon and tree-ring dates are consistent with this. Our historical knowledge of the growth of chivalrous ideals points to the same period. The table is part of the Arthurian legend; but it tells us nothing about the historic war leader of the Britons.

**The Winchester Round Table** can be shown, using historical tools, to have been made almost 1,000 years later than the period of the real King Arthur. History thus separates fact from fiction.

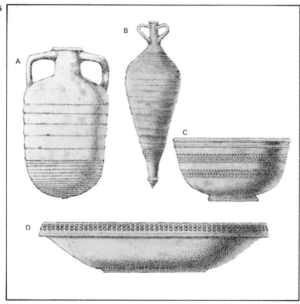

**5 The study of pots** is central to the archaeologist's interpretation of the past. These reconstructed two-handled jars, [A, B] found at Cadbury, each about 50 cm (20 in) tall, once contained Mediterranean wine for church services and princely feasts. The red dish [D] was also from the Mediterranean. Other pots have crosses inside the bowls and may have had a liturgical use. The grey bowl [C] came from Bordeaux, perhaps with wine in wooden casks. Such pots found on sites in Britain reveal trade links and are important for dating, because in Greece similar pots can be dated by coins found with them, and these dates can then be transferred to their British sites.

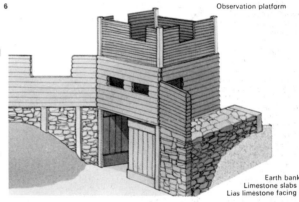

Observation platform

Earth bank
Limestone slabs
Lias limestone facing

**6 Reconstructions of the buildings** can be attempted from the archaeologist's study of the foundations, as in this gateway and rampart of the Arthurian period at Cadbury Castle. The remains consisted of the lower stones of the wall face; the pits in which the timber posts had stood; and dark stains in the ground where wood had rotted. If the tower has been correctly restored, its design may copy that of Roman military gate towers. But the rampart itself, with its use of timber and unmortared stone is very primitive. It reveals the sharp decline of technology in the post-Roman centuries.

**7 Glastonbury, Somerset,** has many ancient legends. In 1191 monks at Glastonbury Abbey claimed to have found the tombs of Arthur and his wife Guenevere. All trace of these tombs subsequently disappeared. The claim attracted great interest at the time, when the legend of Arthur was beginning to spread beyond purely Welsh legend. Although it may have been made to attract visitors to the monastery to contribute to a building programme, it is possible that the pair were indeed buried in the grounds of the Celtic monastery that originally occupied the site. Mediterranean wine jars of the 5th and 6th centuries have been found on Glastonbury Tor, (shown here), about 20km (12 miles) northwest of Cadbury.

**8 Places linked with Arthur** (historic or legendary), are widespread in Britain. Most of the names connected with Arthur or with King Mark and Tristan (Trusty) have no genuine historical significance. They show a popular habit of naming ancient ruins after long-dead heroes. But Mote of Mark and Cadbury Castle both have produced pottery of c. AD 500 and were fortified in Arthur's period – the 5th and 6th centuries. Killibury is probably Arthur's court of Celliwig, that was mentioned in early Welsh traditions. At least six sites are suggested, on place-name grounds, as possible locations for the historic battle of Mt Badon, Arthur's most important victory. The most probable is a hill near Bath.

✕ Possible sites of battle of Mt Badon
🛡 Places associated with Arthurian legend

0    100km

Trusty's Hill
Arthur's Seat
Mote of Mark
Round Table
Camulodunum
Arthur's Stone
Caerwent
Caerleon
Liddington
Camulodunum
Arthur's Stone
Cadbury
Glastonbury
Tintagel
Callington
Killibury
Winchester

# The development of archaeology

Man's interest in his own remote past effectively began with the Renaissance, although the urge to know about our ancestors is an ancient one, Nabonidus, for instance, last King of Babylon, excavated the foundation stone of a temple 3,200 years earlier than his reign to find out how old it was.

## The knowledge of the Renaissance

During the Renaissance two important things happened. The texts of classical authors, such as Lucretius' *De rerum natura*, became widely disseminated by the printing press, so that their discussion of earlier ages of stone, bronze and iron and of the evolution of society from savagery through barbarism into civilization was firmly implanted in the educated minds of the age. Secondly, the age of exploration revealed the New World of America where a stone age technology was still in active use and where the civilization of the Aztec was just developing bronze.

The Renaissance tradition spread from Italy northwards to France and England, where it was reflected in Henry VIII's Palace of Nonsuch, and collecting Greek and Roman statues and vases became a fashionable occupation for the wealthy in Elizabethan and Jacobean England.

The middle classes had a classical education in the grammar schools, where they covered the range of Shakespeare's knowledge but lacked the financial resources to collect or go on the Grand Tour. Their attention therefore turned to the antiquities of their own region. In the work of scholars such as John Leland (*c.* 1506-52) and William Camden (1551–1623) [1], the English antiquarian tradition was born in the sixteenth century, continuing to develop through the seventeenth with such notable figures as John Aubrey (1626–97), Thomas Browne (1605–82) and, later, William Stukeley (1687–1765).

## Developments in Scandinavia

In Scandinavia the work of Johan Bure in Sweden and Ole Worm (1588–1644) in Denmark in the first half of the seventeenth century led to a parallel development, with more state involvement and a greater degree of protection being extended to antiquities.

A similar attitude in England followed the creation of the Royal Society in 1660.

The period of the Enlightenment saw speculation on the social origins of man, and from the stimulus of John Locke (1632–1704), the French and Scottish schools of thought evolved the notion of social typology (the study of types) and the development of society from the family through the band and the tribe to civilized urban groups with kings. This idea, itself a revival of classical thought, was later to prove crucial in the emergence of social anthropology under Edward Tylor (1832–1917) and Lewis Morgan (1818–81).

In the latter part of the eighteenth century evidence accumulated to show that the earth was very old, much older than the biblical date for its creation of 4004 BC. From the work of the geologist James Hutton (1726–97) in 1785 to the publication of the *Principles of Geology* by Charles Lyell (1797–1875) in 1833, a revolution in thought occurred in which the earth was recognized as immensely old and biblical chronology as wrong [Key]. In 1859 the

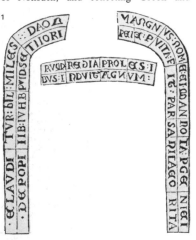

1 **The earliest illustration** of an archaeological monument to appear in a book was a typographical arrangement depicting in a stylized manner the inscription to the hermit Magnus, a prince from Scandinavia. This still stands outside the church of St John sub Castro at Lewes in Sussex. The picture appeared in the late 16th century in the 2nd edition of William Camden's famous *Britannia*, the first serious work in English on the subject of antiquities.

2 **Stonehenge**, in Wiltshire, is an outstanding megalithic monument that has long been one of the most notable and controversial sites in Britain. King James I sent Inigo Jones (1573–1652) to draw plans of it and Jones's account, describing it as a Roman temple, was published in the 1660s, setting off a violent argument in which it was ascribed by various scholars to the Danes, Saxons, Druids and ancient Britons. The first of these views shows the influence of contemporary Scandinavian scholars, particularly Ole Worm. In the late 17th century it was attributed to the Druids although it is much older than this.

3 **The great mound at Grave Creek, Miss.**, was excavated in the mid-19th century, more than 50 years after President Jefferson had undertaken a similar excavation in Virginia. A great stimulus to American archaeology was the continued presence of Stone Age Indians.

4 **Hissarlik in Turkey** was claimed by Heinrich Schliemann as the site of Homer's Troy. Schliemann was obsessed with uncovering the Homeric world and in the 1870s and 1880s excavated at Mycenae and Ithaca as well as Troy. At Hissarlik he uncovered a collection of Bronze Age jewellery which he claimed was "Priam's Treasure" and smuggled out of Turkey. He thought the second of the seven superimposed settlements he excavated was Homer's Troy, but it is now known to be too early.

Royal Society in London heard two of its most distinguished members accept the antiquity of man and in the same year Charles Darwin's *On the Origin of Species by Means of Natural Selection* raised new speculations as to where man had come from.

**Discovery in the Near East**

The middle of the nineteenth century was also the period when the great Near East civilizations were discovered. Mesopotamia saw the work of Austen Layard (1817–94) in the 1840s at Nineveh and the fierce rivalry of French and British archaeologists to loot the mounds of Assyrian and Babylonian sculpture. In the 1870s Heinrich Schliemann (1822–90) [4] dug at Troy and Mycenae and brought to the world the glories of Bronze Age Greece, a previously unknown civilization, the ancestor of which was uncovered at Knossos in Crete from 1900 onwards.

The increased length of man's history and the multitude of new discoveries of the prehistoric period were brought within a chronological scheme of successive Stone, Bronze and Iron Ages. This was first applied to museum material by Christian Thomsen (1788–1865) in Copenhagen in 1816, it was subsequently proved stratigraphically (by the geological study of strata) by his successor Jens Worsaae (1821–85) and elaborated internally by the Swede Oscar Nontelius (1843–1921).

A concern for better excavation methods to acquire archaeological information was typified by the work of Augustus Pitt-Rivers (1827–1900), who between 1880 and 1900 set a standard still unrivalled for comprehensive recording. At the same time in Egypt Flinders Petrie (1853–1942) was trying to do the same under far worse conditions.

In a sense the development of prehistoric studies that began with Gordon Childe (1892–1957) in the 1920s continues. The ancestry of man is being pushed still further back in time under the impact of the work of Louis Leakey (1903–72) in Africa. The parallel development of archaeological thought in the Americas affects Old World ideas more strongly (and vice versa), and archaeology is becoming more of a unified discipline across the world.

This flint hand axe, (top and side views shown), came from Hoxne, Suffolk. John Frere sent it to the Society of Antiquaries in 1797, suggesting that it had a great age, "even beyond that of the known world". Frere's attitude reflects contemporary ideas in geology and about man's antiquity.

**5 Howard Carter** (1873–1939), right, directed the excavation of the tomb of Tutankhamen. In 1922 he located the entrance, cleared it and discovered "wonderful things" inside after a long and frustrating campaign. Tutankhamen was a boy king who died aged 18; the construction of later tombs above his own covered the entrance and preserved it from almost certain looting.

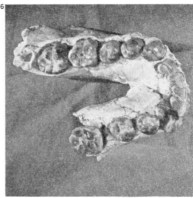

**6 The jawbone** of one of man's earliest ancestors, *Homo habilis*, was found at Olduvai Gorge in Tanzania by Louis and Mary Leakey. Their work there and the later extension of it to Lake Rudolf by their son Richard has taken the ancestry of man back (in less than 20 years) from under one million to nearly five million years. "Handy man" was found to be nearly 1.75 million years old.

**7 Sir Mortimer Wheeler** (1890–1976) worked on sites from Roman Wales to the mysterious Indus civilization in Pakistan. He was also founder of the Institute of Archaeology at London University and did much to make archaeology popular.

**8 The Inca village of Machu Picchu,** high in the Andes, was discovered in 1912 by Hiram Bingham (1875–1956) of Yale University. It was the first time that a late Inca settlement in such a good state of preservation had been found by archaeologists.

# Beginnings of agriculture

Until the Neolithic or New Stone Age the domestication of plants and animals was little practised. Agriculture developed at different times and rates in different places, and took various forms: plant-cultivation, pastoralism and mixed farming. Although the switch from total dependence on food gathering to the beginnings of food production was a gradual evolution, its long-term effects were nothing short of a revolution. Every food plant and animal of importance today was domesticated during the Neolithic.

### The first farmers and herdsmen
Early in the eighth millennium BC cereals were cultivated and animals herded between latitudes 30° and 40° N, over an area stretching for a thousand miles from Anatolia to Iran [1]. This region offered a variety of wild plants and animals that could be domesticated. Early man found wheat and barley growing on the uplands, and goats [4] and sheep grazing on the slopes. Indeed, the wide variety of ecological zones and natural resources would have enabled hunters, fishermen and foodgatherers to live a semi-

sedentary life even after the end of the last Ice Age, about 8000 BC.

Initially the growth of agriculture and herding was slow and haphazard. Wild grain would have been collected and dropped round the settlement and hunters probably captured young animals and brought them home. In these early stages of farming it is not easy to distinguish between wild and domesticated flora and fauna. Animals evolved smaller forms and there were gradual changes, for example in the size and shape of horns. From the number of bones unearthed at Zawi Chemi Shanidar in northern Iraq, it seems that sheep may have been herded on the Iranian plateau as early as 8500 BC and goats not long after.

Evidence of cereal cultivation is harder to prove; cereals are preserved only in exceptional circumstances. Grain carbonized as a result of fire, or impressions left in clay ovens or storage pits, are often the only clues that remain. However, it is known that selection, promoted by some significant mutations, resulted in higher-yielding grain. Some of the evidence provided by Neolithic sites may be

purely circumstantial – the discovery of sickles need not necessarily imply cultivation. Experiments in Anatolia using stone-bladed reaping knives [5] showed that one family would have been able to collect enough wild wheat during three weeks' work to provide for them for a whole year.

### Early Neolithic settlements
Most of the early Neolithic sites were located near springs and were occupied for thousands of years. Enormous mounds or "tells" accumulated from the remains of mud-brick houses and generations of rubbish provide archaeologists with a rich store of information. One of the most thoroughly investigated sites is Tell es Sultan at Jericho, which must have housed as many as 3,000 people during the "Pre-Pottery" Neolithic period around 7000 BC. Catal Hüyük in Anatolia, the largest known trading centre, was four times the size of Pre-Pottery Jericho by 6000 BC and may have been a sizeable settlement much earlier, although the earliest levels have not yet been excavated. It probably had a monopoly of nearby sources of obsidian,

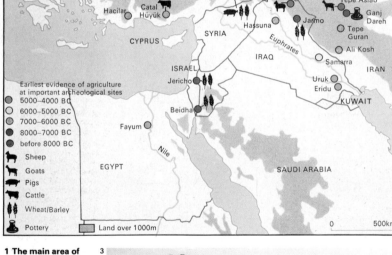

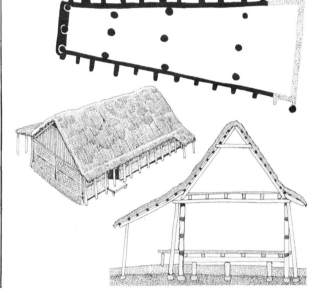

**1 The main area of food production** stretched from the Zagros mountains in Iran to the Taurus mountains of Anatolia and down the Jordan Rift. Earliest signs of herding are in Iran c. 8500 BC. Irrigation was carried out in the Tigris/Euphrates basin c. 5000 BC so that the alluvial land could be farmed.

**3 Tassili N'Ajjer,** an 800km-long (500 miles), eroded sandstone plateau in the Sahara, contains tens of thousands of rock paintings and engravings. The cattle and wild animals that flourished in the equable climate about 3000 BC are superbly depicted, but no other evidence exists to help identify the ancient inhabitants of this region.

**2 The longhouses of central Europe** and Scandinavia are known of from the first half of the 5th millennium BC. The one shown here is a reconstruction of an excavation at Deiringsen-Ruploh in Westphalia. It was just over 16m (52ft) long, about 8m (26ft) wide and the same in height. Long houses were normally rectangular, but the trapezoidal shape (as here) seems to have been a recognized variant. Many long-houses appear to have been divided in two, but whether this was to separate living quarters from storage is not known. The buildings were constructed on a timber frame.

**4 The bezoar** (Capra hircus aegagrus), the wild ancestor of domesticated goats, still lives in the mountains of southwestern Asia. Goats and sheep were kept in herds before 8000 BC, the first animals to be domesticated.

**5 Grain was first harvested with sickles** made from stone insets in a bone or wooden shaft. This example comes from the Fayum, Egypt.

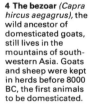

6

the chief material for tool-making: copper and marble were also obtained from the mountains and shells from the Mediterranean. Pottery, weaving and other arts and crafts reached a high standard. Religious beliefs centred on the worship of a fertility goddess, depicted in plaster reliefs, and a cult of the dead: wall paintings show vultures hovering over headless human corpses. However, the dominant theme in the shrines was the bull symbol of virility.

Reasonably secure in their settlements and supported by an agrarian economy Neolithic populations increased rapidly. With irrigation – which may have been introduced at Jericho – it was possible to expand into the lowlands of Mesopotamia. A settlement at Hassuna in the north dates from before 6000 BC, and a thousand years later the alluvial plains of the Tigris/Euphrates were being exploited at Eridu in the far south. Mesopotamia now became the heartland of Neolithic culture, laying the foundations for Sumerian civilization.

Meanwhile food production spread from Anatolia to Greece and on into Europe.

Land cleared by slashing and burning enabled agriculturalists to exploit the fertile soils of the Danube basin; and at the same time the megalith builders [12] were moving round the coasts of western Europe.

### The staple crops of different cultures

The civilizations of western Asia and Europe were founded on wheat and barley, which are adapted to temperate climates and the subtropics, while millet, rice and maize are better suited to the tropics. Rice was cultivated in India earlier than in China, where millet was the main crop (and the pig the main domesticated animal) until about 2000 BC. In subsaharan Africa edible tuber cultivation may have preceded that of cereals (millet and sorghum), although there is no conclusive archaeological evidence. However, the evidence of numerous rock paintings shows that about 3000 BC pastoralists were able to find grazing all over the Sahara [3] in the period before the area became entirely desert. In Mexico primitive maize was cultivated by 5000 BC, but there were no fully sedentary populations in America before 1500 BC.

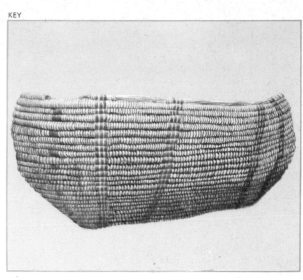

**Wheat and barley** were the staples of Neolithic economy in the Middle East. By about 4500 BC these cereals had spread from there to Egypt. This 40cm-long (16in) basket is made of coiled flax and may have been used for sowing. It was discovered in a grain storage pit in the Fayum.

**6 Skara Brae, in the Orkney Islands,** was occupied by herdsmen and fishermen around 1800 BC. As there was no wood on the island houses and furniture were made of stone. One village includes eight connected huts, each with a hearth, two slabs for beds, and a dresser and wall cupboards.

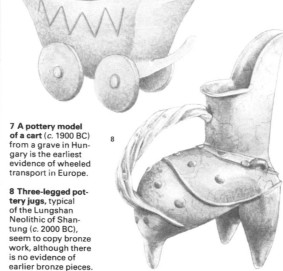

**7 A pottery model of a cart** (c. 1900 BC) from a grave in Hungary is the earliest evidence of wheeled transport in Europe.

**8 Three-legged pottery jugs,** typical of the Lungshan Neolithic of Shantung (c. 2000 BC), seem to copy bronze work, although there is no evidence of earlier bronze pieces.

**9 This beaker from Siyalk, Iran,** was made about 4000 BC, by which time the potter's wheel was in use. The earliest Neolithic settlements in western Asia have no pottery, the first appearing about 7000 BC. In Japan the Jómon culture pottery predates agriculture by several millennia.

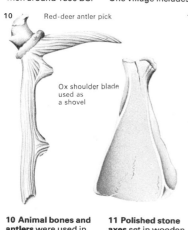

Red-deer antler pick

Ox shoulder blade used as a shovel

**10 Animal bones and antlers** were used in flint mining, which was an important Neolithic industry in western Europe. At Grime's Graves, Norfolk, shafts were sunk through the chalk and galleries tunnelled to reach the flint layers.

Neolithic flint axe

**11 Polished stone axes** set in wooden hafts were used for forest clearance and carpentry. The flints and other rocks used for these highly efficient tools were shaped in "axe factories". Their provenance tells us much about trade routes.

**12 Mnajdra,** one of the many fine megalithic temples in Malta, is trefoil-shaped and dates from the early Copper Age (c. 2800 BC). The first colonists of the island arrived from Sicily about 4000 BC. A thousand years later, collective burials in rock-cut chambers eventually gave rise to elaborate temples unique to Malta. Built of huge upright slabs surmounted by corbelled blocks, they are often decorated with carvings. There was a cult of the dead, with altars for animal sacrifices; corpulent female statues indicate the worship of a mother-goddess. The megalithic tradition extended from the eastern Mediterranean around the coasts of western Europe.

# Early western Asia

The historical term "western Asia" comprises the modern states of Turkey, Syria, Lebanon, Israel, Jordan, Saudi Arabia, Iraq, Iran, and perhaps Afghanistan. In antiquity the centre of the stage was occupied successively by Sumerians, Babylonians, Assyrians, and Persians, with Hittites, Hebrews and Phoenicians also playing their part, and Elamites, Hurrians, Urartians and Aramaeans – to list only some of the best known – in the wings. Their civilizations were mostly lost to knowledge after their fall, and so remained through the Dark Ages; and their recovery was long delayed by restricted access to and exploration of their lands.

## The development of writing
Rapid advances in knowledge came in the mid-nineteenth century, very much as a result of the decipherment of the Old Persian cuneiform script [Key], which through trilingual inscriptions (Old Persian, Babylonian and Elamite) provided the key to the immeasurably greater bulk of Assyrian, Babylonian and Sumerian texts in cuneiform writing of a more difficult kind.

Cuneiform developed from the pictographic script first used by the Sumerians in southern Mesopotamia late in the fourth millennium BC. Their language fell largely into disuse early in the second millennium, but the cuneiform script in which it had been written was used by their political and cultural heirs, the Babylonians, to express their own Semitic language, known as Akkadian, although it was entirely different from Sumerian. Other speakers of Akkadian, in particular the Assyrians, also used cuneiform. The same script, with relatively minor variations, was used elsewhere in western Asia to express other quite different languages, such as Hittite, Elamite, Hurrian and Urartian; and the same principle – varying groups of cuneiform (wedge-shaped) impressions – was used for the simpler Old Persian script of the Achaemenid Empire and for the alphabetic script of the Phoenicians.

## Deciphering the inscriptions
The excavations and study of the cuneiform-inscribed clay tablets and of similar inscriptions on stone and other materials was stimulated by the announcement, in 1872 of the decipherment of an Assyrian version of the biblical story of the Flood, found on a tablet at Nineveh in northern Iraq. Understanding other cuneiform inscriptions was made easier by the Semitic character of the Akkadian language in which many were written – it was related in varying degrees to such known languages as Hebrew, Aramaic and Arabic. The information provided by the inscribed material (nearly all in cuneiform, but with additions particularly from Old Testament Hebrew, Aramaic and hieroglyphic Hittite) has been supplemented by further surface discoveries and, particularly for the prehistoric (generally pre-writing) periods in western Asia, by archaeological excavation.

## The geographical background
There are significant geographical variations in the territories covered by the ancient civilizations of western Asia. The coastlands of the Black Sea and the Mediterranean give way more or less steeply to the Anatolian plateau of central Turkey, mainly watered – around its central desert – by rivers flowing

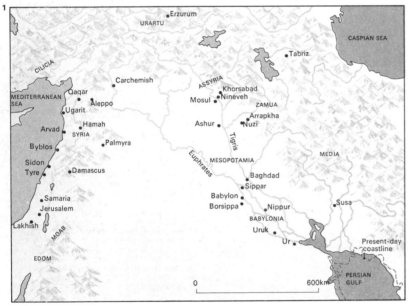

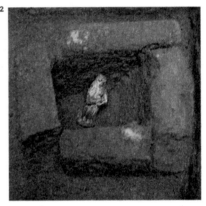

**1 The drama of ancient western Asia** was centred on the riverine plains and adjacent hills and mountains between the Mediterranean and Caspian seas and the Persian Gulf. The area was dominated by the Tigris and Euphrates, the land between being Mesopotamia, but the term is used loosely for a wider area round the rivers. The silt they and their tributaries produced and the water diverted from them by irrigation helped the growth of the towns and later of the capitals of Babylonia and Assyria, whose power and conflicts provided the framework for the history of their times until their decline in the seventh and sixth centuries BC.

**2 A sun-dried clay figurine** from a ninth-century BC palace at Nimrud in northern Iraq bears the inscription, impressed in the clay on the back in Assyrian cuneiform, "Come in, favourable demon; go out, evil demon". Such figurines lay in the brick-built foundation-boxes that are commonly found in the corners and beside the door jambs of important Assyrian buildings of the first millennium.

**3 A main route** from Trabzon and the eastern Black Sea coastal area of Turkey leads southwards up the 2,000m (6,560ft) Zigana Pass, which is open for most of the year. The route continues through high, mountainous country to Erzurum, Tabriz, and Teheran, thus serving as a north-western gateway to Armenia and Persia. It also provided a trade route between those lands and places accessible by ship from Trabzon. The Persian "Royal Road" between Susa in Persia and Sardis in the west used a more southerly route through Diyarbekir and Ankara, where the going was easier. The lands south of Trabzon are typical of much of eastern and northeastern Anatolia.

**4 The wheel** was probably invented in Mesopotamia during the fourth millennium. At that time it was constructed not of rings with spokes but of solid circular discs of planks clamped together, with a "tyre" of broad-headed nails driven into the outer rim. Spokes came later, but the earliest type of wheel still survives in remote areas; this one, for example, is found in a small village in eastern Turkey near Lake Van. Although many notable monuments had been built without the aid of the wheel, including the pyramids, its introduction greatly facilitated farming and transport and proved central to the development and spread of Mesopotamian civilization.

towards those two seas, with the Hittite capital in north central Anatolia close to the modern village of Bogazköy within the bend of the River Kızıl Irmak.

In the south, the Taurus range impedes the way up from the Cilician plain, while in the extreme east and northeast, high ranges (including Mount Ararat, 5,185m [17,011ft] high) restrict movement and cradle the sources of the Euphrates and Tigris. These two rivers, after flowing westwards to begin with, both turn southeast to form most of the Fertile Crescent, watering the plains of Mesopotamia where the capital cities – notably Babylon, Ashur and Nineveh – of their major empires were built [1]. To the west of Mesopotamia lies the desert, and still farther west are the Jordan and Orontes valleys and eventually the Mediterranean coastlands. East of Mesopotamia, valleys wind through the harsh mountains of the Zagros [3] to the dry Iranian plateau with the Elamite capital Susa and the Achaemenid Persian capitals Pasargadae and Persepolis.

Excavations have shown that the settlements of prehistoric man in some of these areas date back to as early as 9000 BC. Agriculture began sometime later. The cultivation of grain ("man's most precious artefact") assured a steady food supply, which led successively to expanding populations, release of labour for pursuits other than food-producing, specialization in craft, trade, government and religion, and so to the development of civilized societies from villages and towns to kingdoms and empires.

Wild cereal plants grew over much of western Asia, and their cultivation seems to have come first in the highland zones, notably in the Zagros mountains of eastern Iraq and western Iran and on the south Anatolian plateau. But as the grain-producing capacity of an inhabited area was bound to be a major factor in accelerating or retarding man's development, the fertility of the Tigris and Euphrates valleys, particularly with the addition of artificial irrigation from those rivers and from their main tributaries (the Habur, Upper and Lower Zab, and Diyala), gave the predominant prosperity in western Asia to the civilization of the Mesopotamian and southern plains.

**Darius the Great of Persia** (r. 521–486 BC) defeated nine princes to secure his throne. He recorded his achievement in detail on the face of the rock at Bisutun in western Iran, on the route from Mesopotamia to Teheran. The sculptures show two attendants behind Darius himself, his right foot planted on the pretender Gaumata, and nine rebels in captivity. The adjacent rock faces bear 11 short cuneiform inscriptions identifying Darius and his foes, with a long trilingual inscription that confirmed and amplified modern knowledge of the scripts, previously known only by similar, much shorter trilinguals.

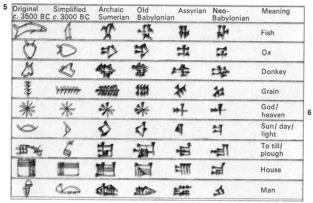

| Original c. 3500 BC | Simplified c. 3000 BC | Archaic Sumerian | Old Babylonian | Assyrian | Neo-Babylonian | Meaning |
|---|---|---|---|---|---|---|
| | | | | | | Fish |
| | | | | | | Ox |
| | | | | | | Donkey |
| | | | | | | Grain |
| | | | | | | God/ heaven |
| | | | | | | Sun/ day/ light |
| | | | | | | To till/ plough |
| | | | | | | House |
| | | | | | | Man |

**5 Sumerian writing** probably evolved from the needs of public economy and administration. As the Sumerian city states developed, records were needed of goods moving in and out of the towns. Clay or gypsum tags were originally attached to objects and bore a seal-impression identifying the owner; line drawings of the objects followed. Drawings were gradually simplified to signs. Later the sign for a common word such as *ti* (arrow) was used for "ti" sounds generally. (*Ti* also meant "life".) The shift to phonetic representation led to the development of written symbols for entire languages.

**6 Fragments of ivory boards** each 33cm (13 in) by 15cm (6in) were found covered in sludge at the bottom of a well in a royal palace at Nimrud. The boards had a raised margin round a recessed portion that probably contained a mixture of beeswax and pigment as a base for a cuneiform text. This unrecessed board carries Sargon's name and the title of the "book" of omens taken from celestial observations.

**7 Hollow "barrel cylinders"** of clay were at times used by the Assyrians for recording texts in cuneiform. This one, about 17cm (6.7in) by 10cm (4in), refers to Esarhaddon and gives a general summary of his conquests and achievements. It also tells of a new palace he has built, with roof-beams of cedar from the Amanus mountains and "doors of sweet-smelling cypress wood". It dates from about 670 BC.

**8 This monolithic basalt water-tank** of the time of Sennacherib (r. 704–681 BC) was reassembled from small fragments, and measures about 3.2m (9.7ft) square by 1m (39in) high. Four corner-figures, almost in the round, represent the god Ea holding a water-dispensing bottle, as do the four figures facing outwards from the centre of each of the four sides. Two priests in fish-garments and holding ritual vessels turn to each of these figures. Two of the sides carry the inscription identifying the king. The detailed interpretation is uncertain, but the water element is clearly treated in an arcane sense; Ea, as god of the deep and of knowledge, may be intercessor between heaven and earth.

# The Sumerians 4000–2000 BC

The partial excavation of the city of Eridu, about 19km (12 miles) southwest of "Ur of the Chaldees", the biblical home of Abraham, has produced the earliest settlements so far discovered in Babylonia, and has vindicated the Sumerians' tradition of its antiquity – they thought of it as the first of the five cities that existed before the Flood. Subsequent pre-dynastic periods of settlement, spanning more than the fourth millennium BC, are named, after the relevant sites, Ubaid, Uruk, and Jamdat Nasr.

The earliest dwellings at Eridu apparently consisted partly of reed huts and partly of mud-brick houses. The following pre-dynastic periods progressed successively through painted pottery, fishing-boats and hunting-slings, flint-headed hoes and hard-baked sickles, writing and the potter's wheel, plough and chariot, sculpture in the round, and vessels of silver, copper and lead.

Writing appeared in the Uruk period, a little before 3000 BC; whether the Sumerians brought it with them, or were already there (having possibly come from Khuzistan, at the foot of the Zagros), is not certain; but there seems no doubt that they invented the art.

The list of Sumerian kings includes a number of monarchs before the Flood, although their position in the archaeological framework and their history are unknown. Whether the Flood of Sumerian and Hebrew tradition is represented by the barren strata of silt found at Ur, Kish and Shuruppak is far from certain. One Ziusudra of Shuruppak, whom we are told survived the Flood, is famous from the *Epic of Gilgamesh* as the man who preserved the seed of living things; but it was at Kish that "kingship was restored to earth" after the flood.

## The First Dynasty of Ur

Little else is known of these kings and leadership passed after a struggle to the famous Gilgamesh of Uruk [8], and from his successors there to the First Dynasty of Ur. The names of some verified monarchs belong to this period, as does probably the splendid Royal Cemetery. Of two vaults at the bottom of a deep shaft, one (partly plundered) presumably contained the king's remains, and the other those of Queen Shub-ad (or Pu-abi) on a bed, magnificently adorned and accompanied by female attendants.

Priceless treasures survived in these and the other major graves: golden harps, bull-headed lyres, a golden dagger with lattice sheath, gold and silver florally decorated combs, golden bowls, huge boat-shaped earrings, thousands of beads in gold, silver and cornelian, and much more; as well as the Royal Standard of Ur showing scenes of war and peace in shell and lapis lazuli.

Little reliable information survives about the history of the period following the First Dynasty of Ur, except at Lagash, where the royal line was inaugurated by Ur-Nanshe, whose power is attested by buildings, works of art (some archaic and crude), and inscriptions, including references to cargoes of timber arriving from the Persian Gulf, and giving the impression of inexperience in the use of writing. His grandson Eannatum rose to a supreme position in Sumer and defeated Mari, on the Euphrates, and Subur, perhaps in the north; the supremacy of Lagash was confirmed by his nephew Entemena.

The history of the rest of the Early

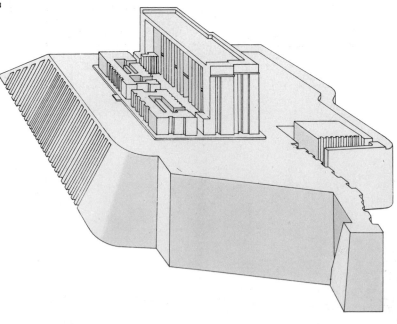

1 **Mount Ararat**, on which, according to the book of Genesis, Noah's Ark came to rest after the Flood, appears also in Sumerian tradition. It is probably more correctly vocalized as Urartu, the name of a kingdom that existed to the south of the mountain during the earlier part of the first millennium BC. The armies of this kingdom pressed long and hard on parts of the northern frontiers of Assyria.

2 **Most of the Fertile Crescent** was made up of the Syrian and lower reaches of the Euphrates and Tigris rivers. In the northern parts of this region there was some rainfall and natural fertility, and in the plains of Sumer and Akkad in the southeast, crops were encouraged by the silt of the rivers and by elaborate irrigation works. The need for these was early recognized by the area's growing civilizations.

3 **Temple architecture** dating from about the end of the fourth millennium is best represented by the White Temple at Uruk, the latest surviving shrine of an irregular mound that was probably an ancestor of the later, more regular ziggurats. The White Temple, approached by three ramps, was built of sun-dried bricks, whitewashed and buttressed, with an altar inside; the building's corners faced points of the compass. A ziggurat, a many-staged temple mount, may have been an attempt to bridge the gulf between man and the gods. It was strongly felt that man should offer residence to a deity, and the erection of a temple-tower may have bolstered belief in contact with such superhuman powers.

4 **Gudea of Lagash**, shown here, was the son-in-law of Ur-Baba, who brought to his city enough wealth to undertake extensive public works. He also patronized a school of sculptors who soon began to produce the finest masterpieces in hardstone. Gudea himself left inscriptions describing the religious observances and daily life of his time. He also enumerated the timbers and ornamental stones used in rebuilding the house of his god Ningirsu, on which he spent nearly all his wealth.

Dynastic period in Lagash and indeed in the whole of Sumer is largely ill-attested, but Urukagina (reigned *c.* 2378–*c.* 2371 BC) with a surprising political maturity instituted social reforms – some apparently intended to lighten burdens imposed on the population by governors and priests. He fell to Lugalzaggisi of Umma, who in turn fell, after a substantial and evidently successful reign, to the great Sargon of Akkad (reigned *c.* 2371–*c.* 2316 BC) [7].

### Sargon the Great, King of Akkad
Sargon rose from obscurity to overthrow Lugalzaggisi, and to subdue the rest of Sumer, Syria, perhaps part of Asia Minor, and much, apparently, of the mountain area of southwestern Iran. Revolt followed, but his grandson Naram-Sin ruled gloriously for 37 years. Sargon's line fell in *c.* 2230 BC to the Gutian tribes from the north or northeast, whose sovereignty left little mark on history and few monuments (although Lagash emerged to a period of great prosperity about that time under Ur-Baba and Gudea) [4], and who were expelled by Utu-khegal of

Uruk; his deputy at Ur, Ur-Nammu [6], seems to have overthrown him, and so founded the dynasty of Ur.

### The Third Dynasty of Ur
Ur-Nammu did not take the title "King of the Four Regions" – perhaps acknowledging his relatively limited authority – but assumed the new title "King of Sumer and Akkad". His 18-year reign was a time of considerable wealth and power, as shown by his many great building works, including the restoration of direct communication by water with the Gulf. His successor Shulgi (reigned *c.* 2095–*c.* 2048 BC) extended his territories in the northeast and east, dealing among others with the Gutians and the Hurrians; he also made his literary mark in his letters and royal hymns, and claims to have been a master performer on eight musical instruments. His second successor Shu-Sin (reigned *c.* 2038–*c.* 2030 BC) had to face the threat of western incursion; Ibbi-Sin (reigned *c.* 2029–*c.* 2006 BC), who claimed victory over these Amorites (under Ishbi-Erra of Mari), later saw his city fall to the Elamites.

**The Mesopotamian harvest** was won only after a long struggle against fierce heat and lack of rainfall. Fertility, celebrated on this seal, took on a central religious significance and the actions of nature were believed to be ruled by the gods.

**5 The Royal Standard**, dating from about 2600 BC, was found in one of the greatest tombs at Ur. It was apparently carried by an attendant wearing a peculiar bead headdress. It shows fully manned four-wheeled chariots, perhaps referring to victory [A], with domestic scenes on the reverse [B]. If it was a "standard" it was very small – 47cm by 20cm (18.5in by 7.5in) for a public display of royal wealth and success.

**8 King Gilgamesh of Uruk** had more legends told about him than any other hero of Babylonian history. The surviving Assyrian *Epic of Gilgamesh* was based on a much larger body of legend in Sumerian. This was so muddled that the king's career is quite unclear, although some of the stories may have been based on fact. He probably repaired a sanctuary at Nippur, and almost certainly built the city wall of Uruk.

**6 Ur-Nammu** (*r. c.* 2113–*c.* 2096 BC), King of Ur, to whom this Sumerian seal was dedicated, may not have been a great warrior. But he did publish certain laws dealing, among other things, with sexual offences and wrongs committed in connection with the lands of others.

**7 The world's first** great empire, under Sargon of Akkad, extended so far that rebellion was almost inevitable, and this evidently occurred even before his death.

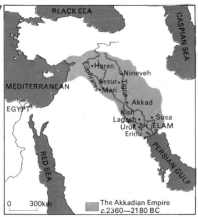

11

# The Babylonians 2000–323 BC

The ferocious sacking and fall of Ur in 2006 BC allowed the Semitic-speaking Amorites under Ishbi-Erra to establish more effectively a dynasty that ruled at Isin for more than two centuries. A few years earlier another Semitic-speaking dynasty arose at Larsa, of slightly longer duration; and the two dynasties in parallel dominated Babylonia for a century until a third power was established – unopposed by them – consisting of more Semitic-speaking Amorites at Babylon early in the nineteenth century.

However, early in the eighteenth century BC, Larsa, under Rim-Sin "the true shepherd", overcame Isin and became the sole major contender with Babylon for the domination of the land [5].

## Hammurabi and his laws

The first five kings of the new dynasty at Babylon were mainly preoccupied with defensive and religious building and by canal-clearing, with little extension of territory. It was left to Hammurabi to engage in victorious campaigns that left his empire stretching from Mari on the Euphrates in the northwest to Elam in the east, and by defeating Larsa to succeed to the traditional "kingship" of Sumer and Akkad.

Apart from his achievement of this relatively ephemeral empire, Hammurabi's fame rests mainly on his code of laws [8], written in Akkadian, a Semitic tongue that had by then – in parallel with political developments – become the principal language of Mesopotamia. Sumerian was retained mainly for religious use, although the civilization it expressed was absorbed by the Semites and continued to flourish.

No evidence has yet been found for the application of Hammurabi's laws in contemporary documents, nor was any appeal made to them; their standing and function are therefore unclear. But they may well have been an attempt to unify practice – notably in land tenure – among diversely regulated areas, with more uniform arrangements perhaps already prevailing in some matters not covered by them.

The reigns of Hammurabi's successors were long and undisturbed, and although in the later eighteenth century BC mention was made in Babylon of the alien Kassites (probably from the mountains in the northeast, and possibly Aryans), it was evidently an attack by the Hittite king Mursilis I in or soon after 1595 BC that brought the long-remembered destruction of Babylon and the downfall of Hammurabi's dynasty. But Mursilis can hardly have contemplated permanent conquest, and the void was filled by a Kassite dynasty later credited with a 576-year rule.

## The dark ages of Babylon

Babylonia absorbed the Kassites, and during a dark age of more than 200 years little was heard of them. In the mid-fourteenth century BC the Kassite king married the daughter of the king of Assyria. But the alliance led to wars that resulted in the temporary conquest and occupation of Babylonia by the outstanding Assyrian soldier-king Tukulti-Ninurta I in 1235 BC. Essentially the Kassites retained Babylonia, but their dynasty fell to the Elamites in 1157 BC.

The Elamites lost political control of Babylonia before the end of the century; it passed to a second dynasty of Isin which,

**1 The great ziggurat of the moon god** at Ur [A] was begun, according to King Nabonidus (r. 555–539 BC), by Ur-Nammu (r. 2113–2096 BC), but may well conceal the remains of an older tower from as far back as the predynastic period. Nabonidus says it was continued but left unfinished by Ur-Nammu's son Shulgi; Nabonidus himself made good the stairways with new treads a metre above the old and raised the level of the terrace. Different in many respects from the Mesopotamian ziggurats, and the largest known, – 100m (328ft) square – is the ziggurat at Dur-Untash in Elam [B], near Susa.

**2 Lilith,** with talons and feathered legs, was a Babylonian-Assyrian goddess who survived in Jewish lore into the Christian era. Traditionally a sinister bringer of death, in this clay relief she holds what may be a measuring rope to indicate the span of man's life. She is mentioned in an early fragment of the *Epic of Gilgamesh,* which also gives some independent evidence corroborating the biblical Flood. The profile used in narrative reliefs was less suited to representing the deity in actual rites; and reliefs over the altars of shrines show the goddess in a frontal view, perhaps to establish a relationship with the worshippers.

**3 This Babylonian tablet,** not yet fully understood, appears to be concerned with theoretical geometry. Most Babylonian mathematical texts are contemporary with the dynasty of Hammurabi (r. 1792–1750 BC); the rest are datable to the last three centuries BC. The earlier history of the Old Babylonian group is not known, beyond the evidence of innumerable economic-administrative texts from the earliest period of Mesopotamian writing, whose number system, based on 60, was retained by the Old Babylonians. But although the content of Old Babylonian mathematics reached a level which can be compared with that of the early Renaissance – it was elementary compared with that of the Greeks.

under Nebuchadrezzar I (reigned 1124–1103 BC), ended Elamite interference. The Isin Dynasty fell after little more than 100 years of political stability. The ensuing age of uncertainty and civil disturbance was relieved by the inauguration of the Eighth Dynasty of Babylon in 977 BC, and for a century Babylonia maintained close contact with the developing power of Assyria.

Shalmaneser III [Key] of Assyria (reigned 858–824 BC) was called upon to help quell a rebellion in Babylonia, at which time the powerful Chaldaean tribes of southern Babylonia were first making their appearance. Wars with Assyria and anarchy at home preceded the emergence of Tiglath-Pileser III (reigned 744–727 BC) as a strong king of Assyria who at length assumed the Babylonian crown. His successor Shalmaneser V (reigned 726–722 BC) ruled both countries for five years, but both Sargon II (reigned 721–705 BC) and Sennacherib (reigned 704–681 BC) found strong antagonists in the Chaldaeans

Babylon's fortunes varied widely in the seventh century, until the rise of the unknown "son of a nobody" Nabopolassar (reigned 625–605 BC) inaugurated a great age of Babylonian civilization under the neo-Babylonian or Chaldaean Dynasty.

**The rise of the neo-Babylonians**
Babylon helped the Medes in the overthrow of Nineveh and the Assyrians in 612 BC. Her brilliant commander Nebuchadrezzar II (reigned 604–562 BC) destroyed Jerusalem and carried off its inhabitants, erected great monuments and buildings, which made Babylon one of the Seven Wonders of the world – this is the period of the "Hanging Gardens".

Nebuchadrezzar's son was murdered, and the decay of Babylonia accelerated under the pious antiquarian Nabonidus [1]; Babylon fell without a fight before the Achaemenid Persian king Cyrus the Great (c. 600–529 BC) in 539 BC. Xerxes (c. 519–465 BC) partly destroyed it in 482 BC; it might have been restored by Alexander the Great (356–323 BC) had he not died there, and thereafter, although its astronomical schools survived, Babylon passed into history.

**The throne-base of Shalmaneser III** found at Nimrud has an inscription on the horizontal surfaces. It includes a separate section referring to the king's campaigns of 851 and 850 BC in Babylonia, in which he helped the Babylonian king to defend his throne against a rebellion. This relief carving on the western vertical face shows Shalmaneser [right] and probably the Babylonian king [left], each with an attendant, under a canopy. They are shaking hands – a unique representation in Mesopotamian art of this modern gesture; whether it implies equality, Babylonian subservience or neither, is unknown.

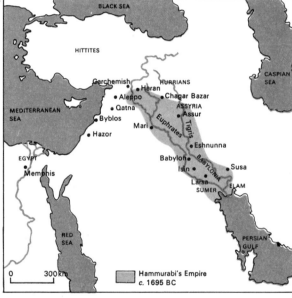

**4 Relief bricks from Babylon**, some showing bulls and mythical creatures, once formed part of the Processional Way. Like most excavated Babylonian remains they are of the neo-Babylonian period.

**5 Babylon dominated western Asia**, more or less, for thirteen and a half centuries. It lay on the lower course of the River Euphrates, an advantage much increased by the development of irrigation systems.

Map labels: BLACK SEA, HITTITES, HURRIANS, CASPIAN SEA, Carchemish, Haran, Chagar Bazar, Aleppo, MEDITERRANEAN SEA, Qatna, ASSYRIA, Assur, Byblos, Mari, Euphrates, Tigris, Hazor, Eshnunna, EGYPT, Babylon, BABYLONIA, Susa, Memphis, Isin, Larsa, ELAM, SUMER, RED SEA, PERSIAN GULF, 0 300km, Hammurabi's Empire c. 1695 BC

**6 Early clay tablets** reveal the importance of sheep and goats– they also use the signs for merchant, cattle and donkey – in the economy of early Sumerian communities. The Akkadian period improved on the quality of the early tablets in the first-ever recording of a Semitic language – Old Akkadian. Their development into the tablets of Babylonia (those shown are Old Babylonian) and Assyria culminated in the calligraphy of the scribes of Assurbanipal's library at Nineveh.

**7 Naram-Sin** (c. 2254– c. 2218) of Akkad, whose Semitic line was an interlude in Sumerian history presaging the supremacy of the Semitic Babylonians, portrayed himself on this stele triumphing over the eastern Iraqi king of Lullubi.

**8 The diorite stele of Hammurabi** was carried off from Babylon by an Elamite invader, perhaps in the 12th century, and taken to Susa, where it was found in the winter of 1901–2. The text is topped by a bas-relief showing Hammurabi receiving the commission to write the laws from Shamash the sun god, god of justice. The Elamites apparently chiselled off parts of the text, but most of these survive on other copies of the code. It has a prologue and an epilogue in semi-poetic style.

# Egypt: the Old and Middle Kingdoms

Successive prehistoric cultures designated by the names of Badarian, Naqada I and Naqada II have been identified from archaeological remains in Upper Egypt but remains from Lower Egypt are scanty and make any sound historical judgment rather difficult. It would appear that two distinct kingdoms evolved in Lower and Upper Egypt [1] and that the unification of the country was brought about by the victory of Upper Egypt over Lower Egypt *c.* 3100 BC. Even after this unification, however, the peoples of ancient Egypt continued to call their country the Two Lands.

## The divine kings of Dynasty I

Traditionally the first ruler of Dynasty I and conqueror of Lower Egypt is known as Menes [2] and he is credited with the foundation of the national capital of Memphis, just south of the Nile Delta. The reigning king was regarded as the living embodiment of the falcon-god Horus and hence divine. During the first dynasty and the next farmers began to use the plough extensively, and irrigation was probably introduced. A national government evolved and writing was developed.

With Dynasty III began the period known as the Old Kingdom (*c.* 2686–2181 BC). The most prominent ruler of Dynasty III was Zoser, for whom the Step-Pyramid complex was built [Key]. Under Snofru, the founder of Dynasty IV, the first true pyramid was constructed and the technique of building pyramids was perfected under his successors Khufu, Khephren and Menkaure. The construction of the pyramids [4] entailed enormous expenditure and organization, and the weakening of the power of the crown at the end of Dynasty IV led to the abandonment of the more expensive techniques.

During Dynasty V the cult of the sun-god Re regained national pre-eminence and the rulers undertook the construction of solar temples for his worship. At the end of Dynasty V magical texts were inscribed on the walls of the burial chamber of the royal pyramids to ensure the safe passage of the ruler's spirit to the after-world. During Dynasties IV to VI periodic campaigns were undertaken against tribesmen in the Sinai peninsula and large-scale expeditions were dispatched to Nubia to extort or trade for

ivory, gold and other precious materials.

At the end of Dynasty VI the growth in power of the provincial governors, the nomarchs, led to the steady weakening of the control of the Memphis hierarchy. Rival dynasties appeared in Heracleopolis and Thebes and the country was plunged into civil war. The confusion was compounded by the infiltration of Asiatic tribesmen from Sinai into the fertile regions of the Delta.

## A period of confusion ends

This chaotic and ill-documented era is known as the First Intermediate Period (*c.* 2181–*c.* 2050 BC). Montuhotep II of Dynasty XI, Prince of Thebes [7], overcame his rivals and reunited Egypt under his rule, although the many nomarchs retained considerable power. He expelled the Libyan and Bedouin raiders, inaugurating the Middle Kingdom in Egypt (*c.* 2050–1786 BC). Montuhotep II had a mortuary temple and tomb built for himself at Deir el-Bahari on the west bank of the Nile opposite Thebes. Montuhotep II's descendant Montuhotep IV was succeeded in unknown circumstances by his vizier

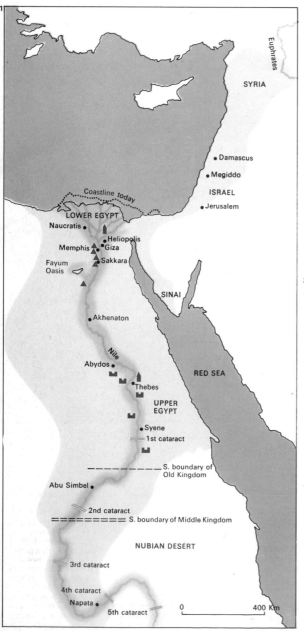

1 **Egypt divides naturally into two areas** – Lower Egypt, which consists of the Nile Delta region, and the long, narrow strip of Upper Egypt, which is confined on both sides by desert. The annual flooding of the Nile brought water for land irrigation and also deposited a rich topsoil. Egypt's agricultural prosperity was based on the river's unfailing predictability.

Legend:
- ▲ Pyramids
- ⬗ Obelisks
- ⌂ Temples
- ☐ Maximum extent of Egyptian Empire (New Kingdom, *c.* 1450 BC)
- ▨ Fertile region

2 **Egypt's unification** was brought about by war. Victories of the early rulers are commemorated on ceremonial palettes such as this one depicting Menes, the first ruler of all Egypt.

3 **The monarch's public image** in the Old and Middle Kingdoms was widely different, a change reflected in the royal statuary. The figure of King Menkaure of Dynasty IV [A] with his queen is an idealized portrait of the god-king. The aftermath of the First Intermediate Period saw the development of a more realistic and intense style, as in the statue of Senusret III [B].

Amenemhat I, who founded Dynasty XII in about 1991 BC.

Amenemhat I founded a new capital at Lisht south of Memphis because Thebes was too far south to serve as an efficient capital. To strengthen his hold on the throne he circulated a spurious prophecy concerning his rise to power and appointed his son Senusret I as co-ruler. Despite these precautions Amenemhat I was assassinated after 30 years of rule but his son managed to secure the throne. The powers of the provincial nobility that might rival the throne were suppressed under Senusret III. Amenemhat I had begun the conquest of Nubia and this expansion was completed under Senusret III, who fixed the southern border at Semna. Apart from one attested incursion into southern Palestine no steps appear to have been taken to exercise direct control in Palestine or Syria, but trade links were strongly maintained. A line of fortifications was built by Amenemhat I in Sinai to deter possible invasions. The rulers of Dynasty XII sponsored a vast land reclamation project in the Fayum area.

The Second Intermediate Period (c. 1786–1570 BC) was marked by a decline in the power of the central government. During Dynasty XIII Asiatic invaders broke through the Egyptian defences and infiltrated the country. These foreigners are commonly known as the Hyksos, although the term should properly be applied to the chiefs only. The Hyksos eventually secured control of most of the country, with the aid of new military weapons such as chariots, and were the founders of Dynasty XV (c. 1674–1570 BC), although it is most unlikely that they ever exercised direct control over Thebes and the south. More probably Thebes was forced to acknowledge the supremacy of the Hyksos ruler in his new capital of Avaris in the Delta.

**The invaders are expelled**
The Hyksos did not rule as foreigners but adopted Egyptian titles and Egyptian culture. As their power weakened, the princes of Thebes of Dynasty XVII were emboldened openly to reject Hyksos rule and, after several campaigns, Kamose and his successor, his brother Ahmose, succeeded in taking Avaris and expelling the invaders.

**King Zoser's Step-Pyramid** at Sakkara, Memphis, was the first major Egyptian building in stone. It was supposedly designed by his vizier Imhotep, who was later deified.

1 Subterranean chamber
2 Queen's chamber
3 King's chamber
4 Entrance
5 Corridor
6 Corridor
7 Grand chamber
8 Vault
9 Shafts

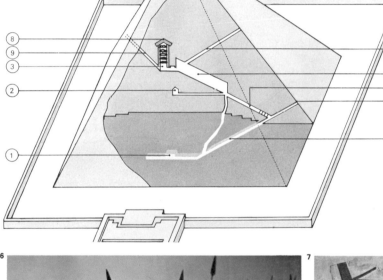

**4 The Great Pyramid** erected at Giza by Khufu, second ruler of Dynasty IV, provides a typical example of the art of the pyramid builder. It is built of limestone blocks and was originally faced with fine white limestone. It was approximately 146m (480ft) in height. After two changes in plan the final resting place of the body, called the King's Chamber, was constructed of granite and approached via the Grand Chamber. The sarcophagus is still in place.

**5 Scribes,** such as . this one depicted in an Old Kingdom statue, were the key to the smooth functioning of the Egyptian administration. Papyrus was used for the recording of daily accounts and business, but very few pieces have survived from this period.

**6 In the afterlife** the same things were felt to be required as in this life. Everyday items, even down to models of retainers like these soldiers, were therefore placed in tombs.

**7 King Montuhotep II** is shown being embraced by Re, the sun-god, in a painted relief from the king's mortuary temple at Deir el-Bahari. The king also prepared tombs for Nefru, his sister and queen, and for several of his concubines. Later rulers of Dynasty XI built similar temples opposite Thebes on the Nile's west bank.

**8 Egypt's lack of certain raw materials,** notably timber, resulted in the growth from early dynastic times of a flourishing trade between Egyptian and Syrian ports. Egypt's influence in Syria and Palestine during the rich period of the Middle Kingdom is reflected in the Egyptian statuary and jewellery found in those regions.

# India: prehistory to 500 BC

The earliest evidence of a literate culture in India dates from about 2300 BC when the Indus civilization emerged from the prehistoric age. This Indus or Harappan civilization (named after the town of Harappa) had its principal centres in the Indus valley, now mainly in Pakistan, but extended westwards to the present Iranian border, eastwards to beyond Delhi and southwards to the Gulf of Broach [1]. Its main cities were at Harappa in the Punjab and Mohenjo-daro in Sind, but there were also a number of smaller towns, including the port of Lothal.

## The nature of settlements
The cities show advanced town planning and the remains testify to a high and diverse material culture [2, 3]. A considerable part of the now fairly arid Indus valley must have been brought under cultivation to yield the surplus crops with which to feed the city populations. Unless there has been a complete change of climate in this area since that time it is obvious that fields were irrigated.

Such a sophisticated civilization required a form of writing. Thousands of steatite (soapstone) seals [Key] have been discovered. In addition to representations of animals, men and gods these present brief inscriptions in as yet undeciphered hieroglyphic script. The seals, some of which have been found as far away as Syria, were probably merchants' seals attached to goods.

## The end of the Indus
Even less is known about the end of the Indus civilization than about its origins. After flourishing for five or six centuries (c. 2300–1750 BC) without undergoing much change it completely disintegrated following a brief decline. Although natural calamities cannot completely be excluded, it now seems that the Indus cities were ravaged by invading nomadic horsemen in the eighteenth century BC. The latter are usually identified as Indo-Aryans, for whose presence there is, however, no reliable evidence until about four centuries after the end of the Indus civilization. It is therefore more likely that the Indus cities were conquered by tribesmen from the mountains who, in their turn, gave way to the Indo-Aryans.

By the thirteenth century BC, the Indo-Aryans – split into numerous tribes who fought each other no less fiercely than the earlier inhabitants – had occupied the Punjab. They subsequently spread into the Ganges valley and southwards into Gujerat and Maharashtra.

A vast collection of religious hymns written in archaic Sanskrit, the *Rigveda*, dates from this early phase (c. 1400–1000 BC). Apparently preserved by oral tradition, the hymns are addressed to many different deities whose help is implored in military and agricultural pursuits. The four Vedic texts, of which the *Rigveda* is the foremost, spawned expositions and commentaries of which the *Upanishads* are the most celebrated. The gods, such as Indra, are usually conceived of as anthropomorphic, but some features – for example speculation about the true nature of the sacrifice – which were to be become characteristic of Hinduism, are already distinguishable.

During the later Vedic period (c. 1000–550 BC) the Indo-Aryans, by then utilizing effective iron tools, spread over

**1 The brown areas on the map** mark the expansion of the Indus civilization, stretching southeast down the coast to beyond the Gulf of Broach and eastwards far beyond present Delhi. The westward expansion into Baluchistan is not shown. All over this vast area – Rupar and Lothal are about 1,600km (1,000 miles) apart – the Indus civilization was uniform, suggesting centralized control. Political control was facilitated by the nature of the land as this civilization flourished in relatively dry areas which, unlike the tropical rain forest, could be cultivated without iron tools.

**2 The ancient Indus city of Mohenjo-daro** was built according to a systematic plan with streets crossing at right-angles and houses opening onto the streets. Elaborate granaries have also been found.

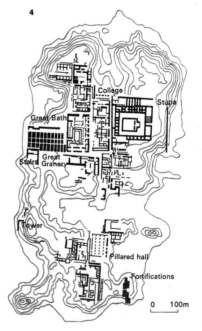

**3 The Great Bath** in the citadel of Mohenjo-daro was built of fine brickwork and presumably used for ceremonial functions. One of the most striking features of the Indus civilization was the importance attached to good water supplies. A well-built bathroom has been found in almost every house, which also possessed proper drainage. As a result each house has its own well, with a deep shaft which was kept in shape by means of terracotta hoops.

**4 The larger Indus cities** all consisted of a citadel mound and a lower city complex stretching eastwards from the citadel. The former was the site of most of the large public buildings such as, in Mohenjo-daro, the Great Bath, the granary and a building that on account of its shape (several courtyards, corridors, rooms and compartments) has tentatively been identified as a college. The lower city was the residential area. This ground plan of Mohenjo-daro shows the grid of the town in the lower part of the city and the houses, which vary greatly in size from those consisting of a single room to large residences boasting more than 20 rooms.

most of northern India including the Ganges valley, burning down the forest to cultivate the fertile land. The gradual progress of this expansion can be traced with the help of a distinctive type of pottery, Painted Grey ware. These people were not urbanized as the Harappans had been. During their expansion they mixed with earlier established forest tribes, introducing them to the horse, and their mode of life changed from semi-nomadic cattle breeders to settled farmers.

This change had important political and cultural implications. The tribal units gave way to kingdoms based not on kinship but on territory. The kingdoms were controlled by warrior classes (*kshatriyas*) headed by the king, and assisted by members of the powerful class of hereditary priests (*brahmins*). These two ruling classes controlled the free peasants, traders and craftsmen who constituted the third class (*vaisyas*), as well as the semi-servile labourers, hunters and fishermen who formed the lowest class of the *sudras*, partly descendants of forest tribes. Some of these, especially those whose way of life was considered unclean or repulsive by the Indo-Aryans, were assigned the status of untouchables. This marked the beginning of the complex caste system.

**The rise of major cities**
During this period major cities developed for the first time since the decline of the Indus cities. The most important were Hastinapura on the Ganges east of present-day Delhi and, in about 500 BC, Rajgir in southern Bihar, with its impressive walls. In the same period most of the basic concepts of Hinduism took shape: not only caste, but also the belief in the transmigration of the soul, in non-violence and in the holiness of the cow. These have all become lasting features of Indian civilization. While the Vedic sacrifice persisted and became more and more complicated, there was also a reaction among those who felt unsatisfied with formal religion and sought higher values in meditation. People of the ruling classes were encouraged to withdraw to a life of contemplation in the forest when their children no longer needed them. On this foundation Siddhartha Gautama (*c.* 563–*c.* 483 BC) instituted Buddhism.

**Three Mohenjo-daro casts** from seals supply valuable information about the ancient Indus civilization, revealing, for example, that cattle had already been domesticated. These seals represent a bull feeding from a manger, an elephant and a rhinoceros. The writing is hieroglyphic but scholars have not yet been able to decipher it.

**5 The earliest true history** of the Indo-Pakistani subcontinent began when, after the middle of the third millennium BC, a high civilization emerged in and about the Indus valley. Once established, the Indus valley civilization flourished for more than six centuries without undergoing any significant change. Its sudden end may have been due to Indo-Aryan invasions, but it seems more likely that these invasions took place when the Indus civilization had already disintegrated. The Indo-Aryans settled in villages in the Punjab and were divided into tribes, about which we know from the *Rigveda*. Between *c.* 1000 and 500 BC Indo-Aryan civiltion gradually spread along the Ganges valley, as we can confirm from later Vedic literature, and early Hinduism took shape.

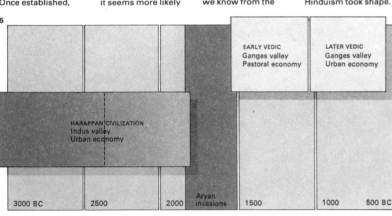

| 5 | | | | EARLY VEDIC Ganges valley Pastoral economy | LATER VEDIC Ganges valley Urban economy |
|---|---|---|---|---|---|

HARAPPAN CIVILIZATION Indus valley Urban economy

| 3000 BC | 2500 | 2000 | Aryan invasions | 1500 | 1000 | 500 BC |

**6 This limestone sculpture** is one of the few surviving stone sculptures of the Indus civilization. It is 19cm (7in) high and is apparently a portrait statuette representing a bearded man with low, receding forehead, elongated eyes and thick lips. The sculpture reveals excellent taste and craftsmanship and gives some impression of the physical appearance of the ancient Indus peoples.

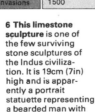

**7 Most seals from Mohenjo-daro** show representations of animals, sometimes natural, sometimes composite or fantastic. This seal shows a three-headed, horned deity seated in an attitude that is reminiscent of the yoga *āsanas* of later times. The god is surrounded by a number of animals. This, among other features, recalls later representations of the god Shiva. The deity has therefore been identified as a proto-Shiva.

**8 The modern inhabitants** of the Mohenjo-daro area, like their predecessors, still use the river as their lifeline. The river was not only important for irrigation of the fields in the vicinity of its banks but it was also essential for communications. The striking uniformity of the Indus civilization would have been impossible without reasonable communications. Representations of boats have been found on stone and terracotta at Mohenjo-daro.

# Minoan civilization 2500–1400 BC

Arthur Evans (1851–1941), the British archaeologist, excavating at Knossos on the island of Crete from 1900 to 1936, uncovered a richly decorated palace, an architectural masterpiece that indicated an early civilization more distinctive and sophisticated then any other European culture hitherto discovered [4]. Other similar palaces have since been revealed – by the Italians at Phaestos, by the French at Mallia, more recently by the Greeks at Zakro – and a balanced picture begins to emerge.

## Beginnings of Minoan civilization

The Minoans (from the name of the legendary King Minos of Knossos), as Evans called the people who lived in Crete, appear mysteriously on the island at the start of the Bronze Age, about 3000 BC, perhaps as immigrants from Anatolia or, as recently argued, from Palestine. The contents of their circular tombs, most frequent on the plain of the Mesara, show that overseas contacts were maintained, contacts that gradually built up into a great trading network across the eastern Mediterranean [1].

By about 2000 BC, economic and social advance had spurred architecture to impressive achievements – the Old Palaces. Their details are much obscured by later additions and alterations, but enough survives at Knossos, at Mallia, and particularly under the west court at Phaestos, to show that building on a lavish scale was already being carried out. The implications for the social organization are of course even greater than for the technical abilities of the builders. The Minoans had achieved civilization.

One of the most obvious criteria of this is the use of writing. The earliest brief inscriptions in Crete are found on seals, where picture symbols appear to belong to a hieroglyphic script. Clay tablets found in the early palace at Phaestos show that by then a simpler syllabic writing had been devised for general use. It may well have been employed mainly for writing on some sort of paper or parchment, but such materials have failed to survive. No convincing translation of these texts, called Linear A, has yet been proposed, so its language remains unknown.

The exact nature of the island's political organization is difficult to discover. The extensive storage capacity of the palaces, for articles such as pottery as well as commodities like olive oil, suggests that they were economic as well as administrative centres, controlling territories within the island. Yet these territories had apparently nothing to fear from each other – there are no walled defences and few signs of weapons or soldiers. Knossos clearly held a leading position, perhaps by controlling overseas trade.

## Height of Minoan culture

Demonstrated by finds of Minoan pottery from as far away as Egypt, by colonies on several Aegean islands, and by the permeation of the mainland culture, overseas trade goes far to explain the wealth of Crete at this period. But Minoan civilization cannot be explained as simply imported from abroad: it is far too individualistic for that.

After apparently natural disasters in about 1700 BC, the palaces were lavishly rebuilt and it is the ruins of these that can be seen today. Building was in limestone, within a timber-frame construction. This added a

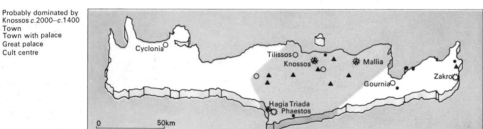

**1 The long narrow island of Crete** was the home of Minoan civilization, the first in Europe. With much of the interior mountainous, Mt Ida topping 2,400m (7,873ft), and the rugged south coast broken only by the plain of Mesara behind Phaestos, there seems little to explain civilization here. But the north coast has a gentler relief and is rich in olives and vines, and the surrounding seas encourage trade and contact over wide areas. The Minoans actively developed their agricultural wealth and foreign commerce.

Map legend:
- Probably dominated by Knossos c.2000–c.1400
- Town
- Town with palace
- Great palace
- Cult centre

Cyclonia, Tilissos, Knossos, Mallia, Gournia, Zakro, Hagia Triada, Phaestos

0 — 50km

**2 Minoan pottery**, after a long and unspectacular development, achieved pre-eminence first in the Kamarais ware of c. 1800 BC. This is wheel-made in elegant shapes, some cups being extremely fine. The studs on the back of this jug from Phaestos suggest the handle-rivets of a metal prototype, as does the shiny black slip. The painted decoration however – the bold, curvilinear, abstract design – could come only from a ceramic tradition.

**3 Elegance of shape** is even more marked in the late Minoan period from 1500 BC. The fashion changed at this time to painting in red on yellow and much greater use was made of naturalistic motifs, though some abstract elements remain. Favourite decorative subjects were flowers – lilies in particular – and sea creatures, such as octopuses, nautili and shells among rocks and seaweed.

**4 The Great Palace of Knossos** had a long history. The plan shows it after its rebuilding in c. 1550 BC. The main entrances [1 and 2] lead by long corridors to the Central Court [3]. Beneath this, deposits have been found going back to 6000 BC. Storerooms for oil and other goods [4] and for pottery [5] hint at the wealth that poured into the building, which controlled at least all of central Crete. The administrative block fronted the court on the west and faced the great staircase to the domestic quarter on the east [6]. Outside the palace to the northwest, a processional way led to a theatre [7].

useful, if not always effective, resilience against earthquake shock, to which Crete is prone, but also added to the fire risk. Ranges of rooms opened on to the great central courts, with well-planned light wells to illuminate inner suites of chambers. Internal walls were plastered and often gaily decorated with the most elaborate and colourful frescoes [9]. Floors were frequently paved with alabaster slabs. But it is perhaps the drainage system, as advanced as any before the eighteenth century AD, which causes the most surprise. The overall impression is a convincing one of light, air and freedom – so different from that of the contemporary civilizations farther east and so much closer to modern ideals.

The art fully bears this out, whether it is a life-sized figure painted in the frescoes, decoration on the magnificent pottery [Key], or minute detail on the carved seal-stones [7, 8]. The colour and naturalism hold an immediate appeal to the modern world.

This great civilization's end is even more hotly debated than its origins, if only because there is so much more evidence on which to base the story. The most widely accepted version, but by no means the only one, would start from the cataclysmic eruption of the volcanic island of Thera, a little over 100km (63 miles) from the north coast of Crete, about 1450 BC. Much of Crete would have been plastered with poisonous ash, shattered by the shock waves of the explosion and pounded by monstrous tidal waves.

**Decline and conquest**
Of the major sites, only Knossos appears to have recovered from this destruction and here there are many signs of a profound change. The new rulers were warriors who used the Linear B script, now recognized as an adaptation of Linear A for writing an early version of the Greek language. This would all seem to point to a conquest of the island by mainlanders, Mycenaeans, who had seized the opportunity given them by the eruption of Thera to oust the Minoans from their control of the profitable sea-routes. Metropolitan Minoan was replaced by provincial Mycenaean and the palaces were lost to sight and memory.

KEY

This pottery figurine displays a courtly elegance typical of the Minoan civilization of Bronze Age Crete. It is 29.5cm (11.6in) high and was found in the Temple Repositories at Knossos, where it was buried c. 1500 BC. The tightly fitting bodice, open to expose the breasts, the embroidered apron and the long flounced skirt are shown frequently on seals and in frescoes. The lioness, if such it is, on her hat and the snakes in her hands are less usual and more sinister. She is probably the earth mother, whose worship is widely attested in shrines and pillar crypts on Minoan sites and in caves and hilltop sanctuaries throughout Crete.

5 **This magnificent stone libation vase** comes from the palace at Zakro, destroyed c. 1450 BC. It shows a sanctuary (centre, left) on a mountain peak, with wild goats on the roof. A bird flies past two pairs of horns used at consecration.

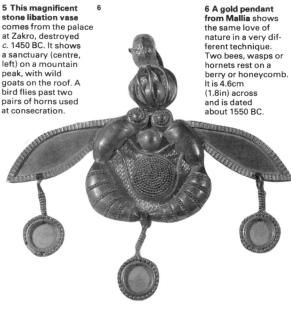

6 **A gold pendant from Mallia** shows the same love of nature in a very different technique. Two bees, wasps or hornets rest on a berry or honeycomb. It is 4.6cm (1.8in) across and is dated about 1550 BC.

7 **On this seal impression**, measuring 2.1cm (0.8in) across, two equestrian acrobats perform in a field full of flowers.

8 **This seal**, in reality only 1.5cm (0.6in) across, demonstrates the mastery of Minoan carvers. It is in blue chalcedony.

9 **Fresco painting** was another spectacular art of the Minoans, although it normally survives only in small fragments. This scene of dolphins and fish decorated the so-called Queen's Megaron in the domestic quarter of Knossos. Other frescoes also show birds, flowers, plants, animals and people.

# The Greek mainland 2800–1100 BC

Homer's *Iliad* and *Odyssey*, written between about 800 and 700 BC, record the exploits of legendary Greek heroes around the time of the Trojan Wars. For centuries the fact that this heroic age ever existed about 1800–1100 BC was in doubt, until Heinrich Schliemann (1822–1890), a German archaeologist, recovered at Troy and Mycenae (from 1874) relics that supported the legends.

## Bronze Age beginnings

This Greek Bronze Age, centred on the Greek mainland, began with the introduction of metal, important both for stimulating trade and for the acquisition of visible wealth. About this time, too, the grain economy of the plains of Thessaly and the north was replaced by one based on grain, olives and the vine, which flourished better in the south. By 2500 BC this economy supported a palace, the House of Tiles, at Lerna in the Plain of Argos. About 2200 BC however, Lerna and many contemporary settlements were destroyed by invaders from the northeast. These were probably the first inhabitants to speak a language recognizably Greek.

At this time the fast potter's wheel and the megaron, a hall with pillared porch, were introduced. Soon after, their civilization showed signs of influence from their contemporary, Minoan Crete [2].

In time, however, strong towns grew up, such as Mycenae. The first real evidence of the flowering of the mainland civilization appears in the shaft graves of Mycenae itself, dating largely from the sixteenth century BC. They contain real solid wealth, in gold, silver and bronze, in crystal, alabaster and clay. We can assume that these were the resting places of a princely or even royal family, ruling a rich and integrated society. Many of the objects [6, 8] reveal a contrast between polished and sophisticated craftsmanship, patently Cretan, and a very un-Cretan emphasis on weapons, armour and military scenes [7]. The owner of the stern gold mask [Key] was no soft courtier but a warring hero, an ancestor of those whom Homer portrayed.

These early Greeks also became seamen. A few of the objects from the shaft graves may be Egyptian work acquired through trade, rather than Cretan or Greek. Desirous

of more trade goods from abroad and supported by local agricultural wealth, the Greeks began overseas ventures of their own, to Troy, to Palestine and Egypt, and to the Lipari Islands beyond the "toe" of Italy.

## Expansion of Mycenaean civilization

But their opportunity came when the power of the Minoans was destroyed, perhaps by the cataclysmic eruption of Thera *c.* 1450 BC. This freed the rich trade routes of the Mediterranean which the Cretans had hitherto controlled. The mainlanders, comparatively untouched by the disaster, made the most of the new situation. Their pottery, valued both for its own sake and for the perfumed oil exported in it, rose sharply in price in both the Levant and Egypt: it was prized, for example, in Akhenaton's newly built Egyptian capital Tell el Amarna, about 1350 BC. Cypriot copper was carried in their ships. A great westwards trade port grew up at Taranto in southern Italy, bringing more copper from Sardinia and the eastern Alps, and amber from the distant Baltic. Crete itself was occupied by the Mycenaeans, and

**1 The Mycenaeans' homeland** was the Peloponnese and adjacent parts of Greece, centred on the Argolid, and Mycenae itself. Here they built their distinctive version of the civilization already flourishing in Crete. As they took over the Minoans' sea trade, so their influence spread to the islands and coasts around the Aegean and beyond. This vast territory was never a unified state. More likely it was a collection of allied kingdoms.

**2 The Mycenaeans** were strongly influenced by the Minoans. This gold cup from Vaphio, near Sparta, if not made in Crete itself must at least have been the work of a mainland craftsman trained in the Minoan tradition.

**3 The syllabic script** came from Crete. Linear B script was extensively used for business documents, such as this stock list of herbs from Mycenae. The language used was an early form of Greek.

**4 The fortified citadel of Tiryns,** *c.* 1330 BC, typifies mainland architecture in the Bronze Age. A tortuous entrance passage [1] leads through the massive walls and an inner portico [2] leads to the first court. The administrative centre took up the whole of the inner court [3] and the megaron [4], with its great central hearth, opening on to it. The main structural fabric consisted of a wooden framework and columns, and sun-dried bricks.

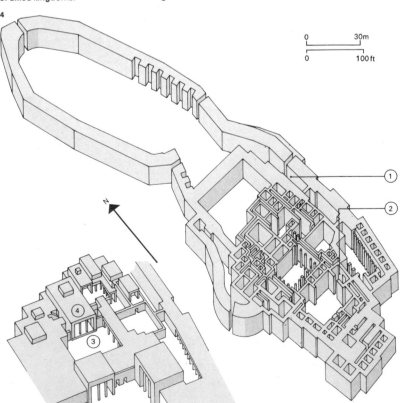

the Palace of Knossos was rebuilt as the seat of the new dynasty.

In the towns of Greece, craftsmen carried out their trades, producing fine metalwork, pottery and perishable goods. The towns themselves grew larger, stronger and better appointed. Walls were heightened and extended, with devices to ensure the safe supply of water. The palaces, still based on the traditional megaron plan, were now elaborately decorated with frescoes. The richly equipped tombs, now great corbelled tholoi (circular buildings first developed at this period) like the Treasury of Atreus [5], show the great architectural skill that had been attained by their builders.

To facilitate such a level of trade, craft and administration, writing was needed. The Minoans on Crete had developed a syllabic script of their own, still undeciphered. This is found inscribed on tablets and archaeologists have called it Linear A. The Mycenaeans adapted it, rather clumsily but adequately, for their Greek tongue (Linear B) [3]. In 1952 Michael Ventris, the English architect, deciphered Linear B and established beyond

doubt that the Mycenaeans, Homer's Achaeans, were linguistically at least the true ancestors of the classical Greeks.

### Mainland civilization declines

The closing stages of Bronze Age Greece are difficult to understand. By one account hardy frontiersmen from the northwest, the Dorians, overran the cities of the south and sacked them all, except Athens. By another, the Mycenaeans lost their expansionist drive towards 1200, engaged in civil war – the siege of Troy exemplifies this – and in effect destroyed themselves. At around this time, there was certainly great unrest over a wide area, and the bands which unsuccessfully attacked Egypt in 1225 BC and again in 1191 BC included Aegean peoples.

In mainland Greece, the succeeding age knew little of what had gone before. Shabby villages replaced the flourishing towns, simple pits the great tombs, and common pots the masterpieces in clay, silver and gold. The one advance in this dismal period, sometimes referred to as the "dark age", was the introduction of iron-working.

KEY

**This gold mask** shows a proud Mycenaean of c. 1550 BC. It was recovered from Shaft Grave V by Heinrich Schliemann in 1876.

**5 Earlier shaft graves** were succeeded at Mycenae by stone-built tholos tombs. The finest is the so-called Treasury of Atreus c. 1320 BC. A walled passage leads to a monumental door in the mound. Inside, a circular chamber is roofed by a corbelled vault. The bodies and grave goods were looted long ago, but other smaller tombs have also been found.

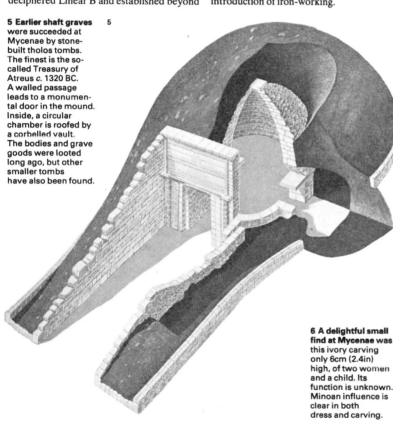

**6 A delightful small find at Mycenae** was this ivory carving only 6cm (2.4in) high, of two women and a child. Its function is unknown. Minoan influence is clear in both dress and carving.

**7 These Mycenaean warriors** may have a comic flavour to our eyes, but the discovery of fortifications, weapons and armour show that warfare was an important factor in life at the time.

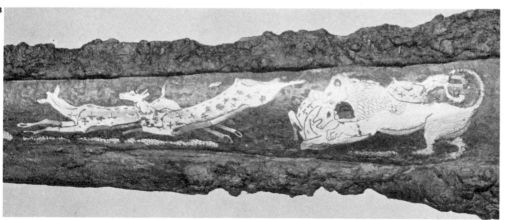

**8 Bronze daggers** from shaft graves of c. 1550 BC reveal great artistic skill in their gold, silver and niello inlay. Some show sea creatures, one shows a hunting cat in Minoan style, but this one has a more ro-

bust mainland subject. A lion is attacking a deer while two more make their escape. The dagger is 23.5cm (9.25in) long and one of the treasures discovered in Shaft Grave IV by Schliemann, the German archaeologist.

21

# Stone Age Britain

Although traces of still earlier occupation are beginning to come to light, the first really clear evidence of human settlement in Britain belongs to a time about a quarter of a million years ago. At that time the country enjoyed a mild climate and favourable environmental conditions between two ice ages.

### Swanscombe man and the ice ages
The population lived in small groups and occupied open-air sites along river valleys and lakesides. They were efficient hunters, catching large game such as now-extinct forms of elephant, and rhinoceros, as well as horse, wild ox, red deer and fallow deer. One of the most important sites of this period, at Swanscombe, just south of the River Thames in Kent, has yielded three fragments of the skull of a fossil man. Swanscombe man is usually classified as the earliest known example of the modern species *Homo sapiens*.

After the occupation of this period, which is sometimes known as the Great Interglacial, there are a number of sites that can be dated either to warmer phases within the next glaciation (c. 200,000–125,000 years ago) or

to the last interglacial period (c. 125,000–100,000 years ago). These sites indicate that men continued to visit Britain, at least during the milder climatic phases. With the beginning of the last ice age, c. 100,000 years ago, modern understanding of human activity in Britain becomes much clearer. Probably on four separate occasions during warmer climatic phases, small groups of hunters moved into Britain across a land-bridge from the continent of Europe and settled in caves [3] and rock-shelters in England and Wales. Some of the best known sites of this date occur in Cheddar Gorge, Somerset, and there is another important group in Derbyshire. Occupation of Britain still remained very sparse and occasional.

### Britain after the ice ages
About 14,000 years ago the climate began to become warmer once again and the ice sheets began their final retreat [1]. As conditions improved, the vegetation altered, and about 10,000 years ago the open tundra of the glacial periods began to be replaced by forests. At first these were forests of birch and pine,

both cold-loving species; later hazel, oak, elm, lime and alder grew too, forming the so-called "Mixed Oak Forest". These changes in flora were accompanied by changes in fauna also: open-country animals such as the horse, reindeer, bison and mammoth disappeared and were replaced by woodland forms such as red deer, roe deer, elk, wild ox and wild boar.

The human population had to adapt to all these changes in climate, vegetation and animal life. Some groups, such as the one that settled at Star Carr in Yorkshire c. 7500 BC, adapted their way of life to forest conditions [5]. They used plant foods such as hazel nuts and learned to hunt the woodland animals that moved singly in the forest, unlike the herd animals that their ancestors had hunted on the tundra. They learned to use timber and they had the first true stone axes.

Other groups settled along the seashore to exploit coastal resources, such as fish and shellfish. During this period Britain became permanently an island. As the ice sheets melted, large quantities of water were released into the sea, and the sea-level (which had been much lower than at the

**1 Ice sheets** covered much of the British Isles at least four times during the Pleistocene period, also known as the Ice Age. During the last and best-known glacial period only half of Britain was covered by ice, but two ice ages earlier, much more of the country was affected – as far south as the valley of the Thames. Temperatures were much lower than today in the glacial periods, and arctic conditions prevailed even south of the ice itself. As a result, there was no human settlement at those times. But the ice ages were separated by warmer "interglacial periods", when temperatures were at least as warm as at present. Shorter mild phases, or "interstadials", occurred within the main ice ages themselves. In these warmer periods, men crossed the land-bridge linking Britain with the European continent and settled, only to retreat to their former homes when the cold returned.

Limits of Devensian glaciation
c. 20,000 years ago
Wolstonian glaciation
c. 200,000 years ago
Anglian glaciation
c. 500,000 years ago

Star Carr

Creswell Crags

Cheddar Gorge · Woodhenge · Swanscombe
Stonehenge

Kents Cavern

0     100km

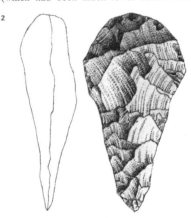

**2 Hand-axes made of flint** are among the earliest tools found in Britain. They could be used for cutting, scraping or hammering. Such axes occur throughout Europe, Africa and southern Asia.

**3 Kent's Cavern, Devon,** and similar caves elsewhere, provided shelter from the elements for the people who settled in Britain during the interstadial periods of the most recent ice age.

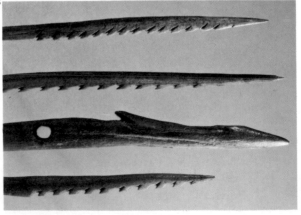

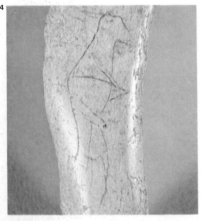

**4 A carving of a male figure,** scratched on an animal's rib bone, is probably about 12,000 years old, and was found in Pin Hole Cave, Derbyshire. The people who inhabited Britain during the last ice age did not decorate their caves with fine many-coloured paintings of animals as their contemporaries at Lascaux, France, or Altamira, Spain, did. Conditions of life at the extremities of Europe were probably too harsh to support such a high level of cultural activity.

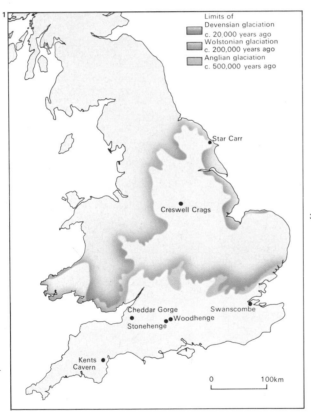

**5 Barbed points of antler** or other bone that might have been used for either hunting or fishing were numerous at Star Carr in eastern Yorkshire, one of the most fully explored Mesolithic sites in Britain. A lakeside platform of felled birch branches supported a small community there which lived by hunting the smaller animals such as deer in about 7500 BC. At that time, after the final retreat of the ice, open birch woodland began to give way to pine.

present during the glacial periods) rose. The last land-bridge connecting Britain to continental Europe was submerged *c.* 6000 BC. The Mesolithic people – as the hunting groups of the post-glacial era are known – probably used boats, both along the coasts and across stretches of water. Both Scotland and Ireland were settled for the first time during the Mesolithic period.

**The introduction of agriculture**
Some time before 4000 BC a new wave of settlers arrived in Britain from the European continent. These Neolithic immigrants introduced a whole new way of life based on farming, rather than on hunting and gathering. They cultivated wheat and barley and they bred domesticated cattle, swine, sheep and goats. They introduced new techniques, including the manufacture of pottery [6] and the production of ground and polished stone implements. These farmers were more numerous than the earlier hunters and they have left far clearer traces of their activities. Not many settlement sites of this period are known, but monumental tombs [Key] sur-

vive, as well as central meeting places or fair-grounds ("causewayed camps"), strange linear earthwork enclosures ("cursus monuments") and, rather later, the sanctuary sites ("henge monuments" [9]), of which the most famous are Avebury and Stonehenge. The sites from which they obtained the raw materials used for axes are also known, such as the mines at Grimes Graves in Norfolk and Great Langdale in Cumbria.

The first farmers in Britain probably had an egalitarian social organization without marked differences in rank or wealth. But it seems likely that by the later part of the Neolithic period, in the third millennium BC, a more hierarchical society had evolved. The construction of the five largest henge monuments probably involved about one million man-hours of work, while the two largest cursus monuments and the artificial mound of Silbury Hill [8] probably required more than ten million man-hours. The organization of manpower, materials and food supply required for these vast projects could have been undertaken only by a ranked society with a chief at its head.

**Monumental tombs,** such as this one at West Kennet, Wiltshire, were often built by the Neolithic inhabitants of Britain. Such tombs were used for many generations, and were closed after each burial and re-opened for the next. The bones of earlier burials were heaped together to make room for the new arrival.

**6 The art of making pots** was one of the skills introduced to Britain by the first farmers. The early pots were hand-made and fired at fairly low temperatures in open pit fires. It is therefore usually assumed that they were made domestically. But even such simple pots were sometimes traded over considerable distances.

**7 This Neolithic wooden figure** shows both male and female sexual characteristics and therefore probably represents a prehistoric deity. Evidence of the religious life of the early settlers is limited in Britain, because few cult figurines of the type common in Europe and Asia have been found. This example comes from the Somerset levels.

**8 Silbury Hill, Wiltshire,** is close to another important Neolithic ritual site at Avebury. It is the largest man-made mound in Europe, and is conical in shape, 40m (131ft) high. It was built in three stages; the first consisted of a gravelly clay core capped by a turf stack within a ring of stakes and covered by mixed materials. This was immediately overlaid by the second stage, which consisted of a chalk mound and a surrounding ditch. In the third stage the ditch was filled in and the chalk mound extended to cover a larger area. The whole process was continuous and took place about 2750 BC. Its purpose remains a mystery. Excavations have shown no sign of burials; it may have been a sanctuary with a temple on top.

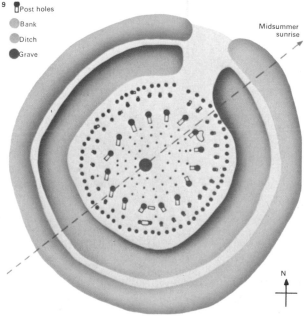

9
Post holes
Bank
Ditch
Grave

Midsummer sunrise

**9 Woodhenge** is an example of a small henge (a circular Neolithic earthwork). It is 3 km (2 miles) north of Stonehenge, and is immediately south of the vast monument of Durrington Walls. Inside Woodhenge there are six concentric rings of holes that originally contained wooden posts. They are thought to be the remains of a wooden building with an open light in the centre. On the axis of the building, near the centre, is a grave of a child about three years old with a cleft skull, one of the few examples of ritual human sacrifice in Britain. The settings of the posts are oval in plan, and the long axis points in the direction of the midsummer sunrise, like the axis of Stonehenge. Woodhenge was built about 2300 BC.

N

# China to 1000 BC

The Chinese have a unique place in history largely due to their natural barriers that protected their great land mass (the size of Europe) and their relative lack of contact with the outside world until the nineteenth century. Their ancient culture did not come to an end like the cultures of ancient Egypt and Greece, but has evolved unbroken from 2500 BC to the present day.

**Earliest human remains**
The earliest human remains so far discovered in China are those of the Peking and Lan-t'ien men, dating back well over half a million years. They were among the first men to make tools and evidence of their descendants has been found in caves in the hills near Chou-k'ou-tien, which contained scraping and cutting stones. These early people were followed by Upper Cavemen who lived about 50,000 years ago. They were able to make fire and lived by hunting, fishing and gathering fruits and edible roots. In the Neolithic age (c. 7000–1600 BC) people made needles, bows and arrows, and ground sharp edges on stones and shells. Antlers were fashioned into sickles and saws and an agricultural and pastoral society arose. The Neolithic period is also characterized by fine pottery [2, 3, 7].

The first farmers lived in beehive-shaped huts which were sunk into the ground for additional warmth and security and covered by thatched roofs supported on wooden posts. Agriculture was helped by the existence of a thick deposit of loess, a very fine soil that is thought to have been blown from the northwest. In some places in the Central Plain it is more than 60m (200ft) deep and, being exceptionally fertile, provides some of the finest agricultural land in the world. Like the Nile mud it is an excellent material for building rammed earth walls or for making bricks. The region's moderate climate supported wild horses, buffalo, deer, wild pigs, sheep and even rhinoceros.

The Central Plain lies between two great rivers – the Huang Ho [1] in the north and the Yangtze in the south. These rivers flow from west to east and carry the loess through the region. It is here that the Bronze Age culture of the Shang or Yin Dynasty was born (c. 1600–c. 1030 BC).

Fortunately the Chinese proved to be expert husbandmen and managed to maintain cereal crops on the same fields for thousands of years.

**The writings of early historians**
There is so far little evidence to support the earliest history of China as related by Chinese historians of the second century BC. They held that the country was first ruled by two groups of three and five emperors made up of legendary figures, who were followed by the Hsia, Shang and Chou dynasties. The existence of the Hsia Dynasty is still in doubt, but archaeological evidence has proved the existence both of the Shang Dynasty and of a central authority with a capital city, Great Shang near An-yang in north Honan. The Shang were mainly agricultural people but they are known for their mastery of bronze casting [Key]. Their bronze ritual vessels, bells and axes exhibit an unsurpassed quality of craftsmanship [5, 9].

Sacrifice played an important part in Shang culture, and people as well as animals were slaughtered to commemorate royal

**1 The floodplains** of the Huang Ho (seen here) and Yangtze rivers provided a natural centre for the growth of Chinese civilization. The rich silt they carried and the annual irrigation encouraged settlements and the growth of agriculture. The Yangtze is the fourth longest river in the world. The Huang Ho or Yellow River derives its common name from its sludgy yellow-brown colour. It is subject to unpredictable floods caused by the melting snows; these have so often devastated the fertile plains that the river was known as "China's sorrow". It flows into the Yellow Sea today but has changed its course many times in its history.

**2 This black pottery tripod vessel** is known as a *li*. It represents the final and most developed phase of Neolithic pottery and comes from Lung-shan in the central Yellow River basin. The three legs are hollow and have the practical advantage of holding the pot upright on the embers and of offering a larger surface to the fire. Pots of this area are characterized by dark burnished surfaces.

**3 This red pottery amphora** was excavated from the Pan-p'o village site in Shensi province and is an excellent example of the red pottery ware of the Yang-shao culture. The pots were often painted with designs based on fish.

**4 Oracle bones,** usually made from the shoulder blades of oxen or the carapaces of tortoises, were used for divination. Questions in the form of pictures were scratched on the surface of the bone and a red-hot iron applied. The heat resulted in cracks radiating from the burn and these enabled the diviner to read the answer to the question. Pictograms were the earliest form of Chinese writing and the symbols are direct ancestors of the modern Chinese script.

**5 The inscription and the human faces** on this bronze ritual food vessel or *ting* (14th–11th centuries BC) allude to human sacrifice; the vessel may have been used in the rites. The sacrifice would have been an offering to an ancestor.

burials and to mark the erection of important buildings. One building excavated at An-yang disclosed guards outside the gates armed with halberds and others along the outside walls. Dogs were distributed along the walls and five chariots complete with charioteers and horses were buried in the central courtyard.

The royal tombs were even more exacting in their needs. Ramps led down to the pit [8] containing the coffin which lay in the centre of the deepest part, usually over a smaller grave containing the body of a dog. The pit contained the bodies of people, horses and dogs as well as chariots and all the furniture and household goods needed for the occupant in the next world. Some people had been beheaded and lay in groups of ten with their heads carefully laid in a separate place. Slaves were occasionally buried alive, and in one tomb 70 living people had apparently been buried with the dead.

The Shang Dynasty prospered. The new bronze tools made a variety of trade possible and exchange of foods became necessary. To facilitate trade, money was introduced in the form of cowrie shells, already one of the world's most popular currencies because of their valuable qualities of size and durability and because they were impossible to forge.

## Calendars and cities
The Shang were a fairly sophisticated people and their astronomers produced an accurate calendar, based on the lunar month, which was corrected by the addition of seven extra lunar months over a period of 19 solar years.

Shang culture spread over central China and traces of it have been found in the Yangtze valley 640km (400 miles) to the south [6]. The Shang method of planning towns in squares can still be seen in Peking. The Shang regarded themselves as the centre of civilization and the name for China still remains Chung-kuo, the Middle Country. However, the rule of Shang was nearing its end. Frequent wars and the oppression of the people by the last ruler, Chou Hsin, finally drove the slaves into revolt. Chou Hsin perished in the flames that destroyed his palace and with this the Chou Dynasty began (c. 1030 BC).

**During the Shang Dynasty** a highly skilled bronze metallurgy was developed, much later than in the West although it was still the earliest bronzework in East Asia. The two main weapons used by the Shang people were the bow and the halberd. This bronze ritual halberd blade from the Shang Dynasty dates from the late 11th century BC.

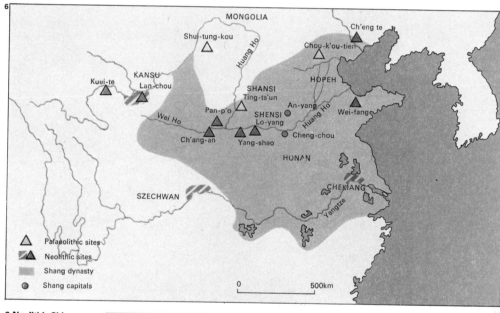

**6 Neolithic China** was centred on the fertile northern plains around the Huang Ho River. The first dynasty, the Shang, ruled first from Cheng-chou and later moved north to An-yang.

**7 The Liang-chu Neolithic culture** flourished within a relatively confined area in the region of Shanghai in the northern Chekiang province. It is characterized by a coarse brick-red or sometimes grey pottery, such as this pottery kettle c. 4000 BC, which frequently adopted curious shapes and forms of a type more usually associated with vessels made from bronze.

**8 Two ramps** lead down to the burial chamber (c. 1100 BC), in the centre of which the coffin is placed over a depression containing the body of a dog. Bodies of funeral sacrifice victims were carefully positioned on the ledge surrounding the coffin. Nothing was left to chance: furniture, clothes, household equipment, food and drink – everything that was needed on earth for the comfort of the deceased was buried with him.

**9 Shang Dynasty bronzes** were mostly discovered at An-yang, the Shang capital; their uses were ceremonial and funerary. Of the food vessels, *chiu* [A] cauldrons had flat bases; the *ting* [B] had three or four legs and handles. Wine beakers of the *chueh* type [C] had tripod bases, handles and spouts; the *ku* [D] was a deep cup with a flaring rim. Of the wine and water jugs, the *hsi-tsun* or *tsun* [E] had animal or bird forms; the *kuang* [F] had a lid in the back of the animal. The *hu* [G], *yu* [H] and *chih* [I] were wine or water jugs. Raised and depressed decoration with animal motifs, *t'ao-t'ieh*, was at first representative and later geometrically stylized.

# Preclassic America to AD 300

The period between 2200 BC and AD 300 saw the rise of the first civilizations in both Mexico, where it is known as the Formative or Preclassic, and Peru. By 1500 BC agricultural villages in both Mesoamerica and South America were developing with craft specialization in such fields as ceramics; society was also moving towards stratification, expressed in the first public architecture. The first truly complex society, the Olmec culture, based in the tropical lowlands of the Mexican Gulf coast, had appeared by 1200 BC. The first great ceremonial centre was San Lorenzo Tenochtitlán, where the whole form of a natural ridge was altered by the construction of ridges and platforms.

## Spread of Olmec culture

During excavations numerous pieces of monumental sculpture in volcanic stone were found, including giant heads deliberately defaced and buried [Key]. The stone itself came from the Tuxtla Mountains many kilometres away and the presence as well as the sophistication of the sculptures indicates an organized labour force, a body of specialist sculptors and a powerful government whose patronage extended from sculptors to lapidaries and potters as well. A further range of sculpture and a large conical pyramid were found at another Olmec centre, La Venta.

Olmec trade spread far into the highlands of Mexico, Oaxaca being a source for various minerals, and the valley of the Río Balsas beyond Mexico City perhaps being the origin of the blue jade favoured by the Olmec; another possible source is even more distant, in Costa Rica. Rock carvings and cave paintings in Olmec style are known from western Mexico, and the carvings continue eastwards into El Salvador. Whether diffusion of this artistic stimulus was commercial, religious, diplomatic or military, it has a good claim to being the first pan-Mesoamerican style. There is some evidence that the Olmec possessed a system of numerical and perhaps other notation, but whether this can be described as "writing" in its true sense is still a matter for argument.

In Peru from about 1000 BC onwards a similar diffusion of the Chavín style occurred. The style involves both birds of prey and feline-human compounds [1] with serpent attributes, and is full of arcane allusion. The style is named after the site of Chavín de Huántar, about 3,000m (9,750ft) up and just below and east of the crest of the Andes in central Peru, where a complex of massive stone buildings with subterranean galleries stand round formal courtyards. Some of the galleries contain sculptures, such as the *Lanzón* that stands in the deepest part of the main structure and portrays a mythical being.

## Chavín influence on arts and crafts

The Chavín style is also found in pottery, and examples of it are known from as far north as Ecuador, while in textiles Chavín influence is found in the Paracas region [4] in southern Peru. Chavín influence continued until about 200 BC, and may have just continued in a provincial form in the sculptures of San Agustín in southern Colombia. The sites at San Agustín cover a wide area on the hills around the modern town and consist of megalithic chambered monuments and feline, fanged sculptures. They are dated

1 **Human and feline characteristics** are combined in a sculpture of a monstrous head projecting from the wall of the Castillo, the main structure at Chavín de Huántar. The undressed but neat masonry contrasts with the sophistication of the carvings. The site lies in a high valley in the upper Amazon basin.

2 **Figures of** *danzantes* – dancers – at the Zapotec centre of Monte Albán, Oaxaca, Mexico, date from about 500 BC and resemble Olmec art of the same period and earlier. The abandoned poses, closed eyes and various details on the bodies suggest that the figures depict slain warriors.

3 **Two sculptured stone slabs** or stelae at Monte Albán bear short inscriptions in a form of hieroglyphic writing, including long bars and round discs that probably denote numbers, a bar equalling 5 and a disc 1. These stelae, dating from about 500 BC, are the earliest dated writing in the ancient Americas.

4 **Part of a richly decorated textile** from the desert cemeteries of the Paracas peninsula, on the coast of south-central Peru, shows a complex design that is repeated similarly on each of the many panels. These textiles have been preserved by the dry climate of the Peruvian coast, and provide an idea of what may have been lost elsewhere.

from AD 1–500, although more radiocarbon dates might vary this.

Elaborate gold work of the Chavín period is found in the Lambayeque valley and other regions of northern Peru. It initiated a tradition of working precious metals that continued until the Spanish conquest. In the Viru valley, south of Trujillo on the Peruvian coast, major centralized settlements developed during the early centuries AD, apparently in response to population pressure and competition for resources. Pucará in southern Peru was an important cultural centre, quite unrelated to Chavín.

From about 500 BC the rise of Zapotec culture [2] in the Valley of Oaxaca in southern Mexico accelerated. The first monumental inscriptions in hieroglyphic script from the New World [3] are found at the great hilltop centre of Monte Albán, together with large stone buildings and low-relief carvings of humans. Another structure, Mound J, could well have been an astronomical observatory. By the end of the Preclassic period Monte Albán already possessed the spacious formal layout, the huge open plazas

and the massive platforms that mark its further development in the Classic.

The Valley of Mexico, after a period of Olmec influence, saw the rise of a number of independent political units round the margins of its broad, shallow lakes. Among these was Cuicuilco, which was destroyed about the time of Christ by an eruption [5].

Teotihuacán, a rival state in the northeast of the valley, grew in the next century into a centralized, planned urban settlement [6] which by AD 150 covered more than 20 sq km (7.7 sq miles), with a growing population. Teotihuacán trade extended a long way eastwards into the Maya area by about AD 400.

### The beginning of the Maya culture
The Maya are the reason for the Classic period formally beginning at AD 300, because that is roughly when they started to erect monuments bearing inscriptions [8] in the Long Count, a complex calendar that enables Maya monuments [7] to be dated to within a day. It now seems that Maya culture itself acquired most of the attributes of civilization during the late Preclassic period.

This giant head of the Olmec period. found at San Lorenzo Tenochtitlán near the Gulf Coast of Mexico, dates from about 1200–900 BC. Several such heads were found at the site, and others are known from La Venta and a number of smaller sites including the early Laguna de los Cerros. They are thought to depict the Olmec rulers and are made of volcanic rock brought at least 100 km (60 miles) from the Tuxtla Mountains, giving strong evidence of the social control exerted. The Olmec culture is the first complex society in Mesoamerica to attain a level that can be described as "civilization" and it stimulated later developments.

5 The circular and stepped pyramid at Cuicuilco in the Valley of Mexico on the edge of present Mexico City was the main structure of a city that flourished at about the time of Christ. It was overwhelmed by an eruption of the volcano Xitle and buried under lava, but has recently been excavated and restored.

6 Teotihuacán, a great city in the northeastern basin of Mexico, began its dramatic rise about 100 BC and from AD 100–700 had a population approaching 200,000. The long Avenue of the Dead runs south from the Pyramid of the Moon to the citadel and market compound in the centre of the city.

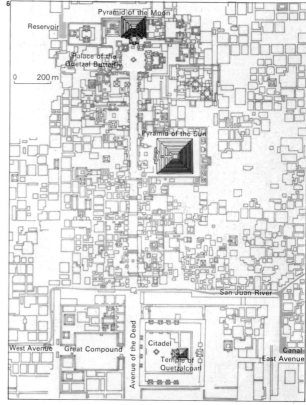

Pyramid of the Moon
Reservoir
Palace of the Quetzal Butterfly
0    200 m
Pyramid of the Sun
San Juan River
West Avenue    Great Compound
Avenue of the Dead
Citadel
Temple of Quetzalcoatl
Canal
East Avenue

7 Reconstruction of Pyramid E–VII–Sub shows a Preclassic temple of about AD 200–300 at the Maya site of Uaxactún, Guatemala, which archaeologists found preserved beneath a later structure.

8 Mayan writing has more than 800 hieroglyphs, few of which have been translated although the Mayan calendar is understood. This is part of an inscription on one of the stelae at Quiriguá, Guatemala.

# Egypt 1570 BC to Alexander the Great

The New Kingdom in Egypt (c. 1570–1085 BC) dates from the victory of Theban forces over the Hyksos rulers of Egypt. New Kingdom Egypt was an empire extending from the northern Sudan to Syria and was one of the major powers of the ancient world. The god of Thebes, Amun, was elevated to the rank of principal deity of the realm and was identified with the sun-god Re in the form Amun-Re, king of the gods [1]. Much of the wealth that flowed into Egypt as a result of its conquests was directed towards the service of Amun and his priesthood.

## The consolidation of Egyptian power

The early kings of Dynasty XVIII were primarily engaged in rendering Egypt safe from any further incursions by the Bedouin in the east or the Nubians in the south. After stabilizing the eastern frontier the Egyptian rulers undertook a series of campaigns to conquer the kingdom of Nubia in the south and to seize its gold mines. The lack of male heirs to the throne from the marriage of the ruler to his full sister led to the increasing importance of the royal heiresses. One such

was Hatshepsut (r.c. 1503– c. 1482 BC), wife and half-sister of Thutmose II, who bore her husband no sons. On his death the child of a concubine, Thutmose III (reigned c. 1504–1450 BC), was placed upon the throne and was presumably destined to marry his half-sister. However, his stepmother Hatshepsut later seized the throne for herself and ruled together with Thutmose III, who was allowed no real power.

On Hatshepsut's death, Thutmose III assumed effective control of the government and immediately embarked on a series of campaigns to subjugate the petty kingdoms in Palestine and most of Syria. He also completed the conquest of Nubia as far as Napata and his immediate successors continued his expansionist policies.

Under Amenhotep III (reigned 1417–1379 BC) the Egyptian court reached the height of its prestige, receiving tribute or trade goods from Syria, Mesopotamia, Anatolia, Crete and even Greece. His son Amenhotep IV or Akhenaton (reigned c. 1379–1362 BC) changed the Egyptian religion by his worship of the sun-god in the

form of Aton, the sun's disc, and moved the capital to the new city of Akhetaten (Amarna). Akhenaton's policy encountered the opposition of the priesthood of the old gods and led to domestic anarchy and the weakening of Egypt's prestige abroad. His successors abandoned his beliefs and order was finally restored in the reign of Horemheb, the last ruler of the dynasty. Upon Horemheb's death the throne passed to his vizier Ramesses I (reigned c. 1320–1318 BC), who founded Dynasty XIX (c. 1320–1200 BC).

## Confrontation with the Hittites

The aim of the rulers of this period was to restore Egypt's power and prestige abroad and to confirm Egypt's dominant position in Palestine in the face of the growth of the power of the Hittite Empire. This rivalry led to a major clash in Year 5 of Ramesses II (reigned 1304–1237 BC) [Key] at the town of Kadesh, where both the Egyptians and Hittites claimed victory. Peace was eventually concluded between the two combatants in Year 21 and sealed in Year 34 by the mar-

1 The ancient cult of the sun-god Re had been eclipsed by the rise of the god Amun, until Akhenaton tried to suppress the worship of all gods except Re. The sun-god was represented in the form of the Aton or sun disc, adored here by his queen Nefertiti.

2 This treasure, a pectoral with solar and lunar emblems [A] and a necklace of the rising sun [B], is from the pyramid tomb of Tutankhamen who succeeded to the throne through his marriage to Akhenaton's daughter and heiress. Bowing to political pressures, he renounced Akhenaton's religion and abandoned Amarna, returning to Thebes and restoring the worship of Amun and other gods. He died c. 1340 BC. His pyramid tomb was the only one left intact. Persistent robberies ended the system of pyramid burials. Instead cliff tombs were cut in the well-guarded Valley of the Kings.

3 Egyptian temples conformed to a common plan. This can be seen clearly in the small temple of the god Khons within the temple complex at Karnak in Thebes. The entrance to the temple was through a pylon (gateway) [1] into an open court [2] with a colonnade along the sides. Off this, along a straight axis, was a hypostyle (pillared hall) [3] leading to the sanctuary [4] where the image of the god lay. Service and storage rooms surrounded the sanctuary. Because each Egyptian ruler was determined to create an enduring reputation through building works, most major temples were forever being enlarged and remodelled by the addition of more courts and rooms to the existing structure.

riage of Ramesses II with a Hittite princess. His successors were faced with increasing threats from Libyan tribesmen and piratical "Sea-Peoples", but these threats were contained by Ramesses III, (reigned *c.* 1198–1166 BC) of Dynasty XX [6].

Under Ramesses III's successors, who were also all named Ramesses, the power of the crown steadily declined in the face of increased Libyan incursions and the growth in the power of local governors, especially that of the high priest of Amun at Thebes. Egypt's foreign possessions in Palestine and Nubia were lost by the end of the dynasty and Egypt itself fell under the control of foreign rulers. Under Dynasty XXI, which ruled from the northern city of Tanis, Thebes was virtually independent under its high priests. The unity of Egypt was restored by the Libyan general Shoshenk I (reigned *c.* 935–914 BC), founder of Dynasty XXII. He installed his own son as high priest of Amun and attempted to restore Egypt's position as a great power by embarking on a major campaign in Palestine. Under his successors the unity of the country was broken by civil wars

and Egypt was partitioned into city states under independent dynasts, mostly of Libyan origin. An independent kingdom had emerged in Nubia in the south and the Nubian kings conquered Egypt in about 712 BC and founded Dynasty XXV.

Nubian rule was terminated by a series of Assyrian invasions that led to the nomination of the prince of Sais as puppet ruler of Egypt. With the help of Greek mercenaries, Psamtik I (reigned *c.* 664–610 BC) of Dynasty XXVI managed to impose his authority on the whole country and broke with Assyria.

**Defeat by Babylonia and Persia**
The rule of Dynasty XXVI (670–525 BC) marked a period of renewed prosperity but Egypt's hopes of restoring her position as a great power were defeated by the Babylonians at the Battle of Carchemish in 605 BC. Ultimately in 525 BC Egypt was absorbed by the Persians and although subsequent revolts re-established Egyptian independence briefly between 404 and 343 BC, the Persians reasserted their domination until the arrival of Alexander the Great in 332 BC.

KEY

**Ramesses II** ensured that his name would be remembered by his extensive building projects. He added the hypostyle hall to the temple of Amun at Karnak and made additions, including this colossus of himself, to the temple of Luxor. On the west bank at Thebes he built his mortuary temple – the Ramesseum. For his favourite queen, Nofretari, a tomb decorated with superb paintings was constructed in the Valley of the Queens. In Nubia he erected the great temple of Abu Simbel, as well as other temples elsewhere in Egypt. He also constructed the city of Pi-Ramesse, his northern capital, possibly using the labour of Hebrew slaves as mentioned in the Bible.

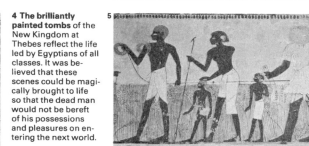

4 **The brilliantly painted tombs** of the New Kingdom at Thebes reflect the life led by Egyptians of all classes. It was believed that these scenes could be magically brought to life so that the dead man would not be bereft of his possessions and pleasures on entering the next world.

5 **The economy of Egypt** was agrarian, most of the people working on the land. In theory all land was held by the crown but in practice large estates were also held by the official classes and the temples. A limited number of peasant proprietors also owned tracts of agricultural land.

6 **The invasion of the "Sea-Peoples"**, including the Philistines and maybe the ancestors of the Sicilians, was repulsed by Ramesses III at the end of the New Kingdom.

7 **Most tombs in the New Kingdom** include a *Book of the Dead* containing spells intended to guarantee the safe passage of the deceased to the afterlife.

# Africa: Kush and Axum

During the course of ancient Egyptian history, the armies of the pharaohs pushed the frontier of their empire ever farther south, along the axis and heart of their civilization, the Nile, towards tropical black Africa. By the time of the New Kingdom (*c.* 1500 BC) all the riverine lands as far as the Fourth Cataract – that is, in the middle of the great S bend of the Nile – had been conquered and to some extent settled by Egyptians. This country, later called Nubia, was known to the Egyptians as Kush and in time a typical late Egyptian civilization flourished there.

### The emergence of the Kushite kingdom

By about 1000 BC the New Kingdom had fallen and Kush emerged as an independent state – independent not only politically from Egypt, but increasingly also culturally. In 200 years its rulers had grown so independent and powerful that in 725 BC they were able to march down the Nile and conquer the whole of Egypt, where they formed Dynasty XXV of the Pharaohs [2].

Kushite control of Egypt, however, was short-lived. Between 676 and 663 BC Assyrian armies invaded and devastated Egypt – first under Esarhaddon and later under Ashurbanipal. The Kushite pharaoh Taharqa retreated southwards to Kush. What had made the mighty Assyrian armies almost invincible over much of the Middle East was their possession of iron weapons, which were much superior to the bronze weapons of their foes. The leaders of Kush had learned a hard lesson and took with them the Assyrian knowledge of iron technology. This was to be the basis for the stability of Kush.

After the withdrawal from Egypt, the rulers of Kush expanded southwards, keeping to the valley of the Nile. The country on either side of the great river was more fertile than it became subsequently and could support large herds of cattle. By the sixth century BC the frontier of Kush had reached just to the south of present-day Khartoum, where the land was well wooded.

### Dominance of the Meroë civilization

The power centre of the empire swung to the south, from the old capital of Napata (near the Fourth Cataract, where the surrounding land had become over-grazed) to Meroë, south of the Atbarah's confluence with the Nile. From this time, the empire is often referred to as Meroë, rather than Kush. Whereas some of the inhabitants of the northern part of Kush were black people, now nearly all the people in the country around Meroë were black and the empire became a black state.

Meroë had abundant iron-ore and wood with which to smelt it. The iron industry of the empire was on a large scale. Immense slag heaps still litter the landscape. The well-armed horsemen of the Meroë army were able to defend the settled lands from attacks of desert nomads. A flourishing trade was maintained with Ptolemaic Egypt, Arabia and even India, via the Red Sea.

By the beginning of the Christian era, however, the civilization of Kush/Meroë had begun to decline. This was the result of internal impoverishment, especially the drying up of once rich grazing and agricultural lands. Attacks by nomads became more difficult to contain, and the empire finally collapsed when invaded by a powerful army

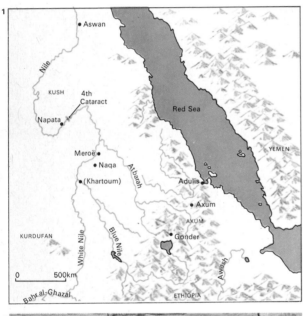

**1 Civilizations of Kush/Meroë** and Axum occupied the northeast corner of Africa: Kush/Meroë in the middle Nile valley south of Egypt and Axum on the high mountain escarpment of northern Ethiopia. Axum was the founding state of the Christian empire of Ethiopia.

**2 Narwa** was governor of Thebes during the reign of one of the Kushite line of pharaohs in the 8th and 7th centuries BC. The Kushites had moved north and ruled Egypt until they were defeated and driven back to their old lands by a new invader – the "iron armies" of the Assyrians.

**3 The Lion God of Kush** was engraved on a temple wall at Naqa (100 BC– AD 100), a centre south of Meröe. The carvings show an Indian influence.

**4 An elephant and war captives** form a temple frieze near Meroë, first century AD. Elephants were used for military and ceremonial purposes at Kush/Meröe.

from neighbouring Axum in AD 350.

The empire of Kush/Meroë had been in existence for over 1,000 years and its cultural achievements were rich and vital [3, 4]. They represented far more than an Africanized form of Egyptian culture. The inhabitants of the empire took their Egyptian heritage, borrowed more from the Hellenistic world and India, and fashioned something unique, including their own form of writing, a cursive script that has to date defied all efforts to decipher it [Key].

### Axum, the rival empire in Ethiopia

Axum, the rival empire of Meroë, had its origin not on the African continent, but in Arabia. A number of small but prosperous states grew up in the Yemen early in the first millennium BC, one of which, Saba, was probably the Sheba of King Solomon's time. By about the seventh century BC Semitic-speaking people from the overpopulated Yemen spilt over the Red Sea to the Horn of Africa, settling as farmers on the northeastern edge of the high plateau of Ethiopia. There they prospered and were able to domi-

nate the indigenous Kushistic-speaking peoples, many of whom gradually accepted the culture and the Semitic language of the newcomers. One group of these, called the Habashat, established a kingdom in the third century BC, centred on Axum [6, 7].

The Hellenistic Greeks were influential at the court of the kings of Axum and prepared the way for the reception of Christianity. The missionary responsible for the conversion of the kingdom in the fourth century AD was a Syrian called Frumentius (c. 300–c. 380). He was made bishop of Axum by the patriarch of Alexandria and within a few decades Christianity had been established there. The rulers of Christian Axum conquered parts of southern Arabia in the sixth century AD, before being driven out by Persian forces; from there on Axum went into gradual decline: the Muslim Arab conquest of Egypt disrupted her Red Sea trade and when the kingdom was devastated by nomads her power withered. Nevertheless, its political, religious and cultural traditions survived to be revived in the Middle Ages deep in the heartlands of Ethiopia.

The mysterious Meroitic script [A] is still unde-ciphered. The Sabaean script [B] of Axum is the fore-runner of modern Amharic, the language of Ethiopia.

**5 Christian art** from vanished Christian kingdoms survived in a church at Faras, near Wadi Halfa, which has now been engulfed by the waters of the Aswan dam. Christian kingdoms succeeded Kush/Meroë after the empire collapsed in the fifth century AD shortly before Egypt became part of the realm of Islam.

**6 Rich in products** that drew Greek, Arabian and Indian merchants alike, Axum was a land of soaring crags, the highest (Rāsdajan) at 4,620m (15,158ft). One of the most difficult African lands to live in or invade, it was to enter European mythology as the home of the legendary Christian king, Prester John.

**7 The tallest surviving stele,** or obelisk, at Axum, is one of the many splendid monuments erected by the rulers of the kingdom of Axum as their wealth grew from trade passing through to Arabia and India.

# The Hittites 1700–1200 BC

A hundred years ago knowledge of the Hittites was derived only from mentions in the Bible and in Mesopotamian records, but then, in the nineteenth century, discoveries began in Turkey of monuments and massive fortifications which had obviously survived from a flourishing and powerful civilization. This civilization was quickly identified as Hittite. What finally brought these peoples into vivid life was the discovery at Boğazköy, the site of the Hittite capital Hattusas, of more than 10,000 cuneiform tablets. The tablets were written in several languages, including Akkadian, Hattian, Hurrian, Luwian and Sumerian as well as Hittite, and were found to be the state archives.

## Origins of Hittite civilization

Little is known about the earliest period of the Hittite civilization before contact with Mesopotamia. The Hittites came into Asia Minor before 2000 BC from Europe or southern Russia. In the middle of the seventeenth century BC King Hattusilas I seems to have united a number of small states and established his administrative centre at Hat-tusas. Hittite power evidently grew rapidly, for in the early sixteenth century BC Mursilis I was able not only to occupy Syria but to march on Babylon, sacking the city and bringing to an end the dynasty of which Hammurabi was the greatest figure. The last king of the so-called Old Kingdom was Telepinus (reigned *c.* 1525–1500 BC), who is best known for his edict laying down rules of conduct for the nobles and the king.

After a period of which there are few records, the Hittite Empire began about 1460 BC. The first king of the new dynasty was apparently Tudhaliyas II, who is said to have captured Aleppo. Mitanni, a state founded by the Hurrians in northern Mesopotamia, seems to have kept further Hittite expansion in check.

The situation changed radically when Suppiluliumas seized the throne in about 1380. He fortified Hattusas and in a brilliant campaign conquered Mitanni and its Syrian satellites. Carchemish, which commanded an important crossing point on the Euphrates, remained independent, but Suppiluliumas then led a second campaign, captured this fortress and occupied all of Syria between the Euphrates and the ocean.

Suppiluliumas died in about 1346 BC; his son Mursilis II proved equally capable, defeating the kingdom of Arzawa to the west and suppressing a revolt in Syria. The next king, Muwattalis, inherited a secure and prosperous empire. But Egypt was determined under Ramesses II (reigned 1304–1237 BC) to regain the possessions and influence she had lost in Syria. The two armies met at Kadesh [7] on the River Orontes. Egypt claimed an overwhelming victory, but the Hittites seem, at least, to have held their own and maintained their ascendancy in Syria. Relations between the two powers improved as Assyria became more of a threat, and in about 1284 BC they signed a treaty of friendship and non-aggression.

## The end of the Hittite Empire

The records of the Hittite Empire end abruptly in the late thirteenth century BC, when Indo-European invaders known as the "Sea-Peoples" poured into the area from Europe. The Hittites fled southwards as the

**1 The impressive sanctuary** of Yazilikaya is open to the air and is cut from the rock outside the walls of Hattusas, the Hittite capital. Spectacular reliefs are carved on the sides of two chambers, which are approached through an elaborate gateway. They depict processions of gods, goddesses and kings, many of the deities being shown with their cult animals, weapons and symbols. Some of the gods are the patrons of Hittite cities and all are named in hieroglyphic script. The principal scene shows the weather god Teshub standing on deified mountains; facing him are his consort and his son and beneath him are the gods of the Hurrian pantheon. During the later years of the empire, Hittite religion came under strong Hurrian influence, as the carvings here illustrate.

**2 The rock carving at Ivriz** in the Taurus Mountains exemplifies the Aramaean style in Hittite sculpture, as is shown in particular by the god's cap and by the ringlets and profiles of both figures. But while the king wears an Assyrian cloak of a kind familiar from the royal statue from Malatya, the god's clothing has little that cannot be paralleled in purely Hittite sculptures, including the clear curved seam above the knees. The combination of relief and script facilitated the grouping (in 1880) of similar monuments reported from elsewhere in Asia Minor, notably at Boğazköy and Yazilikaya, as Hittite. The inscription names the king as Warpalawas (about 730 BC), so dating the relief.

**3 Among the chief deities** in the Anatolian pantheon were the weather god, Teshub [A] and the sun-goddess of Arinna [B]. Teshub is shown in a ninth-century statue in his customary pose, wielding a flash of lightning; for unlike Mesopotamia, Anatolia is a land of cloud and storms. To the sun-goddess, shown in a pendant of the empire period, the king appealed for help in times of war and danger; she was supreme patroness of the Hittite state.

**4 Most surviving Hittite sculpture** takes the form of monumental bas-reliefs in stone, often with inscriptions in hieroglyphic (as distinct from cuneiform) Hittite. The almost total absence of sculpture in the round is partly compensated for by a few beautiful miniature figures like this gold statuette (4.2cm [1.7in] high) of a man, perhaps a king, wearing a full tunic with short sleeves. It was found at Yozgat, near Boğazköy, and dates from about the fourteenth century BC.

Phrygians overran Asia Minor. But although the homeland was lost, the Hittite way of life survived as the refugees established city states in northern Syria, which had so long been under Hittite control. Most of the archaeological evidence comes from this neo-Hittite revival rather than from the early imperial period. The writing of these petty kingdoms is hieroglyphic Hittite, but the language was essentially Luwian, so that we may assume that the Hittites did not necessarily form the majority of the population.

## Structure of Hittite society

The neo-Hittite city states, which were often isolated geographically, were unable to unite effectively against the growing power of Assyria. After exacting tribute over many years and putting down occasional rebellions, Assyria, under Tiglath-Pileser III (reigned 744–727 BC), decided to incorporate the Syrian kingdoms into its empire, and by the end of the eighth century BC the Hittite Empire was little more than a memory.

During the period up to the end of the thirteenth century BC the Hittite king,

although perhaps not quite such a dominant figure as in Mesopotamia, made the final decision on military, religious and judicial matters [4]. On his death he joined the gods, and indeed "he became a god" was a euphemism for the death of a king. The queen was also important, having a role to play in state affairs. Nepotism was institutionalized, most of the highest offices falling to the king's relations. There seems to have been an exclusive caste of privileged nobility and landowners. The common people worked as farmers, craftsmen and labourers, and those of the servant class, while having some legal rights, were little better than slaves.

The brutality that so disfigures the history of Assyria was quite lacking among the Hittites. A city captured in war suffered grave retribution in that it was generally destroyed and its inhabitants enslaved, but we know of no mass killings or systematic torture such as Assyria's enemies could expect. Similarly, punishment for crime was generally based on restitution to the injured party or his relatives, even in the case of murder.

**A double-headed eagle** is carved on the back of a sphinx at Alaja Hüyük in Turkey, a city of the empire period. It is clutching in its talons two hares with their faces turned outwards like the eagle's heads. A figure, now badly damaged but perhaps a goddess, stood on the eagle's back. The same double-headed eagle motif appears also as a base for two standing figures among the sculptures of Yazili-kaya. A double-headed bird appears elsewhere in the ancient world, for example on an early geometric-period ivory from Sparta, and on a shrine at Taxila, and survives on the banners of the Kandyan chiefs.

5

6

**5 In the sphinx gate at Alaja Hüyük** in central Turkey, the sphinxes – unusually for Hittite art – are sculpted partly in the round. Many reliefs were found in the ruins, depicting animals, musicians, jugglers, and a shepherd with his flock. Pre-Hittite tombs of the third millennium were also discovered there and contained silver and bronze animal figures, golden jugs, goblets, and ornaments.

**6 The excavation of Karatepe**, northeast of Adana, revealed a bilingual inscription, one text in hieroglyphic Hittite and the other in Phoenician, which confirmed and amplified the decoding of the Hittite.

**7 Use of the light war chariot**, shown in this drawing of an Egyptian relief, accounted in part for the Hittites' military successes, particularly the drawn battle at Kadesh (1299). Hittite chariots differed from those of Egypt and other nations of the period in that they carried three men – one driver and two fighters – instead of the usual one driver and one fighter. The main tactical aim of the Hittites in battle was to draw the enemy into the open where the chariots would be most effective. But their planning was not based solely on that manoeuvre. A clever ruse, for example, caught the Egyptians entirely by surprise at Kadesh, and only bad luck prevented an overwhelming victory.

7

8

**8 This basalt carving of a lion** from Malatya, dated probably about 1000 BC, is fairly typical of the sculpture of the neo-Hittite period, when the use of stone lions to flank entranceways was not uncommon.

# The Phoenicians 1500–332 BC

The ancient land of Phoenicia covered the coastal strip of modern Israel, Lebanon and Egypt. Its prosperity depended on the waters of the Mediterranean. Phoenician trading ships sailed remarkable distances, opening up new markets and protecting existing routes by establishing trading stations and colonies. The history of Phoenicia is the history of its great cities and colonies, particularly Byblos, Tyre, Sidon, Beirut and Ugarit.

## Foreign influence on Phoenicia

Phoenician cities, like the city states of Classical Greece, maintained their independence from each other. However, independence from their more powerful neighbours was less easy to sustain. In the early sixteenth century BC, Egypt exacted tribute from the cities and then brought them totally under its control. Egyptian influence [6] remained strong in Phoenicia, but the cultural and physical presence of Mesopotamia became increasingly dominant, as the early Phoenician cuneiform script and the evidence of many artefacts makes clear. After a period of Hittite control the Assyrian king Tiglath-Pileser

I (reigned c. 1115–c. 1077 BC) received tribute from the Phoenician cities. Phoenicia then regained its independence of action. A period of great prosperity followed and with it came a remarkable expansion of power throughout and even beyond the Mediterranean.

However, as Assyria's power approached its peak, the Phoenicians again became a tributary people, in thrall first to Ashurnasirpal II and his son Shalmaneser III in the ninth century, and then to Tiglath-Pileser III in the eighth century. In the following century the armies of Esarhaddon overran most of Phoenicia. Tyre held out but eventually fell to the Babylonians in the reign of Nebuchadrezzar II (604–562 BC). Later Phoenicia became part of the Persian Empire of Cyrus the Great. It remained an important sea power, but the powerful contingent that it contributed to the fleet that Xerxes (c. 519–465 BC) led against Greece shared heavily in the defeat at the Battle of Salamis in 480 BC. Alexander the Great (356–323 BC) incorporated Phoenicia into his empire after his victory at the battle of Issus in 333

BC and his capture of Tyre in 332 BC.

From the earliest days of commerce with Egypt and Mesopotamia, the Phoenician economy relied on trade, importing gold, ivory, livestock and corn, and exporting timber, metals, cloth, glass and ships. Its trading vessels often carried the goods of other peoples, taking the produce of the Asian hinterland to Egypt, Greece and Cyprus and later to North Africa, Spain and the Mediterranean islands. Flourishing Phoenician industries included dyeing, which was centred on Sidon and Tyre, metalworking [2], glass-making, pottery and carvings in ivory and bone.

## Phoenicia as a colonial power

Phoenicia's colonizing era began in the twelfth century. It had already planted settlements in Cyprus but it is likely that contacts about this time with the Mycenaeans sparked the imagination and the commercial acumen of Phoenician merchants. In the Aegean, Rhodes and probably Crete had Phoenician settlements, but there is only literary evidence of a Phoenician presence on the Greek

1 The Temple of the Obelisks at Byblos (the most powerful Phoenician city in the Egyptian period) dates from the middle Bronze Age. These open-air sanctuaries were dotted with stelae or pillars erected in honour of the gods or to mark cremations or the burial places of important objects.

2 The Phoenicians were skilled at working gold, an art they learnt from the Mycenaeans and Egyptians. This gold ring dates from the sixth or fifth century BC and was found at Tharros in Sardinia. The scarab on the ring depicts Bes the Egyptian dwarf god.

3 This limestone coffin dates from the thirteenth century BC, but was reused by King Hiram of Byblos in the early tenth century. The king is shown seated on a throne and flanked by winged sphinxes; the drooping lotus in his hand indicates that he has died. Before him is a food-laden table, and a procession of servants is approaching him. Above this scene is a typically Egyptian lotus frieze. Below are four lions which are more reminiscent of Assyrian or Hittite reliefs. On the lid is one of the earliest examples of Phoenician script.

4 King Eshmunazar II of Sidon, who perhaps reigned in the sixth century BC, was buried in this black basalt coffin of wholly Egyptian style. A Phoenician inscription warns against disturbing the body, and tells how Eshmunazar extended Sidon's dominance south to Joppa.

5 The tree of life, fertility symbol of the Babylonians and Assyrians, and the lotus of Egypt are combined on this Phoenician ivory plaque from an Assyrian palace. It shows both the extent of Phoenician trade, and the resultant diverse influences on their culture.

mainland. No more concrete evidence of Phoenician colonization in Italy exists, though there were close trading ties. But in the central and western Mediterranean, the Phoenicians established a chain of colonies, which made them dominant in the area.

Phoenicia also founded several colonies on the North African coast [9] at an early period, including Utica, Hadrumetum (modern Sousse) and Leptis Magna. But the most distinguished of all the settlements, eventually surpassing its mother city, Tyre, in power, was Carthage [7], which dominated – although it did not rule – the Phoenician colonies in the west. The most important of these were Gades (modern Cadiz), Ebesus (Ibiza), which Carthage founded in the middle of the seventh century BC, and Carthago Nova (Cartagena), founded by Hannibal's son-in-law Hasdrubal in 228 between the first and second of the Punic Wars (which ended with the destruction of Carthage by Rome).

A policy of colonization is often accompanied by an impulse towards exploration and the Phoenicians appear to have been enthusiastic explorers. The Greek historian Herodotus reports a story that Phoenician ships circumnavigated Africa, returning in three years to Egypt. Herodotus himself may not have credited this feat, but the details he gives make it possible that the remarkable voyage did take place. According to a much later Roman geographical work, the Carthaginian Himilco sailed from Spain up the Gallic coast to Brittany, and there is a possibility, although no archaeological evidence, that he reached Cornwall in an attempt to gain a share of the tin trade.

### The legacy of a rich literature

Much light has been shed on the mythology and beliefs of the area in pre-Iron Age times by the discovery and decipherment of the cuneiform texts of Ugarit. Although few inscriptions or documents have survived of the once rich Phoenician literature, these relics are important because the Phoenician alphabet was the basis of the Greek alphabet. The Phoenicians spoke a Semitic language which they wrote in an alphabet of 22 consonants with no vowels.

**This Phoenician ivory carving** may be Ishtar, the Mesopotamian fertility goddess. Her Phoenician equivalent Anat (Astarte) was a chief helper of Baal, the Canaanite god.

**6 Egyptian influence** is a feature of almost all the decorated metal bowls found on Phoenician sites. Many, like this bowl (seventh century BC) from Amathus in Cyprus, also have Assyrian characteristics. The outer frieze depicts a Phoenician city besieged by Assyrians and Greeks (as in the detail here). The inner frieze includes Egyptian deities and also Phoenicians with Egyptian amulets.

**7 The precinct of Tanit** at Salammbo was used throughout Carthage's history. Tanit was another name for Anat or Astarte, the chief female deity of the Phoenicians. Many stelae with symbols of Tanit and dedicatory inscriptions have been discovered in the precinct, but the most sensational finds were thousands of urns containing the ashes of cremated babies – clear evidence of infant sacrifice in Carthage.

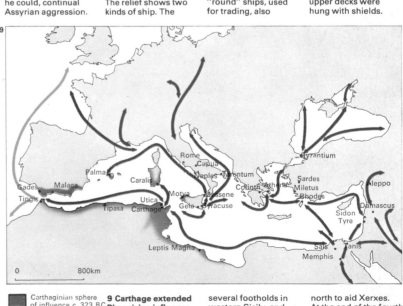

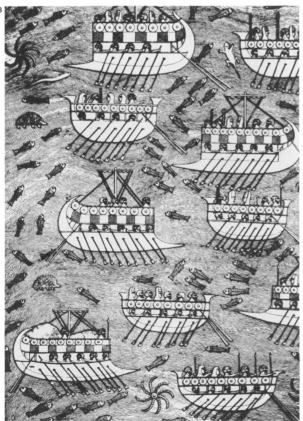

**8 Luli, the king of Tyre and Sidon,** fled to Cyprus in 701 BC. During his reign he formed alliances with Egypt and Judah, and resisted, as far as he could, continual Assyrian aggression.

Eventually, however, Sennacherib (r. 704–681 BC), King of Assyria, forced the departure depicted on this detail of a relief (which is now lost) from Nineveh. The relief shows two kinds of ship. The "long" ships, forerunners of the trireme, were used for war and exploration, and had a double bank of oars, with sails, a ram at the prow, and a high stern. The "round" ships, used for trading, also had two banks of oars but were sailless, with stern and prow of equal height. Both types of ship had steering oars on each side of the stern. The upper decks were hung with shields.

**9 Carthage extended Phoenician influence** in Spain, Sardinia and North Africa. The Phoenicians had several footholds in western Sicily, and in 480 BC the Carthaginians made an abortive invasion of the north to aid Xerxes. At the end of the fourth century they waged an unsuccessful war against Syracuse.

| | |
|---|---|
| ■ | Carthaginian sphere of influence c. 323 BC |
| ■ | Mediterranean trade routes c. 375 BC |
| ■ | 5th-century Phoenician exploration |

0    800km

# The Assyrians 1530–612 BC

The Assyrians, a Semitic people in north-western Mesopotamia, enjoyed a material culture in the mid-third millennium comparable to that of the Sumerians and briefly emerged as a military force under Shamshi-Adad I early in the eighteenth century BC. But for the next four centuries the strongest kingdoms in Mesopotamia were those of the Kassites, who came from the Zagros Mountains to take over Babylonia in the south, and of the Hurrians, who established the state of Mitanni in northwestern Mesopotamia. In the 14th century BC Ashur-uballit led the revived Assyrians into Mitanni after that state had been shattered by Hittite invaders.

## The empire established

Adadnirari I (reigned 1307–1275 BC) pushed Assyria's frontiers up to the Euphrates, and Shalmaneser I (reigned 1274–1245 BC) advanced northwards and finally crushed the Hurrians. The first of the really great Assyrian monarchs was Tiglath-Pileser I (reigned c. 1115– c. 1077 BC), who came to the throne after a period of instability in western Asia. By a succession of military campaigns, which combined brilliance and brutality, he extended Assyria's authority far into the north and northwest, overrunning Syria and exacting tribute even from the rich trading cities of Phoenicia.

Tiglath-Pileser succeeded, though with difficulty, in keeping back incursions by Aramaean peoples from the western desert. But after his death Aramaeans and Chaldaeans overran almost the whole of Mesopotamia, where a kind of Dark Age lasted for more than 150 years. When Adadnirari II came to the Assyrian throne in 912 BC his kingdom was a strip little more than 100 miles long and 50 miles wide. Yet by the middle of the seventh century BC Assyria was the largest and most powerful state in the civilized world.

Ashurnasirpal II (reigned 883–859 BC) [5] was mainly responsible for the restoration of Assyrian dominion. He built up the army into an irresistible fighting unit and led it to the shores of the Mediterranean. At his new capital at Calah (Nimrud) he built a vast palace, the doorway flanked by winged bulls. The glory of Assyria was paid for by the sufferings of its foes, many inscriptions testifying to the tortures inflicted on soldiers and civilians alike. Ashurnasirpal's son Shalmaneser III (reigned 858–824 BC), his father's equal in brutality, continued to conduct annual campaigns [2], but with less success.

## The surge of imperialism

A series of weak rulers and the growing power of the kingdom of Urartu to the north made Assyria's position a precarious one. The situation demanded a decisive and intelligent personality to meet the threat, and the Assyrians were fortunate to find such a one in Tiglath-Pileser III (reigned 745–727 BC). He reasserted Assyrian authority and established a uniform administration. He transformed conquered lands into provinces, each under its own governor and paying a fixed tribute to the central authority in addition to various taxes and duties. Although the governors had considerable authority, they were supervised by the central government, to which they sent regular reports through a remarkably effective system of posting stages. Tiglath-Pileser initiated a policy of

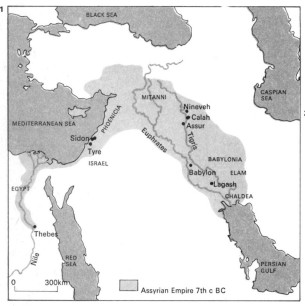

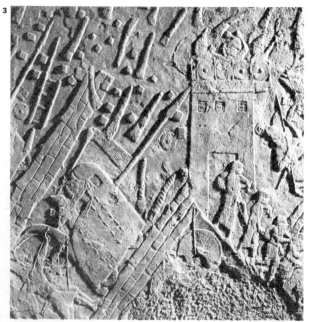

**1 Assyria's empire** reached its greatest extent in the seventh century BC, during Ashurbanipal's reign. He subjected its peoples to merciless repression inflicted by his army, in whose ruthlessness he gloried, and ruled through an efficient administrative system supervised by the central government. Assyrian hegemony collapsed, however, and was followed by a brief resurgence of Babylonian rule.

**2 Jehu, the King of Israel,** is shown bowing to Shalmaneser III (reigned 858–824 BC) on this panel from the gates of Balwat. The panels record many of Shalmaneser's campaigns – against Babylon, northern Mesopotamia, and Syria, which after several wars he failed to subdue entirely. But he was able to force Tyre and Sidon to pay tribute to him and in 841 BC Israel, too, was forced to become a tributary.

**3 Sennacherib's siege of Lachish,** a Judaean city, is portrayed on stone panels from Nineveh. The city's fall was followed by the submission of King Hezekiah of Judah. Many siege machines developed by the Assyrians are represented on stone panels such as the one shown here.

**4 A skin boat on the Tigris** carries perhaps building materials for Sennacherib's palace. Herodotus tells how circular hide boats floated down the Euphrates, carrying one or more donkeys in addition to the cargo. On arrival at Babylon, the boats were broken up and loaded on the donkeys for the return journey overland to Armenia.

mass deportations of defeated or rebellious peoples. By the end of his reign Urartu was no longer a threat and Babylonia, Palestine, Syria and Phoenicia were completely under Assyrian control.

Babylonia, however, was coming increasingly under the influence of the Chaldaean tribes, which dominated the surrounding country, and which remained bitterly hostile to the Assyrians. Sennacherib (reigned 704–681 BC) reacted with characteristic vigour, installing his son on the Babylonian throne. But in 694 BC the Babylonians revolted and invited the help of the king of Elam, who carried off the Assyrian prince to his own country. The brutal war that followed lasted five years and ended with the levelling of the holy city of Babylon by Sennacherib in 689 BC. He made his capital at Nineveh and initiated a vast programme of public works.

Sennacherib was murdered and his son Esarhaddon (reigned 681–669 BC) [Key] at once put in hand the rebuilding of Babylon. He was an able statesman who knew when to temper strength with mercy. Assyrian authority in the east remained supreme and

the Mannaen buffer-state in the north was under Assyrian control. A revolt in Phoenicia was settled by deporting the inhabitants of Sidon and executing its king. But Esarhaddon's most spectacular success was against Egypt. The ruling dynasty there had been fomenting trouble in Phoenicia and Esarhaddon decided to subdue the country.

**The fall of the empire**
Ashurbanipal (reigned 668–c. 627 BC) quelled a rebellion in Egypt and again subdued that country, but as it was too large and too distant an area to occupy permanently [1] its administration was left to local princes. Eventually, Ashurbanipal was forced to withdraw from Egypt since he was involved in a large-scale rebellion headed by his brother, the King of Babylon, in alliance with Elam. Victorious in 648 BC, Ashurbanipal boasted of having the whole world at his feet. Although ruthless, he was also a man of learning. But Assyria could not survive the alliance of Nabopolassar, king in Babylon in 625 BC, with the Medes. Ashur soon fell and in 612 BC Nineveh was destroyed.

**Esarhaddon**, the great imperialist Assyrian ruler, is shown on a stele found at Zenjirli, which lies northeast of the Gulf of Iskenderun and northwest of Aleppo. The king towers over two suppliant prisoners, held by cords through their lips. The standing prisoner may be Ba'alu, King of Tyre, although in that case the stele represents Esarhaddon's wishes rather than the facts, for Ba'alu rejected his terms and the siege was probably concluded only under his successor. The kneeling, negroid, figure may represent either Tarku of Kush or his son Ushanakhuru, who was carried off with his family to Assyria; Tarku also retained control of his land.

**5 Two figures**, one of them (to judge from clothing and inscription) perhaps representing the ninth-century king Ashurnasirpal II of Assyria, stand on either side of a "tree of life". This motif, common in art throughout Western Asia, is a symbol of fertility conferred by the goddess Ishtar.

**6 Ashurnasirpal's son Shalmaneser III** built this dais for the throne in his palace at Fort Shalmaneser, Nimrud. Its vertical faces show relief carvings of tribute. The upper surface has shallow, round hollows to house the feet of throne and footstools, and is covered with inscriptions telling of his reign.

**7 Painted decoration** survived in parts of the palaces at Fort Shalmaneser, including the above figure dressed in a fish cloak with scale-covered legs and holding a pine cone in the fertilization gesture common in the reliefs of Ashurnasirpal.

**8 Servants exercise hunting dogs** in the royal park in this relief from the north palace of Ashurbanipal II at Nineveh. The Assyrians believed that the king was fulfilling a sacred duty in hunting wild animals, and lions were brought to the country so that the king could show his skill in lavish hunts. Ashurbanipal was a "mighty hunter before the lord"; and in his day the lions that infested thickets along the Euphrates destroyed not only flocks and herds but also human beings.

**9 The valley of the River Zab**, in western Iran, a tributary of the Tigris, is typical of the terrain covered by much of the Assyrian Empire. In much of the region mountains ensured that life and communications were centred on the river valleys.

# The Hebrews 1200–322 BC

The name Hebrew is of uncertain origin and meaning. A similar name, Habiru, appears in documents of the fourteenth century BC describing races or classes of people, perhaps semi-nomads, who inhabited the northern fringes of the Arabian desert. "Hebrew" has been associated with Eber, the grandson of Shem (Genesis 24) and the forefather of all the Semitic peoples.

## The twelve tribes of Israel

The early Hebrews were nomads and tradition tells of the migration of Abraham from Mesopotamia into Canaan, an area later called Palestine, on the borders of Egypt. Abraham's grandson Jacob, renamed Israel ("striver with God"), had 12 sons from whom descended the biblical 12 tribes of Israel. The Bible tells how Jacob's sons sold their brother Joseph into slavery in Egypt. When famine broke out in Canaan Joseph, who had found favour in Egypt, received his father and his brothers there and they prospered for many years. Much later, their descendants were enslaved, possibly during the reign of Seti I (reigned c. 1309–1291 BC);

their eventual emergence from captivity was organized by Moses.

Both Moses and the Exodus that he led have an historical stamp because to this day they remain in the consciousness of the Hebrew people [3]. According to tradition Moses was brought up by an Egyptian princess and only later in life did he identify himself with his own Hebrew people. Moses was told by God in a vision to deliver the children of Israel from the captivity of Egypt and lead them into the promised land of Canaan.

The date of this Exodus is uncertain, but it may have taken place in the fourteenth or thirteenth century BC. The captives escaped across the northern end of the Red Sea into the desert and went to Mount Sinai or Horeb. The Law, revealed to Moses on Sinai according to the biblical record, consisted of the Ten Commandments or Decalogue inscribed on stone and later kept in an ark or chest. The longer Law, or the Torah of "five books", the Pentateuch, is traditionally attributed to Moses.

In their present form much in these books suggests a settled agricultural community as

well as a nomadic existence. They include the death of Moses, and the later Temple and rituals were based on them. Moses was followed by Joshua and a series of judges and kings who led the invasion and gradual occupation of Canaan, the eventual goal. Saul was the first Hebrew king, successful in defeating some tribes such as the Amalekites, but was himself killed by the Philistines.

## David, Israel's greatest king

David has always been regarded as a great Hebrew, second only to Moses. He was as successful as Saul in uniting the tribes and was an able administrator [1] as well as a poet – many of the Psalms are attributed to him. David captured Jerusalem from the Jebusites and made it his capital. The ark containing the Law, which had lodged in different places since the desert wanderings, was brought to Jerusalem, and when Solomon inherited this united kingdom he built the Temple in Jerusalem [2, 4, 5] for the ark and a larger palace for himself, financing both by taxation and using forced labour to construct them.

Discontent boiled over after Solomon's

Ancient Israel
Phoenicia
Philistia
Assyrian Empire

**1 Biblical tradition** holds that the ancient Tribes of Israel escaped from slavery in Egypt in the 13th century BC under Moses. After conquering parts of Canaan in the 12th century, Israel reached its peak under David (c. 1000–960 BC), who took Jerusalem and subjugated the surrounding nations [A]. This empire divided after Solomon's death into two smaller and weaker nations, Judah in the south and Israel in the north [B], both declining in the face of Assyrian rule [C].

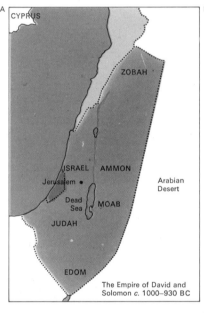

The Empire of David and Solomon c. 1000–930 BC

The Kingdoms of Israel and Judah c. 860 BC

The Kingdom of Judah c. 700 BC

0        150km

**2 The Dome of the Rock,** a Muslim shrine on the spot where Mohammed is believed to have risen to heaven, is on Mount Zion, the site of the Temple of Jerusalem. The Wailing Wall (the western wall of the second Temple) is a place of worship.

**3 The Passover,** the feast celebrating the deliverance of the Hebrews from captivity in Egypt, used to be introduced by a blast on a ram's horn. This woodcut is taken from a book of Jewish customs.

**4 A seven-branched candlestick** of the type used in the Temple of Jerusalem is shown here on the Arch of Titus in Rome, built after the destruction of Jerusalem by the Romans in AD 70.

death and the kingdom was irreparably divided. His weak son Rehoboam managed to hold only the southern country round Jerusalem, in a kingdom that came to be known as Judah (Judaea). His brother, Jeroboam, broke away with ten tribes to form a northern kingdom called Israel, with two rival shrines at Dan and Bethel. The following centuries saw the rivalries of Judah and Israel and the destruction of the northern kingdom by Sargon II of Assyria in 721 [7].

The small kingdom of Judah lingered on in semi-independence for more than a century, until finally it fell in 586 BC and most of its leading figures were taken in captivity to Babylon. The northern tribes of Israel had been scattered and lost (the ten lost tribes) and hence the return from exile after 539 BC was of the leaders of Judah.

**The Hebrew prophets and monotheism**
More important for world religion than these political events was the work of the Hebrew prophets. They were inspired men who were sometimes associated with, but often critical of, the official religion of their time. One of the first, Samuel, was priest, prophet, seer and kingmaker. He chose Saul to be the first king of Israel, and also selected David as Saul's successor. Elijah and his servant and follower Elisha both denounced the prophets of Baal and as a result were hounded by the ruling monarchs of their time.

They were followed by a number of other prophets between the eighth and third centuries, whose messages were soon written down. Amos and Hosea preached at Bethel and in Israel, and Micah and Isaiah [6] in Judah. These men declared the unity of God and His demands of just behaviour from the people, a teaching that is termed "ethical monotheism". Through prophetic influence Deuteronomy, a "second law", was promulgated in Judah in 621 BC by King Josiah, who put down rival shrines and concentrated worship at Jerusalem. Jeremiah preached in Jerusalem before its fall in 586 BC and then went to Egypt, while Ezekiel went to Babylon. The latter denounced heathenism and planned the rebuilding of the Temple, whereas Jeremiah taught a more inward religion of a new covenant with God.

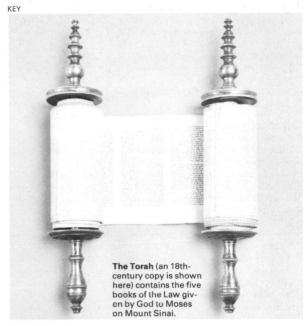

**The Torah** (an 18th-century copy is shown here) contains the five books of the Law given by God to Moses on Mount Sinai.

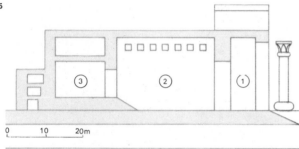

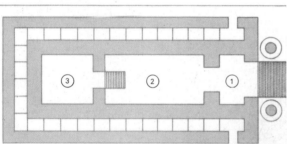

**5 The first Temple of Jerusalem** built by Solomon, of which nothing remains today, was a shrine for the ark, sacred vessels and offerings, with a courtyard for worshippers. It consisted essentially of a hall [1], shrine [2] and inner sanctum [3], or Holy of Holies, where only the high priest was admitted.

**6 In Hebrew history** a number of prophets arose who commented on society and rebuked the insincere practice of religion. Like Isaiah, depicted here by Michelangelo, the prophets taught belief in one God who was just and merciful and required similar qualities from His followers.

**7 Evidence for the relations** of the Hebrews with more powerful neighbours appears in a Mesopotamian relief showing the King of Israel, Jehu, paying tribute on his knees to Shalmaneser III, King of Assyria, about 840 BC. Israel was conquered by the Assyrians in 721 BC, and the southern kingdom of Judah eventually fell in 586 BC.

**8 A Canaanite captive** being led before Pharaoh was depicted in a temple of Ramesses III in Egypt. The Canaanites resembled the Hebrews in appearance, since both were Semites and had fine noses, long hair and beards. They were finally conquered by the Israelites about 1200 BC.

# The Persian Empire of the Achaemenids

The Persian Empire, during the period of its height, between 550 BC and 480 BC, was the greatest in area and accomplishment the world had then known. Centred on an area comprising much of present-day Iran and Afghanistan it contained 40 million people and gave them common law, systems of coinage, postage and irrigation and a magnificent network of roads [1], as well as a liberal and unifying religion. Although the power of the Achaemenid dynasty was broken by Alexander the Great in 330 BC Persian influence revived under the Parthian and Sassanid empires and gave way to the Muslim Arab Empire only in the AD 600s.

## Persia's early history

Persia is the natural bridge between Europe and Asia. Its history dates back to 6000 BC and the country contains some 250,000 archaeological sites [2], a thousand in the plain before Persepolis [5] alone. In about 1500 BC nomadic Aryans from the north arrived, giving the country the name Iran or "Land of the Aryans". In 549 BC their descendants, the Medes, were united with the

Persians in the south by Cyrus the Great who thus founded the Persian Empire, calling it the Achaemenid Empire after an ancestor.

Cyrus [Key] based his empire not merely on territorial conquest but also on international tolerance and understanding. The rights and religions of all the subject states were upheld and their laws and customs respected. After his victory in Babylon in 539 BC, which ended the Jewish captivity, he ordered the temple in Jerusalem to be rebuilt and more than 40,000 Jews left Babylonia and returned to Palestine. His army added the former realms of Assyria, Lydia and Asia Minor to the Persian Empire, making it the largest political organization of pre-Roman antiquity. The conquests of Cyrus had been carried as far as the Mediterranean in the west and the Hindu Kush in the east when he was slain in battle in 529 BC.

Cyrus was followed by his son Cambyses II (ruled 529–522 BC), who had none of his father's virtues but inherited his occasional vice of cruelty. Cambyses II began his reign by putting to death his brother Smerdis and then, lured by the wealth of Egypt, set out to

capture that country. Some 50,000 of his soldiers perished in the campaign and Cambyses unsuccessfully tried to put down the Egyptian religion. In a final outburst he killed his sister and wife Roxana, slew his son Prexaspes and buried 12 of his nobles alive. He died during his return journey to Persia.

## The reign of Darius

Darius the Great (548–486 BC), who won a battle for the succession, had been the commander of the Ten Thousand Immortals, the elite of the Persian forces [7, 8]. His succession was marked by revolts among the conquered states, which he rapidly quelled. In Babylon 3,000 leading citizens were crucified. Realizing how vulnerable the vast empire was to any crisis he reduced military control in favour of wise administration and re-established his realms in a way that became a model of imperial organization. The result was a generation of order and prosperity. Having gained peace and stability at home Darius led his armies first across the Bosporus and the Danube to the Volga, then into the valley of the Indus. The Persian

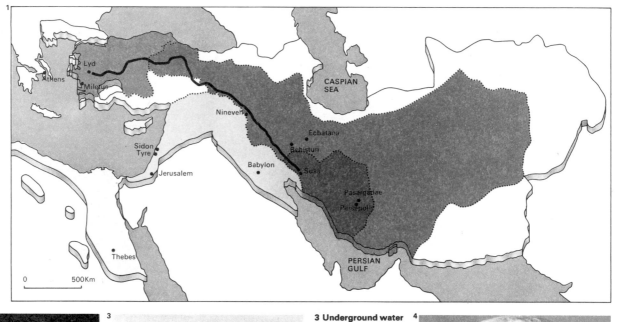

**1 The Persian Empire** in the Achaemenid period was administered through satrapies. To maintain contact with these provinces Darius created roads whose combined length was 2,700km (1,680 miles). At 111 staging posts fresh horses awaited the king's envoys, who could thus traverse the whole system in a week; it took merchant caravans 90 days.

- Kingdom of Persia
- Median Empire annexed 549 BC
- Lydian Empire annexed 546 BC
- Chaldean Empire annexed 538 BC
- Egyptian Empire annexed 525 BC
- Later conquests to 479 BC
- —— Royal Highway

**2 The crushed bowl of Hasanlu,** exquisitely made in gold, shows a weather god in a chariot drawn by a bull, and a battle with a monster. It was found in 1958 during excavations of the citadel of Hasanlu at the northern end of the Solduz valley and was clutched in the hands of a man's skeleton. He was probably trying to escape from a palace that collapsed in flames when the citadel was attacked in 800 BC. The bowl is now in the Teheran Museum Treasure Room.

**3 Underground water tunnels,** called *ghanats*, first introduced to Persia in Achaemenid times, carry mountain water across miles of desert safe from evaporation that would deplete surface canals. A one-man windlass is used to reach the tunnels through shafts sunk at intervals of some 10m (30ft). A digger must work alone in a tunnel only 40 by 60cm (2 by 3ft) in height and width, keeping the channel straight and accurately gauging the amount of fall needed to enable the water to flow steadily to its point of use. These unique water systems contributed as much to the progress of the Persian Empire as the wisdom of its rulers.

**4 A coin of Xerxes I** depicts him in an aggressive pose, but he is best known for leading the Persian forces to defeat at the hands of the Greeks at the Battle of Salamis. Xerxes inherited the empire from his father, Darius I, in 486 BC. In 484 he suppressed a usurper in Egypt in savage fashion and went on to quell a revolt in Babylonia with similar ruthlessness. After early successes in Greece he lost his fleet at Salamis; the Achaemenid decline dates from that point.

40

Empire had by that time achieved its greatest extent and influence.

Agriculture based on both grain and livestock was the mainstay of the country. Artificial irrigation was introduced by means of tunnels [3] many miles long.

The original religion of the country had been the worship of Mithras, identified with the sun, and of Anahita, goddess of water and fertility. This religion was later combined with the worship of a supreme being, Ahura Mazda [9], "the Wise Lord" of the sixth-century prophet Zoroaster, or Zarathustra. As creator and ruler of the world Ahura Mazda clothed himself with the firmament, the sun and moon were his eyes and all forms of nature were his: earth, fire [6], wind and water. To avoid polluting these natural elements Parsees (who still follow Zoroastrian beliefs in India) expose their dead on "towers of silence" to be devoured by vultures.

### The invasion of Greece
Persia's monarchical form of government was supported by her people who believed that the sovereignty of individuals was best maintained by an individual sovereign, the "King of Kings". On the other hand the city state of Athens propounded the idea of democracy, except for slaves and non-citizens. Darius considered the Greek city states and their colonies a danger, and when Ionia revolted and received aid from Sparta and Athens, he crossed the Aegean but was defeated by an Athenian force at Marathon. In the midst of preparations for another attack upon Greece he died in 486 BC.

Xerxes (c. 519–465 BC), son of Darius, crossed the Hellespont with a vast army and defeated the Spartans at Thermopylae. But he was driven out of Europe in 479 BC after incurring the lasting hatred of the Greeks by burning the Acropolis at Athens. The Achaemenid Empire then declined until Alexander the Great (356–323 BC) from Macedon defeated the last of the dynasty, Darius III, at the Battle of Arbela (also called the Battle of Gaugamela) in 331 BC. He routed a huge Persian army and burnt Persepolis, possibly to avenge the destruction of the Acropolis. Thereafter, Persia formed part of the empire of Alexander.

**The tomb of Cyrus the Great** at Pasargadae commemorates an outstanding leader who united the Medes and Persians to form an empire that played an important intermediary role between the civilizations of East and West. Few kings have left such a reputation for tolerance to subject peoples.

**5 The Palace of Persepolis** was begun in 518 BC by Darius and was built mainly under Xerxes I in 486–485 BC. It owes much to its situation with its back to the mountain from which the great terrace was partly carved. The magnificent staircases leading to the terrace were wide enough for eight horsemen to ride abreast up the shallow steps. A procession of Immortals carved in stone decorates the sides of the staircases, followed by lines of courtiers – Medes and Persians – and subject peoples bearing tribute. Iron clamps filled with molten lead lock together some of the blocks of stone of which the terrace is built.

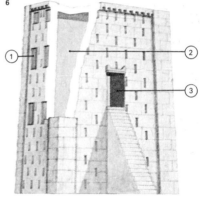

**6 The so-called Fire Temple** at Naqsh-i Rustam near Persepolis stands in front of a cliff in which the four tombs of Darius and his successors are carved. It is about 11m (36ft) high with blind windows [1] of black limestone and a door [3] leading to an empty room [2]. Some authorities believe it to be a Zoroastrian temple for the sacred flame or for holding religious objects.

**7 Persian warriors** owed much of their success to their skill with bows. The arrows were carried in a quiver by the bowman [A] who wore leather shoes and cap and bore a short sword. A bodyguard of Darius the Great [B] wore long robes and carried a long spear with a cut-out shield. Such men, known as the Ten Thousand Immortals, were commanded by Darius during the campaign against Egypt and were the mainstay of his military achievements as emperor.

**8 Depicted in colour** on enamelled brickwork from the palace of Susa, one of the two capitals of the empire of Darius, is a soldier of the Ten Thousand Immortals holding a spear and carrying his bow and quiver. Darius rewarded his loyal bodyguard by having them portrayed on the walls of each palace he built.

**9 Artaxerxes I** (reigned 465–425 BC), a king of the Achaemenid dynasty, is enthroned in the Hall of a Hundred Columns at Persepolis beneath the winged Ahura Mazda, supreme god in the religion of Zoroaster, who was believed to direct the actions of the king as his viceroy, protecting the earth and its ruler.

# India 500 BC — AD 300

The age of Buddha (*c.* 563–*c.* 483 BC) [3, 4] marked the beginning of a world religion and of important developments in the political and socio-economic fields. It was an age in which different religions (such as Jainism) emerged and a period of change in which established values were questioned.

## Trade and political change

In the political field large and expansionist states developed, four of which dominated the scene by 500 BC. The most powerful of these was Magadha in southern Bihar with its capital originally at Rajgir, later at Pataliputra (Patna). The main economic asset was iron but power was also due to energetic rulers who gradually eliminated their rivals by force and diplomacy.

Cottage industries, such as textiles, pottery and metalcraft, flourished and were organized in guilds. Their produce, as well as agricultural surplus, was traded between various north Indian centres and with the Achaemenid (Persian) Empire in the west. Most trade was financed by bankers who supplied the means of transportation and took

the risks. Such activities favoured the rise of a prosperous class that included many who felt dissatisfied with the then rigid divisions of Hindu society. Such people often became enthusiastic patrons of Buddhism and other non-Hindu religions.

These developments were temporarily disturbed by the invasion in 327 BC of Alexander the Great (356–323 BC) who, after conquering the Persian Empire, set out to occupy its Indian provinces. But attracted by the legendary wealth of India, he advanced farther and managed to penetrate the Punjab. Alexander was, however, forced to retreat, soon to be followed by the governors whom he had appointed to rule the territories after his departure [5].

## The glorious Mauryan age

The retreat of Alexander left behind a strong sense of Indian unity which found a leader in the young warrior Chandragupta (*c.* 321–*c.* 297 BC). First he liberated the western provinces and then he marched against Pataliputra, where he defeated the Nanda king of Magadha and so founded the Mau-

ryan Dynasty in 320 BC. In his bid for the throne, Chandragupta was assisted by his able and cunning minister Kautilya, who is regarded as the author of the most important Indian work on statecraft, the *Arthashastra*.

The Mauryan age (320–185 BC) was one of the most glorious periods of Indian history. Chandragupta controlled northern India from the Hindu Kush to Bengal and probably parts of southern India as well. The kingdom was largely centralized, partly because of a network of highways. In 305 BC Chandragupta concluded a treaty with the Greek Seleucus (*c.* 355–281 BC) who sent Megasthenes (*c.* 350–*c.* 290 BC) to the Indian court as an envoy to grant Chandragupta formal rights over Alexander's conquests in India.

The Mauryan Empire [1] reached its zenith under Chandragupta's grandson Ashoka (*c.* 274–*c.* 236 BC), the mightiest king of ancient India. At first Ashoka continued to follow traditional expansionist policies but, after a cruel campaign against Kalinga (the present state of Orissa), he renounced further conquests by force. Instead he substituted conquest by righteous-

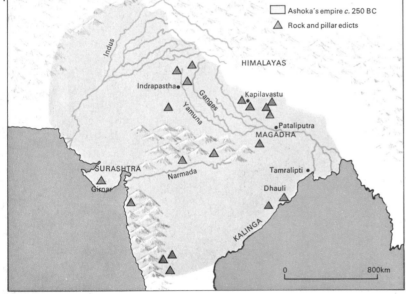

1 □ Ashoka's empire *c.* 250 BC
△ Rock and pillar edicts

INDUS
HIMALAYAS
Indrapastha
Ganges
Yamuna
Kapilavastu
Pataliputra
MAGADHA
SURASHTRA
Narmada
Girnar
Tamralipti
Dhauli
KALINGA
0          800km

**1 The Mauryan Empire** was the greatest of the states of ancient India. It comprised most of the subcontinent, except its southernmost portion, and most of Bengal and Sind. It also included significant parts of present Afghanistan, thus controlling the all-important overland communications with the Middle East. The size can be accurately established on the basis of the sites of the Ashokan rock and pillar edicts. Centralized administration of this vast empire was simplified by a network of highways connecting Pataliputra with the provincial centres.

**2 The rich sculpture** of the eastern gateway of the great stupa at Sanchi shows both pious Buddhist stories and local deities belonging to folk religion but tolerated by Buddhism. The Buddhist stories concern either the important events in the life of Lord Buddha or stories relating to his earlier existences as a man or an animal. Popular religion is represented by various deities such as *yakshas* (tree spirits).

**3 The Buddha** is said to have converted people by performing miracles such as walking on the water, depicted here [A] in the carvings on the gateway at the Sanchi stupa. The presence of Lord Buddha, who is not represented in this early period, must be inferred. Another scene [B] shows Buddha's father paying homage to the tree under which Lord Buddha attained enlightenment. This time the presence of the Buddha has to be inferred from the tree.

**4 The great stupa** (dome-shaped shrine) at Sanchi was built in Ashoka's time, but the railings and the richly sculptured gateways were added during the following two centuries. Sanchi, situated at the centre of India where the main highways from east to west and from north to south crossed, was one of the principal Buddhist centres from at least the time of Ashoka to the 10th century AD; it also gave its name to a school of sculpture.

ness. At about that time Ashoka was converted to Buddhism and became one of its most fervent supporters.

To propagate his ideas Ashoka had edicts engraved on rocks and pillars [Key]. These edicts enjoined upon the population a common ideology based on the concept of loyalty towards one's elders and those in authority and also on justice and mercy for one's neighbours.

## The Indo-Greeks and the Kushan Dynasty

The Mauryan Dynasty continued to rule over vast areas of India until 50 years after Ashoka's death but its authority soon declined. By about 185 BC the army commander Pushyamitra, in one of the earliest recorded military coups, overthrew the last Mauryan king and founded the Sunga Dynasty. The centre of the state was soon moved from Bihar to central India. Pushyamitra was a powerful ruler but his successors could not prevent incursions by the Bactrian Greeks, descendants of some of Alexander's generals. Some were repulsed by the Indians, while others founded short-lived kingdoms in the Punjab and elsewhere. Many of these were influenced by Indian culture and because of this they are usually called Indo-Greeks.

The Indo-Greeks were soon followed by invaders from central Asia and in AD 78 most of northern India was under the control of Kanishka (died *c.* AD 100) [6] of the Kushan Dynasty of Scythian origin (from central Asia). Like other Scythians, Kanishka was a pious Buddhist.

A century later, however, the Kushans had been expelled from India and a Hindu reaction followed. Sanskrit, the language of the sacred texts, developed into a medium of communication among the upper class, in administration and, above all, in literature. The great Sanskrit epics, the *Mahabharata* and the *Ramayana*, although incorporating much older tradition, were probably written down during this period, as were the *Laws of Manu*, the basic code of Hinduism. These three texts together incorporate the basic values of Hinduism and so laid the foundations of the classical age of India in the Gupta period (AD 320–550).

The Ashokan pillars are among the oldest and most splendid monuments of Indian art. They are built of sandstone with a special bright polish and rest on solid foundations below ground level. They are crowned with animal sculptures; this one at Lauriya Nandangarh in northern Bihar has a heraldic lion. Many pillars are also inscribed with Ashokan edicts proclaiming the emperor's authority. This pillar is inscribed with six edicts of the last phase of Ashoka's reign. Earlier scholars have emphasized foreign, especially Persian, influences, but recent research has established them in the Indian tradition.

5 A

Diodotus

B

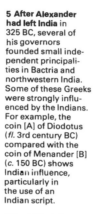

Menander

**5 After Alexander had left India** in 325 BC, several of his governors founded small independent principalities in Bactria and northwestern India. Some of these Greeks were strongly influenced by the Indians. For example, the coin [A] of Diodotus (*fl.* 3rd century BC) compared with the coin of Menander [B] (*c.* 150 BC) shows Indian influence, particularly in the use of an Indian script.

**6 Kanishka I,** the greatest of the Kushan kings, ruled over vast areas of central Asia and also controlled most of northern India eastwards as far as Bihar. This modern illustration is based on a torso of Kanishka (as indicated by the inscription), to which the head has been added from one of Kanishka's coins. The Scythian mantle and boots convey a strong impression of power and authority.

6

7

**7 According to Buddhist tradition,** caves have been used by the community of Buddhist monks since early times, especially as shelters during the rainy season. Although they were gradually replaced by structural monasteries, the tradition was continued in parts of India where numerous caves were excavated between 100 BC and AD 900. The *chaitya* cave at Karli, Maharashtra (*c.* 50 BC) was not used as a dwelling but as a place of worship, as well as for monastic ceremonies. It consists of a long pillared hall with a small stupa, enshrining relics of Lord Buddha, at the end. The rich sculpture of the capitals of the pillars presents a striking contrast to the sober lines of the rest of the cave.

8

**8 Another richly decorated part** of the caves at Karli, Maharashtra, is the façade, which includes the space between the three entrances. In addition to traditional Buddhist scenes, there are usually representations of the pious donors of the caves and especially of the land which was donated for the requisites of the monks. The donors are usually couples, thus illustrating the high status of women in this period in western India.

43

# Buddha and Buddhism

By the sixth century BC the semi-nomadic tribes of northern India had developed into settled agricultural communities ruled by oligarchies or royal dynasties. It was a time of social change and of new ideas. Chief among these, and evolved in opposition to the rituals and hardening caste system of Hinduism, were the philosophical and ethical teachings of Buddhism which were to develop into one of the greatest Oriental religions.

## The life of Buddha

There are many differing accounts of the life of Buddha but the main outline seems clear. Siddhartha Gautama (c. 563–c. 483 BC), who was later to become the Buddha ("the Enlightened One"), was the son of Suddhodana, king of the Sakyas, and his queen Maya. His birthplace, Lumbini, is situated on the northern fringes of the Gangetic valley near Kapilavastu where he spent his early years. After an uneventful childhood the prince, struck by the problem of human suffering, decided to break with the past to seek the supreme truth in meditation. He left home secretly [1] and eventually, after years of seclusion, he attained "enlightenment" seated under the Bodhi tree at Bodhgaya near Gaya in southern Bihar [4]. This subsequently became one of the holiest places of Buddhism and saplings of the tree were taken to different Buddhist countries where they grew into new trees. Soon afterwards the Buddha delivered his first sermon in the Deer Park of Sarnath [5] near Varanasi "setting the wheel of the Law in motion" [Key].

Buddhist doctrine was a Middle Way, avoiding the extremes of mortification and indulgence. It accepted the basic concepts of Hinduism – rebirth and the law of karma, that a man's actions directly control his destiny – but concentrated on ethics as a means to salvation. For Buddha suffering was caused by desire. The abandonment of desire could be achieved by following the "noble eightfold path" of right living and actions. As a result nirvana, the state of bliss in which rebirth ended, would be attained. The ideal of nirvana [3] could best be attained by monastic discipline, but the order of monks (Sangha) depended on the entire community.

Buddha himself preached all over eastern India and received support from the rulers and the emerging merchant class. When at an advanced age he "entered nirvana", he left a monastic order but no written instructions.

## Expansion of Buddhism

For two centuries Buddhism slowly expanded despite difficulties such as the animosity of the Hindu Brahmins who feared for their own privileges. However, when the Indian king Ashoka (reigned c. 274–c. 236 BC) was converted to Buddhism his powerful patronage greatly favoured its expansion. The oldest extant stupas, distinctive monuments built to enshrine relics, belong to this period. Through Ashoka's influence Buddhism was introduced into Sri Lanka, where it has remained the established faith.

For the next few centuries Buddhism spread farther into India with centres located in central India (Bharhut, Sanchi), Maharashtra and Andhra Pradesh where Buddhist art and architecture flourished. In Maharashtra (Nasik, Karle and other places), many caves served as monasteries or halls for worship (the *chaitya* halls). Great stupas

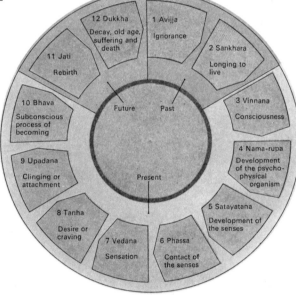

1 The great departure from Kapilavastu is often represented in Buddhist art. Although the future Buddha left secretly at night, sculptors usually show the pomp of a royal procession.

2 In Buddhist philosophy, the Wheel of Existence consists of 12 spokes, each constituting a link in the ever-repeated cycle of life and death. The wheel will revolve as long as ignorance lasts.

(Wheel of Existence labels:)
12 Dukkha — Decay, old age, suffering and death
1 Avijja — Ignorance
11 Jati — Rebirth
2 Sankhara — Longing to live
10 Bhava — Subconscious process of becoming
3 Vinnana — Consciousness
9 Upadana — Clinging or attachment
4 Nama-rupa — Development of the psycho-physical organism
8 Tanha — Desire or craving
5 Satayatana — Development of the senses
7 Vedana — Sensation
6 Phassa — Contact of the senses
Future / Past / Present

3 The fourth great event in Buddha's life is the nirvana, which is neither eternal life nor annihilation but an incomprehensible state of utter bliss. Here Buddha is shown in a symbolic representation of the state of nirvana. This huge sculpture at Gal Vihara, Polannaruva, Sri Lanka, dates from the twelfth century.

4 The Mohabodhi Temple, Bodhgaya, Bihar, marks the spot where Lord Buddha attained "enlightenment" seated under the Bodhi tree. This is perhaps the most hallowed spot in the Buddhist world. The present temple, which replaces an older foundation at the site, was built in the Gupta period (c. 320 – c. 550) but has been restored.

(Amaravati and Nagarjunakonda) also arose in the Andhra country.

Buddhism was always prone to divisions and councils organized to promote unity often had the opposite effect. Early in the Christian era there developed a fundamental division between the adherents of the Great Vehicle (Mahayana) and those of the Lesser Vehicle (Hinayana). The former had monks but emphasized the ideal of the pious layman continually assisting his fellow men by his wisdom and compassion. The historical Buddha and previous Buddhas were worshipped as deities and so were other beings who had taken the vow to become Buddhas (Bodhisattvas). Buddhas and Bodhisattvas received worship in the form of images, thus providing a strong incentive to Buddhist art, which soon included the image of Lord Buddha. Hinayana, however, kept closer to the other teachings.

### The spread outside south Asia
From the beginning of the Christian era Buddhism spread outside south Asia [9]. Buddhism entered China in the first century and subsequently spread to Korea and Japan. In Tibet it took root in the eighth century and developed into Lamaism.

In South-East Asia, too, Mahayana influence, mainly from Bengal, inspired great monuments such as Borobudur in central Java (ninth century) [7] and Ba-yon in Cambodia (twelfth century), but the great expansion of the Theravada school (the monastic version of Hinayana) gained momentum in the eleventh century when the Burmese king Aniruddha (reigned 1044–77) made Theravada the official religion. In the thirteenth century it became the official religion of Thailand and eventually spread to Laos and Cambodia.

Although it has not always guaranteed harmony between these countries, Buddhism has provided Sri Lanka and mainland South-East Asia with a firm ideology and a high standard of education. It has also contributed to great achievements in art and architecture. The astounding temple complex of Pagan (Burma), the splendid pagodas of Mandalay, Bangkok and Ayutha (Thailand), testify to the strength and inspiration of the faith.

In the life of Lord Buddha the first sermon is the third great event (after his birth and "enlightenment"). Buddhists call this event the "turning of the wheel of Law"; the wheel represents the cosmos, and the Law represents the Lord Buddha's philosophy, which offers an explanation of the mysteries of life. The presence of the wheel is suggested by the position of the hands. The sculpture of Sarnath dates from the Gupta period, (c. AD 500). The perfection of the physical shape reflects perfect knowledge; the elongated ears and almond-shaped eyes suggest profound concentration and the monastic robe reveals the perfect body.

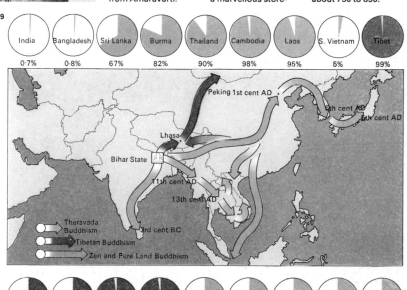

**5 The Wheel of Law** and two deer on this seal suggest the Deer Park of Sarnath. The seal was recovered from the ruins of Nalanda, a great Buddhist monastery in Bihar. Founded in the fifth century, Nalanda became one of the great centres of Buddhist learning, attracting students even from Indonesia and China and enjoying the patronage of numerous kings. The Muslims largely destroyed it c. 1200.

**6 One of the oldest-known** Buddhist images in South-East Asia is this bronze Buddha from Vietnam, dating back to the fifth century. Its style was influenced by Buddhas from Amaravarti.

**7 Borobudur**, situated in the heart of Java, is often described as a stupa (dome-shaped shrine) but although a stupa crowns it, the rest of the structure predominates. It is a marvellous storehouse of sculpture with five lavishly decorated galleries exhibiting pious stories in 1,500 relief panels. It was built by the Sailendras, a Buddhist dynasty in Java from about 750 to 850.

**8 The Mons of southern Thailand** and the Thais of central Thailand became Buddhists by the third century. Despite the Khmer occupation, Buddhism continued to flourish. This Buddha head comes from Lopburi. Although conforming to Buddhist norms, it was modelled to correspond to the aesthetic ideals of the Thais.

**9 The expansion of Buddhism** outside India was a complicated process extending over many centuries. Here the broad outlines of its spread are shown, together with the percentage of Buddhists in various countries today. Buddhism was spread by monks who sometimes acted as advisers to kings.

| India | Bangladesh | Sri Lanka | Burma | Thailand | Cambodia | Laos | S. Vietnam | Tibet |
|-------|-----------|-----------|-------|----------|----------|------|-----------|-------|
| 0·7% | 0·8% | 67% | 82% | 90% | 98% | 95% | 5% | 99% |

Peking 1st cent AD
Lhasa
Bihar State
11th cent AD
13th cent AD
3rd cent BC
6th cent AD

Theravada Buddhism
Tibetan Buddhism
Zen and Pure Land Buddhism

| Nepal | Sikkim | Mongolia | Bhutan | Japan | Korea | China | N. Vietnam | Malaysia |
|-------|--------|----------|--------|-------|-------|-------|-----------|----------|
| 40% | 35% | 98% | 98% | 78% | 70% | 40% | 80% | 25% |

# Europe 1200–500 BC

By 1200 BC the Bronze Age was fully mature among the Urnfield peoples, predecessors of the Celts who were by 800–700 BC to become the dominant and most progressive element in European society for several hundred years. The Urnfield peoples lived north of the Alps and belong to the prehistoric phase of European evolution; their name was given to them by archaeologists because they introduced a new burial rite into Europe. Burial in barrows was replaced by cremation, the burnt bones then being placed in an urn and interred in large flat cemeteries or Urnfields.

## Technological revolution

With some exceptions – Basques, Finns, Iberians – the Europeans were of Indo-European origin and thus had linguistic and cultural traditions in common. The Urnfield peoples, who were farmers living in villages or large homestead complexes, may have spoken some form of Celtic dialect as the distribution of their monuments corresponds with the oldest recognizable Celtic place-names. These Urnfield peoples are generally regarded as being "proto-Celtic" and there seems to be little difference between them and their immediate descendants, the Celts of the Hallstatt culture.

The Urnfield period saw not only improved agriculture in Europe but also great developments in metalworking. It was a time of expansion and of warfare, and archaeological evidence shows that the central Europeans possessed quite sophisticated bronze weapons. Towards the end of the period, about 800 BC, Europe experienced a major technological revolution initiated by the Celts. They introduced the use of iron into Europe north of the Alps, and with it all the superiority in weapons and edge tools which the use of iron made possible. The areas of initial development coincide closely with Urnfield settlements in the Danube and Rhine regions.

Apart from evidence of some contact with people from the Steppes, everything suggests a continuity of the indigenous population enriched and empowered by the discovery of iron. This first phase of Celtic culture is known to archaeologists as Hallstatt after a village in the Salzkammergut in Austria.

The Hallstatt site has provided dramatic and comprehensive evidence about the early Iron Age in Europe. The community there derived much of its wealth from large salt mines. Both the preserving and healing powers of salt were recognized at an early stage. But it was also a valuable trading commodity, being perhaps the chief export from the Hallstatt Celts to the Graeco-Etruscan world. Evidence from many sites points to the importance of this trade which passed between the two regions through Greek colonies in the northern Mediterranean. A leading colony was Massalia (Marseille) which was founded about 600 BC.

## Workers and aristocrats

The equipment, dress, foods and eating habits of workers are all too often unknown in a society solely concerned with its aristocracy, the wealth of which is attested by the richness of the burials. Clothing and leather helmets have been preserved at Hallstatt. Their wooden bowls and other eating utensils have remained intact and numerous seeds

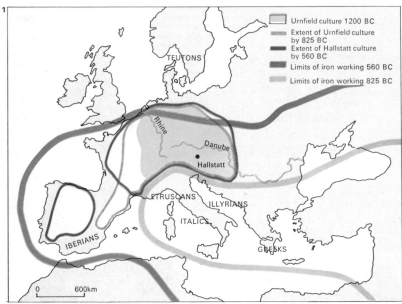

**1 The Urnfield culture** developed around the Danube and Rhine and by 825 BC had reached Spain. The Hallstatt culture, which began in the same place and superseded the Urnfield, by 560 BC covered most of Spain and Portugal. By then iron working, introduced from the east, had spread through most of Europe. The Hallstatt culture is named after a key archaeological site in Austria.

Map legend:
- Urnfield culture 1200 BC
- Extent of Urnfield culture by 825 BC
- Extent of Hallstatt culture by 560 BC
- Limits of iron working 560 BC
- Limits of iron working 825 BC

**2 In Irish tradition** this stone with its spiral designs marked an entrance to the "otherworld". It dates from c. 2500 BC, foreshadowing Celtic designs of some 2,000 years later.

**3 Hallstatt ceramic skill** and restrained decorative elegance are shown in this painted pottery urn from Burrenhof, Germany, dating from about 620 BC.

**4 A gold armband** from Dover of about 1000 BC anticipates Celtic work.

**5 Irish goldsmiths** made this gold-plated lead pendant about 800 BC.

**6 Later Celtic symmetry** is seen in a gold-plated Irish ring of about 1000 BC.

and fruit stones provide some indication of their typical diet.

Information about the aristocrats comes from a vast cemetery which points to great changes in burial customs and personal equipment coinciding with the development of a culture based on iron, a more abundant metal and cheaper for practical purposes than bronze. Chieftains were no longer cremated and placed in humble urns but were buried with much pomp.

## Burial ceremony

The richest graves consisted of a wooden chamber, usually of oak and covered by a mound decorated by a commemorative stone figure [Key], sacred tree, or stone pillar. The deceased was placed under his status symbol, a four-wheeled wagon. Horse trappings were present, but there seems to be no evidence for the burial of the horses themselves; perhaps they were sacrificed to the gods and ritually eaten, or burnt. All the warrior's fine military equipment was placed in the tomb with him – his sword and spear, helmet, neck and arm ornaments and other things he had valued. Pots no doubt full of ale or imported wine for the "other world" feast, and joints of meat were laid beside him to sustain him on his journey. According to the Old Irish tales, once the actual burial rite was completed, the ceremony would be followed by feasting and funerary games.

The Hallstatt period lasted until about 500 BC and laid the foundations for the full flowering of Celtic culture in Europe at that time. There was some intermarriage with the Teutonic peoples to the north – both Teuton and German are Celtic names – and the Celts were probably overlords, making up the aristocracy of these closely related peoples. The Hallstatt phase of the Celts manifested itself deep into Spain. Hallstatt art [3, 7, 8, 9] tended to be linear, influenced by Greek Geometric, the naturalism of Urnfield bird and animal art, and old indigenous motifs, magical and symbolic. It was to become an important element in the magnificent magico-religious art [11] of the La Tène period that followed, and in the important contribution of Irish art [4, 5, 6, 10] to the Western Church in early Christian times.

KEY

**This stone statue** of a Hallstatt warrior or divinized hero, dates from the end of the 6th century BC. The figure was found on a Hirshlanden burial mound, broken where it had fallen. The cult of graves and ancestors was strong among the Celts and this anthropomorphic figure links the prehistoric world with that of the historical Celtic world in all its flourishing vigour. In this sense, it epitomizes all that had gone before and anticipates the strength of Celtic culture in its later phase. The Hallstatt peoples had close trade links with the Etruscans, another important bronze-using culture.

**7 Warfare, whether as necessity** or as an aristocratic sport, dominated most aspects of Celtic culture. Emphasis was laid not only on efficient weapons but also on the appearance of the warriors. Although not usually worn into battle, helmets were popular headgear. This bronze helmet from Italy probably dates from the Hallstatt period and is a particularly fine example of Celtic work.

7

8

**8 A Greek bronze crater** for mixing wine, weighing 208kg (460lb), was found in the burial of the priestess at Vix. It shows that as early as the 6th century BC the Celtic and Mediterranean worlds were in close contact. This may have been a gift of peace, friendship or trade.

**9 The Celts were skilled metalworkers.** They introduced iron into northern Europe by 800 BC but continued to use bronze with exquisite results. This detail of a bronze bowl handle from the 6th century gives some indication of the sophisticated craftsmanship of the Hallstatt culture.

9

**10 This gold dress-fastener** from County Galway (Castlekelly) in Ireland dates from about 700 BC and measures 28cm (11in) across. Such objects not only provide proof of Celtic pride in personal ornamentation but also reveal the exquisite skill and harmony of Celtic craftsmen and their predecessors in their use of various metals as a medium of their art.

**11 The severed head** – the true godhead – with one, two or three faces was the supreme object of Celtic worship. This Janus head from a sanctuary in France about 250 BC looks back and also forward, possibly to the "otherworld".

11

10

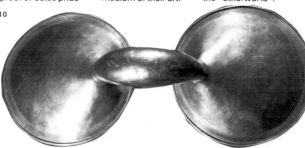

# The Greeks to the rise of Athens

Some time about 1200 BC, Greek civilization underwent a major change. Dorian tribes moved through the peninsula from the north and settled, mainly in the Peloponnese. The existing peoples were assimilated or confined into smaller areas, and Ionians and Aeolians in particular were pushed out across the sea to found cities in Asia Minor.

## The development of institutions

Major social changes must have accompanied this upheaval, but little detail is known of the next 400 years; much of what we do know comes from the two epic poems by Homer, the *Iliad* and the *Odyssey*. It is, however, possible to identify several important developments that were of major significance for subsequent Greek civilization. The use of iron became widespread for tools and weapons [2]; a phonetic alphabet was developed and more or less standardized; and a feeling of national consciousness arose – a racial and intellectual identity bound up in the use of the word *Hellas* to describe the whole Greek world. At the same time a pantheon of gods that appear in Homer's

poems was formed, religious ceremonies developed and the importance of shrines such as Delphi became generally accepted, and the city state was adopted as the most important political, economic and social unit.

The rugged geography of Greece played a major part in making the inhabitants of each valley regard themselves as a separate entity and Greece became a patchwork of small states each of which guarded its independence jealously [3]. They varied greatly in size; Athens succeeded in subduing Attica and no other states developed there, while Thebes failed to overcome Boeotia and at least 12 states existed there. Writing in the fourth century BC, Aristotle mentions the existence of at least 150 states.

The size of the city state was important for Greek political development because a firm belief developed that a satisfactory political unit must be small and totally independent. A Greek had a series of loyalties to *Hellas*, to his city state and to his tribe within the state – but loyalty to the city was the most powerful and the idea of a larger political unit was never developed. During this period the

Greeks also evolved the belief that government must be based on a known constitutional and legal framework.

## Agriculture, trade and politics

Economically, agriculture was all-important [Key] and as the cities developed, the link between them and the country remained strong. However, some states became increasingly involved in trade and industry [6] and a definite class of traders and craftsmen evolved. Politically, by the mid-seventh century BC most states had moved away from the monarchies described by Homer and were ruled by oligarchies of the richest and most powerful citizens. A privileged or noble class held all political, military and religious power and there was usually tension between them and the common people.

This tension was made worse by increasing population and a safety valve was found in colonization [4]. States organized expeditions to found new cities overseas, but once founded these new cities were completely independent of, although they

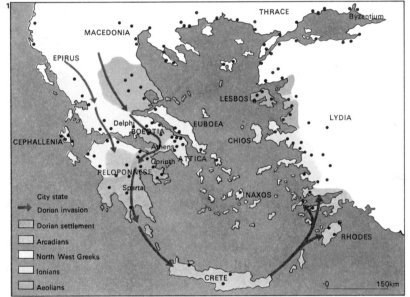

1 **Little is known of the history** of Greece between the arrival of the Dorians (c. 1200 BC) and the dawn of the Archaic period (c. 800 BC). Homer describes a society of small agricultural communities grouped round citadels and led by kings and aristocracies that still retained many of the features of Mycenaean civilization and had little trade or commerce. By the time of Hesiod (8th century BC), whose narrative poems give a description of the early Archaic period, trade and commerce were increasing, monarchy had generally been replaced by oligarchy and the city was becoming the focus of political life.

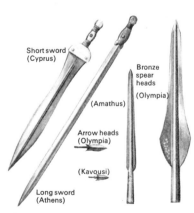

Bell corset

Helmet (Argos)

Earliest Corinthian helmet

Illyrian helmet

Greave (900-800 BC)

Archaic greaves

3 **The landscape of Greece,** with its limited fertile plains and harsh mountains, became a significant factor in the rise of small communities such as Corinth (shown here). Travel was difficult and economic and political life tended to be concentrated in confined areas. The Greeks were convinced that these small independent units were the most natural size for a satisfactory political life. This attitude, combined with constant diplomatic and military manoeuvring between states, meant that wider unity was never attempted, although the idea of a distinct Greek identity and a feeling of cultural superiority to outsiders did exist.

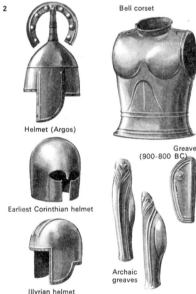

Short sword (Cyprus)

(Amathus)

Arrow heads (Olympia)

(Kavousi)

Long sword (Athens)

Bronze spear heads (Olympia)

2 **Bronze arms and armour** were used by the aristocratic warriors of Homer's poems, who fought in individual combat. But iron began to supersede bronze before 700 BC and tactics changed fundamentally, with heavily armed infantry (hop-

lites) fighting in a well-disciplined mass formation – the phalanx. Many hoplites came from outside the aristocracy (although they had to be wealthy enough to provide their own equipment) and this helped to weaken the old social order.

retained close links with, their mother cities. From about 750 BC migration established Greek cities throughout the Mediterranean.

Colonization did not solve the problem of class struggle and the archaic Greek world (Greece between 800 and 500 BC) saw the widespread appearance of tyrants, a word originally applied by the Greeks to men who seized power unconstitutionally and ruled – either well or badly – without legal backing.

### New political systems

In Athens attempts were made by Solon (c. 640–c. 559 BC) to remove the economic problems that lay at the root of the class struggle and reform the legal framework of the state to protect the weak. Power was seized in 545 by Pisistratus (c. 600–527 BC) who increased the rights of the common people and brought the nobility under the rule of law. These developments formalized the democratic system that ruled Athens for the next two centuries.

The same pattern was followed in other states; tyrants rarely lasted long. Some states, such as Sparta with its peculiar constitution,

and Corinth with a strong oligarchy, avoided the tyrannical stage completely.

Until the middle of the sixth century BC the Greeks were largely unaffected by outsiders, apart from trading contacts [5]. The situation altered when the Lydians extended their power over the Greek states of Asia Minor and were succeeded in 546 by the Persians. Neither overlordship was oppressive, but in 499 the Greeks rose in revolt and succeeded in temporarily reasserting their independence. There was, however, little unity among them or support from the mainland, and in 494 the Persian emperor Darius was able to crush the revolt. He followed this up by reimposing his power in Thrace and Macedonia and then in 490 launching a major invasion of Greece.

Athens, as the largest state, was his immediate target and she called for help from the others, but before this could arrive her troops, who were significantly outnumbered, met and decisively defeated the Persians at Marathon. Darius' army withdrew, leaving the Greeks still disunited but convinced of their superiority over the "barbarians".

**Greek agriculture,** represented by the olive harvest shown on this 6th-century BC amphora, was always faced with the difficulty of providing sufficient food from the relatively small area of fertile land. The natural consequence of an expanding population faced with a limited food supply was emigration, first across the Ionian Sea and then throughout the Mediterranean. But overpopulation was only part of the reason for emigrating: the nature of aristocratic control of land resources meant that the distribution of agricultural land was by no means equitable; the resulting social tensions naturally encouraged the tendency to emigrate.

**4 Colonization was** used to send surplus and disaffected populations to found cities in new regions. The first phase began about 750 BC with expeditions to the west, where the Greeks found the Phoenicians already well established in many areas. They were able to settle in Sicily, southern Italy, France and Libya. About 650 BC the Greeks began to move into the Black Sea region until there were colonies round almost all its shores. By the 6th century BC, the colonies were sending enough food back to Greece to feed the expanding population and thus reduce emigration.

**5 The Greeks traded with the Phoenicians,** the Egyptians and the people of the Middle East as well as between colonies and mother cities. In states bordering the sea, such as Athens and Corinth, trade became an important source of wealth. Shipbuilding and navigation were therefore vital skills.

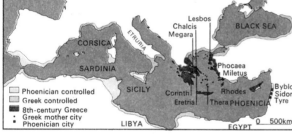

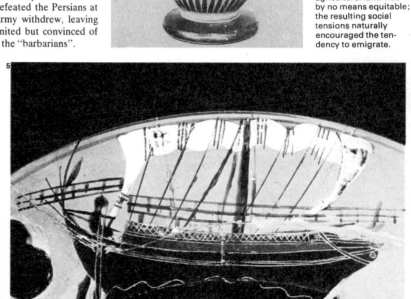

**6 Trade and commerce** were free to develop after the city states had been established, and the system of barter was replaced by more regulated methods. Various systems of weights and measures were developed (such as this one on an Attic black-figure amphora, showing men using a balance scale), but no single system became dominant. Precious metals were used for exchange either in the shape of weapons or as pieces valued by weight. By the end of the 7th century money had been invented. The issuing of coinage soon became the privilege of governments and not of individuals.

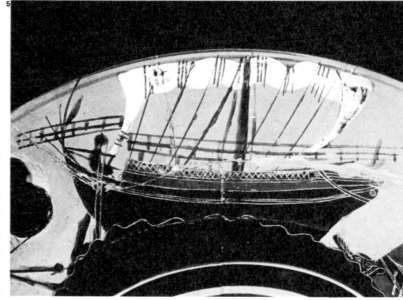

**7 Priene in Asia Minor** was a model of Greek town planning. Most cities grew haphazardly, but few were as well planned or showed so clearly the essentials of a small city state of only about 4,000 inhabitants. The citadel or Acropolis [1] stood at the top of the cliff with the main city below it. The principal features were the sanctuary of Demeter and other gods [2]; the huge theatre [3], possibly the oldest Hellenistic example, which could accommodate an audience of 5,000; housing blocks [4], each with four to six dwellings; buildings for the council and courts [5, 6]; the agora [11], which was the market-place and heart of the community, adjoining the main street [8]; the sanctuary of Zeus [7]; the gymnasium [9]; and the stadium [10].

# Classical Greece

In 480 BC the Persians under Xerxes launched a second invasion of Greece. A large army advanced across the Hellespont and down the peninsula; it was briefly halted by the heroism of 300 Spartans under their king, Leonidas, who held the narrow pass at Thermopylae until outflanked. They fought to the last man. Athens was occupied but shortly afterwards its fleet, led by the statesman Themistocles (c. 528–c. 460 BC), annihilated the Persian force at Salamis [1]. Xerxes' army fell back northwards and in 479 BC it was defeated at Plataea by a largely Peloponnesian army under the Spartan Pausanias. If the Greeks had not defeated the Persians, the history of Europe might have been very different – a dominant Persian civilization would have left Europe with quite another set of values and institutions.

## The golden age of Athens
The Persians withdrew but their threat remained and a defensive league of many of the Aegean islands and Greek states in Asia Minor was set up in 478 BC under Athenian leadership, with its headquarters at Delos [4].

A navy was established, maintained by contributions of money or ships.

Soon Athens, as the most powerful Greek state, came to dominate the Delian League and, under the guidance of her statesmen Cimon (died 449 BC) and Pericles (c. 490–429 BC), became a maritime empire in all but name. The democratic system was refined under Pericles, and the great buildings and cultural achievements that were to make Athens famous grew from trade.

Inevitably, the power of Athens aroused jealousy and fear, particularly in Sparta, which continued to dominate the Peloponnesian states, and Corinth, the other great trading state. There was sporadic warfare during the 450s BC and Athens built up a land empire in Megara, Boeotia and Achaea, but this was abandoned in 445 BC after concluding a truce with her rivals. Hostilities broke out again in 431 between the rival alliances and Athens, secure behind the Long Walls linking her with her major port of Piraeus [5], allowed the Spartans to invade Attica and instead concentrated on using her maritime power to wear down her enemies.

Pericles died of plague in 429, but his strategy was continued by Cleon (died 422 BC). Neither side could decisively defeat the other, and a peace was reached in 421. This lasted only two years before fighting broke out again; in 415 the war party in Athens led by Alcibiades (c. 450–404 BC) persuaded the people to launch a major expedition to invade Sicily and capture Syracuse. The venture was a ghastly failure, and in 413 the bulk of the Athenian army and navy were destroyed. Despite the disaster Athens fought on, although her enemies were now being financed by the Persians and several of her allies revolted. In 405 the remainder of the Athenian navy was surprised and destroyed at Aegospotami by Spartans under Lysander (died 395 BC), who then besieged the city. When it surrendered in 404, an oligarchy replaced democracy, and the Spartans took over the Athenian Empire.

## Decline of Spartan rule
This Spartan supremacy was short-lived; spurred on by the exploits of Xenophon's Ten Thousand – Greek mercenaries who

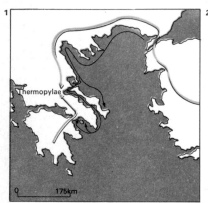

**1 After the Persians overran Athens**, the refugees fled with the Greek navy to Salamis. There, by a stratagem the Greeks trapped the Persians and destroyed an entire corps as well as 200 Persian ships for a loss of only 40 of their own.

→ Route of Persian army
→ Route of Greek army
▨ Route of Persian navy
⬡ Island of Salamis

**2 An Athenian trireme** was the type of warship that defeated the Persians at Salamis and was the mainstay of the powerful navy built up under the direction of Themistocles at the beginning of the 5th century. The navy was significant in the democratic system, for it was largely manned by the poorer citizens and provided them not only with a livelihood but also with a source of pride and power. Since much of the wealth and power of Athens came from trade and her maritime empire, the common people could assert that they were the backbone of the state and should play a major part in its political life.

**3 This Athenian four drachma coin** shows the owl of Athena, who was the patron goddess of the city. Athens' naval and trading domination of the Aegean gave the city great wealth which was lavished on fine buildings and the arts, and allowed its citizens the leisure to participate in the democratic system or to make contributions to philosophy and literature. Even during its decline, Athens remained the acknowledged intellectual and artistic leader of Greece.

□ Sparta and allies (the Peloponnesian League) 431 BC
▨ Athens and allies 431 BC
▨ Neutral Greek states 431 BC
✶ Revolts

**4 After the defeat of the Persians**, Athens used its navy to secure the Aegean against them and to liberate the Greek states in Asia Minor. Soon the defensive Delian League was turned into an aggressive empire with Athens intervening directly in the internal affairs of allied states. Sparta's fear of this expansion caused it to encourage revolts and oligarchic governments, and led in 431 to the start of the Peloponnesian war which engulfed most of Greece.

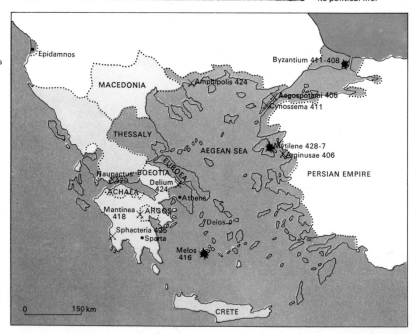

made an epic march across the Persian Empire – a crusade was launched to regain the freedom of the Greek states in Asia Minor, but the Persians encouraged the Spartans' allies to turn against them and the attempt had to be abandoned in 387, leaving them under Persian domination.

The next 50 years show the worst features of the Greek political system of the Classical age, with petty jealousies and continual military rivalry preventing the emergence of any wider unity. Athens recovered quickly, democracy was restored in 403 and by 377 she was again leading a naval confederacy against Sparta. However, it was Thebes that became the next dominant power when it destroyed the Spartan army at Leuctra in 371. After a decade she too began to decline, and Phocis, by capturing the treasure of Delphi, was able to hire mercenaries and set up a temporary mastery.

**The Hellenistic age**
Interstate rivalries continued and prevented the Greeks from realizing that a new threat was growing in the north. The Macedonians had hitherto been a loose confederation of tribes, but in 359 Philip II (382–336 BC) became king. A fine organizer, general and diplomat, he unified the tribes in his own kingdom and then went on to annex Thessaly in 352 and Thrace in 342.

The Athenians were the first of the Greeks to become aware of this new danger, for Philip's power threatened their lucrative trade routes to the Black Sea. However, years of relative peace had made the people of Athens apathetic and lacking in military zeal. A few orators such as Demosthenes (died 322 BC) tried to arouse them to the danger to their trade and to their city, and to exhort them to put an end to traditional rivalries so that the Greek states could unite against this new peril. Eventually a Greek league was formed, but in 338 Philip routed its armies at the battle of Chaeronea and occupied Thebes. Athens prepared to continue its resistance but there was little support elsewhere and at the Congress of Corinth a new league of Greek states was set up under Macedonian leadership. The independence of the free city states was at an end.

KEY

A Greek hoplite is shown killing his Persian enemy on this vase. The Greek Classical age is usually taken as beginning with Pausanias' defeat of the second Persian invasion in 479 BC and ending with the establishment of Macedonian power over all Greece in 320. Many of the great achievements of the Greeks flowed directly from the feeling of security and superiority that followed the Persian defeat, but with their devotion to the small city state and their obsession with political and military manoeuvring, the Greeks failed to develop a wider political unity which could have resisted the rising power of Macedon.

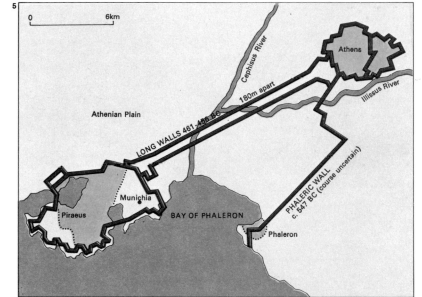

5 Themistocles began the development of Piraeus as the base for Athens' navy and its vital trading and commercial port. The Long Walls were built to link it with the city and give Athens the means to maintain her maritime power even when its territory was invaded. It was symbolic that when Athens was defeated in 404, the Spartans insisted on the immediate demolition of the walls.

6 The hoplites were heavily armed soldiers trained to fight in a highly disciplined phalanx (a solid formation). They were usually recruited from the merchant citizens who thereby won great political power.

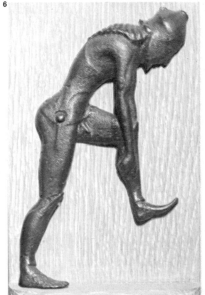

7 Throughout the Classical age there was almost continual fighting between city states. This weakened the Greeks politically, but did not prevent a flowering of the arts, literature and philosophy. The above relief comes from a Hellenistic sarcophagus found at Tyre and depicts The Death of Hector. The achievements of Athens have tended to overshadow the fact that many other states, both on the Greek mainland and in Asia Minor, also produced great artists and writers.

8 The Temple of Athena at Delphi, whose oracle was presided over by Apollo, was part of the widely respected shrine in ancient Greece. Religion in the Classical age was an affair of sacrifices and ceremonies by the state or individual that contained little moral guidance or mystical experience. However, a belief in the same gods and legends did promote the feeling of a common culture which was added to by semi-religious festivals such as the Olympic games.

# Classical Greek society

Classical Greece was the birthplace of many of the most influential Western ideas in art, literature, philosophy and science. Its other great contribution was in politics, for it was there that the ideals of democracy were first developed. In all these areas Athens was pre-eminent, a fact recognized even by her contemporaries. In two centuries she produced a succession of outstanding writers, artists, scientists and philosophers. Many who were not natives were attracted to the city, and there are few important figures in Greek cultural life who were not associated with Athens for at least part of their careers.

## Athens and democracy

The city state of Athens, with an area of about 2,500 square kilometres (1,000 square miles), was the largest of the many city states into which Greece was divided. Her population at its peak was about 260,000, of which about 45,000 were male citizens and about 70,000 slaves. The rest were women, children and resident foreigners or *metics*. Corinth may have had a population of 90,000; Thebes, Corcyra and Acragas about

50,000 each; and the other states anything down to 5,000.

Politics in all these city states was a very intimate affair and this profoundly affected the Athenian concept of democracy [1]. It was based on direct participation, rather than representation, with every citizen having an equal opportunity to hold high office. In common with many other Greek states, Athens went through the transition from oligarchy (a small number of individuals holding power) to tyranny (a single all-powerful ruler) with struggles between rich and poor before the reforms of Cleisthenes in 508 BC established a democratic framework.

The essence of this democracy was the citizen body or *Demos*. Citizenship was a jealously guarded right, rarely given to foreigners and never to women [5] or slaves. All power was vested in the *Demos* which met in public assembly about every ten days [2]. There, any citizen could put forward proposals for laws or action which were discussed and voted on, and the civil and religious officials were chosen. Juries were selected from volunteers, and the business of the Assembly

was prepared by a Council of 500, the *Boulê*, elected by the ten tribes into which the citizens were divided.

## Rights and duties

Every Athenian citizen had the right and duty to serve the state but, because there were more than 1,000 offices to be filled each year, the system could work only if there were enough men with both the time and inclination to devote their lives to public service. It is a remarkable fact that at no time was Athens short of able men to serve with little or no reward, and it was only during the fourth century BC that a small payment was introduced to help the poorest citizens to participate fully.

Athenians gained their wealth from land, trade and commerce. At the beginning of the fifth century Athens was a major exporter of pottery, oil and wine and an importer of fish, timber and wheat on which it was largely dependent. In Athens, in particular, a definite class of capitalists and an urban proletariat developed. Their leisure resulted from the widespread use of slaves to under-

1

**1 The hub of Athenian democracy** was the Pnyx where the Assembly of citizens gathered for its regular meetings. Public and social life was a gregarious and open-air affair with informal discussion, theatre and sports providing the most common interests.

**2 Fifth-century Athenian democracy** was based upon the power of the Assembly of citizens to vote on all major decisions. Public officials were responsible to the Assembly and were chosen by the ten citizen tribes for limited terms; only the ten military commanders or *strategoi* were elected and could serve for more than a year. Popular control over both the magistrates and the law could also be exercised through the courts where the large citizen juries had legislative as well as judicial powers and could try a law as unconstitutional.

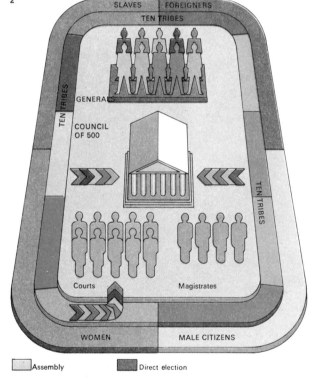

2

Assembly     Direct election

Nomination and lot

**3 A Negro slave** follows a member of the leisured class. Athenian democracy, with its large number of official jobs being filled by unpaid or low-paid citizens, depended on a plentiful supply of men with the inclination and leisure to undertake them. Athenian civic responsibility and pride in the system meant that there was never a lack of volunteers and this was helped by the wealth from land and commerce which flowed into the city. The large-scale use of slaves freed citizens for public service. Athenian thinkers saw no contradiction between the individual rights and freedom on which their system was based and the slaves upon which it depended.

3

4

**4 A heifer is led to sacrifice** in a religious ceremony. Greek religion was supervised by the state – the correct prayers and sacrifices were carried out by elected priests or private individuals – but there was little of the moral certainty and interference in private affairs that characterized later religions. The gods were irrational and arbitrary and had to be placated, often by sacrifices; their conduct provided little guidance.

take many of the most basic jobs [3]. Despite this influence of the wealthy, it is also remarkable that Athenian democracy saw few of the direct confrontations between rich and poor of the kind that caused continual unrest in most other city states.

All citizens and *metics* were liable for military service, but usually only the more wealthy were called up because troops were expected to equip themselves. By the early seventh century BC the typical Greek soldier was a heavily – and expensively – armed hoplite infantryman [6]. At the height of the Peloponnesian war Athens put about 16,000 hoplites into the field; few other states could raise as many. In Athens the navy was especially important and had an intake of about 12,000 citizens a year.

### Sparta: a military state

No other state reached such a fully developed system of democracy as Athens. Its main rival for much of the period was Sparta, whose political and social system is remembered as representing the political opposite of everything that democracy stands for. By 600 BC

Sparta had become a unique military state; Laconia and Messenia had been conquered and their populations either enslaved (*helots*) or deprived of political rights and forced to support the Spartans through taxation and food and manpower supplies.

To prevent revolt or secession, Sparta became a military camp. The citizen body was never large – probably never much more than 5,000 – but everyone was a professional soldier devoted from childhood to absolute discipline and the art of war. Two hereditary kings commanded the army in the field and were members of the ruling council of elders who were elected for life from citizens over 60. Five elected *ephors* had civil and judicial functions. No other Greek state approached Sparta in exclusiveness or xenophobia – even trade and commerce were largely disdained. A total refusal to admit new citizens led to a declining population and eventual defeat.

Sparta has remained the model of a closed and totally disciplined society, but it was Athens whose pursuit of individual freedom and democracy gave the modern world two of its most precious and lasting ideals.

**Pericles** (*c.* 490–429 BC) was the great Athenian statesman under whose leadership the city became the richest and most powerful Greek state. He was responsible for the building of the fine temples and monuments on the Acropolis.

**5 Women in Classical Greece** were the other great "slave" class; they had no political or legal rights and were excluded from all public affairs. Their place was in the home with the children. Their absence from much social life led to widespread development of homosexual relationships and the institution of the *hetaira* – high-class courtesans outside conventional mores.

**6 Spartan infantrymen** (hoplites) were normally well and expensively equipped. The Spartan political system of a totally mobilized citizenry devoted to military service (boys were sent to barracks at the age of seven and not allowed other interests) was unique in Greece and gave Sparta far greater importance than its relatively small size justified. Most other states relied upon temporary conscription to fight the frequent wars that were endemic to Greek life. But a class of professional mercenaries did grow up during the 4th century, possibly as many as 50,000 in all, some fighting for the Persians.

**7 Gods and goddesses** with Athena holding a shield inscribed with an owl are shown on this Greek vase. The pantheon was featured in the epics of Homer and was the basis of the religion of Classical Greece. The gods were conceived of in human form with human emotions. They often interfered in human activities and could be invoked or calmed by prayer and sacrifice. There was little belief in an afterlife; religion was strictly temporal, devoted to a pleasant existence.

**8 Athletic competitions** and the cult of the well-trained and healthy body played an important part in everyday social life, the gymnasium or stadium being a popular meeting place where men could talk and hold political or philosophical discussions. The Greeks dated their history from the first Olympic games in 776 BC, a festival which, with contestants from all over the Greek world, provided an opportunity for Greeks to gather together as a nation.

# Alexander the Great

Alexander, the son of Philip of Macedon and Olympia, princess of Epirus, was born at Pella in Macedon in 356 BC and died in Babylon in 323 BC. The pupil of the philosopher Aristotle between the ages of 13 and 16, he succeeded to the Macedonian throne in 336 BC on the assassination of his father, whose cavalry he had commanded two years earlier at the battle of Chaeronea. This battle had finally ended Athenian hopes of regaining the leadership of Greece, giving hegemony to the Macedonians who were, at best, peripheral Greeks. It also marked the victory of the soldier over the rhetorician, for it had been Demosthenes, the Athenian orator (c. 383–322 BC), who had most attacked the Macedonians and their king.

## Securing the frontiers of Macedonia
During the next 13 years Alexander was to establish the greatest empire the ancient world had ever known [4], stretching from the Libyan frontier to the Punjab. His exploits gave rise to stories and legends in all the languages of Europe and many of those of Asia.

Upon his accession he marched south into Greece and, asserting Macedonian supremacy, had himself elected by the Greek League as a leader of an Asian expedition, one that had already been planned by his father. The oracle of Delphi hailed him as invincible. In 335 BC he campaigned towards the Danube, to secure Macedonia's northern frontier. On rumours of his death, a revolt broke out in Greece with the support of leading Athenians: Alexander marched south covering 386km (240 miles) in a fortnight. When the revolt continued he sacked Thebes, killing 6,000 people and enslaving the survivors, sparing only the temples and the house of Pindar (c. 522–c. 440 BC), one of the greatest of Greek poets. His base thus secured, he prepared for the campaign for which his father had raised him. He also needed the riches of Persia to pay his father's debts to the Macedonian army.

## The victory over Darius
Alexander crossed the Hellespont in 334 BC, with 30,000 infantry, 5,000 cavalry and a corps of specialists. He paid a visit to Troy

and at the River Granicus fought a battle that opened Asia Minor to his southward drive. He defeated Darius, the Persian king (who fled, leaving his family), at the Issus [2] in 333 BC and continued until his advance was held up at Tyre, which fell in July 332 BC.

After the sack of Tyre, Alexander went to Egypt, where he founded the city of Alexandria. On visiting the shrine of Amon at Siwah Oasis, he was greeted as pharaoh, son of Ammon, an event that gave rise to stories of his divine origin. In 331 BC, he marched eastwards to the Euphrates and fought another battle at Gaugamela, but Darius once again escaped; Alexander received the surrender of Babylon and Susa with their riches. In 330 BC he captured Persepolis; then he sent the Thessalians and Greeks home, apparently planning a Persian-Macedonian empire. While he was campaigning eastwards Darius was assassinated.

Alexander next marched into Afghanistan and Transoxiana, partly to pursue a rebellious general, and thence to Samarkand and Alexandria Eschate (present-day Leninabad). There were further revolts until

**1 The battle of the Hydaspes** (Jhelum) in the Punjab, shown here on this coin, was one of Alexander's most skilfully planned and executed victories, greatly extending his empire. His tactics were greatly influenced by the horse's natural fear of the elephant. The defeated Indian ruler Porus became an ally. During this battle Alexander's famous charger Bucephalus died and was given a full imperial funeral.

**2 This mosaic from Pompeii,** copied from a painting by Philoxenus, shows Alexander commanding his army against the Persians, under Darius, at the Battle of the Issus, 333 BC. Darius fled, leaving his queen and family together with a vast amount of wealth to the Macedonians.

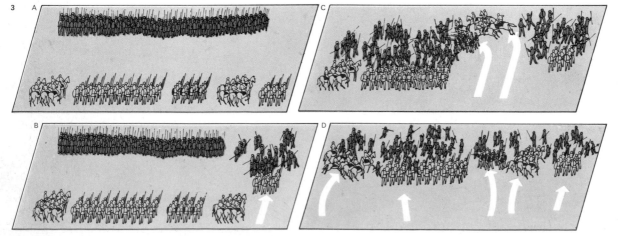

**3 Alexander placed the phalanx** at the centre of his battle order [A]. Fighting was initiated on the extreme right [B]. At the right moment Alexander would lead his companions, supported by the household infantry, in a charge that penetrated the gap in the enemy line [C]. As the enemy ranks broke, he wheeled his companions to take the flank to relieve the left and centre of his army. As the enemy retreated, he pressed home his advantage with his full force [D].

328 BC, the year of his marriage to Roxana, daughter of the king of Bactria, a marriage that seems to have been symbolic of East-West fusion. At the same time his absolutism increased. His murder of his commander and friend Clitus in a drunken brawl angered the Macedonians.

In 327 BC he led his men into India, one army marching through the Khyber Pass while the other, which he commanded, fought its way through Swat. The final battle was fought on the Hydaspes (Jhelum) [1]; after the defeat of Porus, an Indian prince, Alexander's soldiers refused to go farther.

### Return from the East

On his return to Susa, Alexander found a state of corruption and oppression. He set about a ruthless campaign of punishment. This was followed by a scheme for settling Greeks and Macedonians in Asia and Asians in Europe as part of a plan for fusing the two regions. A more immediate project was the marriage of Alexander and Hephaestion (his closest friend and lover) to two of the daughters of Darius, while another 80 Macedonian officers married daughters of Persian nobles.

Asian soldiers had already been trained in Macedonian military methods and were now admitted to the army; others were recruited to the cavalry and Persian officers to the royal bodyguard. In 324 BC his 10,000 Macedonians, already disturbed by the new army policy, mutinied. Alexander ordered 13 of their leaders to be killed on the spot, appointed more Persians and Medes to Macedonian posts and transferred regimental names to what the Europeans considered barbarian regiments. The Macedonians then set off on the return march.

Plans were now made for a campaign into Arabia, but Alexander developed fever and on 13 June 323 BC he died, not yet 33 years old. His empire began to disintegrate almost at once as the various regional commanders assumed the titles of kings in their own right. Although Alexander was renowned primarily for his military conquests, his most enduring achievement was to extend the influence of the Greeks to a vast area of the ancient world, and to widen the basis of Hellenic culture through contact with the East.

KEY

**Alexander** is wearing the ram's horn head-dress on this coin.

**4 The extent of Alexander's** campaign over 14 years explain the rapid collapse of his empire after his death. There was no consolidation and the vast distances precluded real integration.

**5 A picture from the** Flemish *Alexander Romance* (a 13th-century legend cycle) shows him preparing to fly in a basket attached to two griffins, which are to be lured upwards by a lump of meat on a stick. Another illustration from the same source shows him in a glass "submarine", an idea that also occurs in a Malay story depicting Alexander. Both pictures imply his dominion over land, sea and air.

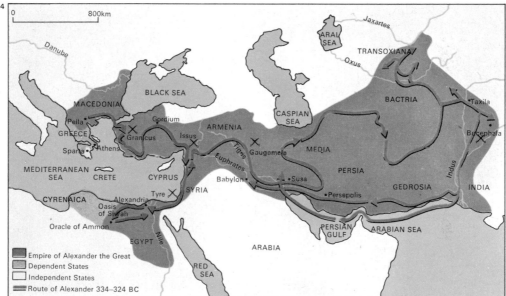

0 ___ 800km

Empire of Alexander the Great
Dependent States
Independent States
Route of Alexander 334–324 BC

**6 The Alexander legend** is told in many languages, from Middle English to Malay, throughout the countries of Europe, the Middle East and India. He is depicted in many forms – Burgundian king, Armenian horseman, Persian prince. (One sultan in the 15th century had his own features depicted as Alexander's.) In the Muslim world he was held to be a pious follower of Islam who fought pagans and spread the faith. He was identified with the Two-horned One mentioned in the Koran, almost a thousand years after his death. In this Persian painting (1595–6) he is being asked to spare pagan idols.

# Greek science

The earliest stirrings of Greek science are found in the eighth century BC in the Homeric poems with descriptions of the stars and an unusual concept of the universe as a sphere [1]. Other civilizations had been content with hemispherical skies but it was the Greek love of symmerical shapes that led them to the concept of a spherical universe.

## Greek studies of the universe

The first Greek scientific men whose names are known – Thales, Anaximander and Anaximenes – came from the eastern seaboard of the Aegean and lived during the sixth century BC. Thales accepted the spherical universe and believed that water was the basic substance from which everything was formed. Anaximander, who thought some indefinable substance (not water) was the basic material, taught that the earth was cylindrical in shape and, like Anaximenes, he believed the heavenly bodies were holes in a dark sky through which shone a surrounding fiery zone. The most important sixth-century scientist was Pythagoras, best known for his proof of the relationship between the sides of

any right-angled triangle. He also investigated musical harmony, which led him to suggest that there was a divine relationship between numbers, music and the universe.

Significant developments in the fourth century BC followed the establishment by Plato (c. 427–347 BC) of an academy in Athens, where he laid great stress on the mathematical nature of the universe. His pupil Aristotle (384–322 BC), the greatest scientific philosopher of antiquity, set up his own academy – the Lyceum – also in Athens. He adopted the theory, first formulated by Empedocles in the fifth century BC, of the Four Elements – earth, air, fire and water – as the fundamental components of all matter. Astronomically, Aristotle discussed whether or not the earth moved in space but, on the basis of the available evidence, he tended to favour a fixed earth in the centre of the universe. Aristotle also discussed the nature of change and especially of motion, as well as teaching that there was a fundamental difference between celestial and terrestrial bodies. The former were eternal and changeless, and all change, he believed, must occur below the

sphere of the moon, the nearest body to the earth. He also rejected the idea, proposed in the fifth century BC by Democritus and Leucippus, that the universe is composed of separate and indestructible atoms.

## Investigations in the pure sciences

Although it was Aristotle's views about the physical universe that exerted the most profound influence on science for the following 2,000 years, he was at his best in the biological field. He carefully described the compound stomach of ruminants such as the cow and the habits of bees and the diseases they suffered; he studied the placental dogfish that reproduces its young live rather as a mammal does and made a general study of sexual reproduction [2]. He also studied plants, although it was his friend and disciple Theophrastus (c. 372 – c. 286 BC), who was the founder of botanical science. Aristotle emphasized the important notion that there is a continuous order of being stretching from inanimate matter up to man.

Following the claim by Eudoxus (c. 408–c. 355 BC) that heavenly bodies moved

**1 A Victorian illustration** of the Homeric universe shows a disc-shaped earth with Greece as its centre, floating on water and surrounded by the sphere of the universe. The sun is rising in the east and the moon is shown high in the sky. Most Greek philosophers thought that the sun, moon and planets all orbited the earth: their innovatory idea was that the heavens were an all-embracing sphere, a more perfect shape than a dome or hemisphere. There was no evidence to support this view of the universe; it was adopted purely for aesthetic reasons. But the belief that the earth was at the centre of the universe remained until Copernicus' work in the 16th century.

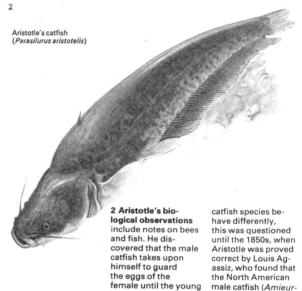

Aristotle's catfish
(*Parasilurus aristotelis*)

**2 Aristotle's biological observations** include notes on bees and fish. He discovered that the male catfish takes upon himself to guard the eggs of the female until the young hatch. Since other catfish species behave differently, this was questioned until the 1850s, when Aristotle was proved correct by Louis Agassiz, who found that the North American male catfish (*Amieurus*) does the same.

**3 Archimedes in his bath** (from a 16th-century engraving) is a reminder of his discovery that a body displaces fluid equivalent to its volume. This means that, regardless of shape, objects of equal density and weight displace the same quantity of fluid. Archimedes used the new principle to determine if a crown made for the king of Syracuse was of unalloyed gold. The crown displaced more water than the same weight of pure gold, proving that it contained other metal.

**4 The Archimedean screw** for raising water may have originated before Archimedes but was attributed to his mechanical skill. Driven by a handle or foot pedals, the spiralling screw rotates in a cylinder, drawing the water upwards.

*c*. 1000 BC, there are socketed axes, true swords [4] and beaten metal objects, including shields and vessels. From the Middle Bronze Age onwards settlements are known; these include embanked enclosures and after *c*. 1200 BC the defended hilltop settlements known as hill-forts [7].

## The first use of iron

The introduction of iron technology was not a sudden event. Some iron objects were occasionally used as early as *c*. 700 BC, but iron did not come into general use for another 200 years. The main factor in the development of the Iron Age was the continuing culture of the Bronze Age. The principal types of settlements – farmsteads, villages and hill-forts – all developed from Bronze Age antecedents, as did the round post-built house, which is one of the main Iron Age dwelling forms. However, there was certainly trade with Europe and, later in the Iron Age, there were also two limited movements of people from continental Europe. The first was a migration from France that brought the practice of chariot burials [6] into Yorkshire perhaps as early as the late fifth century BC. The second was a movement from northeast France into southeast England in the first century BC. This can be identified with a historically known people, the Belgae, who were described by Julius Caesar (*c*. 100–44 BC).

Insular Iron Age communities were gradually developing an urban way of life during the second half of the first millennium BC, but the Belgae introduced a more organized urbanism already developed in Europe. They lived in large defended settlements known as *oppida*, which can be regarded as true towns; they were organized on a tribal basis and society was highly stratified, with a wealthy aristocracy at the top and slaves at the bottom, separated by a "middle class" of craftsmen and by the bulk of the peasantry who were engaged in primary production. They used the potter's wheel and they minted coins, both skills previously unknown in Britain. They traded abundantly with their Romanized relatives in Gaul and were partly Romanized by the time of the Claudian invasion of AD 43.

**Decorated bronze mirrors** are among the finest products of British craftsmen in the Early Iron Age and they must have been highly prized by their aristocratic women owners, with whom they were sometimes buried. This example, dating from the early 1st century AD, was found at Desborough, Northamptonshire. Its reflecting surface was made of polished bronze and its back was decorated with intricate patterns. The engraved area was probably set out with a pair of compasses; the outline was then engraved and the filling of parts of the pattern completed by chasing. Wear on the inside of the ring on the handle suggests that the mirror was suspended when it was not being used.

5

**5 Dartmoor was an attractive area for** prehistoric settlement and because it has been little exploited since early times it has many sites available for archaeological exploration. Stone was readily available there for use as a building material, and so the footings of walls of huts and of enclosures are still visible, as in this example at Grimspound. Few sites have yielded clear dating evidence but most were probably built in the Bronze Age. The huts are circular and vary in diameter from 3m (10ft) to 12m (39ft). Only the footings were of stone; the rest of the structure was timber, thatch and turf. The buildings were conical in shape.

6

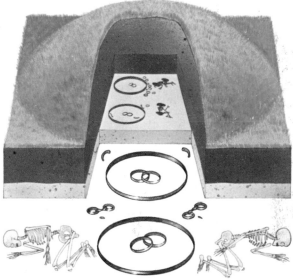

**6 Chariot burials** have been found of some of the warrior aristocrats of the Iron Age in Yorkshire. In this example from Danes' graves, two bodies were buried in a crouched position on the floor of a rectangular grave pit under a round barrow. With them were the remains of a dismantled chariot and several items of harness fittings. In other burials the chariot was buried intact and on one occasion two horses had been buried with the vehicle. This special type of burial does not occur elsewhere in Britain but is well known in continental Europe. It may have been introduced by settlers from France, perhaps from Burgundy, where there are close parallels with the Yorkshire burials.

7

8

**7 Hill-forts, or fortified settlements** on hilltops, were first used in the later part of the Bronze Age, but most of them belong to the Iron Age. This example, Badbury Rings, Dorset, had a long development and may have lasted into the Roman period. The area enclosed is *c*. 7 hectares (17 acres), and is surrounded by two substantial banks and ditches, as well as a third, much slighter one outside them. One of the entrances turns inwards and the other has additional outworks. Hill-forts that have been excavated have revealed continuous intensive occupation, organized internal planning and some public buildings and provision for craftsmen. These hill-forts can be considered the first true urban settlements in Britain.

**8 This large chalk-cut horse** is situated just northwest of the hill-fort of Uffington Castle, Oxfordshire. It measures 110m (360 ft) in length and is a maximum of 40m (132 ft) in height and has been cut down to the natural chalk in broad terraces. Such hill figures are impossible to date accurately, but on stylistic grounds this horse is usually thought to have been cut in the late pre-Roman Iron Age, and to have been the first hill figure in Britain. But some scholars give it a much later date. Its dramatically curved and attenuated form resembles horses portrayed by Iron Age craftsmen in other media, such as those found on coins or on wooden buckets decorated in sheet bronze, known from Aylesford and Marlborough. It may have been the symbol of a local tribe.

# The Celts 500 BC-AD 450

From the beginning of the second phase of Celtic culture, known to archaeologists as La Tène, our knowledge becomes much more detailed. The archaeological record is filled out by written accounts that give a fuller, more detailed identity to peoples previously distinguished by the remaining artefacts of their material culture alone. For the first 500 years of this period of European history, the story is basically that of the astonishing growth and development of the Celtic world and its gradual decline with the rise of Rome and the establishment of the Roman Empire.

## The development of Celtic culture

The term La Tène is applied to this period of Celtic culture that extends from about 500 BC and is the period of their greatest attainments. Like Hallstatt for the first phase of c. 700–c. 500 BC, the name La Tène is taken from the name of a major archaeological site. In the nineteenth century a large variety of religious offerings [3] were found at La Tène on the shores of Lake Neuchâtel in Switzerland, and these findings, like those discovered at Hallstatt, testify to the changes in the

equipment and way of life experienced by the Celts. As with Celts of the Hallstatt culture, their altered life-style was developed more or less simultaneously, and with great rapidity, over much of Europe.

The Celts were still highly aristocratic in their social organization; kingship was common among the tribes and below the king were the warrior aristocracy and freemen farmers. The Celts had a highly evolved religion [5, 6] with the powerful priesthood – the Druids – which itself formed a major class. In addition there were slaves.

The Celts had taken to using a light two-wheeled war chariot pulled by two small ponies, and the artistic skill of their craftsmen in metalwork, always remarkable, had advanced to new heights. At the same time, a revolution had taken place in their art style. The old Urnfield and Hallstatt patterns, the fine animal art of the Scythians, Greek foliage motifs, and elements from styles formed much farther east had been merged into a brilliantly original art – subtle and elusive, and full of magical significance. From 500 BC this new aspect of Celtic culture

spread rapidly and by 300 BC it was dominant from the Baltic to the Mediterranean and from the Black Sea to the Atlantic.

## Celtic society and warfare

The early Celts did not make written records, they recorded their history orally. However, unlike the earlier Hallstatt culture, that of La Tène is nevertheless well documented; much of our knowledge about the daily life of the Celts has been provided by contemporary Greek and Roman writers.

To them the Celts were tall, muscular and fair-skinned, qualities most attributable to the warrior class and reaching their ideal in the *gaestatae* ("spear-bearers") who were a highly specialized class of Celtic warriors.

Warfare was an essential part of the Celtic life. Armed with highly efficient iron weapons the Celts swept through central Europe in the fourth and third centuries, overcoming their Etruscan neighbours in about 400 BC, sacking Rome in 390 and plundering the shrine at Delphi in 279.

But the Celts were not only warriors. They achieved a high level of material

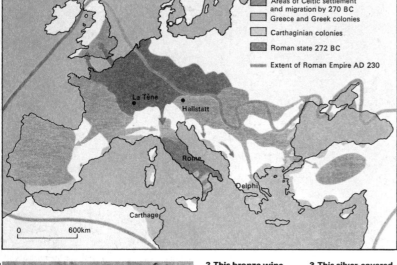

**1 La Tène, a key** archaeological site in Switzerland, is the name given to the period of Celtic culture in Europe that lasted from approximately 500 BC until the time of Roman expansion during the 2nd and 1st centuries BC. As the map shows, by about 270 BC the Celts had migrated into France and the Iberian Peninsula, parts of the British Isles and to some extent eastwards into central Europe. From this time, however, they gradually lost ground to Rome. By the mid-1st century BC the Roman dominance was assured.

Map legend:
- La Tène culture
- Areas of Celtic settlement and migration by 270 BC
- Greece and Greek colonies
- Carthaginian colonies
- Roman state 272 BC
- Extent of Roman Empire AD 230

La Tène · Hallstatt · Rome · Delphi · Carthage

0    600km

**2 This bronze wine flagon** is one of a pair from Basse-Yutz in Lorraine. Inlaid with coral, it demonstrates elements that contributed to the subtlety and charm of La Tène art. The wolf-like animals forming the handles and on the lid link these pieces with the Bronze Age cult of water birds.

**3 This silver-covered iron votive torque** (bracelet) weighs about 6kg (13 lb). Both ends have sacred ox heads, each with its own twisted necklace. Too heavy to be worn, it was probably hung on a stone or wooden divine image. It comes from Trichtingen, Württemberg, in Germany.

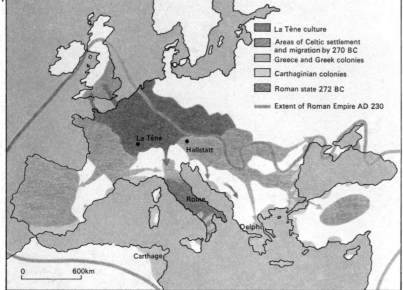

**4 Warfare was the main influence** on Celtic architecture. Fortified dwellings built for defence were common. One such was the crannog [A]. Found mainly in Ireland, crannogs were artificial islands built of timber, clay, peat and brushwood. Dwellings were constructed on top of the island. This crannog, from the La Tène period, is in County Antrim. The most famous Celtic fortifications were the hill-forts (*oppida*) [B]. This hill-fort, seen from the air, is in Somerset.

civilization using their mastery of iron-working to open up new land and develop agriculture. Their economy was based on mixed farming – the cultivation of grains and vegetables, and cattle raising – and on trade. These two aspects  expansionist warfare and domestic settlement -- can best be seen in their hill forts (*oppida*), the remains of which are scattered throughout Europe. Originally built as hill-top forts for defence only they varied considerably in size, some developing into major towns. One such was the *oppidum* at Bibracte near Autun in France which covered more than 130 hectares (330 acres) and had houses, streets and possibly shops.

**The rise of the Roman Empire**
It was the rise of Rome – a little town on the bank of the Tiber – into a great, organized civilization which, by 225 BC and after bitter fighting, defeated the Celts at Telamon in Italy, and took the first major step towards subduing them forever. Even after actual subjugation, the Celtic traditions and language continued to survive but in forms modified to agree with the needs of Roman

institutions. Only Ireland and much of Scotland escaped Roman domination in the British Isles. It was there that the old Celtic traditions and way of life survived and were written down by the scribes of a Celtic Church, of the fifth century AD and deeply sympathetic to the heritage of its people.

The Roman Empire lasted into the fifth century. But from the third century it was endangered by increasingly powerful "barbarians". It was these barbarians from the north, east of the Rhine and from the vast steppelands of the eastern continent who, during the fifth century AD, eventually wrecked the Roman Empire and laid the foundations of feudal Europe. The people of the Roman Empire had become used to living in towns and obeying a single, absolute government. The barbarians knew no such control, living in tribes without towns and led by chieftains who gained their power through the dictates of tribal custom and tradition. These pagan peoples struck deeply at the growing Christian Church in Europe, a Church to which Celtic missionaries from Ireland were to contribute profoundly.

**A bronze figure of a dying Gaul** was recovered from the hill-fort at Alesia, Alise-Ste-Reine, where Vercingetorix, the young Celtic leader, king and commander of all the Gallic confederates, made his last great stand against Julius Caesar in 52 BC. For a time he managed to repulse Caesar and cause him heavy losses, but after a final bitter battle he was defeated. In spite of the dignified and noble way he surrendered in order to save his fellow countrymen, Caesar held him prisoner in Rome for six years and then ordered his belated execution.

**5 The god Cernunnos,** "The Horned One", figures as the Lord of the Wild Beasts on one of the inner plates of the great votive silver cauldron found at Gundestrup, Jutland, Denmark. He wears the antlers of a stag.

**6 The cock** [A] was believed to avert evil with its crow and thus in Britain it was considered unlucky to eat it. The peculiar three horns on the bull [B] conveyed an idea of its supernatural qualities as the number three held religious significance.

**7 Belief in the "evil eye"** goes far back into Celtic minds. The eye on this stone figure of a boar god dates from about the 1st century BC.

6 A

B

8

**8 An early example of La Tène art style** is shown here. The bronze plaque from a double burial at Waldalgesheim (c. 325 BC) shows a mask-like face, a torque round the neck and, on the head, traces of a leaf-crown which is a token of divinity. The hands are raised in the Celtic attitude of prayer. This bronze is one of a pair.

**9 Bronze decorated mirrors** are among the most splendid pieces of Celtic art. This example, from a woman's grave at Birdlip, Glos, is pre-Christian.

9

# The Etruscans

Far less is known about the Etruscans than about their contemporaries, the Greeks and Romans. The reason lies mainly in the total loss of their literature, which leaves them from our point of view inarticulate. But whereas their writings consist almost solely of brief funerary inscriptions, their other material remains offer much greater scope for archaeological research.

## Origins of the Etruscans

The long-standing controversy over this people's origins seems at last to be dying down. Ancient records began it: Herodotus declared that the Etruscans sailed from Lydia in Anatolia to colonize a new territory in the west; and Dionysius of Halicarnassus argued that they were natives of Italy. Today both views are regarded favourably, and both are at least partly right.

Certainly the argument for continuity between the Villanovan settlements in northern Italy (c. 1100–700 BC) and cemeteries of the ninth century BC and the Etruscan cities and cemeteries of the early seventh century BC on the same sites is

stronger than ever. Most of the population and much of the culture can be traced beyond this, back into the Bronze Age. Conversely, at several stages new ideas and cultural traits from abroad could well have arrived with bands of new immigrants.

The result was a great flowering of culture in the seventh and sixth centuries BC, which built on local foundations, themselves supported by the wealth of the metal resources of Etruria (present-day Tuscany) [1], but strongly influenced by Greece and many other east Mediterranean lands. Indeed this variety provides a strong argument against Herodotus' story of a homeland in Lydia.

Etruscan civilization as a whole is puzzling. The general impression is very Greek. Only on closer inspection of the details does it become apparent that, however Greek in inspiration, everything has been transmuted and absorbed. This, and the grafting on of other Asiatic ideas, like divination and tumulus tomb building, and the development of purely local traits like the high-quality black *bucchero* pottery, enable historians to think of Etruscan civilization as

something in its own right, not merely a provincial version of the civilization of Greece. Yet politically the two peoples appear to have been bitter enemies, Etruscan history having as its constant theme the attempt to bar the Greeks from the Tyrrhenian Sea. By one sea battle, the Greeks were expelled from Corsica in 535 BC, at the height of the Etruscan political domination.

The Phoenicians played a part in this story too, as intermediaries between Etruria and the Orient. Here political relations were more cordial, Etruria and Carthage being often in alliance against their common enemy, the Greeks. At Pyrgi, a port of Cerveteri, a dedication was found to Uni (Juno) – the goddess Astarte – engraved on gold plates in parallel texts, one in Phoenician, the other one in Etruscan.

## Clues to language

The tablets found at Pyrgi proved of great help in advancing our knowledge of the Etruscan language, the most important unifying link between the Etruscan peoples. Since they had adopted the Greek alphabet

**1 The Etruscan home territory** lay between the Arno and the lower Po. It was there that the distinctive civilization arose and reached its highest development. At its widest, c. 535 BC, Etruscan power extended to the Alpine foothills and south to the Gulf of Salerno. But this was not an empire; instead it was a loose federation of independent city states with no common front.

1

0        300km

ALPS

Po    Melpum

Spina
Felsina
Arno
Volterra  ETRURIA
Populonia    Perugia
Vetulonia  Chiusi
Vulci
Tarquinii  Veii
Caere  Rome

APENNINES

TYRRHENIAN SEA

■ Etruscan power at its greatest extent c. 540 BC
□ Etruscan sphere of influence

**4 Jewellery** reached a high level of development with the Etruscan civilization. The Etruscans were particularly skilled goldsmiths and a number of superb pieces decorated with fine granulation have survived. This fibula or safety pin dates from between 700–600 BC. It is an exquisite piece, demonstrating the quality and originality achieved by the Etruscans.

**2 Bronze cists** (caskets) held women's personal possessions, jewellery and toiletries. They were engraved with mythical scenes and were fitted with cast feet, handles and ornaments. This fine example from Palestrina (c. 300 BC) shows an engraving of Bellerophon holding Pegasus.

**3 Mirrors of polished bronze** assisted Etruscan ladies at their toiletries. The reverse side of mirrors such as this (c. 540–530 BC) was often engraved with mythical scenes – in this example Orion is crossing the sea – in an incised drawing. Mirrors were objects commonly buried with the dead.

3

**5 The Apollo of Veii**, together with figures of Mercury, Hercules and Latona, strode along the roof ridge of the Portonaccio temple at Veii. The sculptor was Vulca, who modelled Apollo in terracotta about 500 BC. Apollo has a frightening aspect, not in the least softened by his smile, and is different from the Apollos which the Greeks have left. The Etruscans clearly owed much to the Greeks, but they translated any borrowings into their own idiom.

with little change, there has never been any great problem in deciphering their writings. Translating them has proved much more difficult because all attempts at identifying the language with a known one have failed. It seems to have been the only survivor of those tongues spoken before Indo-European was introduced into the area. Little by little, however, the scholars' competence in translation increased, beginning with such tomb inscriptions as "X son of Y, aged Z years". But the few longer texts are obscure ritual documents, and yield so far little more than the general drift. The longest of such texts so far discovered was written on linen.

### Etruscan culture
United by language, the Etruscans were less uniform in culture. There are clear differences (as in tomb architecture) between the Etruscan cities, mirroring their political independence. All, however, give a picture of an energetic, happy people with a bold and attractive art. Although much of the evidence comes from tombs [6, 7, 8], it is by no means a sombre picture. Their temples and cities too

were architecturally exciting, and their civil engineering of a high order. A ship canal at Cosa, the channelling of streams below ground to prevent soil erosion, and their practice of tunnelling rivers below roads instead of building bridges over them, demonstrates these skills.

What survives from Etruscan civilization is to be found in the romantic ruined sites and cemeteries, and vast museum collections looted from these. But their place in history is assured by their contribution to Roman civilization. The end of the Etruscans probably came in the fourth century BC, because they had failed to present a common front and so fell individually to the Romans. However, the Romans' origins lay beneath the shadow of their rich and powerful neighbours and enemies. Much of the Greek civilization they adopted came to them not only through Etruscan hands but in Etruscanized form. What was non-Greek in Roman life was often pure Etruscan; for example, the realism of their portraiture and their religious practices and divination. Many Roman families had, and were proud of, Etruscan origins.

**This married couple** is sculpted in life-size on the lid of a terracotta sarcophagus from Cerveteri (Caere).

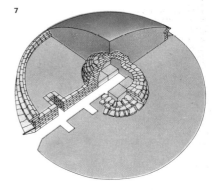

**6 The Tomb of the Reliefs at Cerveteri** is carved in the solid rock to represent a room in a house, with raftered ceiling supported on pillars, proto-Ionic capitals and bed niches in the walls. A series of funerary beds, each with two pillows, some even with a footstool and slippers awaiting their owners, is then added in stucco. Above the niches are displayed pieces of armour and weapons in relief – shields, helmets, leg armour, swords. The central pillars are decorated with a wide variety of tools and implements used in day-to-day life. This tomb is the only one of its kind.

**7 Types of tombs** differed from city to city. At Populonia, a corbel-vaulted chamber of stone was covered by a hemispheric barrow within a stone retaining wall. The Tomb of the Chariots, shown here, contained two chariots fitted with bronze and iron decoration on ivory, and a bronze trumpet as well as gold jewellery and fragments of weapons and armour. The tomb dates from the 7th century BC. Many tumulus tombs were also erected at Cerveteri.

**8 The Tarquinian tomb type** was a rectangular chamber cut in the rock and approached by a sloping ramp. The chambers were then plastered and painted with vivid scenes of the highest beauty and significance. On the end wall of the Tomb of Hunting and Fishing (c. 520 BC), the funeral feast occupies the gable, with a frieze of mourning wreaths below. Fish leap all around the men in their boat, and a slinger ashore attempts to bring down one of the many gaily coloured birds that cover the ceiling. The funeral banquet was a common motif, coupled in other tombs with frescoes that pictured dancing and athletic contests in honour of the dead.

# Early Rome: the kingdom and the republic

The origins of the city that founded the mighty Roman Empire are obscure. The traditional account, recorded by Livy, is that Romulus and Remus [Key] founded a city on the Palatine Hill [2] on 21 April 753 BC. At least the date agrees with the archaeological evidence, which shows that shepherds settled on the Palatine about the middle of the eighth century. They joined with other communities in the area in the early sixth century to establish a city around a site that later became the Roman Forum but which had for a period been used as a cemetery [1].

Of the six kings said to have followed Romulus the first three were almost certainly legendary, but the fourth, Tarquinius Priscus, was Etruscan. His reign marks the beginning of a period of Etruscan control.

## Expansion under the republic

Etruscan rule and the monarchy ended simultaneously with the expulsion of King Tarquinius Superbus, traditionally in 509 BC. Two elected consuls and a senate, composed entirely of wealthy aristocrats known as patricians, controlled Rome's affairs.

During the next 200 years the policy in Italy was directed towards expansion, conquest and consolidation.

Soon after the foundation of the republic Rome played a leading part in the formation of the Latin League, an alliance of the cities of Latium, the western region of central Italy. In 390 BC the Celtic Senones and other Gallic peoples overran northern Italy and captured all Rome except the Capitol. They left on payment of a ransom and Rome profited from the bitter lesson by building the Servian Wall, which made it the most strongly defended city in Italy.

From this secure springboard Rome engaged confidently in a number of wars, which resulted in its obtaining undisputed mastery over the whole of Italy from the Po valley southwards. In 340 BC the cities of the Latin League rose against Rome but found themselves no match for their powerful partner. Rome imposed separate terms on each vanquished city, awarding some Roman citizenship, some part citizenship and punishing others, but in each case stipulating that the city should trade only with Rome. The

next struggle, against the Samnites in the south, was much harder. A Roman army was forced to surrender at the Battle of the Caudine Forks, but by 290 BC the war was won. Victory over the Greek cities then gave Rome control over the whole peninsula, a position it consolidated through alliances and the establishment of citizen colonies [4] but above all by the threat of its army.

By this time the plebeians had seen many of their grievances rectified. They had their own council, the *concilium plebis*, and their own officers, the tribunes. In 445 BC they received the right to marry into the patrician class and in 366 BC the first plebeian consul was elected. From 287 BC measures passed by the *concilium plebis* had the force of law. For the moment social conflict was muted although these changes had done little to alleviate the poverty of most of the plebeians.

## The Punic Wars

Rome's advance into the south of Italy had brought it face to face with the Carthaginians (*Poeni*), who were ensconced in western Sicily and appeared to have designs on the

**1 The Seven Hills of Rome** are flat-topped spurs rising from a low, formerly marshy, plateau. The Palatine, Quirinal and Esquiline were the first to be settled, the Capitoline and Aventine the last. A unified city began to emerge when villages on the Palatine, Esquiline and Caelian came together in the early 7th century BC. The first wall round the city was built according to tradition in the 6th, which was apparently a period of great building activity under the Etruscan kings. The Cloaca Maxima, a sophisticated drainage system, and the temple of Jupiter Capitolinus both date from this early period.

1 Circus Maximus
2 Circus Flaminius
3 Senate House
4 Record Office Temples
5 Juno Moneto
6 Jupiter Capitolinus
7 Saturn
8 Castor and Pollux
9 Vesta
10 Jupiter the Victor Markets, Bridges
11 Aemilian Bridge
12 Fabrician Bridge
13 Fish Market
14 Vegetable Market
15 Cattle Market

A Portico and Theatre of Pompey
B Shipyards

**2 A village of huts on the Palatine,** one of which is shown here in reconstruction, was discovered after World War II. It dates from the mid-8th century BC and so seems to support the legend of the foundation of Rome by Romulus and Remus. Crude in construction, these huts were the homes of the farmers and shepherds of Latin origin who are the earliest known inhabitants of the city. There is now archaeological evidence that Latium, the area surrounding Rome, was colonized in the 12th century BC by Late Bronze Age people who came from the east by sea, thus reinforcing the legend handed down to us by Livy that Rome's environs were settled by refugee Trojans under the leadership of Aeneas.

**3 Aeneas,** who escaped from Troy after the Trojan War, was said to have founded Rome. This legend was enshrined in the *Aeneid* by Virgil (70–19 BC). This fourth-century manuscript vividly illustrates the dangers of his voyage to Latium.

**4 The formation of a new Roman colony** was formally recognized when the founder guided a bronze plough, drawn by a bull and a cow, round its boundaries. Colonies were useful as a means of garrisoning vulnerable areas and also for moving surplus population and giving them employment. A few colonies were created as early as the 5th century, but the number increased as Rome's dominions spread because citizen colonies could be founded only in Roman territory.

eastern part. In the First Punic War (264–241 BC) Rome, after several near disasters, built their first fleet and eventually mastered Sicily [7]. The ostensible cause of the Second Punic War (218–201 BC) was an attack by the Carthaginian general Hannibal on Saguntum, a city on the eastern coast of Spain allied to Rome. Hannibal with 40,000 men and a train of elephants made a remarkable march through Gaul and over the Alps [6]. He inflicted severe defeats on Roman armies at Trebbia, Lake Trasimene and Cannae, but then the delaying tactics of Fabius and the loyalty to Rome of most of its Italian allies began to have their effect. A crucial blow was the defeat at the Metaurus River in 207 BC of Hannibal's brother Hasdrubal, who was bringing reinforcements from Spain.

Rome opened up a second front, the young and brilliant Scipio (later given the title of Africanus Major) capturing Carthago Nova and then driving the Carthaginians out of Spain completely. In 204 BC Scipio led an invasion force from Sicily into Africa. Hannibal was forced to retire from Italy but the

war ended with his defeat at Zama. The Third Punic War (149–146 BC) began when Carthage attacked Rome's ally Massinissa, king of Numidia (modern Algeria). After a desperate siege Carthage was captured in 146 BC and razed to the ground.

## Influence of the Gracchi

During the second century BC Rome controlled almost the whole of the Mediterranean area, but storm clouds gathered at home. The patricians and rich plebeians kept a stranglehold on government and, perhaps of more immediate concern, on land. A champion of the poor arose in the person of Tiberius Gracchus, a tribune of the plebeians, who in 133 BC introduced a land bill intended to reduce drastically the large estates held by a few rich men. Rioters incited by apprehensive senators murdered Tiberius, but ten years later his brother Gaius tried to reduce the price of corn and generally to break the power of the senate. But proposals to extend the citizenship to all Rome's Latin allies were too radical and brought about his political ruin and death.

**5 The three surviving columns** of the Temple of Castor and Pollux in the Roman Forum were once part of a colonnade that ran round a shrine to the divine twins, who were also known as the Dioscuri. The tradition was that the temple was built following a battle between the Romans and the Latins at Lake Regillus in 499 or 496 BC. The twins fought on the Roman side and carried the news of the Romans' victory back to the city. The temple may, in fact, have been built much earlier, in the misty period of the kings. It lies within the boundary of the early Palatine villages. It was restored in the 2nd century BC and in the 1st century AD.

**6 This Spanish coin shows Hannibal** [A] on one side and an elephant [B] on the other. The elephants in the force that Hannibal led over the Alps were African forest elephants, which at that time were to be found round the

Atlas Mountains, the Moroccan coast and the oasis of Ghadames in Tunisia. They were much smaller than bush elephants and were better suited to the kind of forced march they had to undertake. They terrified primitive tribes.

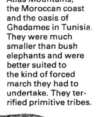

6 A

**7 To make an effective challenge** to Carthage's domination of the western Mediterranean, Rome had to become a naval power. A large fleet was constructed and equipped with boarding devices to allow for hand-to-hand fighting, at which the Romans excelled. As a result, after initial reverses they inflicted naval defeat on Carthage in the First Punic War.

**8 This Roman soldier of the 6th century BC** has a breastplate, helmet, sword and spears. Up to about 400 BC soldiers received no pay and only the rich could afford to do military service. A professional army was set up about 100 BC.

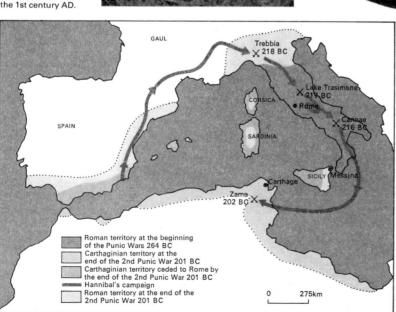

7

GAUL

Trebbia
✕ 218 BC

Lake Trasimene
✕ 217 BC

CORSICA
● Rome

Cannae
✕ 216 BC

SPAIN

SARDINIA

SICILY ● Messina

● Carthage

Zama
202 BC ✕

Roman territory at the beginning of the Punic Wars 264 BC
Carthaginian territory at the end of the 2nd Punic War 201 BC
Carthaginian territory ceded to Rome by the end of the 2nd Punic War 201 BC
Hannibal's campaign
Roman territory at the end of the 2nd Punic War 201 BC

0          275km

# Rome: the organization of the republic

Republican Rome (509–27 BC) is often regarded as a democratic state. Certainly later Roman writers looked back nostalgically on what seemed a golden age of political and social order and agreed morality. There was a theoretical balance between the powers of the magistrates, the Senate and the plebeians. But in fact most of the early republican period was an age of bitter conflict between the nobles of the Senate, anxious to keep their privileges, and the plebeians, equally anxious to have a share of the benefits. It was not until the third century that the plebeians were able to make laws on their own account. Their admission to all the magistracies only created an alliance of the nobility and rich ambitious plebeians, forming an oligarchy as exclusive as the former patrician nobility had been in earlier years.

## The political structure of the republic

The Senate and the *concilium plebis* (people's assembly) formed the legislative branch of the republic and the magistrates [1] the executive. The 300 senators [5] were chosen from ex-magistrates by the censors (those who watched over public morals). The Senate was basically an advisory body with overriding financial control. It initiated legislation and in practice made the vital decisions on war and peace and foreign policy in general. It also assigned provinces to senior magistrates at the end of their year of office. The *concilium plebis*, which represented the plebeians, was able to initiate legislation, its resolutions having the force of law after 287 BC, but in general it merely accepted or rejected proposed legislation.

The chief executives during the Roman Republic were the two consuls. They were elected (from candidates proposed by the Senate) by the *comitia centuriata*, an assembly in which wealthy citizens had disproportionate voting strength. The consuls had immense power, presiding over the Senate and acting as supreme commanders in war. Beneath them were the praetors, whose numbers varied from two to eight and whose main duties concerned the administration of the law. Four quaestors were in charge of the state finances. The two censors supervised state contracts and public morals and, during the late republic, checked and if necessary expelled members of the Senate.

Streets, temples, public works, the grain supply and the public games were the responsibility of individual *aediles*. Twelve *lictors* preceded consuls and two preceded praetors, clearing the way and carrying bundles of rods known as *fasces*. The ten tribunes were entrusted with the defence of the plebeians, having the power of veto against actions of magistrates and against laws. In the second century BC the tribunes became entitled to sit in the Senate.

## The power of the consuls

At the end of their year of office the *imperium* (power) of the consuls and praetors was transferred from Rome to one of the provinces. The Senate decided which provinces should be consular and which praetorian; to avoid corruption this decision was taken before the election of the magistrates. The actual province each magistrate received was decided by lot. *Imperium* did not extend beyond the province's boundaries, as was shown when Julius Caesar, by crossing the

1

Civil
Quaestors
Tribunes
Aediles
Censors
Praetors
Consuls
Generals
Pontifex maximus
Flamines (priests)
Military
Religious

**1 Most of the civil officers of Rome** [in the green band] had legal functions as well as administrative. The generals had military responsibilities only. The *pontifex maximus* was head of the state religion.

**2 The basilica at Pompeii**, measuring 56×21m (185×70ft), was built in the first century BC and was the centre of economic life. Most Roman cities had one of these rectangular roofed halls where business transactions were concluded. They generally stood near the Forum. Some basilicas included arcades and galleries and their design influenced later Christian basilicas.

2

4

3

**3 The demobilization of Roman soldiers** is portrayed on this relief (*c.* 1st century BC). The scribe on the left takes down details from a discharged soldier who holds his certificate, while others wait their turn.

**4 The *tabularium*** or record office [centre left] was built in 78 BC to the plans of Sulla (138–78 BC). It housed the state archives and was probably an annexe of the Treasury. The upper part is a palace (*c.* 1500).

Rubicon in 49 BC, in effect declared war on the Senate. Governors might keep their provinces for only one year or by *prorogatio* might have their command extended.

The most important religious figure was the chief priest, the *pontifex maximus*. He was the elected head of the college of priests, which also included the vestal virgins [7] (who kept the sacred fire burning in the Temple of Vesta) and the *flamines*, each of whom was responsible for the cult of one of the gods. Outside the college were the augurs who from certain signs, such as the behaviour of birds, decided whether a certain course of action was advisable.

The Romans worshipped many gods, most of them originally Greek. The chief god was Jupiter, to whom a temple was founded on the Capitol at the time of King Tarquinius Superbus (reigned 534–510 BC). Religious festivals were held throughout the year [6], among the most important being the Lupercalia, held on the Palatine on February 15, and the Saturnalia on December 17.

The security of the republic and its steady expansion into a great empire depended on the discipline and courage of its army. The record of victories over powers as formidable as Carthage, Macedonia and Syria was remarkable considering that it was still a citizen militia summoned by the consuls to meet specific emergencies. Only citizens with certain property qualifications were eligible, although an equal number of allies also served. Clearly the quality of commanders and centurions must have been high. Not until the reforms of Marius (157–86 BC) was a professional volunteer army formed.

**Taxation and tax-collecting**

Most Roman taxation was indirect and included customs duties and a number of special taxes, such as that on the freeing of slaves. The *tributum*, a direct tax, was levied mainly in time of war. The censors decided which taxes were applicable to the various classes, while the quaestors administered their collection. But more and more, tax-collecting in the provinces was farmed out to *publicani*. They were closely associated with the wealthy *equites*, the second social class, who waxed fat on the proceeds.

**The magistrates of Rome** had great power and influence. Civil lawsuits were heard first by a magistrate, such as the one shown here, before going to a judge for settlement. In the late republican period criminal cases were tried before special courts, where the penalties were generally exile, loss of citizenship or hard labour. The most important achievement of the Roman legal system was the classification of its code in order to clarify citizens' rights. The laws were published in 450 BC at the instigation of the plebeians. The body of Roman law, many of the principles of which are still very much in use, has had a vast influence in the West.

5

6

**5 The Senate** was the principal advisory body of Rome. This 19th-century painting by Maccari shows Appius Claudius persuading the Senate to reject peace proposals from Pyrrhus of Epirus in 280 BC.

**6 In the Temple of Vespasian** at Pompeii there are sacrificial scenes on an altar dedicated to the Roman imperial cult. Ritual sacrifices of animals such as pigs, sheep and bulls were an ancient element in the complex of Roman cults. Their purpose was to encourage divine beneficence.

**7 The six Vestal Virgins** lived in the House of the Vestals in the Forum. They began their service as children and could retire after 30 years. If they allowed the sacred fire to go out they were whipped by the *pontifex maximus*, under whose authority they came.

# Roman life

In Rome, as in all societies, the sort of life the people led depended very much on the social class to which they belonged. In general the class system was based on wealth rather than birth, although often the two criteria merged. The highest class was composed of the members of the Senate, who for most of the republican period were *nobiles*, or nobles. The second class, the *equites*, or knights, derived most of their considerable wealth from business activities such as banking. Members of the upper classes wielded authority not only over their own families but as patrons over a number of semi-dependants known as clients. The third class of full citizens, the plebeians, after a long struggle won complete political equality. Once they were permitted to hold the magistracies they could move into the highest social class, because former magistrates were automatically *ex officio* members of the Senate.

## The Roman slaves

At the base of the social pyramid were the slaves. The settled order of Roman life depended on the toil of slaves, who might well make up half the population of a town. A slave was under the absolute control of his master during the period of the republic.

During the imperial period the treatment of slaves improved somewhat, some protection being given to them against savage masters. More important, slaves were able to look forward more confidently to eventual *manumission*, or freeing. Many freedmen became extremely wealthy and influential and their sons became full Roman citizens. The life of slaves varied greatly, particularly between town and country. In the country they were likely to work long hours carrying out arduous tasks on *latifundia*, or estates, and on farms or in mills, while in the towns they might be comparatively well treated.

## Careers and education

The son of a rich upper-class family might well have political ambitions. But he would generally start by training as a lawyer and become either an advocate in the courts or a legal consultant. Other professions were not thought really respectable. For much of the republic most doctors, architects and dentists were slaves or freedmen. Writers could expect to make little money from their work unless they could rely on some wealthy patron to encourage them, as Maecenas encouraged Virgil. But most Romans were far from rich or influential. Although manual labour was thought unworthy of a citizen, they struggled to make a living as bakers, shopkeepers and craftsmen of all kinds, generally employing one or two slaves to assist them. Some young men might enter the army which, after the reforms of Marius the consul at the end of the second century BC, was a professional force manned by voluntary recruits who received a small land-holding on retirement.

Most children of Roman citizens received some formal education although only boys could expect to go beyond the primary stage. Under the empire some education was provided free for poor students but generally parent paid a small fee. Between the ages of 7 and 12, children received a somewhat rough-and-ready grounding in reading, writing and arithmetic from a *litterator*. They could then, if they chose, move on to a *gram-*

**1 The ruins of Pompeii** were preserved beneath ashes after the eruption, described by Pliny the Younger, of Vesuvius in AD 79. Excavations revealed a unique record of Roman daily life.

**2 This poulterer's shop** was located in Ostia, once the port of Rome. Cicero regarded shopkeeping as near the bottom of the list of employments suitable for people of taste – but better than dancing.

**3 Every upper-class Roman** visited baths – like the Stabian baths of Pompeii – daily with his oil flask, towels and other toiletries. He progressed from the tepid to the hot bath, from the sweat room to the cold bath. Refreshments and massage were available. Many baths had separate sections for women.

**4 All baking** was apparently done at home until the 2nd century BC. The exhausting work of turning the grinding mills was for slaves helped by donkeys. A bakery like this one was uncovered at Pompeii. The oven in it contained a large number of loaves, still intact and weighing about 900g (2lb) each.

*maticus*, under whom they studied Greek and Latin literature and received an introduction to geometry and advanced arithmetic. The third stage in schooling was study under a *rhetor*, or orator, to learn the principles of effective public speaking, an ability that was important for success in politics and in the law courts. Finally the more ambitious and wealthy students might progress to the equivalent of university level. They studied either law, under an established lawyer or at a law school, or Greek oratory and philosophy, which involved attendance at one of the great centres of Greek learning, the most popular of which were at Athens and Rhodes.

**Spectator and participatory sports**
Sports among the Romans were in two categories, spectator sports and participatory sports. In the first group were the public spectacles staged in the amphitheatres, the "bread and circuses" of which the satirist Juvenal contemptuously wrote. These included musical performances, readings of verse and theatrical performances, which were sometimes staged with extraordinary lavishness. What really drew the crowds were gladiatorial contests to the death between men or between men and beasts, and also the thrilling and dangerous chariot races, which might be run between individual charioteers or between teams of chariots.

The Romans did not place the same emphasis on physical exercise as the Greeks, but many young men of the upper classes were enthusiastic riders and hunters. Many also enjoyed boxing and wrestling and there were several ball games, such as *harpastum* and *trigon*, the details of which are rather obscure. Children played many of the games that children have played through the ages – hoops, tops, pitch and toss, marbles, hide-and-seek and leap-frog. In general the adult Roman preferred gambling games above all other leisure activities, except perhaps drinking (there were about 120 taverns in Pompeii). Throwing dice, *tesserae*, and knucklestones, *tali*, were the favourite methods of gaming. Dice, which like modern dice carried numbers from one to six, were also used to determine the player's moves in various board games.

**Roman shopkeepers** worked long hours. Their produce was brought into the city at night to avoid the traffic congestion of the day. This relief of a greengrocer's shop in Ostia includes illustrations of various vegetables.

**5 The life of Herculaneum**, a residential town between Naples and Pompeii, was revealed only after arduous excavations; the eruption of Vesuvius in AD 79 covered it with a thick layer of mud. However, the mud preserved much of the original town. Here a mosaic shows a man and woman served by a slave.

**6 The house of Menander** at Pompeii was more a country villa than a town house. The main reception room in the centre of Roman villas was the *atrium*, which was luxuriously furnished with tiles, marbles and fresco paintings. In the middle of the floor was the *impluvium*, a pool into which rainwater fell.

**7 A number of houses at Herculaneum** have kept their second storeys. The house shown here, the Cása del Graticcio, still contains its original beds in two small rooms on the upper floor, together with other furnishings. The house was clearly divided into many small apartments; large blocks of flats, often shoddily built, were a common feature of towns and cities in imperial times.

**8 This sandstone relief from Gaul** shows a school scene: a teacher is seated between his two pupils who are opening their scrolls for the lesson. Discipline was severe and corporal punishment was frequent. Sons of wealthy families were escorted to and from school by a household slave or freedman known as a *paedagogus*, who was sometimes also a tutor. The children wore warm cloaks and thick shoes to protect them against the rigours of the northern climate.

**9 Many Roman houses had a *lararium*,** a private chapel to *lares*, spirits of the hearth to whom offerings of food and flowers were made. Closely related was the worship of the *penates*, the guardians of the store cupboard.

# From the civil wars to Caesar's empire

The period between about 100 BC and 42 BC, leading up to the fall of the Roman Republic and its replacement by the Roman Empire, was one of disorder and disunity in which ambitious men used ruthless methods in their efforts to secure or maintain dominance. Julius Caesar (100–44 BC) was the outstanding figure but Marius, Sulla and Pompey all contributed to the end of the old form of government.

## Political conflicts

In 108 BC Marius, champion of the popular party against undue senatorial power, was elected to the first of his seven consulships. An outstanding general, he proved less skilful as a politician and his influence began to wane. In 90 BC a new popular leader, Drusus, revived advocacy of an extension of citizenship to all Italians. His murder precipitated the Social War in which Rome was hard pressed by a rising of its allies, finally triumphing only by conceding most of the allies' demands.

The popular cause was left in some disarray. When most of the Eastern Empire rebelled under the lead of Mithridates (c. 133–63 BC), king of Pontus [3], command of the campaign of suppression was given to Sulla (138–78 BC), an aristocrat [5]. The popular party had the command transferred to Marius but Sulla forthwith marched on Rome, forcing Marius to flee. He pushed through measures against his opponents, then left for the East. Marius returned and began a slaughter of political enemies.

Sulla returned to Italy from the East in 83 BC and with the help of two powerful commanders, Pompey (106–48 BC) and Crassus (c. 115–53 BC), fought his way to Rome. There he began a reign of terror, massacring his opponents and making himself dictator. He drastically reduced the powers of the tribunes and the consuls and increased those of the Senate, but after he resigned in 79 BC the inability of the Senate to use its powers effectively was revealed. Corruption grew, particularly in the provinces. In Spain, Pompey fought a long campaign against Sertorius, a supporter of Marius. Meanwhile Spartacus (died 71 BC) led a slave uprising, terrorizing southern Italy for two years.

Pompey and Crassus joined forces to gain control of Rome, securing their illegal election as consuls in 70 BC. They soon swept away Sulla's legislation favouring the Senate and pinned their colours to the populist mast. Pompey demonstrated his military and organizational ability by speedily clearing the eastern Mediterranean of the growing menace of piracy. In 66 BC he was given virtually a free hand in the East.

## The First Triumvirate

On his return Pompey received a cold reception from the Senate and he joined with Crassus and Julius Caesar [Key], who had returned from governing Spain, in forming the First Triumvirate. They forced through legislation by appealing to the Assembly over the heads of the Senate. Pompey received approval of his Eastern settlement and Caesar, after his consulship in 59 BC, was granted command in Gaul for five years.

In 55 BC Pompey and Crassus were consuls while Caesar received a five-year extension of his command. Crassus disappeared from the scene when an ill-conceived attack

**1 Jugurtha, grandson of Masinissa**, seized the throne of Numidia in 112 BC, killing several Romans in the process. Rome sent an army against him but the war dragged on in spite of some Roman successes. Marius, who became consul in 108 BC, led an army enlisted from the poor of Rome to Africa and defeated Jugurtha. After being exhibited as part of Marius' triumph, Jugurtha was strangled.

**2 A relief from the Temple of Fortuna Primigenia** at Praeneste shows a warship of the 1st century BC with soldiers prepared for hand-to-hand fighting.

**3 Mithridates VI, King of Pontus**, controlled the Crimea and much of southern Russia. In 88 BC he began a struggle against Rome that was to last for 25 years. He occupied Asia Minor and invaded Greece before making peace with Sulla. A second war in 83 BC was soon ended but a third Mithridatic war lasted from 74 to 66 BC, when Pompey made Pontus and Bithynia a Roman province. Mithridates killed himself when his son Pharnaces led an uprising against him.

**4 Pompey the Great** (Gnaeus Pompeius Magnus) lacked the military genius of Caesar and was less skilful politically. He was however a brilliant administrator and ruthless general who achieved power less by creating opportunities for himself than by waiting for situations to arise in which he would be called on to lead.

**5 Lucius Cornelius Sulla** made his military reputation in the Social War. Elected consul in 88 BC, he received the command against Mithridates. Later he used the office of dictator to massacre his opponents and force through pro-Senate legislation. He reformed the criminal law setting up *quaestiones* (new courts for particular crimes).

on Parthia ended with his death at the disastrous Battle of Carrhae. Pompey received Spain as his province but preferred to stay in Rome, intriguing with his supporters against Caesar, whose successful campaigns in Gaul [6, 8] were proving an embarrassment. Caesar, having conquered the whole of Gaul and made two exploratory invasions of Britain, was now ready to return to Rome backed by his devoted legions.

After fruitless attempts to reach a compromise or reconciliation, the Senate in 49 BC ordered Caesar to disband his army. Caesar at once crossed the Rubicon, the river dividing his province from Italy, and marched on Rome, so plunging Italy into civil war. Pompey hastily left for Greece, hoping to mobilize the resources of the East. Caesar soon mastered Rome and went on to crush forces favourable to Pompey in Spain, to defeat Pompey himself at Pharsalus in Thessaly in 48 BC, and finally to pursue him to Egypt where Pompey was murdered. Delaying his campaign, Caesar began his celebrated affair with the Egyptian queen, Cleopatra VII (69–30 BC) [9]. But within

two years he controlled Roman Africa. Finally he sealed his authority by quelling a revolt by Pompey's sons in Spain.

### End of the republic
The main basis of Caesar's authority was the office of dictator, which he held twice before receiving it for ten years in 47 BC. He packed the Senate with his supporters, nominated some of the magistrates and although denying any ambition for kingship, finally accepted the dictatorship for life. Brutus (85–42 BC) and Cassius (died 42 BC) organized his assassination at a Senate meeting on 15 March 44 BC. They hoped to save the republic but it had been fatally weakened: the only question was who would be Rome's first emperor. Mark Antony (c. 83–30 BC), Lepidus (died 13 BC) and Octavian (63 BC–AD 14), Caesar's heir, were the three contestants. In 43 BC they formed the Second Triumvirate, issuing proscriptions for the deaths of many. Caesar's death was avenged when Octavian and Antony defeated Brutus and Cassius at Philippi in 42 BC. Octavian was soon to become sole ruler.

Julius Caesar, born in 100 BC, was the son of a leading patrician family. His aunt was the wife of the popular leader Marius and his own wife, Cornelia, was a daughter of Cinna, Marius' successor. These connections displeased the conservative Sulla and Caesar left Rome. On Sulla's death he returned and made a reputation as a barrister and political orator. Moving up the political hierarchy, he became quaestor in Spain. After Cornelia died, he married Sulla's wealthy granddaughter Pompeia and set out to become a popular party leader. His election as praetor for 62 BC provided a springboard for his swift rise to absolute power in Rome.

**6** BRITAIN
54
55
Eburones 54 × × 55
Nervii 57 × × 53
56 × Agedincum 52
Alesia 52 × × 58
Avaricum 52 × Bibracte 58
GAUL × Lugdunum 58
Gergovia 52
× 56
Ilerda 49
SPAIN ITALY · Rome
× Munda 45
Dyrrhachium 48
MACEDONIA
Pharsalus 48
PONTUS
Zela 47
AFRICA
Thapsus 46
Alexandria 47
EGYPT
0            700km

**6 Successful campaigns** were waged by Julius Caesar between 58 and 51 BC against the Helvetii, Belgae, Veneti and the Aquitani. He conquered the whole of Gaul and made it a new province, Transalpine Gaul. He twice landed in Britain, near Walmer or Deal in 55 and near Sandwich in 54 BC. The second expedition was on quite a large scale and Caesar penetrated northward beyond St Albans.

**7**

**7 Standard equipment of a legionary** in the later republican period was a *gladium* (short sword) and a *scutum* (shield).

▨ Roman dominions in 63BC
▢ Conquests of Julius Caesar
× Campaigns in Gaul and Spain
☒ Civil war campaigns

**8 The triumphal arch at Orange,** France, is the third largest Roman arch extant. It commemorates

Caesar's victories over the Gauls with reliefs of prisoners-of-war and captured armour. The capture

of the port of Massilia is commemorated by such designs as anchors, prows and ropes.

**9 Cleopatra, Queen of Egypt,** was the mistress of Caesar and Antony. She bore Caesar a son and

followed him to Rome. After Caesar's death, she returned to Egypt, marrying Mark Antony in 37 BC.

**8**

**9**

**10**

**10 A Roman siege tower** was divided into several storeys and was up to 55m (180ft) tall according to the height of the wall to be attacked. It was hauled along a prepared causeway by ropes and capstans. Archers fired on the defenders from the upper storeys while on the bottom floor a battering-ram pounded the base of the wall. A boarding bridge could be let down from the top.

# Rome: the expansion of the empire

Octavian became the undisputed master of the Roman Republic and Empire following his victory over Mark Antony at the Battle of Actium in 31 BC. There is no doubt that he intended to establish a personal dynasty, but he was too clever a politician to ignore the strength of republican feeling in Rome. When he returned from the East in 29 BC he ostensibly restored the republic and set out to establish absolute power within it.

## Augustus: "first among equals"

The Senate voted Octavian the honorary titles of "Princeps" (first citizen) and "Augustus", by which he was known thereafter [Key]. Additionally, he received consular status and the power of a tribune with the right to summon the Senate, introduce business, veto decisions, nominate candidates for elections and issue edicts. This was how Augustus was able to influence the government of Rome and Italy and put in hand massive development programmes [2].

The government of the empire was divided between the older, settled provinces, governed by proconsuls elected by the Senate, and the newer, military provinces that were ruled through legates appointed by Augustus as a proconsul with special powers over all others [1]. The army was reorganized under the emperor's direct control into a force of 28 legions of professionals recruited for 20–25 years. It was drawn from Roman citizens plus an equal number of auxiliaries enlisted from provincial territories. This system, of emperors ruling with the Senate, was to endure for more than 200 years.

The most important immediate task was to restore order to the empire and secure its frontiers. Augustus's first expeditions were to Gaul and Spain, each of which was reorganized into three provinces. The River Danube line was secured with a series of military provinces garrisoned by large legionary forces [3], and attempts were made from 12 BC to push forward across the Rhine to the Elbe. But the annihilation of three legions under Varus by the Germans in AD 9 forced Augustus to accept the Rhine as his boundary. In the east, peace was made with the Parthian Empire and a buffer state was established in Armenia. Internally, brigandage and piracy were stamped out and taxation and the administration of Roman law put on a uniform basis.

Augustus died in AD 14 and under his successor, Tiberius (reigned 14–37), his policies of establishing order were continued so well that the incompetence of Caligula (reigned 37–41) caused little lasting harm. Under Claudius (reigned 41–54) the conquest of Britain was begun and Mauretania (now Morocco and Algeria) was occupied.

## Problems of succession

A major weakness of the Augustan imperial system was that the succession was never formulated and when in AD 68 the last of his direct house, the unstable Nero, was killed, four rival candidates for emperor were put forward by different sections of the army. Following a terrible civil war, Vespasian (reigned 69–79) was successful and developed a system whereby each emperor "adopted" his successor, thus giving the empire stability.

Under Trajan (reigned 98–117) the frontiers of the empire were again extended and

**1 The Roman Empire, at its height** in the 2nd century AD, was theoretically divided into provinces controlled by the Senate and the emperor. In reality, the emperor had the power to intervene in senatorial provinces. Italy itself was ruled according to a modified version of the republican constitution.

Imperial provinces
Senatorial provinces
Province or area controlled sporadically from AD 60

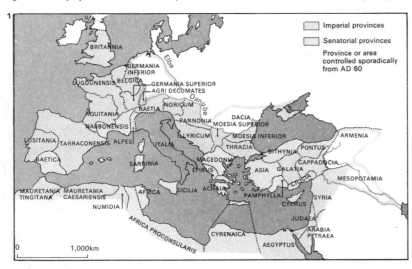

**3 Legionaries and Germans** were often at war in the 1st century, as seen in a contemporary relief. The empire failed to find secure frontiers and barbarian invasions played a major part in its collapse. In the relatively remote east a client state in Armenia usually provided a reasonable buffer against the Persian and Parthian empires, but in the west, far closer to the heart of the empire, constant vigilance was needed. Of the 28 legions established by Augustus more than half were always stationed in the provinces bordering the Rhine and Danube. Augustus attempted to gain the more easily defensible Elbe-Danube river line, but failed to secure it.

**2 The Roman Forum** (now in ruins) was the centre of the government of the empire. Augustus and his successors symbolized their power in a series of impressive public buildings. The administration of all parts of the empire remained almost entirely in the hands of native Romans, who held both governorships and lesser posts until well into the 2nd century. Yet an increasing number of provincials succeeded in working their way up the administrative ladder, first from the western provinces and then from the eastern. By AD 200, 57% of the Senate were provincials.

**4 The theatre at Palmyra** in Syria is typical of the fine buildings – temples, amphitheatres, aqueducts and baths – that were built in all the provinces of the empire. Just as they tolerated other religions, the Romans took care not to interfere with the social customs of the peoples they conquered. The civilizations of Greece and the East continued to flourish, but provincials were inevitably influenced by the example of Roman culture.

72

Dacia, Armenia and Mesopotamia were added [8]; but the last two were abandoned by Hadrian (reigned 117–138). Hadrian concentrated on improving existing imperial defences – building a wall across northern England and a fortified line between the Danube and the Rhine – and travelled throughout the empire inspecting the imperial administration and legal systems.

**Peace and prosperity**
Under the Antonine emperors (so called because of the family name of Hadrian's successor Antoninus) the empire was at its most peaceful. A man could travel in safety from Britain to Arabia along superb roads and secure seaways [5]; trade flourished [6] and a single culture, two languages – Latin and Greek – and a single system of law and administration covered the whole empire. Great cities with fine public buildings grew up in the provinces [4], where the people strove to become Roman citizens.

There were, however, underlying weaknesses. Rome had grown rich in booty and taxation from the provinces and economic activity tended to be one-way, with wealth and produce flowing to Rome but little produced in return. This caused jealousy in the provinces and an increasing idleness within Italy [7], problems made worse by the widespread use of slaves for all productive labour and a steady decline in the population. It became more and more difficult to find native citizens to undertake the many administrative and military duties on which the government of the empire depended. As a result an increasing number of provincials reached high administrative positions.

Under Marcus Aurelius (reigned 161–180) [9] the peace ended. In the east a Parthian attack was defeated but the returning troops brought back a terrible plague which devastated the whole empire and further reduced its manpower. On the Rhine and Danube frontiers the barbarians were being forced forward by a massive migration of Goths in central Europe, and in 167 several tribes crossed the Danube and Alps and swept into Italy. Dacia was also overrun and Marcus spent the rest of his reign fighting to restore the frontiers.

**The Emperor Augustus** is shown here as Pontifex Maximus (High Priest). The state religion of the Roman Republic continued under the empire. The emperors were deified after their deaths and sometimes they were worshipped during their lifetimes by people in the Roman provinces. Other religions were tolerated as long as they accepted the divinity of the emperor, and many Eastern cults such as Mithraism or the worship of Isis, which provided greater mysticism and colour, became popular. Only Judaism and Christianity, because they denied the divinity of the emperor, were in disfavour, but there was little direct persecution.

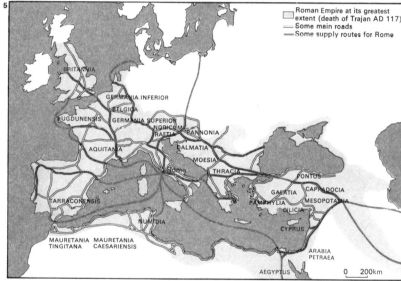

**5 The network of roads and sea routes** that held the empire together was built to enable troops, tax collectors and administrators to travel swiftly. But the great roads also allowed traders to cover the whole empire easily and the Roman world became an economic common market, with goods from one area available everywhere.

**6 The loading of a Roman grain ship** is shown in this picture. Egypt and North Africa were the granary of the empire and the importance of the grain trade, which provided a free ration for every citizen in the capital, was recognized by placing the trade directly under the personal control of the emperor.

**8 Legionaries and their captives** are shown here on Trajan's Column, a memorial in Rome to the Emperor's victories in Dacia. Trajan brought the empire to its largest extent with legions crossing the Danube into Dacia and down the Tigris and Euphrates to the Persian Gulf. But these areas were never fully pacified and their defence was a drain on the empire's military and financial resources.

**9 Marcus Aurelius,** shown here addressing his troops, was a civilized, highly educated man and a staunch follower of the Stoic philosophy. He was fated to spend most of his reign struggling against the first great onrush of barbarians that threatened to overwhelm the empire. For the first time in centuries a foreign invader swept over the Alps into Italy and Aquileia was besieged. Only by conscripting every fit man, including gladiators and brigands, was Marcus able to drive back the barbarians, restore the River Danube line and begin the work of reconquering Dacia. His reign marked the end of the enduring imperial peace.

**7 Races – especially chariot races –** and gladiatorial games became increasingly popular and important under the empire. Thus the emperor and rich patricians courted the popularity of the Roman mob by providing ever more lavish spectacles. The distribution of free bread and the frequency of free entertainments helped to insulate the Roman people from economic and political reality and played a major part in dissolving civic responsibility.

# Roman rule in Britain

The Romans ruled Britain, or at least its southern half, for more than 300 years. The northern frontier was always a problem, but much of England enjoyed a peaceful and prosperous existence as one of the provinces of the Roman Empire. The people, particularly in the towns, adopted many of the social and religious practices of their occupiers. The final collapse of Roman power resulted as much from civil strife in Italy as from unrest among the Britons.

## Patterns of conquest

A century separated the Romans' first tentative probes into Britain and their full-scale expedition of conquest. Britain fascinated the Romans as a strange romantic land in much the same way as the New World fascinated the Elizabethans. But the Romans also coveted its mineral wealth and realized its important strategic position. Julius Caesar (c. 100–44BC) was anxious to cut off the aid that the Britons were giving to the Gauls. His first landing, in 55 BC, achieved little of substance. In his second attempt the following year he marched north and probably captured the defenders' stronghold at Wheathampstead, Hertfordshire.

The Emperor Claudius [1], anxious to give some shine to his exceptionally dull image, ordered the conquest of Britain in AD 43. The troops of four legions (3,000 to 6,000 men in each), plus auxiliary regiments of provincials, landed and made their main base at Richborough. The invaders soon won a major victory on the River Medway. The main British force under Caractacus (died AD 54) withdrew and avoided further pitched battles. Claudius himself made a brief visit to lead his forces triumphantly into Colchester (Camulodunum).

The south and Midlands up to the Trent and Severn rivers were occupied without much opposition being met. But in Wales Caractacus led a stubborn resistance based on guerrilla tactics. When he was eventually inveigled into the open he was defeated, and was taken prisoner to Rome and exhibited in the triumph awarded to the successful Roman general. By AD 61 the Romans controlled England as far north as the River Humber. But in that year Boadicea (Boudicca) [3], Queen of the Iceni in East Anglia, led a revolt which spread so quickly that the governor, Suetonius Paulinus, was forced to abandon Colchester, London (Londinium) and St Albans (Verulamium). Inevitably the greater armed power, skill and discipline of the Romans prevailed and the rebellion was crushed with savage reprisals.

## Consolidation and administration

By AD 80 the whole of Wales had been subdued. The new governor, Agricola (AD 37–93), pushed the frontier northwards to the Forth and Clyde, and at the Battle of Mons Graupius gained the whole of lowland Scotland. But as elsewhere in their empire, the Romans found it difficult to maintain their expanding frontiers securely. A period of consolidation led to the building of Hadrian's Wall [4] between the Tyne and the Solway during the AD 120s. Under the Emperor Antoninus Pius further attempts were made to subdue Scotland, and the Antonine Wall was built linking the Firth of Forth and the Firth of Clyde. Hadrian's Wall fell into disuse for a period but by about AD

1 A bronze head of Claudius, Emperor of Rome from AD 41 to 54, was found in the River Alde in Suffolk. Claudius instigated and took a close personal interest in the conquest of Britain, which was important for his own prestige. During the 16 days that he spent campaigning in Britain he led his troops from the Thames and quickly captured Colchester. He also received the surrender of many tribes.

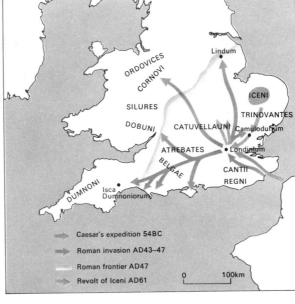

2 The two Roman invasions came about for different reasons. Julius Caesar saw the British campaign as a diversion from his main task of subduing Gaul, and retired after achieving his aim of defeating the British chief Cassivellaunus. By comparison Claudius hoped to confirm his own dubious power in Rome and at the same time saw the creation of a new colony in Britain as a means to balance the great power of the generals on the Rhine. Southeast Britain was the centre of both Celtic and Roman Britain at this time; the Fosse Way was the frontier of Roman Britain in AD 47, and served as a springboard for advances into south Wales in AD 49 and north Wales in AD 61.

Lindum
ORDOVICES
CORNOVI
SILURES
DOBUNI
ICENI
TRINOVANTES
CATUVELLAUNI · Camulodunum
ATREBATES · Londinium
BELGAE CANTII
DUMNONI REGNI
Isca
Dumnoniorum

→ Caesar's expedition 54BC
→ Roman invasion AD43–47
— Roman frontier AD47
→ Revolt of Iceni AD61
0    100km

3 Boadicea, warrior queen of the Iceni in East Anglia, riding in her war chariot, symbolizes revolt against Roman oppression. This massive sculpture, executed by Thomas Thornycroft in 1902, stands nationalistically at the west end of Westminster Bridge, London.

4 A long stretch of Hadrian's Wall that is better preserved than most runs along the Whin Sill escarpment near the large fort of Housesteads. The wall runs for 117.5km (73.5 miles – 80 Roman miles) from Wallsend-on-Tyne to Bowness-on-Solway. It was built in the AD 120s, after a visit by the Emperor Hadrian, to help to defend the empire's most northerly frontier from invasions by the Picts. It was several times overrun and rebuilt, before the border was finally abandoned to the Picts in AD 383.

200 it again formed the northern frontier.

The first capital of the province of Britannia was Colchester, but London soon succeeded it as the centre of administration and trade. The bridge over the Thames there was the focal point of the road network and of the sea trade routes. London was burnt during Boadicea's rebellion but was quickly rebuilt and became one of the largest cities in the Roman Empire. The governor was assisted by an *iuridicus* who was responsible for justice in the civilian zone, and by many civil servants. Taxation and the treasury were under an independent *procurator*.

In the early third century Britain was divided into two provinces. London was the capital of Britannia Superior and York (Eburacum) became the capital of Britannia Inferior. Later, four provinces and then five were created. Communities had considerable control over their own affairs and the *coloniae* (important towns) [7] of Colchester, Lincoln (Lindum) and Gloucester (Glevum) were virtually self-governing.

Most Britons lived a settled, peaceful life under civil rule. But the territories between the Humber and Hadrian's Wall, much of Wales and some other areas, were under military rule and were controlled through a network of large garrison bases and smaller fortresses. The movement of troops was aided by an excellent road system. Roads and forts [6] always followed close on conquests. Important roads were Watling Street, from Dover (Dubrae) to Chester (Deva), Ermine Street, from London to York, and the Fosse Way, from Lincoln to near Axminster.

## Withdrawal and abandonment

In the fourth century Saxon raiders became a serious threat to the southeast coast while the Picts and Scots increased pressure on the northern frontier, destroying Hadrian's Wall and overrunning much of the north in AD 367. The situation was temporarily restored but Roman forces began to withdraw, and by the early fifth century had completely abandoned the island. The last appeal for help was rejected by the authorities in Rome in AD 446 and the Anglo-Saxons began the process of effacing or transforming many of the signs of Roman occupation.

**The arrogant attitude of the Romans** towards the conquered Britons in the early years of their occupation is graphically illustrated by this scene of a Roman cavalryman trampling a Briton under his horse's hoofs. The horseman, named Longinus, came from Sofia, in modern Bulgaria, and was a *duplicarius* (junior officer) in a Thracian cavalry detachment. The scene was carved on a tombstone found on the site of Colchester. The troops of Boadicea (died AD 62) defaced the tomb, overthrew the headstone, and burnt Colchester as an act of vengeance after the Romans had violently taken over the territory of the Iceni, flogged Boadicea and raped her daughters.

**5 This reconstructed Roman boat** is typical of the craft used by the Romans to bring troops and supplies from Gaul and up the main rivers of southern Britain. But communication by road was soon developed as the most efficient means of military control.

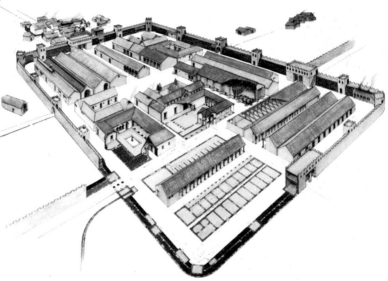

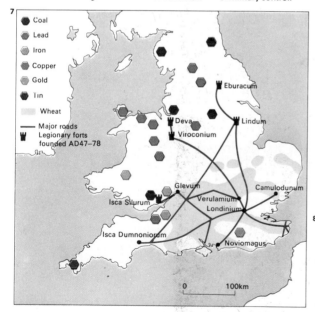

**7 The map of Roman Britain** during the early decades of conquest and control shows roads, towns, frontiers, fort systems and industrial and agricultural regions. Throughout their empire, the Romans put the emphasis on urban rather than on rural life. The first of many towns they founded in Britain was at Colchester, while other towns developed from the settlements outside the military stations. The largest element of local government was the *civitas* (community), which was based on already existing tribal groupings. The most important towns received the title of *colonia* or *municipium*. Such towns were permitted to elect a town senate, which provided magistrates for administrative duties.

Map legend:
- Coal
- Lead
- Iron
- Copper
- Gold
- Tin
- Wheat
- Major roads
- Legionary forts founded AD47–78

Map labels: Eburacum, Deva, Lindum, Viroconium, Glevum, Camulodunum, Verulamium, Isca Silurum, Londinium, Isca Dumnoniorum, Noviomagus

0    100km

**6 The typical Roman fort** would hold 500 to 1,000 men. Each fort was strengthened by a wall with an earth rampart banked against it. From the main gate (*porta praetoria*) a main street (*via praetoria*) led to the headquarters building (*principia*). From there the other main street led to the side gateways, the *porta principalis dextra* and *porta principalis sinistra*. Within the fort there would usually be barracks for the troops and their officers, a workshop, granaries, stables, armouries, the regimental chapel and the commandant's house. Water would be supplied by an aqueduct running from a nearby river. Civilian settlements were often built and grew up outside the walls of the fort to provide a measure of comfort. Forts were built along Hadrian's Wall at regular intervals in order to repel aggressive barbarian tribesmen.

**8 The Roman fort of Anderida** at Pevensey in Sussex was built *c.* AD 280 to defend the south coast against Germanic invaders. A chain of these forts was built from Norfolk to the Isle of Wight to protect important harbours against the incursions of Saxon sea raiders. Others were built on the west coast. In AD 491 the Saxons stormed Anderida and slaughtered everyone in it. Today the fort stands several miles away from the shore because of the silting of the harbours.

# Life in Roman Britain

In Celtic times Britain was already a prosperous country. The Romans rapidly increased its prosperity. Their colonial policy aimed at winning the approval of the upper classes by founding new centres such as Lincoln in the countryside, or by introducing Roman civilization to existing tribal centres. Their way of life affected the lower classes only slightly and gradually.

## Life in the towns

At the centre of the typical Roman town [3] was the *forum,* round which were grouped buildings such as the *basilica* (hall of justice and public meeting-place), *curia* (council chamber), temples, baths and shops. The shape of each town was essentially that of Rome itself. The streets were paved and some had main drains beneath them to which house drains could be linked. Principal buildings were constructed of stone, with timber buildings surrounding them, and in the bigger towns wealthy Romans and Britons owned houses built of brick.

Labourers and craftsmen lived in simple rectangular houses made of wood, set with their longer dimension at right-angles to the street. They doubled as shop-front and workshop, the living rooms being set behind the working areas or on an upper floor and equipped with furniture and utensils that were usually homemade. Merchants' houses were larger, and made of brick, with an internal courtyard. They might have a hypocaust [7](a system of underfloor central heating), a flush latrine (fed by rainwater collected in a lead tank on the roof), mosaic floors [Key] and brightly frescoed interior walls.

In Roman eyes the bath house was an essential feature of civilized life and even the smallest town had one, centrally placed and open to all. Amphitheatres were important, apart from the entertainment they provided, for the urban solidarity they demonstrated. The Romans enjoyed violent entertainments: as well as chariot races in which blood was shed accidentally, there were gladiatorial performances in which it was shed deliberately. Amphitheatres seating perhaps 5,000 spectators can still be seen at Silchester and Dorchester. Theatres existed in only the most important towns, such as St Albans [5].

Britons who lived in the towns, or visited them regularly, probably adopted the dress of the Romans. Those who, as Roman citizens, were entitled to wear a toga probably did so on formal occasions. Others wore tunics and, out of doors, hooded cloaks. Soldiers serving at Hadrian's Wall are known to have worn socks and underpants.

There was considerable interchange between Roman and Briton. Soldiers on the northern frontier, for instance, spoke a British dialect of Latin and drank not only imported wine but also "Celtic beer". Civilian settlements grew up beside forts and even in its most remote outposts the Roman army lived constantly in the company of the people it had conquered.

## Agriculture and industry

Within Roman Britain the pattern of agricultural life seems to have changed little; even in their *coloniae,* or settlements of veteran soldiers, the Romans do not seem to have brought to bear their improved agricul-

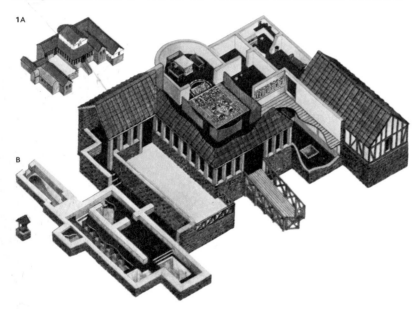

1 **The Roman villa at Lullingstone, in Kent** (shown here in model [A] and cutaway [B]) was built on an ancient site. The first stone house to appear on the site was probably built by a British farmer in the 1st century AD. By the end of that century it was occupied by a Roman and was greatly expanded by the addition of baths and other rooms. The house stood empty for most of the 3rd century until it was taken over by a prosperous Romano-British family. During the 4th century its celebrated mosaic floor was laid in a new reception room and another room was converted into a Christian chapel. The house was abandoned in about 400.

2 **Pottery figurines** fashioned to represent diners and reciters were excavated from a Roman child's grave at Colchester. The stocky build and general facial characteristics of the figurines suggest that they depict men from northern Italy. It is known that after AD 49, veteran soldiers, mostly Italian, increasingly settled at Colchester and raised families. Eventually there were several thousand members of this community.

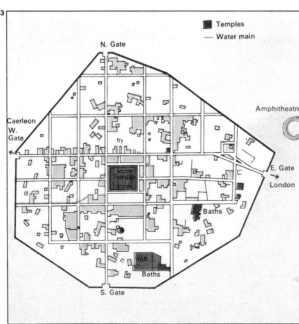

3 **Silchester**, in Hampshire, is the only Roman town in Britain that has been completely excavated. The first town on the site, where seven main Roman roads met, is thought to have been founded about AD 45. It is a typically Roman town in its grid-iron arrangement, buildings such as baths and temples, its residential areas and its open spaces. The centre, as in Rome itself, was the *forum,* a large square surrounded by public buildings and shops. The most important building was the *basilica,* a long hall where business was transacted. The shops in the forum were more elaborate than the ordinary shops, which served also as houses and sometimes as workshops.

Temples ■
Water main —

N. Gate
Caerleon W. Gate
Forum
Amphitheatre
E. Gate
London
Baths
Inn
Baths
S. Gate

4 **St Martin's Church, Canterbury,** is probably the oldest Christian church in Britain. It is also the only building in the country that was used for Christian worship in both Roman and Anglo-Saxon times. Before being adapted for Christian use, the site had served as a pagan temple for Romano-Celtic religions. The Kentish queen Bertha worshipped there in the 6th century and St Augustine used it as his headquarters for his mission to re-Christianize England in 597. The western wall is Roman and was probably the wall of the church of Durovernum, built in the 3rd or 4th century. Few other buildings in Roman towns have been identified as specifically Christian edifices; usually small square rooms were set aside for worship.

tural technology. Most villas [1] were comparatively simple and even the most luxurious were primarily productive farms.

Agriculture was the means of subsistence of most people in Roman Britain [8]; after that came textiles, above all wool. Numerous varieties of weave have been recently unearthed at Vindolanda, near Hadrian's Wall, where remains of a tannery were also found. Wine, olive oil and works of skilful craftsmanship were imported into Britain, but in return Britain exported wool and, after native potters had learnt from the Romans, pottery such as Castor ware. Mineral deposits were worked by the Romans to a much greater degree than ever before.

**The Roman ideals**
The roads that fostered the urban way of life, and made Britain for the first time a living unity, were built primarily for the uses of the army and the administration. For those who used them there were *mansiones* (staging-posts) provided at regular intervals of ten Roman miles. A typical *mansio* had six guest rooms, a heated dining room, a

kitchen and a small bath house, all of which, together with the staff, had to be maintained by the local community. Another significant way in which Britain was now unified was in the law, which probably did much to spread the use of Latin among the upper classes.

There was great variety in the practice of religion. Claudius had from the first introduced emperor worship, but this was a comparatively small part of a Roman's typical round of religious duties. The Romans had done their utmost to stamp out Druidism, for they violently disapproved of its human sacrifices, but they were otherwise tolerant either of the religions they had imported, such as Mithraism, originally from Persia, or of the native religion, of which little is known. The chief Celtic deity seems to have been a figure whom the Romans identified with Hercules [9]. Christianity made some converts, mostly in the fourth century [4].

When the Romans departed, the country quickly lapsed from its civilized ways. But the memory of Rome remained for centuries afterwards an ideal to which the emergent nation had continual recourse.

**Mosaics,** such as this 2nd-century depiction of autumn from a villa at Corinium (Cirencester), were put in many public and private buildings of Roman Britain. They often represented mythical scenes. The invaders tried to bring their Mediterranean style of life to Britain, adapting it as little as possible.

**5 The theatre at Verulamium** (St Albans), which was built in about AD 140, is one of only three found in Britain. It was used not only for plays but also for dancing, wrestling and bear-baiting. The audience sat on a semicircular bank of raised seats, with leading citizens occupying the front rows.

**6 Romano-British farmhouses** were generally single-storey buildings with rooms leading into one another rather than off a corridor. There were usually a number of buildings in addition to the living quarters.

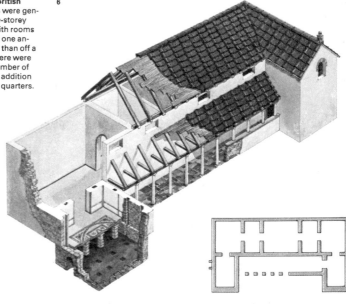

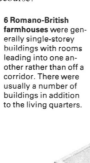

**7 The central heating system** (part of which is shown) at Chedworth Roman villa, near Cheltenham, worked by means of a hypocaust. In every Roman villa in Britain, one or more rooms were heated by the same means. The principle of the hypocaust was simple but effective. It consisted basically of a furnace below ground-level, which was fed with charcoal by a stoke-hole located in an outside wall. The hot air from the furnace was drawn through channels under the floors (which were supported by tiled pillars) and from there up through small flues in the walls. In Mediterranean lands hypocausts were usually installed only for heating the baths, but the rigorous British climate demanded a more elaborate and effective system.

**8 This bronze statuette** of a British ploughman was found at Piercebridge in County Durham. Belgic immigrants from northeast Gaul before and after Caesar's invasions introduced the heavy *caruca*, which went deeper than the Celtic plough (shown here). The Romans used the Belgic plough, and Celtic farmers became confined to the areas of lighter soil.

**9 The Cerne giant** was cut in the chalk of a hillside north of Cerne Abbas in Dorset in the late Roman period. The figure stands 55m (180ft) tall and holds a club. It has been suggested that the giant is a British adaptation of the cult of Hercules, which was early introduced into Britain by the Romans and has been found in various parts of the country.

# Roman remains in Britain

The remains of the Roman occupation of Britain that survive represent only a fragment of the civilization the Romans imported. So much has disappeared largely because the Anglo-Saxons had no use for the towns, roads, fortifications and villas the Romans had constructed, and, abandoning the Roman urban style of living, returned to the land. The remains lay unappreciated until the eighteenth century, and urban development from the medieval era to the present has all but obliterated many Roman towns.

## Roman roads and towns

The most universal and unmistakable evidence of their existence left by the Romans is their road system, essential to the swift movement of troops and an efficient administration. Most of the more than 8,000km (5,000 miles) of sturdily constructed roads they laid down have been overlaid by modern highways, but are easily identifiable by the straightness of their alignment [2]. The finest stretches of intact road are found in the north, where the embankment (*agger*) of the road was often metalled with stone paving as,

for instance, at Blackstone Edge [Key]; in the south less durable gravel, chalk or small stones were used.

Not very much remains above ground of the towns that the network of roads was designed to link. In London fragments of the old Roman wall stand isolated, and there is a temple to Mithras similar to that found near Hadrian's Wall [8]. However, quite a good picture of life in the city can be built up from the numerous artefacts found in it [7]. At Silchester in Hampshire the complete circuit of the walls is intact, and the outline of the town's small amphitheatre is visible, as is the amphitheatre at Cirencester. At St Albans the southeasternmost of the four gates has been excavated: it was 30m (100ft) wide, with massive circular towers, and from it a street 12m (40ft) wide led into the city through a triumphal arch. Little of this remains, although there are stretches of wall and tessellated pavements (pavements of small cubical coloured stones) and hypocausts (underfloor heating systems) that testify to the wealth and high standard of living of the inhabitants. There is also there a

theatre which became the town's rubbish dump in medieval times.

Something of the former grandeur of provincial capitals can be seen at Bath [3], York, Lincoln and Caerwent in Gwent; this last was a religious centre where a temple and a bathhouse have been excavated. The Multangular Tower at York still rises amid intermittent stretches of wall; at Lincoln traffic still passes through the Newport Arch, formerly part of the great north gate.

### Villas in Britain

Roman villas, ranging from enormous village-like settlements to simple farmhouses of five or six rooms, are most common in the milder and more Romanized south, particularly in the southeast, the Cotswolds and Hampshire. Only a few of the more than 500 known or suspected Roman villas in Britain have been properly excavated.

The largest and most splendid of these villas was only recently discovered at Fishbourne near Chichester; it was built in the first century AD and contained not only elaborate decoration but the only Roman

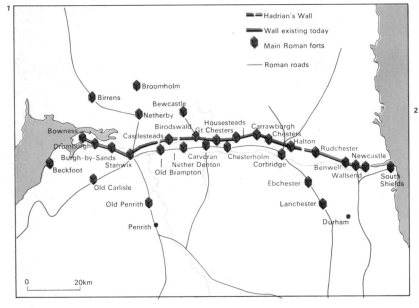

1 **The vast complex of Hadrian's Wall** is the largest Roman site in Britain. This map shows the course of the wall, linking the Tyne and the Solway, its many forts and the system of roads and towns that supplied it.

Hadrian's Wall
Wall existing today
Main Roman forts
Roman roads

Broomholm
Birrens
Bewcastle
Netherby
Bowness
Birdoswald
Housesteads
Gt Chesters
Carrawburgh
Castlesteads
Chesters
Drumburgh
Halton
Rudchester
Burgh-by-Sands
Carvoran
Chesterholm
Newcastle
Stanwix
Nether Denton
Corbridge
Benwell
Beckfoot
Old Brampton
Wallsend
South Shields
Old Carlisle
Ebchester
Old Penrith
Lanchester
Penrith
Durham

0   20km

2 **The Fosse Way**, in an aerial view near Hinckley, a town in Leicestershire, is typically Roman in its straightness. Roman roadbuilders always took the shortest route between two places, crossing rather than

circling hills. Running from Lincoln towards Axminster in Devon, the Fosse Way, built after the first phase of conquest, was one of the earliest and straightest of all the roads constructed by the Romans in Britain.

3 **The Great Bath at Aquae Sulis**, modern Bath, is surrounded by a modern portico (in the Roman Doric order) but otherwise is substantially as it was in Roman times. The Great Bath is one of three plunge baths created in the 1st century AD, and filled by a natural hot spring with waters at 48.5°C (120°F) of renowned curative properties. Originally unroofed, it was later covered with a great barrel vault. Roman Bath was an elegant and sophisticated spa town with numerous luxurious villas in the surrounding country. It was visited not only by Britons but also by foreigners. Numbers of inscriptions found there are dedicated to the presiding goddess of healing, Minerva Sulis, from whom the town gained its name.

4 **The most elegant mirror** found in ancient Britain, this fine piece of Roman silverwork was once the property of a rich citizen of Viroconium, now Wroxeter. The town was known for its large *forum* and splendid baths. The mirror is 29cm (11.5 in) in diameter, and its skilful workmanship perhaps indicates that it was imported from Italy. The handle consists of two thick strands of interlocking silver wire, each of which bears two floral roundels. The mirror is now in Shrewsbury museum.

formal garden to have been found north of the Alps. A villa at Chedworth in Gloucestershire is particularly well preserved; both Chedworth and Fishbourne have museums attached, with a wide range of artefacts used by the inhabitants. Of other examples, Bignor Villa in Sussex is notable for its fine mosaics and the view it offers of Roman Stane Street climbing the Downs; and the villa at Lullingstone in Kent is interesting archaeologically because it is a small but elegant building that has undergone a number of structural alterations.

## Around Hadrian's Wall

Something of what it cost to maintain and protect the Roman civilization can be seen from the straggling remnants of Hadrian's Wall [1]. The wall itself is 2m (6.5ft) high, and wide enough to walk upon; it has a ditch to the north 2.75m (9ft) deep and 8m (27ft) wide. Along its length are 17 forts of which the best preserved are Chesters, Housesteads and Greatchesters, but at every Roman mile (1,480m or 1,620 yards) there was a smaller bastion. A major rampart, 3m (10ft) deep and 6m (20ft) wide at the top, runs parallel to the wall 55 to 75m (60 to 82ft) to the south, and between the wall and the rampart runs a road. The Antonine Wall is also visible in Scotland, between the Forth and Clyde.

Numerous fortresses and civilian settlements surround Hadrian's Wall to the south, notably Vindolanda, where a detailed picture of everyday military and civilian life (and the earliest example of writing in Britain) has emerged from excavations. Corstopitum (Corbridge) [5] was once an important supply base and there is now a museum there with a good collection of Romano-British sculpture, including the "Corbridge Lion". Naturally, most military remains are in the frontier areas, to the north and the west of England, but in the southeast are the forts of the Saxon Shore, erected at the end of the third century AD to combat Saxon raiders. Reculver, Richborough, Pevensey, Portchester and, on the east coast, Burgh Castle are the best examples. Lastly, the Roman *pharos* (lighthouse) at Dover testifies to that port's position as the gateway to and from the heart of the empire.

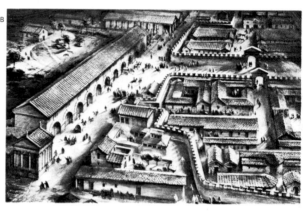

At **Blackstone Edge above Littleborough** in Lancashire there is a long stretch of paved Roman road almost 5m (16ft) wide. It has a shallow trough built of shaped stones that runs down its centre. This may have been for drainage, but was more probably filled with turf to provide horses or oxen with a secure footing as they toiled uphill. Beneath the stone paving, so as to provide a firm base, was an embankment (*agger*) of earth or rubble, with a trench running on either side. This ensured that the road was drained. Not until the 18th century were roads of such a quality to be seen once more in Britain. They were built not for stimulating trade, but for the fast movement of troops and for administrative uses.

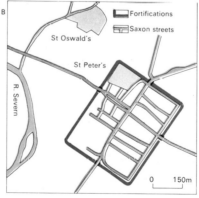

**5 The Roman fort of Corstopitum,** standing near Corbridge on the north bank of the River Tyne, is shown as it is now [A], and as it might have been [B]. The extensive 4th-century remains are typically square in basic plan. The town was both an important fort and supply base, and a wealthy civilian settlement. Its main buildings consist of two large granaries, a general storehouse in a courtyard, several temples and a fountain fed by an aqueduct.

**6 These three plans** show the development of the Roman city [A] of Gloucester, in late Saxon times [B], and in the Middle Ages [C]. Its development, in a pattern recurrent in Britain, reflects its defensible site near a bend in the Severn. Saxon Gloucester contained a shrunken community inside the Roman walls. But a growing population and burgeoning trade in medieval times caused expansion, especially towards the river and to the north.

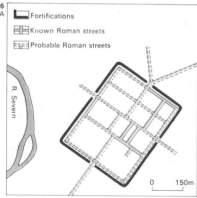

**7 A Roman kitchen,** reconstructed in the Museum of London, is fully equipped with Roman utensils found in the city. Food was cooked in copper pans over charcoal (stored in the arch below) on a stone hearth.

**8 This Mithraeum,** or temple to Mithras, the favourite god of the legionaries, is in the fort of Carrawburgh on Hadrian's Wall. At the head of a nave flanked by benches for the worshippers, stood three altars, on one of which Mithras is carved with a halo.

# Christ and the Apostles

Jesus Christ was an orthodox Jew. Born in about 4 BC, he was crucified outside the walls of Jerusalem in about AD 30. He certainly gave Christianity its original impetus, but it is less certain that he meant to found a Church. His disciples came to think of him as the promised "Messiah" (the Hebrew form of the Greek "Christ"), and then gave to him the value and honour they reserved for the one God alone.

The figure of Jesus and his teaching still dominates Western imagination nearly 2,000 years after his death. Today more than 1,000 million people in many parts of the world describe themselves as Christians.

When Jesus lived there was in Judaism a variety of emphases and interpretations leading to controversies between parties. The evidence of the Dead Sea Scrolls [4] and other contemporary sources suggest that the teaching of Jesus had much in common with some of the sects current during his lifetime.

Responsibility for his death is still disputed. According to the Gospels he was crucified on the orders of the Roman governor at the insistence of the Jewish religious establishment. The Gospels suggest he was condemned for blasphemy (which was a capital offence) because he claimed to be the Messiah, although such a claim was not technically blasphemous in Jewish law.

## The historical Jesus
The only detailed records we have of the life of Jesus are the Gospels, which were written by Christians for Christians. What were believed to be sayings of Jesus and stories about him circulated first by word of mouth. Collections of such sayings and stories were doubtless later written down, and it was from such sources that the four Gospels were compiled. They were written in Greek, although Jesus spoke in Aramaic. The first of the Gospels, St Mark's, was written in about AD 62.

The Gospels present us with highly interpreted history, and it has been impossible to disentangle fact from interpretation.

The earliest records (St Paul's Epistles and St Mark's Gospel) do not describe Jesus' birth. According to the later accounts of St Luke and St Matthew Jesus was born at Bethlehem of a virgin mother, Mary, his conception in her womb being due to the creative power of God's spirit. Jesus' home town was Nazareth in Galilee [1].

Jesus was baptized in about 26, when he was about 30, by his cousin John the Baptist [5]. Immediately after his baptism he went into spiritual retreat in the desert. Then he began teaching in Galilee, healing the sick in body and mind and proclaiming the imminent arrival of the kingdom (more accurately the kingly rule) of God.

Many have found its essence distilled in the Sermon on the Mount – a compilation of his sayings masterfully arranged. It emphasizes the need for spiritual rebirth and describes the heroic goodness that follows as a consequence. The teaching of Jesus had a challenging directness. He called men away from the letter of the Jewish law to its spirit. This led him to criticize severely the Jewish leaders of his day.

## Arrest and crucifixion
Whatever the precise form of his criticisms, Jesus was marked down by the religious authorities as a public enemy. And this con-

1 **Christianity began** in the northern Jewish province of Galilee, away from the religious centre of Jerusalem, and Jesus spent most of his ministry among simple country people. Traditionally, some Apostles travelled as far as Persia and India. The most widely travelled Apostle, Paul, was a Jew but a Roman citizen born at Tarsus in what is now Turkey. He took the Gospel both to Asia Minor and to Greece.

2 **Capernaum**, where the remains of this synagogue are still visible, is at the north end of the Sea of Galilee. It is mentioned several times in the Gospels in connection with Jesus' mission.

3 **Christ is transfigured** with Elias and Moses representing the Prophets and the Law, while John, Peter and James crouch before the light in this painting from a 12th-century church in Cyprus.

4 **The Dead Sea Scrolls** were discovered between 1947 and 1956 in caves to the northwestern end of the Dead Sea. They contain most of the books of the Old Testament and some other hitherto unknown Jewish writings in Hebrew and Aramaic from a monastic community at Qumran. Most of the manuscripts are made from leather and papyrus and are kept at the Israel Museum in Jerusalem.

cerned the civil (Roman) authorities because his wide popular support might involve disturbances. He probably realized that his life was threatened. On a visit to Jerusalem in about AD 30 to observe the Jewish Passover He provided his enemies with an occasion to arrest him by physically assaulting the money changers and traders in the Temple. He was eventually arrested by the Temple guard while he was praying in the Garden of Gethsemane – Judas Iscariot no doubt leading them to the place and betraying the identity of Jesus by kissing him. The Jewish leaders handed him over to the Roman governor, Pontius Pilate, who ordered his crucifixion (a Roman form of execution for slaves and low criminals) with two thieves at Golgotha.

**The early Church**
From the third day after the crucifixion the followers of Jesus became utterly convinced that he was alive. They were sure that he appeared and spoke to them as recognizably himself though now glorified. At a slightly later date the news was spread that certain women had gone to his tomb to anoint his dead body and had found the tomb empty, except for the graveclothes.

At the harvest festival of Pentecost, some five weeks after the crucifixion, the disciples believed themselves visited by the spirit of God sent down by the exalted Jesus. From then on they went about preaching that Jesus was the Messiah crucified and raised from the dead, through whom eternal salvation was offered to all.

Paul became the chief Apostle to the Gentiles (non-Jews) after a dramatic conversion to Jesus' teachings on the road to Damascus. Greek-speaking and a Roman citizen, he began the transformation of Christianity into a world religion for everybody. He travelled extensively, preaching in Asia Minor and Greece [8]. He was eventually arrested in Jerusalem, used his right as a Roman citizen to appeal to Caesar, and is said to have been executed in Rome at the same time as St Peter, about AD 60.

According to legend, St John, "the disciple whom Jesus loved", lived to an old age in exile. St John's Gospel is a profound meditation on the life and teaching of Jesus.

The image or name of Jesus Christ and the Gospel open at the words "I am the Light of the World" appear in many mosaics, including this 12th-century work on a ceiling in Palermo.

5 Jesus was baptized in the River Jordan by John the Baptist. In this sixth-century mosaic from Ravenna, the figure on the left represents the river god of the Jordan. Baptism is the method of entry into the Christian community.

6 Jesus celebrated his Last Supper with his disciples on the night before his death. This meal is the distinctive Christian ceremony called the Lord's Supper, Holy Communion, Eucharist, Liturgy and Mass. This sixth-century mosaic at Ravenna shows 11 disciples reclining with Christ. The two fish recall the miraculous feeding of the multitude.

7 A fifth-century ivory carving depicts the women who went to the rockhewn sepulchre of Jesus at dawn on Easter Sunday and found that he had risen from the dead.

8 Paul went on his first preaching tour to Asia Minor. A return visit continued over into Greece and a third journey covered much the same ground. The final journey by sea went through Crete, Malta and Sicily to Rome.

St Paul's journeys 1 2 3 4

# Rome: soldier emperors to Constantine

After the murder of the Roman Emperor Commodus in AD 193 four rivals disputed the imperial succession. There was a costly civil war in which several major cities, including Antioch, Byzantium and Lyons, were sacked before Septimius Severus (reigned 193–211) was successful. Order was restored, but the military basis of imperial power then became more obvious.

## Political anarchy and religious persecution

Septimius was succeeded by a family dynasty, but because a settled system of succession was lacking and because the legions increasingly realized that they had the power both to elect and to destroy emperors [1] there was continual unrest, with rivals being set up by local troops. In the 74 years from the death of Septimius to the accession of Diocletian (245–313) in 284 there were 27 emperors and many usurpers.

This political anarchy came at the worst possible time, for the barbarians were again pressing on the empire's frontiers. In 236 Alemanni and Franks crossed into Gaul and Goths poured over the Danube in 247

raiding the Balkans and killing the Emperor Decius (200–251). The Romans were forced either to allow the barbarians to settle within the frontiers or to buy them off.

In the east a new Persian dynasty, the Sassanids, invaded Syria and Asia Minor and then captured the Emperor Valerian (193–260) in 260 [2]. His son and co-regent Gallienus (reigned 253–68) had to put down five rivals before recovering the lost eastern provinces. Aurelian (reigned 270–75) finally abandoned Dacia but began restoring the Danube and Rhine frontiers. The work was completed by Probus (reigned 276–82).

The unrest was accompanied by a breakdown of civil order and a collapse of the economy. Inevitably, men searched for scapegoats and the most obvious ones were the Christians. The Romans had always been highly tolerant of religions provided they accepted the divinity of the emperor, and many Oriental cults, including the worship of Mithras and Isis, had become widely popular. But the Christians, who refused to sacrifice to the emperor, were an easy target. They were barbarously persecuted by Decius and even

more so by Valerian (reigned 253–60) [3].

Despite all the disasters, civilized life continued and the third century saw the work of some of the greatest commentators on Roman law – Papinian, Paulus and Ulpian – and considerable literary achievements.

## Division of the empire

There was a desperate need for reorganization and in 285 Diocletian established a totally new governmental system [Key]. The empire was divided into Eastern and Western parts, each ruled by an "Augustus" with a "Caesar" as his deputy. The Augusti were to resign after 20 years and be succeeded by their Caesars. The imperial court moved away from Rome [4] and the provinces were replaced by dioceses ruled by a massive new bureaucracy and a reformed army. The whole system was supported by a new currency and heavy taxation and the emperors became absolute monarchs.

Diocletian's reforms did not solve the succession problem and when he and his co-Augustus Maximian (reigned 286–305) resigned in 305 chaos followed. In 312

1 **The Praetorian Guard** were the élite bodyguards of the emperors. They were the first body of Roman soldiers to realize they had the power to make emperors and, if need be, to break them too;

during the third century their example was followed by troops in the provinces. Anarchy ensued as local garrisons set up their own emperors and tried to dominate the empire.

2 **The Emperor Valerian** was forced to kneel to the Persian ruler in the worst disaster that befell Rome in the third century. The internal chaos of the empire coincided with renewed pressure

from barbarian tribes in the West and from the Persians in the East. The cohesion of the empire was further weakened as threatened areas took action independently of Rome to defend themselves.

3 **Roman persecution of Christians** [A], which reached its height under Decius and Valerian, contrasted with general religious toleration, limited only by the importance given to the unity of the empire. Provided the adherents of a religion were prepared to pay homage to the divine emperor, they were free to worship and make converts. Many Eastern cults such as Mithraism [B] flourished but the exclusiveness of Christians and their refusal to do homage caused them to be treated as a treasonable sect and to be deprived of citizenship.

Constantine (c. 285–337) emerged victorious in the Western Empire in a battle at the Milvian Bridge, during which his armies fought under the Christian cross. In gratitude he made Christianity the official religion of the empire. In 324, on the death of the Eastern Emperor Licinius (reigned 311–23), Constantine reunited the empire and moved his capital to Byzantium, which was rebuilt as a totally Christian city with the name Constantinople. Henceforth the Eastern Empire and Christianity were to be closely identified.

Constantine's death in 337 led to a division of the empire between his two sons; fighting followed until it was briefly reunited in 353. In 355, the Western Empire was placed under Julian, who briefly reunited the empire between 361 and 363. But thereafter the split became permanent.

The difference between the two halves was steadily being emphasized by the presence of barbarians in the West [6], as more tribes were settled within the frontiers, and by the development of a Christianity-dominated absolute empire in the East. In the West the army was by then almost entirely recruited from barbarians; as a result, its resistance was severely reduced.

## Major barbarian invasions

Towards the end of the fourth century came renewed major invasions; in 376 the Visigoths were allowed to cross the Danube to settle, but they were so badly treated that they revolted in 378 and killed the Emperor Valens (c. 328–78) at Adrianople.

Other groups also crossed the frontiers; the Vandals moved through France and Spain to set up an independent kingdom in North Africa; Jutes, Angles and Saxons occupied Britain; Franks and Burgundians settled in northern France and Ostrogoths in Italy. By the middle of the fifth century the Western Empire had been almost completely occupied by barbarians, although a Romanized administration and culture survived. It came as no great surprise when German troops in Italy elected Odoacer, the Ostrogoth (reigned 476–93), as king and he deposed Romulus Augustulus (reigned 475–6) ending emperors in the West.

Representing Diocletian's tetrarchy, this statue from St Mark's in Venice shows two Augusti clasping their Caesars, the deputies who would succeed them after 20 years. The chaos and disasters of the 3rd century forced Diocletian to impose major changes on the empire. His reforms, which were the first alterations to the system established by Augustus, can be seen as formalizing the practices of the years of anarchy when emperors reacted on an *ad hoc* basis to barbarian invasion and civil strife. The emperor and his deputies became full-time military leaders and the whole system was supported by stringent new laws.

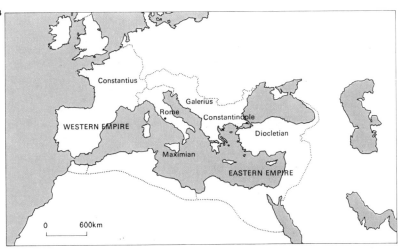

4 The reforms of Diocletian fundamentally altered the empire, splitting it into two almost independent halves. He and his Caesar Galerius were in charge of the crucial Danube and Eastern provinces, while Maximian and Constantius ruled the West. The emperors moved their headquarters nearer to the frontiers. Diocletian ruled from Nicomedia, near Constantinople.

5 Constantine the Great made the momentous decision that Christianity was to be the official religion of the empire. He also reunited the empire and moved the imperial capital from Rome to the strategically placed city of Byzantium (Constantinople), which he had rebuilt as a purely Christian city. Constantine identified with his new faith and put the whole weight of empire behind it.

6 This detail from a sarcophagus shows Roman soldiers subduing barbarians. Some fighting emperors during the third century were able to hold the frontiers and push back invaders but generally the barbarians were allowed to enter the empire, settle and infiltrate the army and administrative structure. During the fourth and early fifth centuries in the West the barbarian kingdoms took shape and their rise merged almost imperceptibly with the decline of the empire.

7 The influence of the Roman Empire continued as a civilizing force long after its fall. The massive grandeur of its buildings, such as these at Palmyra, remained as a visible reminder, while Rome's intellectual legacy was permanent.

# Early Oriental and Western science

Modern scholarship has made it clear that in Roman times there was considerable cross-fertilization between different civilizations. The Roman Empire itself, with its emphasis on foreign trade, provided regular links between the diverse civilizations of Europe, Africa, India and even China.

## The extent of Roman technology

The vastness of the empire posed immense problems in peace-keeping, in government and administration. On these counts the Romans excelled. They developed military technology, constructing large mechanized catapults, mechanical arrow ejectors and crossbows originally invented by the Chinese in the third century BC, elaborate battering-rams and wheeled siege towers, Assyrian inventions of the ninth century BC. The large standing army required not only weapons but clothing and food and here again the Romans used the most modern techniques, establishing in the south of France, for instance, water-operated multiple flour-grinding mills.

Roman roads stretched throughout the empire. Most were gravelled or stone set on concrete with curbstones and drainage channels. Since the empire extended into climates much colder and damper than that of Rome, forms of central heating and damp-proofing were common, at least in the houses built for Roman officials. Heated baths were also common in cities and army camps all over the empire. For their shipping, the Romans followed the example of Sostratos who, in the third century BC, built a huge lighthouse at Alexandria and constructed lighthouses at many other ports [1].

Yet, expert though the Romans were in the art of running an empire and in using up-to-date technology to help them, they made no progress in pure science. Such science as they knew they obtained from the Greeks. In the first century AD, Pliny (23–79) had written his *Naturalis Historia*, a vast compendium on all known science, but this was primarily a compilation of Greek science. Galen (*c*. 130–*c*. 200) [2], the greatest medical man of Roman times, was a Greek national. As a physician and surgeon to the gladiators, Galen obtained valuable knowledge about wounds and various internal organs and later he became personal physician to the Emperor Marcus Aurelius (121–180). He took many pupils and promoted his interpretation of the operation of the human body, which was based on the idea that the liver was the main organ of the venous and arterial systems.

## Advances in other centres

It was not until the third century AD that there was a turn from the Greek concentration on geometry. Then, in Alexandria, the mathematicians Diophantus and Pappus recommended the study of numbers and evolved a kind of algebra. Their work was extended by later generations and particularly by the Muslim civilization, where algebra became highly developed. The "arabic" numerals [Key], which had originally been devised in India, were adopted.

Arithmetic and a form of algebra also characterized Chinese mathematics. It was in China that the abacus was invented and it became such a useful calculator that it is still common in Japan today.

In the West, some 1,800 years and more

**1 A Roman lighthouse**, erected at Dover, was one of many such aids to shipping, a typical use of technology by the vast and efficient Roman administration. Lighting was by means of a fire, usually of wood and tarry substances, contained at the top of the building. The lighthouse was built in a stepped form like the famous Pharos at Alexandria (3rd century BC).

**2 Trajan's Column** was erected by the Roman Emperor Trajan (*c*. 53–117) to celebrate his victories. Built of marble and more than 30m (100ft) high, it was set up in the Forum in Rome in 113. This section shows Roman legionaries being treated on the battlefield. It was here and in gladiatorial combat that Galen and other surgeons learned the basics of anatomy.

**3 A crane** is depicted on this section of Trajan's Column. The pulley block and ropes, and the men inside the treadmill at the bottom, can be seen clearly. Cranes such as this were found well into medieval times.

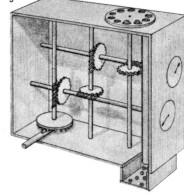

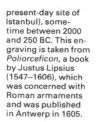

**4 A euthytonon** was a type of mechanical crossbow that was so large it had to be mounted on a stand and fired by a trigger mechanism. This improvement is usually credited to the mechanician Philo who worked at Byzantium (on the present-day site of Istanbul), sometime between 2000 and 250 BC. This engraving is taken from *Poliorceficon*, a book by Justus Lipsius (1547–1606), which was concerned with Roman armaments and was published in Antwerp in 1605.

**5 Roman taximeters** were operated by the wheels of the carriages. Worms and gear wheels reduced the rotations until dials and a counter could be run at a convenient speed. The dials had pointers that indicated the distance travelled by the carriage. The counting disc (at the top of the taximeter) allowed pebbles to drop into a holder at the bottom of the meter. By counting the number of pebbles in the holder, the fare could easily be worked out.

before the Roman conquest, astronomical observations were being made in Britain with great accuracy by using stone circles, of which Stonehenge is probably the greatest example. The Chaldeans (flourished 1000–540 BC) had discovered that eclipses occurred in cycles. Yet it was not until early in the second century AD that accurate eclipse predictions and studies of the earth and heavens were regularly made in China; however in the same period technological advances were accomplished. Chang Heng had invented a seismograph for recording earthquake shocks and the art of papermaking was established [7]. By the eighth and ninth centuries AD the Chinese had also invented gunpowder [6] and block printing, as well as the first clock ever to be made with an escapement – the large water clock in Sian [8]. Moreover Chinese technology brought in the first efficient form of horse harness, the sternpost rudder for ships, the manufacture of silk and most importantly, the compass which was in widespread use by the 1100s.

Alchemy, the forerunner of chemistry, was an ancient art of obscure origins that sought, among other things, to transform base metals such as lead into silver and gold. Carried westward, it was developed in Alexandria particularly by Zosimos in the fourth century AD, along with the important process of distillation.

## Medicine and the Chinese influence

Medicine, too, was not free of mysticism and superstition, but herbal drugs were discovered and used by the Chinese, who in their pharmacopoeia had drugs against malaria and for bronchial diseases, while in India more than 500 drugs came into use, including an early form of tranquillizer. It was in China that the technique of acupuncture evolved.

After the Greeks the progress of science was slow and piecemeal, in the West at least, and seems virtually to have halted for some 600 years. Fortunately, though, the Muslims collected and collated all knowledge of Greek science and, with additions from India and the Far East, all this information filtered through to the West from the twelfth century AD onwards, thus paving the way for the great scientific revival 400 years later.

Pythagoras (right), using an abacus, seems to be competing against Boethius (475–524) [left] who is using arabic numerals.

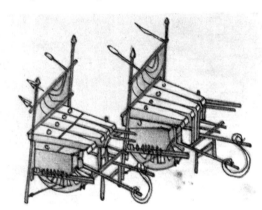

**6 Gunpowder**, first invented by the Chinese, was originally used for fireworks and only later adapted for war. Shown here are early wheelbarrow-like rocket launchers. Gunpowder was first mentioned by Chinese Taoist alchemists about five centuries before it appeared in Europe (*c.* 13th century AD). The development of the gun is more obscure because at first gunpowder was used only in rockets and bombs.

**7 Paper was another Chinese invention** that only gradually reached the West over many centuries. Known in China in the 1st century AD, the necessary technique did not reach even the Muslim world until the 8th century, and it was 400 more years before knowledge of it penetrated to Spain and southern France. Once in the West, it still took 200 years more to reach Germany and 100 more to reach England.

**8 The first mechanical clock** was Chinese, invented in the 8th century by I-Hsing. It was driven by an elaborately engineered waterwheel which acted as an escapement – the essence of all mechanical clocks. This clock was built by Su Sung about 1050. The clock was probably known in the West in the 9th century. The first European clocks with mechanical escapements were made in the 13th century.

**9 Scientific chemistry** developed slowly. Practical chemistry, on the other hand, was part of everyday life – as epitomized here in this copy of a 12th-century Arabic manuscript showing the preparation of perfumes. Attempts were made by the Greeks and the Muslims to classify natural substances and build chemistry into a science but success did not come until the 17th century.

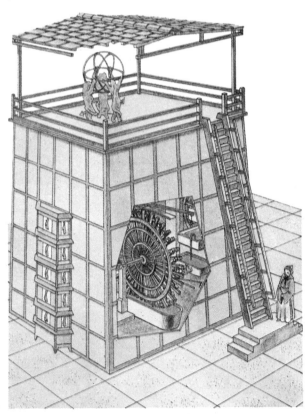

# India 300–1200

After centuries of political fragmentation and foreign domination northern India was once more united under the Gupta dynasty (c. AD 320–550), India's classical age. In southern India another great state gradually took shape under the Pallavas.

## The Gupta dynasty and its empire

The Gupta kings, especially Samudra Gupta (reigned 330–75), Chandra Gupta II (reigned 375–415) and Kumara Gupta (reigned 415–55), founded and maintained, both by conquest and diplomacy, a great empire controlling nearly all of northern India. Good communications, security and relative prosperity created an atmosphere in which Indian culture attained unequalled heights. Thus the works of the poet Kalidasa (flourished fifth century AD) achieved such a degree of perfection that they were often imitated but never surpassed. In art and architecture, too, Indian genius revealed itself in its most accomplished form of refinement and symbolism, but without the overemphasis of detail that typifies much Indian art after about the seventh century.

The material prosperity of India in this period is emphasized in the accounts of a Chinese Buddhist pilgrim, Fa-hsien (flourished 399–414), who visited India in the fifth century, and by the discovery of many gold coins of the Gupta Empire [5].

At the beginning of the sixth century the Huns invaded India from the northwest and penetrated as far as central India. This invasion has often been described as the main cause of the downfall of the Guptas, but it can be argued that the Huns would never have succeeded if the Gupta Empire had not declined owing to internal factors.

## The expulsion of the Huns from India

Although the Huns were expelled after 30 years, northern India became divided between rival powers in Surashtra, Uttar Pradesh and Bengal. There were important changes too in southern India in the present states of Madras and Kerala. A prosperous and cultured society, as reflected in classical Tamil literature, flourished in this area at least from the beginning of the Christian era. In the fourth century AD, the Pallavas made

Kanchi (Conjeevaram) the centre of a large kingdom. Although much smaller than the Gupta Empire in the north it was still of great importance. The Pallavas established a successful form of power-sharing between central and local government, which promoted political stability. The east coast of southern India remained under Pallava control until about 880, and from then until 1200 under that of the Cholas.

The Pallavas patronized the Brahmins who, in their turn, provided excellent educational facilities. In art and architecture a particular Dravidian style (named after the language spoken in central and southern India), culminating in the monolithic sanctuaries and rock reliefs of Mamallapuram (the "Seven Pagodas"), was developed [2]. The Pallavas contributed more than any other Indians to the expansion of Indian civilization into South-East Asia.

## The influence of Harsha of Kanauj

Most of northern India was temporarily united by Harsha of Kanauj (606–47) whose career, admirably described by a Sanskrit

**1 On the relief panel** of this temple of the Gupta period, Vishnu is represented during his cosmic sleep on the coils of the seven-headed Naga. His consort, Lakshmi, is at his feet.

**2 The greatest temple foundation** by the Pallava dynasty of Kanchi, southern India, is the complex of Mamallapuram or Mahabalipuram, popularly known as the Seven Pagodas, south of

Madras. The complex, built in 625–74, comprises a number of caves, a group of beautiful monolithic structures (the so-called *rathas*) and this splendid Shore Temple, dedicated to Shiva.

**3 Frescoes depicting beautiful maidens** are painted on the side of a huge rock at Sigiriya, Sri Lanka, where a fortified royal residence was built in the fifth century.

**4 One of the most striking forms** of the god Shiva is that of the four-armed Nataraja, dancing on top of a demon and surrounded by a halo with flames destroying the world at the end of an aeon. This is one of the finest bronzes of the Chola period (eleventh century).

**5 The numerous gold coins** of the Guptas (the Bayana hoard alone contains 1,021 specimens) are an important source for the history of the period. Their distribution gives an idea of the areas controlled by various Gupta kings and the frequency of the minting reflects economic activity. The representations show how the Gupta kings wished the world to see them. This king appears as a fearless hunter slaughtering a lion with a bow and arrow.

writer (Bana) and a Chinese pilgrim (Hsüan Tsang, in 630–43), reflects high standards of government and reasonable prosperity.

After the time of Harsha northern India showed progressive political fragmentation with larger states tending to split into smaller units which at first paid homage to the central authority but gradually became independent. Harsha's capital, Kanauj, was made the capital of the Pratihara dynasty in 750. The latter ruled paramount over the present states of Uttar Pradesh, Punjab and Rajasthan, but before the end of the ninth century their effective authority was limited to parts of the Punjab and Uttar Pradesh while different Rajput dynasties, originally of tribal descent, ruled in Rajasthan. Bihar and Bengal were under the Buddhist Pala dynasty (c. 750–1150) but from the tenth century they shared with minor dynasties.

During such divisions the Muslim Mahmud of Ghazni (Afghanistan) (971–1030) invaded and plundered northern India many times between 1000 and 1026 [7]. These were destructive raids, carried out mainly for booty. Although many Indian armies fought bravely, their resistance proved ineffective through internal rivalries and military miscalculations, such as over-reliance on elephants. Further political, but not cultural, decline led to new Muslim invasions and by the end of the twelfth century most of northern India had come under the control of the Muslim sultanate of Delhi.

Sanskrit literature of the post-Harsha period offers many excellent works, although few of the quality of the earlier periods. The most important historical text of ancient India, the *Kashmir Chronicle*, belongs to the twelfth century. In art and architecture some of the greatest achievements, such as the temples of Orissa and Khajuraho, belong to this late period.

There was no decline in southern India where the Cholas established one of the greatest Indian empires. Their kings invaded Sri Lanka and Bengal and even undertook a great maritime expedition to South-East Asia. While northern India suffered political fragmentation and Muslim invasions, the Chola kingdom established conditions in which Hinduism flourished.

**Vishnu**, one of the principal gods of Hinduism and the supreme deity for the Vaishnavas, some of whom find a close analogy between religious experience and sexual love, has revealed himself as a saviour of mankind in many different forms, in particular in ten descents (*avataras*) as a man or as an animal. His most celebrated *avatara* was as Krishna, the divine shepherd and king-philosopher. Of the animal *avataras*, the Boar (*varaha*), shown here with elaborate ornamentation, is most frequently represented. In Hindu mythology the god is believed to have descended in this form to rescue the earth, which had sunk in the ocean.

6

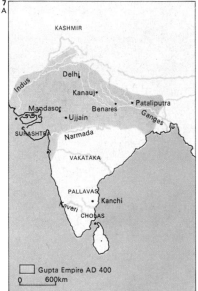

7
A

KASHMIR

Indus

Delhi

Kanauj

Mandasor

• Benares • Pataliputra

• Ujjain

Ganges

Narmada

SURASHTRA

VAKATAKA

PALLAVAS

Kaveri

• Kanchi

CHOLAS

Gupta Empire AD 400

0 600km

B

KASHMIR

• Peshawar

Ghazni

• Lahore

Indus

• Multan

Delhi

Brahmaputra

SIND

Kanauj

PRATIHARAS

Benares

Ganges

• Ujjain

PALAS

Narmada

Godavari

CHAULUKYAS

CHOLAS

Indian Empire of Mahmud of Ghazni 1030

0 600km

**6 An older Shiva temple** at Orissa shows the typical shape (*shikhara*) of a southern India temple. It is built on a platform in front of a pool that is used for ritual ablutions.

**7 Although the Gupta Empire** [A] represented the peak of classical Indian culture, its influence hardly reached the south. After its fall, the north was rarely united, while the Pallava and Chola dynasties brought continuity to the south. Despite the lack of cohesion, the north easily resisted the Muslims and lost only Sind until the growth of Mahmud of Ghazni's empire [B] as a powerful and aggressive neighbour. Mahmud was not impelled by religious motives but Muslim raids continued until the establishment of the Muslim Sultanate of Delhi in 1206, marking the start of permanent Muslim influence in India.

8

**8 Puri** is one of the great religious centres, attracting countless pilgrims from all over India during the annual cart festival of Jagannath (Juggernaut). The god used to be a tribal deity.

**9 Although they were meant for monks**, there is little trace of puritanism in the Buddhist caves of the western Deccan. This relief, probably of the sixth century, depicts Tārās, a kind of female saviour, who is performing a devotional dance.

9

# China 1000 BC – AD 618

The Shang dynasty (c. 1600–c. 1030 BC), the first in the recorded history of China, was overthrown in about 1030 BC by a group of tribesmen from west China called the Chou. Their dynasty was to be China's longest, and its notable contribution to Chinese history was that it witnessed the birth and popular acceptance of Confucian philosophy.

## The Chou and the Ch'in dynasties

The Chou period (c. 1030–221 BC) saw many important developments. The realm was extended to the sea in the east, the Yangtze River in the south and to the borders of Szechwan in the southwest. As this expansion continued, semi-independent states emerged which, although paying tribute to the emperor and his court, were more concerned with culture and religion than with political authority.

The delicate balance of power between the emperor's vassal states finally collapsed and the "Warring States" period began (475–221 BC). During this period of violent struggle, philosophical and moral thought flourished and a new, educated class arose.

Chief among the philosophers was Confucius (551–479 BC), whose teachings emphasized duties to the family and society rather than preoccupation with the dead. The influence of his thought signalled the decline of the old feudalism and began a tradition of close association between philosophical thought and political practice in China.

This was also a period of great technological change. Iron superseded the use of bronze, especially in weaponry; irrigation improved harvests; and the invention of the breast harness vastly improved the efficiency of the horse.

Gradually the smaller and weaker states were absorbed by the militarily and economically stronger states, until the chief contenders were the Chou in the south and the Ch'in in the west. Eventually the Ch'in became supreme rulers and in 221 BC China was for the first time unified under Shih Huang Ti (259–210 BC), the "First Emperor" [3]. He abolished the political system of the Chou and returned to the old feudal system, dividing the country into 36 provinces over which he set officials directly responsible to

himself. He completed and strengthened the Great Wall [1], today stretching 2,400km (1,500 miles) from southern Kansu province to the coast east of Peking. The written language was simplified and unified over the whole country. Weights, measures and coinage were standardized. Shih Huang Ti is remembered as a despotic but practical emperor who burned existing literature, exempting only works on agriculture, medicine, pharmacy and divination. After the First Emperor's death the structure soon collapsed under the feeble rule of the second emperor who was murdered in 207, bringing the Ch'in dynasty to an end.

## The Han dynasty: education and wealth

Out of the chaos that followed there emerged a successful candidate for the throne, Liu Pang (247–195 BC), who founded the Han dynasty in 206 BC [2]. Initially the Han endeavoured to rule with the Ch'in system. But after about a century the principle of hereditary local power was curtailed and candidates for local government were selected by open examinations [4]. In 124 BC

**1 The Great Wall of China** was commenced under the Chou dynasty in the fourth and third centuries BC. It was designed to protect the Chinese people from attacks by the nomadic tribes who occupied the steppe lands in the far north and west. Building went on under ensuing dynasties and various sections of the wall were connected until, during the Ming dynasty (1368–1644), it extended for 2,400km (1,500 miles).

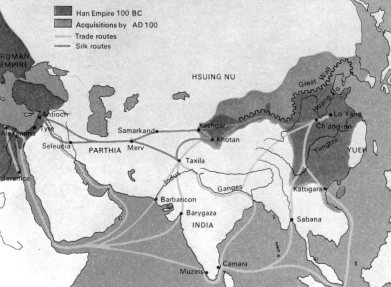

**2 China expanded under Han rule,** after unification by the Ch'in. The growing silk trade had to be made secure, but central Asia remained vulnerable to barbarian threats.

Han Empire 100 BC
Acquisitions by AD 100
Trade routes
Silk routes

ROMAN EMPIRE — Antioch — Tyre — Alexandria — Seleucia — Berenice — PARTHIA — Merv — Samarkand — Kashgar — Khotan — Taxila — Indus — Barbaricon — Barygaza — Ganges — INDIA — Muziris — Camara — Sabana — Kattigara — HSUING NU — Great Wall — Huang Ho — Lo Yang — Ch'ang-an — Yangtze — YUEH

**3 Standardization** of weights and measures was first ordered by Shih Huang Ti, First Emperor of all China. It was one of a number of measures to consolidate his rule, including standardization of the language, censuses and the construction of a defensive road system. After his death taxation and the forced labour system led to peasants' revolts and the eventual collapse of the dynasty.

**4 A Han official** in his carriage is drawn by slaves. His attendant follows in the rear. During the Han dynasty a large bureaucracy was established to implement the growing powers of the state. The officials, usually nobles, were the product of the Confucian training of the official class. The Confucian ethical code required that the official class should possess wisdom, integrity, righteousness, conscientiousness, loyalty, altruism, love and humanity. Confucius insisted on the importance of education and training: "By nature men are pretty much alike; it is learning and practice that set them apart". The ruler's power could be forfeited.

**5 A bronze axle-cap** dating from the mid-Chou period (seventh century BC). The linchpin that held the wheel in place is decorated with a tiger's head. Chariots from which such axles came would probably be ceremonial, or for state use. Although chariots were also widely used in warfare, they were reduced to an auxiliary role as the raids by the mobile, northern horsemen increased.

an Imperial University was set up for the study of Confucian classics; its students were trained for government and rapidly increased until by the end of the dynasty they numbered nearly 30,000. Provincial schools were also established. Education and the growth of the civil service was greatly assisted by the invention of paper, and ink and brushes replaced sharp writing tools.

Under state patronage the arts revived and the early wealth of the Han dynasty can be seen from their rich tombs [6]. Most of the attainments of this period reflect the needs of a growing state bureaucracy – engineers developed irrigation methods and water clocks, and sundials and seismographs were also invented [9].

Until this time there had been little contact between China and the outside world, but under Han rule the empire was extended. Caravan routes were opened up, including the Old Silk Road which followed a chain of oases skirting the foothills of the Tarim basin. China sent ambassadors abroad along with its ever-popular silk, and products were exchanged as far afield as the outposts of the Greek world. Ideas travelled with the trade, most notable of which was Buddhism [10], introduced from India under the Han and which by the seventh century had become a major force in China.

Under the Ch'in and the Han, China for the first time became a great state. But the mandarins, so carefully picked by scholarly examinations, became corrupt and sided with the great landlords in their oppression of the peasants. The Han dynasty was brought to an end by widespread revolt in AD 220.

### Disintegration of the empire

During the next three and a half centuries there was a succession of short-lived ruling dynasties. It was not until AD 581 that the country was at last reunited under the Sui dynasty. Prosperity increased, taxes were reduced, irrigation improved and public lands were distributed so that each family had some land of its own. But the extravagant second emperor increased taxation. In AD 618 he was assassinated by one of his officers, Li Shih-min (Emperor Li Yüan), who founded the Tang dynasty.

**A rubbing from a Han stone relief** shows a mounted barbarian archer at full gallop. The reins are looped on the horse's neck leaving the archer's hands free to loose off the arrow. Firing from the saddle he had great speed and mobility. Such raiders were a constant threat to the Han.

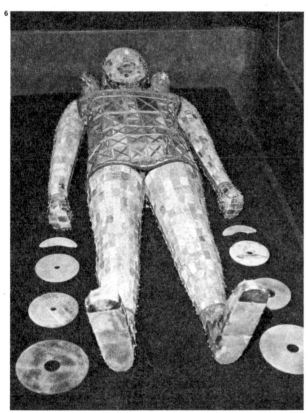

**6 Princess Tou Wan** was buried in this jade suit. She was consort of Prince Liu Sheng, who died some years before her, in 113 BC. Their tombs were accidentally discovered by some soldiers in 1968 in a cliff on the Ling mountain in the province of Hopei. The massive stone doors, which led to the burial chambers, were sealed by molten iron. The tombs were some 12.5m (40ft) square and beneath the collapsed jade suits lay some ash, all that was left of the royal couple. Jade was believed to have magical properties of preserving for eternity anything kept in it. The suits were made in 12 parts so that they totally encased the body.

**7 A celestial horse** of the Han dynasty was excavated in 1969 from a tomb at Wu-wei in Kansu province. Flying horses were a recurrent motif in Han art.

**8 This bridge, at An-chi,** built in AD 610, shows the remarkable sophistication of Chinese engineering, long pre-dating Western achievements. The building of canals and roads, needed for the transport of grain and the maintenance of peace, was fostered under Sui rule. The Grand Canal, built by forced labour, linked the Huang Ho and Yangtze rivers and connected the political centres of the north with the economically important Yangtze region.

**9 The earliest known Chinese seismograph** depicts eight dragons, each holding a ball in its mouth. Around the base of the vessel sit eight toads with open mouths. An earthquake at any point of the compass causes the dragon facing that direction to drop the ball it is holding into the mouth of the toad below, thus indicating the direction of the tremor. This instrument was invented during the Han period by a famous astronomer, mathematician, poet and writer, Chang Heng.

**10 The Buddhist school of sculptors** produced this white marble stele in the early part of the fifth century AD. It shows the Buddha Sakyamuni in a posture denoting him as the bestower of fearlessness. The Buddha is seated under some sal trees surrounded by his disciples and Bodhisattvas, including Ananda his favourite disciple, and Mahakasyapa, who became leader after his death. Above him float goddesses holding garlands of flowers.

# Confucius and Confucianism

Thousands of oracle bones [1] which survive from the Shang dynasty (c. 1600–c. 1030 BC) give archaeologists clues to the form of religion in ancient China. From texts incised on these bones, a picture emerges of a world regulated by spirits of deceased kings (ti), ancestors, nature gods and guardian spirits. The Shang dynasty was overthrown by the Chou (c. 1030–221 BC) who believed that their dynasty had a mandate from heaven to rule the land. Heaven (T'ien) or the "supreme ancestor" (Shang Ti) was believed to govern the universe, fix the seasons, give fertility to men and animals and order the cycle of death and renewal. The emperor was also a priest who performed rituals to ensure the orderly succession of nature.

## The life of Confucius

Documents have survived from the Chou period, which are quoted, and may even have been edited, by Confucius. They form part of the ancient tradition, which includes the complementary forces of yin and yang [Key] and reverence towards heaven and ancestors [5], that Confucius inherited. Elements of Chou religion were transmitted by later Confucian teachers. Confucius is the Latinized form of K'ung Fu-tzu, Master K'ung, who was born in the city state of Lu in northern China in 551 BC and died in 479 BC. Confucius came from an aristocratic family but grew up in comparative poverty and, being disappointed in a political career, found his true work in training young men for public service [2].

Confucius founded his own private school, one of the first in China, and without claiming originality taught what he considered to be the best ancient wisdom. He discussed the arts of life in a city state, the study of old documents, and the Book of Poetry which included ritual hymns of early Chou rulers. But while claiming to preserve or restore earlier tradition, Confucius interpreted the documents in his own way and formulated an ethical and moral system that has influenced China ever since.

When he was about 50, Confucius was given office in the state council – some have claimed that he was prime minister of Lu – but he was dissatisfied with office and he travelled to neighbouring states without success and meeting much hardship. He returned home a disappointed man and spent his last years in teaching and study.

## The literature and teachings of Confucius

Confucius is traditionally credited with authorship, or at least editorship, of the five Confucian classics: the Book of Poetry, the Book of History, the Book of Changes, the Spring and Autumn Annals, and the Book of Rites, but few of these writings can be safely attributed to him. His true teachings are contained in the Analects (Lun-yu), a small book of his sayings recorded by his pupils. Modern specialists consider that some of these chapters are not authentic, but they are traditionally held to be the words of the Master. The Analects teach a way of goodness (jen) which includes courtesy, loyalty and unselfishness. Rulers should seek it, but it is almost a saintly quality. The ideal prince should rule by goodness and govern his conduct by ritual (li). This ritual is not confined to religious worship but is concerned with dress, good manners and personal morality. Confucius

1 **Oracle bones** were inscribed with questions to the spirits about the future. The bones were heated and the resultant cracks were "read".

2 **This painting** on silk from the Ming dynasty (1368–1644) shows Confucius as the ideal teacher, the "uncrowned king". During his life, he was a tutor to the sons of aristocrats and wandered from state to state, hoping to find some rulers who would put his teachings into practice. However, he met only with indifference and on occasion hostility. Indeed Confucius was unrecognized in his own lifetime as a moral teacher except by his small band of disciples.

3 **The tomb of Confucius** can still be seen at Chufu, in the province of Shantung. In front of the tomb stands a stone tablet and altar with candlesticks and incense vessels. The tablet bears a simple inscription: "Ancient Most Holy Teacher".

4 **Court officials in China,** such as this mandarin, even before the beginning of the Christian era were appointed to study the Confucian classics. Eventually the study of these works became universal among the educated classes and examinations in them had to be passed before service to the state could be undertaken or promotion gained; eventually a large Confucian-trained bureaucracy developed.

described this as the Way of the True Gentleman and it is his ideal. He also advocated filial piety (*hsiao*) to parents and ancestors and proposed a hierarchy of relationships: ruler and subject, father and son, older and younger brother, husband and wife, and friend with friend. Confucius believed in the Supreme Being, but held that service to God is meaningless if service to man is neglected.

Confucius and his contemporary Lao Tze (*c.* 604–531 BC) were teachers rather than founders of religions, but their supposed writings became the sacred scriptures of Confucianism and Taoism respectively, and part of the whole culture of China [8]. The teaching of Confucius was continued and extended a century later by Mencius (372–289 BC) and Hsun Tzu. Within a few centuries Confucian teachings became the orthodox doctrines of the state and the guiding lines of the official classes [4].

**The role of Confucius in history**
Confucius was neither a god nor a prophet, and it is often asserted that Confucianism is not a religion, but this statement should be qualified in order to be properly understood.

Before the Christian era, emperors offered sacrifice at the tomb of Confucius [3] – a practice that continued for many centuries. Yet Confucius was not a god with images but an ancestor or great sage, revered as the Teacher of Ten Thousand Generations. Nevertheless, the tradition of Chinese veneration of ancestors and Confucius' own emphasis on filial piety led to ancestral ceremonies being associated with Confucianism. The role of the emperor, and his performance of rituals on behalf of the people [6], further added to the complexities of Confucianism as did the moral and social teaching of Confucius himself.

In modern times Confucius has been alternately attacked as a feudal aristocrat and revered as the greatest teacher of ancient China. The dead are still venerated in China, and much time and money continue to be spent on preserving temples [7] and graves. Modern China, despite the shift away from tradition, brought about by the Marxist ideals practised by its rulers, still continues to be profoundly influenced by Confucianism.

P'an Ku, a mythological figure, here holds the symbols of yin and yang which appear in Confucian thought.

5 Bronze ritual vessels were used in sacrifices and ceremonies from ancient times. These vessels, grouped on or around the altar, bore stylized designs and masks. Their inscriptions describe royal or religious ceremonies, traditions that have influenced Confucian thought.

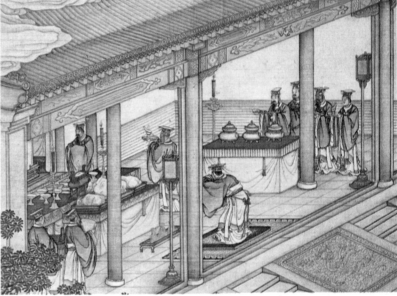

6 The offering of sacrifice and praising of the king for his laws is pictured in this illustration from the *Shih Ching*, a Confucian classic.

7 The Temple of Heaven in Peking, with its three roofs, gold-capped shrine and blue tiles, is one of the finest buildings in China. Here the emperor himself acted as high priest for the people. It is still a national monument today.

8 This fanciful picture illustrates the meeting of three ways of thought in ancient China. Confucius, left, as a scholar, may never have met Lao Tze, shown, right as an old man, and the Buddha, as a, centre, monk, may never have been to China. But Confucian morality and ceremony, Taoist nature mysticism, and Buddhist ascetism and devotion played formative parts in the traditional structure of Chinese religion, art and social life.

# China 618–1368

The Emperor Li Yüan, who founded the T'ang dynasty (618–907), was followed by his son, the Emperor T'ai Tsung (reigned 627–49) under whose rule China became the most powerful and the largest empire on earth. The security China enjoyed in this position encouraged trade with the outside world and brought in a rich horde of goods. The trade also carried scientific ideas westwards beyond the borders of China [8].

## Art, commerce and religion
Chinese arts flourished during the T'ang dynasty [3, 4] particularly poetry, and it produced such poets as Wang Wei, Li Po and Tu Fu. The earliest known printing commenced in this fruitful period and paper money was first issued [1]. Money-lenders thrived in the numerous markets and the growth of commerce brought prosperous trade with merchants from Japan, central Asia, Arabia, Turkey and the Mediterranean.

The emperor was as tolerant of the religions that the foreigners introduced as he was of the merchants themselves. Although a Taoist, he supported Confucianism for reasons of state and treated Buddhists with great respect. Zoroastrian temples and Nestorian Christian churches also existed in the capital Ch'ang-an, modern day Peking.

## Wu Tse-t'ien – an efficient empress
The peace and prosperity that T'ai Tsung brought to the empire was continued by his former concubine, Wu Tse-t'ien, who came to the throne in 683 and ruled China with ruthless ability until she was forced to abdicate in 705 at the age of 82. She was a profound believer in Buddhism and was the first and only female "Son of Heaven". Much of the progress and stability of the country was due to the fact that civil service officials [2] were selected by examinations held under controlled procedures. The empress also permitted women to sit the examinations for government posts.

The main function of the government was the collection of revenue and the promotion of the agriculture on which it mainly depended. For this purpose the country was divided into districts controlled by magistrates. The people were divided into three groups mutually responsible for each other's conduct and for tax payments – encouraging a sense of collective responsibility that is still a feature of China today.

T'ang influence spread far afield, to such an extent that the Japanese capital of Nara was modelled on Ch'ang-an. In the west it clashed with Islam. Muslim armies had advanced, bringing their faith as far as Samarkand and Bokhara. Eventually they conquered central Asia, severing the overland route between China and the West. Trading continued by sea, but the power of China began to wane and as it weakened she became less tolerant of foreigners and their religions. In 845 all foreign religions were proscribed and a ban was placed on Buddhists and their rich but unproductive monasteries [9]. Disastrous revolts and invasions decimated the population and in 907 the T'ang dynasty ended in ruins.

## Five dynasties and the Mongols
The T'ang dynasty was followed by a period called the Five Dynasties between 907 and 960, when, as a Chinese poet said, "States

**1 The *Diamond Sutra*,** the world's oldest printed book, dates from AD 868, nearly six centuries before the first printing in Europe. With gunpowder and the magnetic compass, printing was one of the revolutionary inventions developed by China long before the West. The consequent growth in literacy meant that increasingly the civil service (for which, in theory, recruiting had always been democratic) was drawn from a wider circle of families. Printing facilitated the great expansion of the economy that characterized the Sung dynasty by making possible the introduction of paper money and credit notes.

**2 This T'ang mandarin** was one of the highly educated, privileged and wealthy élite who comprised the mandarinate or civil service. The continuity and resilience of the large state bureaucracy from earliest times is one of the more remarkable features of Chinese history. Its officials, selected by public examination, collected taxes, supervised state projects and the nationalized salt and iron industries (under state control since the Han dynasty) and administered local areas. They also supervised the merchant communities and foreign trade, a despised business largely in the hands of immigrants, but strictly controlled by the state.

**3 A fine example of the elegant work** that was produced in the classical period of Chinese civilization is this white T'ang porcelain spitoon of the late 9th century. It comes from Hsing-chou in the modern province of Hopei and exemplifies the best of the high-fired ceramic ware produced there. Under the T'ang, Ch'ang-an was a thriving capital, one of the cultural centres of the East. Its wealth came partly from the prosperous western trade – Chinese goods were much in demand along the Silk Route. The T'ang is often seen as the artistic complement to the great scientific and technological achievements of the preceding Sui dynasty: the T'ang literary achievement in prose, as in verse, remains unsurpassed.

**4 This silver wine flask** of the T'ang dynasty is a typical piece of Chinese metalwork displaying strong foreign influence. Under this dynasty the capital, Ch'ang-an (now Peking), was probably the most cosmopolitan city in the world and as the empire expanded, merchandise arrived from all quarters. The flask is modelled on the leather water bottle widely used by travelling merchants.

**5 Gunpowder was discovered by Taoist** alchemists in about the 9th century and was first used strictly peacefully. By AD 1000 simple bombs, grenades and rockets were being made, but it was the Mongols who first exploited gunpowder for military ends. They probably used a type of cannon in their campaigns against the Sung troops and certainly employed Chinese engineers. The Mongols captured the Sung fleet which was armed with trebuchets for firing bombs. Although gunpowder was a Chinese invention, it did not have the revolutionary effects on Chinese society that it had in Europe. Illustrated is a Chinese rocket of the Sung dynasty.

rose and fell as candles gutter in the wind". In 960 the Sung dynasty was founded by Chao Kuang-Yin. The war-weary country was at last glad to accept established rule and welcomed the new emperor, who took the title Sung T'ai Tsu. China was still threatened from the north and in 1044 an indemnified peace treaty was concluded with the Hsia, a former tributary kingdom. Gunpowder, which had been discovered during the T'ang period but had been used only for fireworks, was now used to produce the first military rockets in history [5]. The loss of the northern part of the country was partly offset by sea trade, which had been considerably helped by the Chinese discovery of the compass. Large ocean-going junks [6] carried cargoes of tea, silk, porcelain, paintings and other works of art to the East Indies, Africa and India. Another important invention was the abacus [Key], the first calculating machine and one still widely used.

The Sung dynasty ended in a similar manner to the previous empires. Corruption at court and discontent among the people permitted the ascendancy of the latest nomad

empire of the north, the Mongol nation. The new invasion started in the thirteenth century when Genghis Khan (1167–1227) invaded northern China [7]. By 1223 he had conquered most of the country north of the Yellow River and defeated the Hsia, killing about 90 per cent of the population [10]. However, it was not until 1264 that his grandson Kublai Khan (1215–94) was able to move his capital from Karakorum in Mongolia to Peking, and, in 1279 he overcame his former allies the southern Sung.

Mongol rule or, as it was officially known, the Yüan dynasty (1264–1368), was successful in uniting the Chinese and Mongol empires and under Kublai Khan Mongol power reached its peak. But the invaders were eventually overcome. Kublai Khan's successors did not have his ability and the oppression of the Chinese by hordes of foreign officials led to the formation of secret societies and to revolts. In 1356 Nanking fell to a peasant movement led by a monk, Chu Yüan Chang, who finally became first emperor of the new and purely Chinese dynasty, the Ming, in 1368.

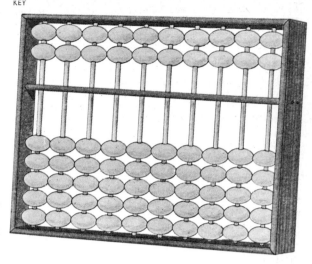

KEY

**The abacus**, introduced during the Sung dynasty, is still widely used today in all areas of commerce. Under the T'ang and Sung the economy underwent a rapid expansion, similar to that which occurred in 17th century Europe, but despite this Chinese society remained essentially feudal.

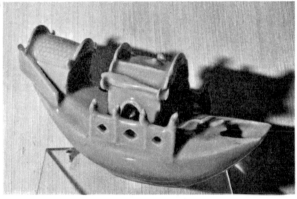

6 **Maritime commerce** expanded greatly during the Sung dynasty. Seagoing junks, such as the porcelain model here, carried cargoes of silk and porcelain to the East Indies, India and the east coast of Africa. Undoubtedly improvements in navigation (which was greatly aided by the invention of the floating compass in AD 1021) contributed to these ambitious trading expeditions.

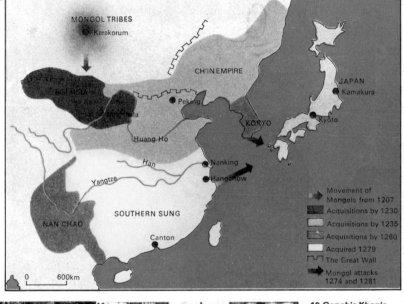

7 **The Mongol conquest of China** was finally completed in 1279. The Sung had previously allied with the Mongols against the Ch'in in the north but were eventually encircled by Mongol conquest.

Movement of Mongols from 1207
Acquisitions by 1230
Acquisitions by 1235
Acquisitions by 1260
Acquired 1279
The Great Wall
Mongol attacks 1274 and 1281

8 **This medical drawing** from a Persian textbook of the 14th century is in fact of Chinese origin and shows the widespread influence of Chinese science.

9 **Buddhist temples** carved from rock caves were features of the Yun-kang and Lung-men periods (in the 5th and 6th centuries AD). The last of them (like the Fen-lai-feng cave temple near Hangchow, of which a detail is shown) were carved in the late 13th century (in the Yüan dynasty). Buddhism in China reached its peak in the middle of the T'ang dynasty, but thereafter the faith was gradually absorbed into traditional Chinese customs and philosophical beliefs.

10 **Genghis Khan's army** capturing a Chinese town is recorded in this painting. The Mongols came to rule almost all of eastern Asia as part of an empire stretching across Asia to Hungary and the Black Sea. After the conquest of the Sung in the south, China was for the first time ruled by foreign invaders. The Chinese-style Yüan dynasty ruled China for less than 100 years. Under the Mongols trade routes across Asia were safeguarded and a variety of religions, including Christianity, were permitted. Kublai Khan was the first Yüan emperor, but after his death Mongol rule was shortlived, ending in a series of rebellions and, finally, expulsion.

# Japan 200 BC – AD 1185

By the first century AD successive waves of settlers from the Asian mainland, coming mostly through Korea, had brought three crucial skills to Japan. The casting of iron and bronze produced more effective tools and weapons. The potter's wheel speeded the production of earthenware. But more important than these was knowledge of rice and irrigation which replaced hunting and fishing with settled agriculture. The resulting Yayoi culture was based on farming villages [2], which had little or nothing by way of large-scale political organization.

## Unification of Japan
In the third century AD a Chinese chronicle, *Wei Chih*, described Japan as a country of more than "100 communities" that had been unified by Queen Pimiko. Some clan (Uji) leaders had sufficient power to organize the construction of vast chambered tombs; one such family claimed descent from the sun goddess, and emerged as head of a loose confederation of powerful clans.

By the sixth century this embryonic Yamato Imperial House [Key] had organized Japanese intervention in Korean civil conflicts. This brought contact with Chinese ideas and skills which swept down the Korean peninsula, leading to a second and more radical transformation of Japanese life.

Buddhism [3], Confucianism, medicine, astronomy, Chinese-style architecture and the Chinese script all entered Japan in the sixth and seventh centuries [1]. Scholars travelled to China [5] and soon Japan's central rulers sought to model their state upon the bureaucracy of China's T'ang Empire. In 592 Shotoku Taishi [4] became regent and began a programme of spreading Buddhism and widening the power of the Yamato Imperial House.

In 646, measures known as the Taika Reforms included the imperial control of rice land, systematic taxation, and a nationwide network of imperial officials. At the centre of the new state was to be a Chinese-style capital with palaces, temples and broad straight avenues linking public buildings. China's system of civil service examinations was never reproduced, however. Powerful provincial families remained remarkably independent and a conscription system proved inefficient. Yet the legal codes of 702 were detailed and far-reaching and Heijo (Nara) contained impressive structures that still survive.

At the close of the eighth century the political influence of Buddhism had become so great that one priest, Dokyo, attempted to capture the imperial throne. Partly in response to this danger the court set up a new capital at Heian (Kyōto) in 794.

## Rise of Fujiwara
After 50 years of stable administration, events at court produced new threats to imperial authority. The Fujiwara family had been loyal state servants throughout earlier centuries but now they used intermarriage and masterly intrigue to dominate palace appointments. In 857 Fujiwara Yoshifusa became grand minister. Soon after, his grandson was made child-emperor with himself as regent. Later Fujiwara remained regents after infant emperors reached maturity, and throughout the eleventh century they wielded overwhelming power.

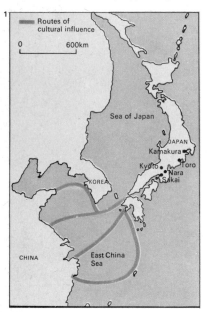

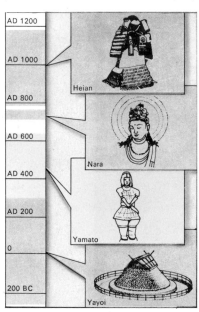

1 **Routes by which Chinese** culture and Buddhism entered Japan were established by the 9th and 10th centuries. Contacts dated from c. AD 400 when the King of Paekche, in Korea, sent scholars to Japan with Confucian writings. Koreans brought Buddhist writings and sculptures in the 6th century and Japan then began sending official embassies and students to T'ang China.

2 **A house of the Yayoi period** (250 BC – AD 300) was reconstructed at Toro in the suburbs of Shizuoka where the foundations exist of 11 houses, granaries and irrigation channels for paddies.

3 **A mural painting of a Buddhist deity** in the Kondo of Hōryūji temple, Nara, is in the style of contemporary T'ang painting of the 7th or 8th century and reveals the Indian origins of T'ang and Korean Buddhism. Only fragments of these murals remain, but in China no similar works survive at all.

4 **Shotoku Taishi** (571–621) made a profound study of Buddhism and founded such important temples as Hōryūji in Nara. He also tried to introduce Confucian ideas into the Japanese state and proclaimed a code of government in 604. The painting shows him in Chinese-style robes and is in the manner of a Chinese imperial portrait.

The Heian capital was the scene of outstanding cultural achievements. Whereas the dominant arts of Nara had been in the Chinese T'ang style, the new regime severed links with the continent and developed artistic styles that were authentic expressions of Japanese sensibilities. Architecture became less flamboyant and more refined. Vivid picture scrolls illustrated historical and literary themes. A new phonetic script supplemented Chinese characters, and permitted more supple forms of expression [7]. *The Tale of Genji* (c. 1010–20), Japan's most famous novel, was written by a court lady of the Heian capital.

**Warrior families and court life**
Parallel with the weakening of imperial authority came the rise of provincial families with new sources of power. To maintain law and order and combat northern aborigines, these lords increased their armies and became increasingly oblivious of imperial control. Their independent estates (*shoen*) paid little to the capital but stimulated the economic development of other territories.

These new centres of agriculture and organization produced leaders with a practical military ethic indifferent to many of the pretensions of court life.

In the eleventh century courtiers recognized the might of this new class and invited the powerful Taira and Minamoto families to aid them in suppressing dangerous rebellions. The Fujiwara may have hoped to control these robust warriors [6] but soon the Taira had replaced them as the effective masters of palace and throne. Taira Kiyomori used force and intrigue to overpower his rivals and in 1180 made his infant grandson emperor. After 20 years of dominance the Taira appeared unchallenged in the capital, but military power was now the only determinant of politics and the Minamoto rebelled against the new overlords of Heian Kyo.

From 1180 to 1185, these two families and their coalitions were embroiled in nationwide warfare. By 1184, the land forces of the Taira were annihilated and a year later their navy was destroyed. Now the Minamoto [8] were masters of Japan. Warriors ruled from their capital at Kamakura.

A *haniwa* is a hollow pottery figure, designed to house a spirit, which was often placed on the burial mounds of clan leaders and members of the imperial family. This figurine of an armoured warrior comes from the Yamato period (c. AD 300–c. 625); figures also exist in the form of animals, buildings and boats, as well as men and women. The idea of an anthropomorphic grave-statue was native to the Shinto tradition; when Buddhist craftsmen came to influence the Japanese artists, they brought refinements, but not the basic idea. Japanese *haniwa* differ from Chinese statues by having a hollow "eye" allegedly the entrance for the spirit within.

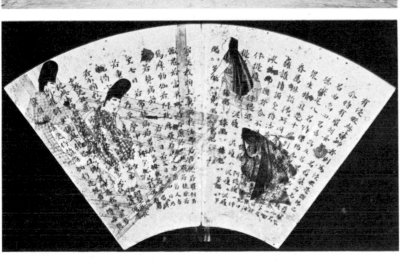

**5 Naindaimon, an imposing Chinese-style** structure, is the main gateway to Todaiji Temple. The style of the gateway reflects the architectural trend towards strength and simplicity that typified the Kamakura period and indicates the wide cultural links Japan developed with T'ang China.

**6 Japanese armour** of the Kamakura period shows the artistry associated with the late Heian period and the rise of a provincial military class that demanded very high skills of workmanship. Warriors often donated fine armour to important shrines. Their personal code emphasized simple dignity and courage.

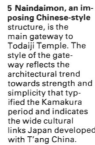

**7 This hand-painted copy of a *sutra*** (Buddhist scripture) dates from the late Heian period. It was believed that copying *sutras* by hand was one way to gain re-birth in Paradise. This was a feature of the Buddhist cult – the Jodo cult – which arose in the late 12th century and laid great stress on afterlife.

**8 Minamoto Yoritomo** (1147–99) led the armies that destroyed the power of the Taira family in 1185. This conflict, immortalized in *The Tale of Genji*, inspired many important works of literature. Shown here in formal dress, Yoritomo set up his capital in his own territory, far from the imperial capital.

# The rise of medieval Western Christendom

The barbarians who destroyed the Western Empires in the fifth and sixth centuries were either pagans or Arian heretics who denied the unity of God the Father and Son and violently rejected Roman Christianity. By the sixth century Europe needed to be reconverted. Missionary activity from Rome followed the growth of Benedictine monasticism and a rejuvenation of the papacy. St Benedict (c. 480–c. 547) lived in Italy when it was ruled by the Arian Ostrogoths. About the year 500 he had begun a hermetical life at Subiaco with emphasis on the performance of the liturgy and on a community life of moderate self-denial. In c. 529 he founded the Abbey of Monte Cassino, one of the bulwarks of Christianity and civilization in early medieval Europe. He also wrote a Rule for his monks that was humane and ensured the durability of his ideas and institutions [Key].

## The Papacy – spiritual and temporal

The medieval papacy was founded by Pope Gregory the Great (c. 540–604) [2], who was a firm supporter and propagator of monasticism. He became pope in 590, a time

when the power of the Byzantine governors of Italy was rapidly declining and the Arian Lombards threatened to reduce the Papacy to little more than a Lombard bishopric. Gregory himself managed the Church estates in central and southern Italy, organized the defences of Rome, appointed governors of the leading Italian cities and in 592–3 made peace with the Lombards without reference to the Eastern Emperor. The Papacy henceforth existed as a temporal as well as a spiritual power in the West.

The Franks were the first of the barbarians to be converted when Clovis (465–511), founder of the Merovignian monarchy, was baptized, probably in 497.

Gregory dispatched St Augustine to England in 597 with monks from his own Roman monastery to begin the reconversion of Britain. But Britain was reconverted from two different directions because the Irish, who had remained Christian after the mission of St Patrick in 444 [7], had sent St Columba to Scotland c. 563 to found the monastery of Iona and convert the Picts. In c. 635 St Aidan went from Iona to Lindisfarne to convert the

English in Northumbria. There the Roman and the Irish traditions met and the result was the most advanced and flourishing culture of seventh- and eighth-century Europe [3].

## Anglo-Irish influence

The Irish also penetrated deep into mainland Europe [4]. In 590 St Columban established monasteries at Anagratum and Luxeuil in the Vosges. Expelled from Burgundy for criticism of the behaviour of the court, he went to Italy to found the monastery of Bobbio, which set an example that was the most important impetus to the conversion of the Lombards. These and other Irish monasteries reintroduced the Catholic faith and brought with them their libraries, both classical and Christian, which had remained safe in Ireland during the migration period. The influence of the Irish on European culture can hardly be overemphasized.

Frisia and Germany were converted from Britain in the eighth century. Willibrord (c. 658–739), the apostle of the Frisians, was a Northumbrian who had joined a monastery in Ireland. Boniface (c. 680–754), an

**1 Orthodox Christianity** in the later Roman world reached its greatest extent c. 600. North Africa, Rome and Ravenna were reconquered from the Arian Goths by Justinian in the mid-6th century. In the north, the Irish had been converted about 430, the Franks in 496, the Burgundians in 516 and the Visigoths in 589. The Anglo-Saxon missions began in 597. The new Christian unity of the Mediterranean, however, lasted only until the Arabs in the 7th century conquered an empire from Syria to Spain including three of the five original patriarchates, Antioch, Jerusalem and Alexandria.

Map labels: IRISH, DANES, ANGLO-SAXONS, BRITISH, SAXONS, BRETONS, AVARS, FRANKS, LOMBARDS, BURGUNDIANS, BASQUES, Rome, VISIGOTHS, Byzantium (Constantinople), BERBERS, EASTERN ROMAN EMPIRE, Antioch, Jerusalem, Alexandria, ARABS

0   500 km

Majority are Christian by 600
+ Patriarchates
Eastern Roman Empire

**2 Gregory I** (centre) was elected pope at a time when Rome was under strong pressure from the Arian Lombards. But his energy, dedication and grasp of administration enabled him to give the Roman Church a status it had never previously enjoyed. He established the principle of papal authority in temporal affairs both by his diplomatic initiatives and by asserting control of the "patrimony of Peter" which later grew into the papal states. By sending Augustine to England in 597, he made sure that the Church in Britain would look to Rome rather than Byzantium. Gregorian chant is named after him.

**3 The Ruthwell Cross**, possibly either a mass or preaching cross, is the finest monument of Northumbrian art during the British cultural renaissance of the 7th century.

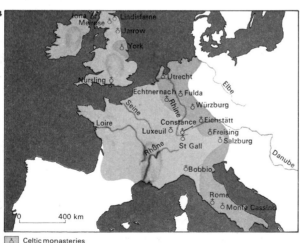

Map labels: Iona, Lindisfarne, Melrose, Jarrow, York, Nursling, Utrecht, Echternach, Fulda, Würzburg, Luxeuil, Constance, Eichstätt, Loire, Seine, Rhine, Freising, Salzburg, St Gall, Rhône, Elbe, Danube, Bobbio, Rome, Monte Cassino

0   400 km

Celtic monasteries and their influence
Anglo-Saxon monasteries and their influence

**4 Many European monasteries** were founded by missionaries from Ireland where Christianity and classical learning had been preserved. Others were founded by their Anglo-Saxon converts.

**5 The Gatehouse of Lorsch Abbey**, in Hessen, West Germany, is an example of Charlemagne's impressive programme of new church building.

Englishman, continued the Frisian mission in 716, and in 719 was appointed by Gregory II to convert the Germans. He laid the foundations for the Carolingian Church and was martyred in Frisia in 754 [6].

The Arian Visigoths in Spain were converted to Christianity at the Third Council of Toledo in 589 (although Muslim invaders were soon to dominate the country). In northeastern Europe, conversions were delayed longer. Sweden and Denmark were only temporarily converted by St Anskar in the ninth century, Poland and Hungary in the late tenth and Norway at sword point by St Olav early in the eleventh century.

In the meantime the emperor of the Franks, Charlemagne (742–814), had imported Anglo-Irish missionaries to establish the basis of Carolingian Christianity, backed by energetic church building [5]. The late eighth century also saw an alliance between the pope and the Frankish emperors against the Lombards and the creation of the idea of the Holy Roman Empire. Anglo-Saxons, Germans and Franks all visited Rome, accepted the lead of the Papacy and bought relics for their native dioceses [8].

The rise of the Holy Roman Empire saw a marked decline in the standards of the Church. There was widespread simony (the selling of ecclesiastical appointments), monasteries became rich and lax, and the Papacy itself was corrupt.

## Church reform

Reform of the Church began at the house of Cluny, a Benedictine monastery in Burgundy [9]. Under Abbot Odo the Benedictine Rule was strictly enforced. The spirit of Cluniac reform permeated all aspects of Western Christianity, culminating in the pontificates of Leo IX [10] and Gregory VII (1073–85).

In 1054, the last year of Leo IX's pontificate, the Western Church broke with the Eastern. The Patriarch of Constantinople would not accept the universal supremacy of Rome, nor the people of the East the liturgy and practice of the Roman Church. Leo IX and the Emperor sought a political settlement between East and West to thwart their common enemy, the Normans, but the rift in religious practice was too wide to heal.

The Benedictine Rule was the cornerstone of the early medieval Church. It contained strict yet reasonable regulations for monastic life, in contrast to the ascetic excesses of Eastern monasticism. The Rule stressed the value of religious community life, humility, self-denial and the performance of the liturgy. For 600 years after Benedict's death in c. 547 there was no other monastic rule in the West. Its followers have included 20 popes and many pioneer missionaries. The learning and education of Benedictine monasteries in the Dark Ages also provided the only training for administrators faced with the increasingly complex problems of government.

6 The story of the martyrdom of St Ursula is the most famous of the martyrdom legends from the barbarian period. The saint, together with her companions, was murdered by the Huns in Cologne in 454 still protesting her virginity and her faith. Her triumphal funeral is shown in a painting by Vittore Carpaccio (1490). The cult of local martyrs became increasingly important during the reconversion period, at which time the supposed number of St Ursula's companions was increased to 11,000 by a clerical error. A notable missionary martyr was St Boniface, who went to Frisia and was murdered at Dokkum in the mid-8th century with 30 other monks.

7 St Patrick, a Romano-Britain is credited with converting Ireland between 430 and 461. Ireland was the only country to escape the invasions of the 5th and 6th centuries. Christianity was preserved, along with many manuscripts containing both secular Latin and Christian literature. Irish missionary impetus was a prime factor in the re-education of Europe but its loosely ordered yet ascetic monasticism conflicted with the usages of the Roman Church after the reforms of Gregory the Great. This conflict was resolved at the Synod of Whitby (664) and led to period of peace which saw the creation of a British culture unrivalled in the rest of Europe.

8 Relics became an essential part of the furnishings of every church in the 9th century. They were housed in the greatest magnificence, as in the High Altar of St Ambrose, Milan, decorated by the German Volfinius about 835.

9 The Abbey of Cluny saw the start of the reform of the Benedictine system with a strict adherence to the Rule and stress on the splendour of the liturgy. This is the third church at Cluny dedicated to these ideals.

10 Leo IX, who was pope from 1049–54, was an ardent supporter of Cluniac reform. He began to improve papal standards.

# The barbarian invasions

"Barbarian" was a term of abuse used by the Romans to describe anyone outside the Mediterranean civilization of Greece and Rome. Since the time of Caesar the frontiers of the Roman Empire had been menaced by invading Germanic peoples, many of whom were conquered, after which they settled as fairly peaceable – though armed – colonists.

The frontier that extended from the North Sea to the Black Sea via the Rhine and Danube was under renewed pressure in the fourth century from a fresh wave of hostile German peoples: Franks, Saxons, Burgundians, Visigoths, Ostrogoths, Sueves, Alans, Vandals and Gepids [Key]. Their societies were based on the clan and their tribes were relatively small in number, ranging from about 25,000 to 120,000; all able-bodied men were soldiers and farming was done by slaves. Their armies, supported by a powerful cavalry, proved too strong for the last of the Roman legions. The barbarians were converts to Arianism, a heresy abhorrent to orthodox Christians because it denied Christ's divinity. The westward pressure of these peoples at the end of the fourth century was due to overpopulation and shortage of food as well as the arrival of the Huns, a fierce nomadic Mongol people from central Asia who came to pillage rather than to settle.

## Eastern Roman Empire

The Eastern Roman Empire was threatened by barbarians on all fronts [2]. In Asia Minor it was under pressure first from the Sassanian Persians and later, after 622, from the rapid expansion of Islam. On the Danube and in the Balkans the threat of the Germans and Huns was ever present.

After the death of Theodosius the Great in 395 the Visigoths rose in Lower Moesia under Alaric (c. 370–410). The Eastern emperor Arcadius persuaded them to move west where Alaric was made Master of the Soldiers in Illyricum (coastal region of modern Yugoslavia); it was therefore as a Roman general that Alaric led a German invasion of Italy in 401–3. He invaded Italy again in 408 and in 410 captured Rome.

In 406 vast armies of Vandals, Sueves and Alans crossed the Rhine into Gaul which was already troubled by internal conflicts in the imperial administration. External attack and internal conflict led to the withdrawal of the last legions from Britain where the Angles, Saxons and Jutes were now free to invade. The Vandals ravaged Gaul, moved into Spain in 408 and, in 429 under the leadership of Gaiseric (c. 390–477), accomplished the most crippling blow of all to the Western Empire – the invasion of Africa. In 442 Gaiseric was recognized as the independent ruler of North Africa on which Rome depended for the bulk of her food.

## The first German empires

By 416 the Burgundians in Gaul had established the first German kingdoms within the old imperial frontiers and with the Franks scattered across northern France the pattern of post-Roman western Europe was beginning to emerge. But any hopes of peace were shattered by the Huns, who for nearly a century had been stable in what is now Hungary, threatening east and west alike and building up an enforced alliance of subject German peoples. In 450 the empire refused to buy off the Huns with any more gold so, led

**1 At the time of their invasion** of Gaul in the 5th century, all freemen within the Frankish tribe were warriors. The Frankish army was mainly infantry rather than cavalry. Their most redoubtable weapon was the battleaxe, the *fran-* *cisca* [1], although they also fought with a cutting sword [2] and bows and arrows [3]. Because metal was scarce the round shield [4] was made of wood covered with stretched hide. They wore close-fitting tunics [5] and plumed helmets [6].

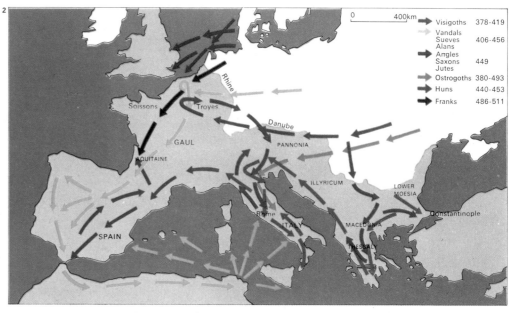

**2 A chaotic wandering of barbarians** within the confines of the Western Empire followed the collapse of the Rhine and Danube frontier. The barbarians, although quite unco-ordinated, had four targets: Constantinople, Macedonia and Thrace; Italy; northeastern Roman Gaul; and North Africa, the granary of the Western Empire. Without any preconceived plan of attack, the citadels of the empire fell according to a "domino" pattern. Westward pressure was intensified as more tribes arrived from the east, in particular the Huns. The crucial blow to the empire was the Vandal invasion of Africa which, by 429, left Rome surrounded and the Vandals controlling the western Mediterranean.

| Visigoths | 378-419 |
| Vandals Sueves Alans | 406-456 |
| Angles Saxons Jutes | 449 |
| Ostrogoths | 380-493 |
| Huns | 440-453 |
| Franks | 486-511 |

**3 The barbarians** gradually formed independent kingdoms in the west. They expropriated some property but left much of the Roman landed aristocracy and administration intact. Roman and Teutonic societies existed side by side in an uneasy balance, the military strength of the invaders bringing the defensive capacity that defeated the Huns in 452. The Huns remained nomadic and never founded a lasting kingdom. The barbarian kingdoms were the origins of the national boundaries of medieval western Europe.

Kingdom of Visigoths
Kingdom of the Franks
Kingdom of the Burgundians
Kingdom of the Ostrogoths
Kingdom of the Vandals

by Attila (c. 406–53), they invaded Gaul. The Huns, with their powerful horses and incredible stamina, were considered almost invincible and were only halted near Troyes in 452 when the Franks and the Visigoths joined forces with the Romans. Attila turned south and menaced Rome, but died in 453 [7]. The destruction was widespread but the Germans had saved the legacy of Roman civilization in the west.

The Franks gradually consolidated their power in Gaul. Under Clovis I (465–511) they created a united and non-heretical Christian Gaul (Council of Orleans, 511) and Clovis was recognized by the Eastern emperor as the ruler of a country that roughly corresponds to modern France. He was baptised following his victory over the Alemanni.

After the deposition of Augustulus, the last Western emperor, in 476, the German soldier Odoacer (died 493) became the ruler of Italy. Meanwhile the Ostrogoths had left the Black Sea area and after the downfall of the Huns had moved into Pannonia and thence to Illyricum. Led by Theoderic from 471 they ravaged Macedonia and Thessaly

and in 487 marched on Constantinople. Theoderic was bought off by the emperor Zeno, who persuaded him to go to Italy and overthrow Odoacer. Theoderic defeated Odoacer on the River Adda in 490 and after a three-year siege of Ravenna Odoacer gave in. Theoderic assassinated him and established the Ostrogothic kingdom in Italy [8].

**The Eastern Empire**
The Eastern Empire averted most dangers from the Germans and the Huns by passing them over to the west, but the Balkans were ruined and depopulated and the Bulgars were able to threaten Constantinople in 493 and 499. In the east the emperor Justinian (c. 482–565) fought for 35 years against the Persian king Chosroes (reigned 531–79). The balance of power in the Mediterranean was temporarily reversed by Justinian's reconquest of Africa (533–4) and Italy (536–54); yet all this effort was wasted when, in the following century, the Arabs overran all imperial lands from the Middle East to North Africa, besieging Constantinople annually until their fleet's defeat there in 718.

KEY

1 Jutes
2 Angles
3 Saxons
4 Franks
5 Burgundians
6 Thuringians
7 Sueves
8 Vandals
9 Ostrogoths
10 Visigoths
11 Gepids
12 Alans
13 Huns

Barbarian tribes c.395
Tribes not invading the Roman Empire 395-511

**The positions of the barbarian tribes** to the east of the Roman frontier along the Rhine and Danube rivers changed constantly. The pressure on Rome's increasingly ill-defended northeastern frontier was kept up by the arrival of new warring peoples who were impelled relentlessly westwards from central Asia by hunger and nomadic life style. The Huns invaded Italy in 452.

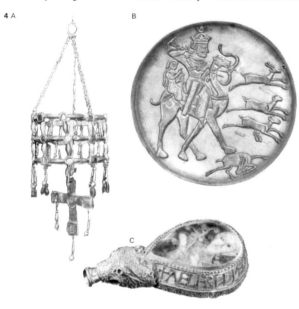

4 **The highest achievement** of barbarian art was in its metalwork. The 6th-century silver-gilt dish from Sassanian Persia [B] was the equal of any contemporary east Roman metalwork. In the west, work ranged from the sternly Teutonic Visigothic crown [A] to the Anglo-Saxon Alfred Jewel [C]. This is made of continental cloisonné enamel and has classical motifs and a figure of Spring (or Christ).

5 **The Mausoleum of Theoderic** is the tomb of the first king of Ostrogothic Italy. It was built about 530 and is circular in shape, surmounted by a monolithic dome of Istrian stone weighing 477 tonnes.

6 **The Breviary of Alaric II**, king of the Visigoths, an illuminated detail of which is shown here, is a collection of Roman law. Alaric's capital was Toulouse and his kingdom stretched into Spain. The breviary, which was completed in 506, is an important source of late Roman law and is the result of an established Arian German barbarian king seeking to codify and reconcile his native tribal law with that of the lands of the old Roman Empire over which he found himself ruling.

7 **Raphael's fresco** of "The Repulse of Attila" (1513) shows Attila and his Huns confronted by Pope Leo I, protected only by the miraculous intervention of St Peter and St Paul. Attila, repulsed by the Romans and Visigoths near Troyes in 452 and by Leo in Italy, retired to Pannonia and died on his wedding night of a burst blood vessel – four events which saved the legacy of Roman civilization.

8 **German barbarians**, when converted to Christianity, adopted the Arian heresy that denied the divinity of Christ. Theoderic, having established the capital of his Italian kingdom at Ravenna, built an Arian cathedral and baptistery. The mosaics in the baptistery show the formalized presentation of the Baptism of Christ with the Apostles moving towards an altar-throne; a scene, the Etimasia, taken from the fourth chapter of the Apocalypse. The existence of Arian and Catholic buildings side by side in the same city exemplifies the spirit of co-existence that prevailed in Theoderic's Italy.

# Anglo-Saxon settlement

In the course of the fifth and sixth centuries the once-unified Roman province of Britain was split into a collection of petty kingdoms, barbarian Saxon in the south and east, Celtic in the west and north. The Venerable Bede (673–735) [Key], was clear about the origins of the barbarian invaders and the date of their arrival. They came, he said, in about 450 from three tribes, the Angles, Saxons and Jutes. Modern archaeological research has confirmed that the main regions from which distinct groups of settlers came were indeed Angeln, part of Schleswig and southern Denmark, and Lower Saxony, between the Elbe and Weser river mouths [2]. The identity and origins of the Jutes remains more problematic. Peoples not mentioned by Bede, including Frisians and Franks, also played some part. None of these peoples appears to have retained a separate cultural identity for long after their arrival.

## The earliest Saxon settlements

Contrary to Bede's opinion, there were already Saxons living in Britain before the Roman withdrawal. Sea pirates, known generally as "Saxons", were raiding the eastern and southern coasts of Britain throughout the fourth century [1]. By the late fourth century it was common practice in the Roman army to employ mercenary bands under their own leaders, who fought, often against peoples related to themselves, in return for land and money.

There are large cemeteries in eastern England which contain thousands of cremated burials, many in pots similar to those at equivalent sites of the fourth and fifth centuries on the Continent [3]. Mucking, a village in Essex near Tilbury on the Thames, where occupation began early [7], is a site of some strategic importance, where Saxons would not have been able to settle so early without a position of some power, whether won by treaty or force.

When the regular Roman army withdrew from Britain in 410 the British leaders had to look after their own defence but continued the practice of employing mercenaries. Gildas, a Celtic monk who lived in the sixth century, wrote in graphic but perhaps exaggerated terms of the result of this policy: the barbarians rebelled against their employers and "fire and slaughter spread from sea to sea over the entire island". The story, recounted by Bede, of Hengist and Horsa, mercenaries who rose up against Vortigern who had hired them to protect Kent from the Picts, may have been a significant, although not the only, incident in this rebellion.

## The survival of Romano-British society

Gildas was writing within living memory of the events he described, in a period of peace established after a British revival and defeat of the Anglo-Saxons, perhaps under the leadership of Arthur. Frequently the penetration must have been peaceful and gradual. As late as the mid-fifth century the native British had time to indulge in religious dispute, and St Germanus had to visit them twice from Gaul to combat the Pelagian heresy (which denied original sin). Despite the general decay of town life, he visited Verulamium (St Albans), a city in eastern Britain, which contained a functioning water system well into the fifth century.

During the invasions, many of the British

1 The "Saxon Shore" forts, shown here in a Roman map, were part of a system built in the 3rd century to protect the south and east coasts of Roman Britain from raids by barbarians. Some of these forts may have been manned by Saxons who stayed after the Roman withdrawal.

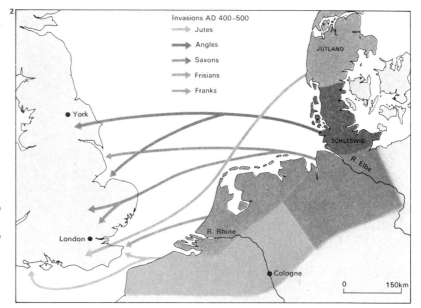

2 The 5th century invasions came from the far coasts of the North Sea. The Saxons were from Germany between the Elbe and Weser rivers, the Angles from Denmark and the Franks from the Rhineland. Other tribes came from Frisia. They had been driven from their homes by tribes from the east.

Invasions AD 400–500
→ Jutes
→ Angles
→ Saxons
→ Frisians
→ Franks

York · JUTLAND · SCHLESWIG · R. Elbe · London · R. Rhine · Cologne

0      150km

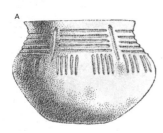

3 Early Anglo-Saxon pots survive in large numbers because they were used for the burial of cremated bodies. They were often clumsy and badly fired, although elaborately decorated. The Continental ancestors of the settlers also used these pots, so they can now aid in tracing the various tribes in Britain. The Continental Angles made pots with linear grooved patterns [A], while the Saxons preferred bizarre bossed and stamped decoration [B]. In England these styles became mixed, suggesting a quick loss of separate tribal identity. With the spread of Christianity, burial rather than cremation in pots became the rule. Use of the Romano-British potter's wheel died out by 500.

4 An Anglo-Saxon ship found at Sutton Hoo, Suffolk, in 1939, was the cenotaph or memorial of a great king, and contained much glorious jewellery and many domestic utensils. It is not certain which king the ship commemorated, but he may have been Raedwald of East Anglia. It dates from before the final acceptance of Christianity in that kingdom (c. 650). The invaders were sea-faring people, and ships played an important role in their mythology and religion. The Sutton Hoo ship, which was almost 29m (89ft) in length, is the best example of the boats they used. It was primarily a rowing boat, but may have had a sail. It probably had an elaborate carved figure head on the prow.

aristocracy may have emigrated or been killed, yet it is unlikely that all the existing population could have been slaughtered. Enslavement or absorption through marriage with the invaders were more likely. It is significant that the Anglo-Saxon language absorbed very few Celtic words other than names of natural features; but the Anglo-Saxon word for "Briton" also meant "slave". The barbarian invaders of France, by comparison, were not sufficiently numerous to eliminate the language, which became an amalgam of Germanic speech and Latin. But the distribution of placenames with a British origin suggests that the bulk of the Saxon settlers arrived and settled in the eastern half of the country. Anglo-Saxon penetration to the west was slow, and the invaders may have lived alongside the Britons, instead of displacing them, as was once thought.

**The Anglo-Saxon kingdoms**
The small warrior bands and groups of migrants, organized by family and clan, evolved gradually into petty kingdoms, of which seven developed into stable entities [9].

These kingdoms have given the name "Heptarchy" to Anglo-Saxon England from the sixth to the ninth century. Frontiers were not constant, kingship was personal rather than hereditary, and the balance of power was constantly changing. The most powerful king at any one time might be known as the "bretwalda", a name meaning perhaps "British leader" or "power wielder". The bretwalda had an informal power over the other kings. Raedwald (died 625), King of East Anglia, who was perhaps commemorated in the great ship burial at Sutton Hoo [4], may have been such a bretwalda.

Until the seventh century the Saxons were pagan. Their conversion to Christianity [6] resulted from two missions, the official Roman one by St Augustine (died 604), who arrived in Kent in 597, and the Celtic monastic one from Ireland [8], which won most favour in Northumbria. Differences in practice between these two, especially concerning the calculation of the date of Easter, led to dispute, which was resolved for Northumbria at the Synod of Whitby in 664 in favour of the Roman tradition.

KEY

**The Venerable Bede** was a monk who wrote the best surviving account of the early Anglo-Saxon period. Working in the early 8th century, he aimed to tell the story of the Church in England. He tried to be more critical of the sources he used (such as earlier chronicles as well as legends and hagiographies) than previous writers and is considered to have been the first English historian. Writing at Jarrow in his native kingdom of Northumbria, he tended to regard Celtic Christianity as heretical, but he admired its great men, especially St. Columba (521–97) who brought Irish Christianity to Scotland, and St Aidan (d. 651), bishop of Lindisfarne.

**5 East Anglia** was settled earlier and more densely than any other region, being the part of Britain closest to the invaders' homelands. From the pattern of 5th-century burial grounds in England it appears that the immigrants sailed up the rivers and settled along the valleys and Roman roads. Some invaders sailed up the Wash and moved both south and north. Cemeteries at North Elmham in Norfolk and Loveden Hill in Lincoln contain thousands of burials, and show that by the mid-5th century much of the population was already barbarian. The kingdom of East Anglia soon became wealthy as can be seen by the treasures found in the Sutton Hoo ship burial of c. 625.

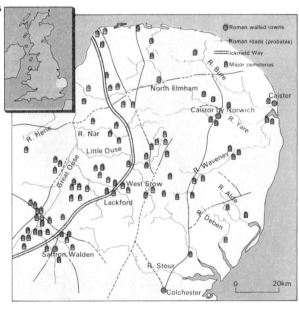

Roman walled towns
Roman roads (probable)
Icknield Way
Major cemeteries

North Elmham
Caister
Caistor by Norwich
R. Bure
R. Nene
R. Nar
R. Yare
Little Ouse
R. Waveney
Great Ouse
West Stow
R. Alde
Lackford
R. Deben
Saffron Walden
R. Stour
Colchester
0    20km

**6 The Franks Casket,** a small whalebone box, was made in Northumbria c. 700. Its decorative carvings include pagan and Christian myths, and its inscriptions are in both Latin script and Germanic runes. This panel shows the Adoration of the Magi and the story of Weland the Smith from Germanic mythology. The Anglo-Saxons often added Christian elements to their existing myths, as can be most clearly seen in the epic poem *Beowulf*, probably written after 700. But the Church was important in secular affairs by the 7th century, and many kings gave land and wealth to monasteries.

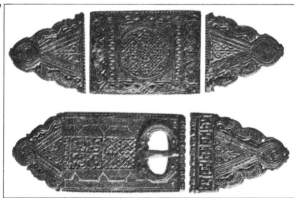

**7 This bronze gilt belt-set** was found in a grave in Mucking, Essex. It belongs to a type current in the late Roman army but is in a style found only in England, indicating there was a close relationship between the barbarians and the Roman army.

**8 St Cuthbert** (d. 687) was one of the best-loved Irish or Celtic churchmen of Anglo-Saxon England. He is seen here being presented with a book by King Athelstan. Although he had a Celtic training, he supported the decisions of the Synod of Whitby which ended the confusion over the date of Easter. A holy man known for his piety and humility, he was bishop of Lindisfarne. Miracles were said to occur at his tomb, now in Durham cathedral. His history was recorded by the Venerable Bede.

**9 The kingdoms of the Heptarchy** were often in conflict with one another and sometimes sought help from the Celtic kingdoms of Gwynnedd in Wales or Dalriada in Scotland. The centre of power altered quickly.

Anglo-Saxon kingdoms
British/Celtic kingdoms
Northumbria
Mercia
East Anglia
Essex
Wessex
Kent
Sussex
0    100km

# The Celts and Christianity

Prior to the Roman conquest, much of western and central Europe was dominated by Celtic tribes of Indo-European origin. Skilled in the use of iron, which they introduced into northern Europe, the Celts flourished from about 700 BC. They achieved a high level of material culture and also developed a highly complex religion and mythology which formed an integral part of their society. Celtic art reflected the importance of religion, and geometrical or magic symbols and cult animals are repeated on objects from all periods of Celtic history – pagan and Christian alike.

## The finest phase of Celtic culture

Celtic culture reached its finest achievements during the La Tène period which began in about 500 BC and, in Europe, lasted until its absorption by Rome. Information about the Celts of this period is obtained both from archaeological evidence and also from Greek and Roman authors. They have recorded details of tribes, kings, nobles and place-names, all of which give important information about the Celtic languages, which have survived in a modified but recognizable form in Britain, Ireland and Brittany.

The Celts did not commit their religious beliefs and traditional learning to writing until after the arrival of Christianity in Ireland in the fifth century. The comments of the classical writers of the time when Rome's armies destroyed the Celtic world in Europe therefore have a unique importance. Almost fanatical in their religious fervour, the pagan Celts were dominated by powerful, highly aristocratic priests, the Druids, who often combined the role of king with their priesthood. Tribal in social organization, the Celts also possessed the oldest and most complex legal system in Europe. Every man had his rights, and crimes from murder to the smallest wrong were listed and categorized.

## Celtic spiritual tradition

The Celts were highly conservative in matters of tradition. Non-literate, they had a complex oral tradition and were natural scholars with a deep admiration for intellectual power and a passionate love of words. The beauty of nature is depicted in some of their richest poems; its appeal to the Celts came at a time when their neighbours had little care for such intense spirituality.

It is understandable then that Christianity had such an early and widespread success in Ireland, the only country in western Europe to be totally untouched by Roman arms. Ireland fell in the fifth century, not to disciplined Roman soldiers, but to the equally disciplined Roman Church. All the Celtic fervour for religion was now transferred to the service of Christianity – a very Celtic type of Christianity, noted for its austere devotions and the selfless dedication of its clerics. The detailed and sophisticated laws were now transformed for Christian purposes; the glorious art once used to adorn the pagan warriors and their shrines and honour the gods now served to praise God in the form of superbly illuminated manuscripts [2, 3], the old pagan symbolism of spirals and circles taking on a new meaning.

In a Europe torn by invasion and disaster of every kind, Ireland remained a haven of peace and learning, far from the terrible ravages of the northern barbarians who from

1 **St Columba** founded his monastery in Iona in AD 563. He was the first of numerous missionaries and scholars who, as shown on the map, established centres of sanctity and learning in Western Europe. The movement was represented by such figures as Aidan in England (635), Columba, in France, Switzerland and Italy (from 590), Feuillen in Belgium (c. 650), Kilian in central Germany (martyred c. 689) and Fearghal in Austria (mid-eighth century). Many of the Irish exiles were scholars, or monks wanting to evangelize the new pagan tribes who had overrun the Roman Empire.

2 **Illuminated manuscripts** are one of the great glories of European art, as this page from the seventh-century *Book of Durrow* shows. As Ireland remained untouched by the Roman Empire, its art retained its original style.

3 **The great period of Irish manuscript** illumination was from the late seventh to the early ninth centuries AD. In these unique works, vitality in the design is combined with austere representations of divine figures, showing by their elongated, sombre faces their long link with the Celtic past. In the *Book of Kells*, St Matthew is surrounded by decorated panels and motifs, which were familiar from the art of Ireland's pagan past.

406 were burning the churches and the towns of Europe and desecrating and destroying all that was sacred and beautiful. The early Irish Church favoured the monastic system and during the fifth and sixth centuries monasteries sprang up throughout Ireland.

### The Age of Saints
This long period of tranquillity and learning was known as the Age of Saints. It was a time when the churchmen and their guests were occupied in studying the Gospels and illuminating the manuscripts, while the Christian scribes were busily committing to writing the old pagan oral traditions and poems of their country for, although Christians, they were also Celts and loyalty to the archaic traditions of their old and much-loved country was strong.

Only the coming of the Vikings at the end of the eighth century broke the spell that had made Ireland the cultural centre of the Western world. In the sixth and seventh centuries many Irish churchmen, such as St Columba (521–97), Aidan (died 651) and St Columban (543–615) travelled far over

Europe, founding monasteries and churches, converting the heathen, teaching in the courts, establishing their own schools and inspiring all who came into contact with them by their austere devotion to their calling [1]. Following the Viking invasion, exiled monks continued to travel throughout Europe.

Their rich literature and that of their neighbours, the Welsh, profoundly influenced the evolution of medieval literature and provided new and thrilling themes for the enrichment of the troubadours' repertoires for the entertainment of the rich courts of later medieval Europe.

The Celtic story in Europe does not end in the romances of the courts of Eleanor of Aquitaine and her contemporaries in the twelfth century. In the eighteenth century the famous Ossianic controversy fascinated Europe. Although the poems of the legendary Gaelic bard, Ossian, were subsequently proved to be a mixture of traditional Gaelic folk poetry and poems attributed to James Macpherson (1736–96) they nevertheless inspired writers, painters, musicians and antiquarians with a fresh interest in the Celts.

**This two-faced stone figure** from Boa Island in County Fermanagh dates from the first century BC. It forms a link with the old pagan world of the Celtic past and the flowering of Celtic religious and artistic genius in the Christian era. It is impossible to say how long paganism lingered in Ireland after the arrival of Christianity. As Roman law and administration never interrupted the traditions of tribal life and religious awareness, the transition from pagan gods to the Christian God was complicated by the survival of some elements of Celtic pagan tradition. But by the fifth century, Christianity was firmly established.

**4 The finest of all Irish brooches** is the Tara brooch [A] (c. early eighth century). Both sides of the brooch are richly decorated, the back [B] being in a better state of preservation than the front.

**5 The Ardagh Chalice** [A] was found in Co Limerick in Ireland. The contrast of plain surface (silver) decorated with studs and gold filigree makes a striking impact. One of the more beautiful details is on the underside [B] of the foot of the bowl.

**6 High crosses** were free-standing monuments decorated with Christian or pagan symbols. One of the finest is the ninth-century South Cross at Castledermot, Co Kildare. These crosses presumably stood in the monastic precincts and were of varying heights with the wheel-shaped arcs joining the arms and shaft, and set on a substantial base.

**7 Glendalough in Co Wicklow** was a place of beauty and sanctity, sacred to St Kevin. Known as St Kevin's Kitchen (c. ninth century), the building has a vaulted ceiling which supports a corbelled roof in an ingenious manner. Small ecclesiastic buildings of this kind were probably widely distributed in early Christian Ireland, providing testimony to the spread of Christianity in that remote region, far from Rome.

# The Byzantine Empire

In AD 293, the Emperor Diocletian decided, for military and administrative reasons, to shift the centre of the Roman Empire eastwards. From its origin as a new Rome, the Byzantine Empire became a vital trade and cultural link between Europe and Asia and a bastion within which Graeco-Roman civilization developed new and magnificent forms. Byzantium later found itself in doctrinal and political conflict with the Western popes and emperors but, as a Christian empire, it resisted Arab, Slav and Turkish invaders for more than 11 centuries.

## The founding of Constantinople

Both Diocletian (245–313) and Constantine I (c. 285–337) sought a better base than Rome, closer to the troop-recruiting grounds of Anatolia and the Balkans. Constantine's choice fell upon a town on the Bosporus which had been the site of an ancient Greek city, Byzantium. Constantinople, as the new capital was called, had a fine harbour and was almost unassailable [Key]. The scale on which it was conceived surpassed anything in the ancient world. Constantine was deter-

mined to found an urban centre to which men throughout his empire could direct their loyalties. He believed a common religion could also provide a powerful cohesive force. He had been converted to Christianity in 312 and in 330 dedicated Constantinople to the Virgin Mary.

The close association of Church and state and the prestige and near impregnability of the capital gave the eastern sector of the Roman Empire remarkable unity after Theodosius (346–95) left the empire split into two. While the Western Empire was swept away in 476, the Eastern, or Byzantine, Empire was able to resist attacks on the Balkans by the Visigoths and Ostrogoths. In the fourth and fifth centuries an intellectual élite created the science of theology from Greek logic and the Christian revelation.

Although theology helped to strengthen the people's faith, it also led to religious discord. Many of the Byzantine Empire's later problems can be attributed to factional struggles in which theological differences hardened into political ones that could be exploited by invaders. The Christological con-

troversy, which came to a head in the fifth century, was concerned with the relationship between the human and divine aspects of Christ's nature. The followers of Nestorius, Patriarch of Constantinople, stressed the human side while the Monophysites, based at Alexandria, stressed the divine. An equally bitter controversy, which reached its height in the eighth century, was iconoclasm – opposition to the worship of images.

## The Justinian era

The empire reached its apogee under Justinian the Great (c. 482–565), a brilliant administrator with wide-reaching military ambitions [6]. His general, Belisarius, reasserted Christian-Roman authority over large areas of the former Western Empire. Justinian greatly expanded the capital and built Hagia Sophia [8] which was intended to provide a centre of worship for all Christendom. Perhaps Justinian's greatest achievement was the codification of Roman law. His *Codex Justinianus* remained in the Middle Ages the main legal source book in Europe.

Byzantium nevertheless became increas-

**1 The Byzantine Empire** under Justinian I grew from an exclusively Eastern power in 527 [A] to an empire controlling by 565 many former territories of imperial Rome [B]. Germanic invaders were ousted from many areas of the Mediterranean.

527 / 565 / 0 300 km / Constantinople

**2 The recovery of many areas** which the empire had lost to the Slavs, Germans and Arabs in the 7th and 8th centuries was completed by the conquests of Basil II ("the Bulgar slayer") [A]. But Normans and Turks had made large inroads by 1092 [B].

1025 / 1092 / Constantinople

**3 Dismembered by Turkish attacks** and by internal feuds, the empire had shrunk in 1350 to a corner of the Balkans and some land in Greece [A]. By 1402, even the Balkan territory was lost [B] and Constantinople was soon to fall.

1350 / 1402 / Constantinople

**4 A patrician couple** of the 6th century had a similar social status to their traditional Roman counterparts. As a middle class emerged, mobility between plebeian and patrician classes was higher than in Rome.

5 A / B

**5 Byzantine coins** reflected a change to a predominantly Greek culture after the 7th century. The Latin inscription on the gold solidus [A] gave way to one in the new official language of Greek [B].

**6 Justinian I** ("reigned" 527–65) is the central figure in a glowing mosaic from the Church of S. Vitale, Ravenna. Justinian made a determined effort to reunite the old Roman Empire under Christianity. Byzantine churches, such as at Ravenna were built after Justinian's general, Belisarius, overran Italy as far north as Milan in the years following 535. Justinian's military, cultural and administrative achievements earned him the title of "The Great". His consort, Theodora, daughter of an animal keeper, was influential in Byzantine court politics.

**7 The dromon** was a Byzantine development of the traditional Greek galley. Much Byzantine trade was carried by sea and the empire kept large and efficient mercantile and naval fleets. The dockyards along the Marmara coast were the finest found in Europe until the 12th century.

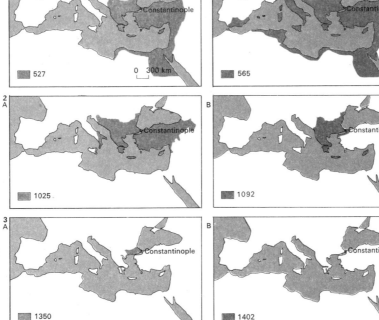

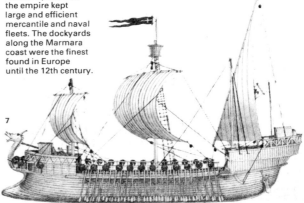

ingly Greek in character after the reign of Justinian and Greek replaced Latin as the official language [5]. The conquests in the west were short-lived and the ravages of plague weakened the empire's ability to resist Persian attacks in the east. Aided by dissident Monophysites, the Persians had occupied most of Egypt, Syria and Palestine by 615. A greater menace appeared in 637 when the Arabs, five years after the death of the prophet Mohammed, overran Syria and Palestine. Later they took North Africa, Sicily and the important grain lands of Egypt while their fleets secured Cyprus, Rhodes and several other islands.

## Revival and decline (867–1453)
As its boundaries shrank, the empire regained its ethnic unity and acquired renewed strength. From 867, under a Macedonian dynasty, it took the initiative against the Muslims and by the time of the death of Basil II (958–1025) its borders reached from the Danube to Crete and from southern Italy to Syria [2]. During this last period of greatness, trade flourished [9] and

missionaries spread Christianity throughout the Balkans and into Russia.

The Turks were soon to bring the empire to its knees, however. The defeat of Romanus IV by the Seljuks in 1071 and subsequent capture of Anatolia were the beginning of the end. From then until 1453 the empire was steadily eroded by intrigues, attacks and religious conflicts [3]. The Crusaders, whose help was enlisted against the Seljuks, fell out with the Byzantines and exploited a quarrel to take Constantinople in 1204 and set up a number of semi-independent Latin states. Religious schisms and trade rivalries prevented any concerted western effort against the Ottoman Turks who made Byzantium a vassal state in 1371. Although only Constantinople and a few outposts along the Sea of Marmara remained by 1453, it took the Sultan Mehmet II (1431–81) [10] nearly two months to capture the great city itself. With his final victory the old Byzantine world from the Balkans to Palestine was once again united, this time under the Ottoman state, which dominated the Mediterranean for the next 200 years.

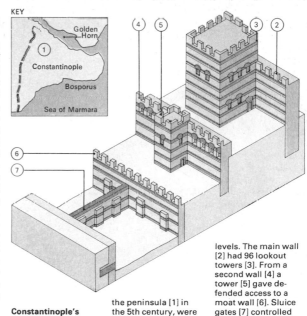

**Constantinople's walls,** built across the peninsula [1] in the 5th century, were defensible at varying levels. The main wall [2] had 96 lookout towers [3]. From a second wall [4] a tower [5] gave defended access to a moat wall [6]. Sluice gates [7] controlled water in the moat.

**8 Hagia Sophia** (Church of Holy Wisdom), built during the reign of Justinian I, was completed in only five years. Intended to provide a spiritual centre for the empire, it is the largest Christian church in the Eastern world and is exceeded in splendour only by St Peter's in Rome. The most famous of many architects who worked on the project were Anthemius of Tralles and Isidorus of Miletus. The over-

all design shows little classical influence, although Justinian despoiled classical buildings in Athens, Ephesus, Rome and Baalbek for marble. Technically, the most striking feature is the massive central dome [1] which measures 31m (100ft) across. Its thrust is borne by four arches [2], joined by pendentives [3]

which separate the semi-domes [4 and 5]. Lesser semi-domes [6] flank the main piers [7]. The thrust from [5] is taken at the west by an arch [8] supported on piers [9]. Vaulting [10] transfers the outward thrust to a series of flying buttresses [11]. Buttresses [12] support the dome's north and south thrust. By building domes on

arches [13 and 14], large areas could be spanned. The exterior brickwork is plastered. Brick domes and semi-domes are lead-covered. Interior walls, piers and floors are clad in various marbles, and vaults and domes in rich mosaics. The church was used as a mosque after 1453 and has been a museum since 1933.

**9 Major trade routes** of the 11th century reached a natural junction at Constantinople and the city became a great east-west market. A duty of 10% was levied on imports reaching Hieron from the Black Sea, Abydos from the Mediterranean, Trebizond from Asia, and Salonika from the Balkans. Byzantine craftsmen were famed for their working of gold, silver, amber, ivory and all kinds of precious stones.

■ Byzantine Empire in 1045
▭ Trade flow
• Customs houses

| | |
|---|---|
| 1 Amber | 9 Timber |
| 2 Ivory | 10 Spices |
| 3 Gems | 11 Salt |
| 4 Minerals | 12 Weapons |
| 5 Gold | 13 Slaves |
| 6 Textiles | 14 Wax |
| 7 Cotton | 15 Furs |
| 8 Silk | 16 Dried fish |

**10 Sultan Mehmet II** gave the Ottoman Empire a European outlook when he took Constantinople in 1453 and made it a centre of learning and religious tolerance. Although autocratic, he was a gifted administrator. Gentile Bellini, who painted this portrait, was one of several Italian artists he patronized.

# Mohammed and Islam

Mohammed (Mahomet) was born in Mecca in west-central Arabia in *c.* 570. He had an unhappy childhood: his father, mother and grandfather died before he was eight and left him in the care of an uncle. At the age of 25 he married a wealthy widow, Khadija, who bore him six children, and for 24 years they lived happily together. Only after her death in 619 did Mohammed take other wives, to strengthen ties with important families and to seek – unsuccessfully – a male heir.

## The visions of Mohammed

When he was 40 years old Mohammed, who loved solitude, was in a cave on Mount Hira outside Mecca when he had visions of the angel Gabriel calling him to "recite" in the name of God the creator. He received revelations that were to become the first parts of the Koran ("recitation"). Mohammed conveyed these teachings to a group of friends who believed with him in the unity of God.

At first the little group, which met for prayers to God (Allah), was ignored or scorned, but as their numbers grew they were persecuted. Some took refuge for a time in Christian Ethiopia. They were called Muslims (Moslems) – "surrendered men" – in the religion of Islam they had "surrendered" or submitted to the one God. Early converts were made from Yathrib, a town 200km (120 miles) north of Mecca, and Mohammed was invited to go there. In 622 the *hegira* (migration) took place and Mohammed and his followers moved from Mecca to Yathrib, henceforth called Medina the "city" of the prophet. The Muslim year is dated from the *hegira*.

At Medina, Mohammed built a mosque and a house, and sent his followers on raids to provide funds and ensure protection against armies from Mecca. There were battles at Badr and Uhud and finally Mohammed's armies and influence grew so that in 630 he was able to capture the city of Mecca almost without loss [1]. He rode around the Kaaba shrine [4] and had its idols destroyed.

## After the death of the prophet

The death of the prophet in 632 was sudden, but after some hesitation his friend, the elderly Abu Bakr (573–634), was appointed as caliph – successor to the prophet and vice-regent of God. Arabian tribes that had been bound to Mohammed by oath began to break away but Abu Bakr sent armies to establish Muslim rule. They were so successful that his forces broke out of Arabia into the rest of southwestern Asia. Abu Bakr died two years after his appointment, but under his successors, the caliphs Omar and Othman, Arab armies rapidly conquered Mesopotamia and entered Persia, while others entered Syria. Jerusalem surrendered to them and Omar visited the Christian churches there and the site of the ancient Jewish temple where later a great shrine was built, incorrectly called the Mosque of Omar but more properly the Dome of the Rock, one of the most holy places of Islam. Arab armies went to Egypt, where Alexandria surrendered; then after some delay they travelled along North Africa and in 711 crossed into Spain at Gibraltar. They even penetrated into the heart of France, where between Tours and Poitiers the Muslim armies met Frankish forces under Charles Martel in 732. After seven days of fierce skirmishes the Arabs were forced to retreat southwards.

**1 This painting** is from a copy of *Siyar-i-Nabi* (Life of the Prophet) and shows Mohammed and Abu Bakr on their way to Mecca from Medina. The prophet is traditionally depicted faceless with a flaming halo. The paintings of Islamic art are unique in that the historical events depicted take a secondary place to the intensity of the religious feeling. This work is in the 16th-century Ottoman court style, yet it has an almost contemporary realism.

**2 The Prophet Mohammed** was a "warner", calling men to turn from idols to worship the one true God (Allah). There are no contemporary pictures of the prophet but later artists have pictured him as an Eastern holy man.

**3 The Koran** is the sacred book of Islam. All Muslims know some of its verses by heart and use them in daily prayers. Illuminated copies of the Koran in gold and bright colours were written by hand by skilled scribes.

They remained in southern France for some years but Spain was the limit of their rule and here they remained for centuries until the fall of Granada in 1492, after which Muslims and Jews were expelled from Spain. In the east, Persia came completely under Muslim rule as well as a large part of India. The Muslims preserved much of the cultures they encountered and transmitted them, taking Indian numerals as Arabic numerals to Europe and preserving Greek medicine, astronomy and philosophy during the period of the Dark Ages in Europe.

## The importance of the Koran

Mohammed, who is said to have been illiterate, passed the Koran, the divine Word, to his followers and it was written down by scribes at his recitation or from memory [3]. The final official version was completed under Othman, about 20 years after the death of Mohammed. The Koran is in Arabic, in 112 *suras* (chapters) the first of which is always recited in daily prayers. Most of the early chapters are long and deal with religious and social matters, while the later ones are short and challenging in content.

The Koran teaches faith in God, the coming judgement against unbelief, and the ideas of heaven and hell; it also sets out duties appropriate to marriage, the family and social life. Many stories in it are parallel to some in the Old and New Testaments and Adam, Abraham, Moses and Jesus appear as prophets. The religious duties of Islam are taught in Five Pillars: confession of faith in one God and Mohammed as his apostle, prayer five times a day [5, 7], alms-giving of a proportion of one's income, fasting from all food and drink during the hours of day throughout the whole of Ramadan (the ninth month of the year) and pilgrimage to Mecca at least once in a lifetime.

All men and women are bound to perform these religious and social duties, with exemptions for the young, sick and old. Islam is an international religion, with perhaps 500 million followers, mostly in Asia and Africa. The Arabic language prevails in the southern Mediterranean and many Near Eastern countries, and is used by all Muslims to recite the Koran and in formal prayers.

**"Praise be to Allah"**, the first words of the Koran, is a favourite text inscribed on the walls of mosques.

4

6

**4 In the centre of Mecca** stands the Kaaba (cube), a stone building covered with a black cloth, towards which Muslims turn in prayer and round which they go at times of pilgrimage.

**5 Five times every day** Muslims are called to prayer from a mosque or minaret tower. The *muezzin* calls that "God is most great, there is no god but God, Mohammed is the Apostle of God, come to prayers, come to salvation".

5

**6 The Royal Mosque Masjid-i-Shah**, in Isfahan, Iran, was built in the 17th century for Shah Abbas the Great. It is composed of porches, halls, domes and minarets covered with blue tiles and mosaics. Long friezes of elegant lettering proclaim the glory of God.

**7 Prayer rugs**, such as this 18th-century Persian rug, are famous products of Muslim craftsmen. Large ones cover the floors of mosques.

7

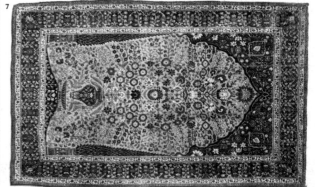

# Arabs and the rise of Islam

Arab expansion was a tribal conquest of civilization. Such conquests are commonplace in history, but the Arabs are the only people who started a new civilization as a result of their conquest. This came about by a combination of two special circumstances. First, on the side of the conquerors there was a unique fusion of religious conviction [2] and tribal military force. The Arabs conquered the Middle East [4] in the name of a monotheism that sanctified their tribal heritage over and against the conquered civilizations and their conquests were so successful that they had no need to come to terms with those civilizations anyway. Thus the Arabs could avoid being culturally absorbed by the peoples they had conquered.

Second, on the side of the conquered peoples there prevailed in Egypt, Syria and Iraq a unique type of provincial culture. Having lost their own civilizations some 1,400 years before when they first came under the rule of alien empires, these provinces had not yet been fully assimilated by Byzantium and Iran. As a result, they were less committed to these civilizations and the

Arabs were exposed only to a culture filtered through a provincial milieu and language. These provincial cultures, pale versions of their imperial civilizations, could thus be reshaped by the Arabs.

The strength of the Arab position as against the weakness of provincial culture is the keynote of early Islamic history politically, culturally and ethnically.

## The political influence
Politically, the strength of the Arab position determined the evolution of the Arab conquest society. With the Umayyad dynasty [4] (661–750) the capital was moved from Medina to Syria where a tribal confederacy formed the basis of the caliphs' power; in the provinces the tribal armies were placed under tribal leaders in a system of indirect rule. Within some 40 years kinship ties had been eroded and the tribal armies gave way to professional soldiers and civilians.

Normally, the loss of the tribal organization means that the conquerors must borrow the political organization of their subjects or suffer political disintegration; either way the

conquered civilizations eventually win. But among the Arabs the sanctity of the tribal past meant that neither of these eventualities came to pass and the obsolete organization was retained until the third civil war (744), which was followed by the Abbasid revolution. It was thus that the Abbasids (750–1258) [3] had to govern an Islamic empire as opposed to an Arab conquest society without losing the link with the tribal past, a problem that eventually proved insoluble. Although the Arabs attempted in various ways to foster an imperial ideal and aristocracy within Islam on the Iranian model, the fourth civil war (811–13) meant the failure of such attempts, the adoption of slave armies [5] as the instrument of government and, soon afterwards, the dissolution of the unitary state. The delay, however, meant that meanwhile Islamic civilization had developed sufficiently to survive.

## Islamic culture and learning
Culturally, Arab strength accounts for the character of Islamic learning. The core of Islam is a revealed law, actually created in

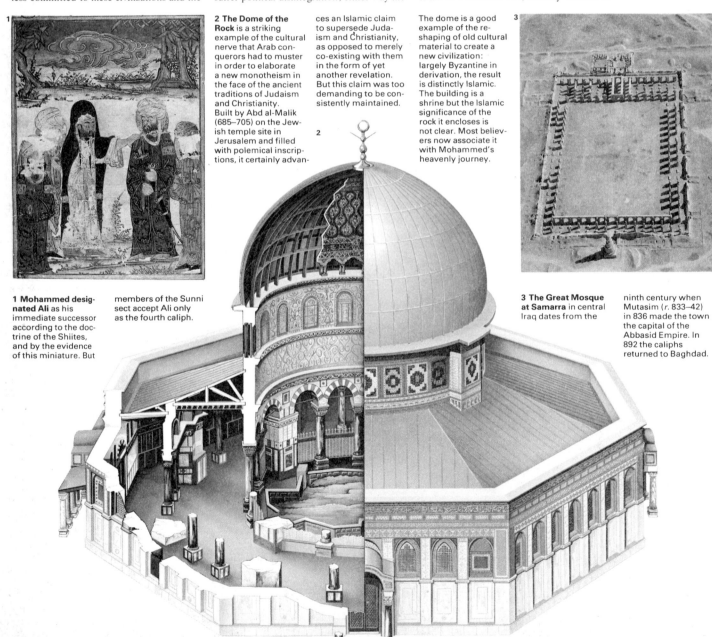

**2 The Dome of the Rock** is a striking example of the cultural nerve that Arab conquerors had to muster in order to elaborate a new monotheism in the face of the ancient traditions of Judaism and Christianity. Built by Abd al-Malik (685–705) on the Jewish temple site in Jerusalem and filled with polemical inscriptions, it certainly advan-ces an Islamic claim to supersede Judaism and Christianity, as opposed to merely co-existing with them in the form of yet another revelation. But this claim was too demanding to be consistently maintained.

The dome is a good example of the re-shaping of old cultural material to create a new civilization: largely Byzantine in derivation, the result is distinctly Islamic. The building is a shrine but the Islamic significance of the rock it encloses is not clear. Most believ-ers now associate it with Mohammed's heavenly journey.

**1 Mohammed designated Ali** as his immediate successor according to the doctrine of the Shiites, and by the evidence of this miniature. But members of the Sunni sect accept Ali only as the fourth caliph.

**3 The Great Mosque at Samarra** in central Iraq dates from the ninth century when Mutasim (r. 833–42) in 836 made the town the capital of the Abbasid Empire. In 892 the caliphs returned to Baghdad.

Iraq in the eighth and ninth centuries from a variety of foreign materials, but in theory based exclusively on the Koran and the Prophet's works. It was the learned laity studying Islamic law who came to be seen as the heirs to Mohammed's preaching.

It follows that it was not difficult to create an Islamic scholarship, overwhelmingly Arab in orientation; but it was not so easy to create an Islamic philosophy and science. The Arabs did inherit Greek philosophy from the conquered provinces, but being neither Arab nor Islamic, such teaching was regarded as ungodly wisdom. Although philosophy continued to be cultivated, it was gradually relegated to marginal and heretical circles.

### Ethnic development

Ethnically, the weakness of provincial culture explains the overwhelming Arab influence on the Middle East. Islam began as a religion for Arabs, but could not remain so when the non-Arabs began to convert to it. From being an ethnic faith on the Judaic model it had to become a universal belief on the Christian model, but the transition was never quite completed. Mohammed was an Arab who, unlike Jesus, had never ceased to be honoured in his own community and in his name the Arabs had conquered a kingdom that was very much of this world [Key]. The notion that a Muslim was in some sense an Arab, and Islamic civilization in some sense Arabian, therefore proved extremely tenacious. In the ninth and tenth centuries non-Arab converts, especially Iranians, attempted to disentangle Islam from its Arab origins, insisting that Islam was a faith that could be combined with any identity and culture; but the success of these so-called *shuubis* was limited. The three provinces – Egypt, Syria and Iraq – all became Arab countries, while Iran, not a province but an empire, retained its Iranian identity but largely lost its Iranian civilization. Only where Islam has spread peacefully, as in parts of black Africa and Java, has it proved flexible enough to combine with a local culture. In the Middle East the ancient intransigence of Islam *vis-à-vis* such cultures has a modern sequel in the preference for Arab as opposed to Egyptian, Syrian or Iraqi nationalism.

**Camel-breeding Bedouin tribesmen** roamed over most of Arabia before the days of oil. South Arabia had sufficient internal resources to maintain stable state structures, while in the north external resources were often available in the form of commercial revenues or imperial subsidies. But most of the peninsula was too poor to support a non-tribal organization. Here Mohammed was the first, but not the last, to create a state in the name of a religious doctrine. By uniting the tribesmen as believers and calling on them to wage war against the unbelievers, he provided a rationale for a conquest of the fertile lands that culminated in the formation of a vast empire.

**4 The unification of Arabia** is traditionally credited to Mohammed and was accomplished before his death in 632. Egypt and Syria were taken from the Byzantines and Iraq, and the Iranian plateau from the Sasanids between 632 and 656, when civil war broke out. The first Umayyad caliph, Muawiya (*r.* 661–80), resumed Arab expansion in North Africa and eastern Iran, while a second thrust under Walid I (*r.* 705–15) pushed the Arabs into Spain and India; but a last attempt to conquer Constantinople in 715–16 failed. At the end of the Umayyad period (750) the limits of Arab expansion were the Pyrenees, the Sahara, the Caucasus and Turkestan. Further expansion, whether Arab or Islamic, became the work of local dynasties, militant fraternities and missionaries and merchants, and such expansion continued far beyond 950.

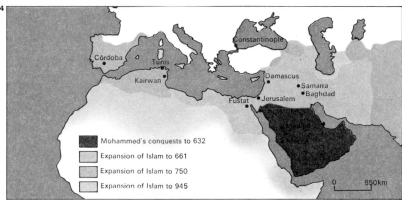

**5 A mounted archer** (detail from a Palmyra fresco) typifies the kind of Turkish slave soldier from Transoxania who swelled the ranks of the Islamic armies. Transoxania, which was once the eastern frontier of Iran, is now wholly Turkish. Divided into well-entrenched principalities, it was a difficult place for the Arabs to conquer. As a result, Iranian culture survived and it was in this marginal province that the revival of Iranian literature in Islam took place from the tenth century onwards. Transoxania was exposed to Turkish tribes and after several invasions was overrun, eventually to become Turkish.

**6 A hoard of Arab coins** from a tenth-century Viking grave in Sweden represents payment for the slaves, fur and honey that were exported to the Muslims by the Vikings who colonized Russia.

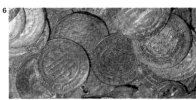

**7 Harun ar-Rashid** is one of the few caliphs to have fired Western imagination, thanks to *The Arabian Nights' Entertainments*. His reign (786-809) fell in the period following the transfer of the capital from Syria to the culturally richer Iraq, but politically his days were troubled. Faced with revolts and sectarian discontent, he divided his lands between his sons; this provoked a fourth civil war which, disastrously for royal power, was won not by the caliphate but by a provincial army.

**8 Kairwan,** in Tunisia, was founded as a garrison city for the settlement of Arab soldiers. It soon became a centre of learning and orthodoxy in North Africa, which was at that time inhabited overwhelmingly by Berbers. On conversion, the Berbers repeatedly made use of the programme of tribal state formation and conquest enshrined in the Prophet's career, in the name of a doctrine that was sometimes reformist, sometimes heretical. Although North Africa is extensively Arabized today, it still has a substantial Berber population. But Arab or Berber, Islam among North African tribesmen is highly distinctive, centring on holy men often identified as descendants of the Prophet.

# Charlemagne and the Carolingian Empire

The Carolingians, a dynasty named after Charles Martel ("the Hammer") and his grandson Charlemagne, became the leading aristocratic family among the Franks in the seventh century. The family's power and prestige were greatly increased during the rule of Charles Martel (c. 688–741) who united the Frankish kingdom, halted the advance of the Arabs at the Battle of Poitiers in 732 [1] and began a political relationship with the Papacy that led to the foundation of the Holy Roman Empire. Charles Martel's son Pepin (c. 715–68), the father of Charlemagne, ruled from 747 and was anointed king with papal approval in 754. In 753 Pope Stephen sought the aid of the Franks against the Lombards who, having taken Italy, were threatening Rome. The king of the Franks became a regular ally of the pope, and the Carolingian house was invited to divide Italy with the Papacy.

## The Frankish dynasty

The Franks traditionally considered their kings as being of divine origin and saw the tribe as the possession of its royal family. The Frankish state as such only existed under strong kings such as Clovis (465–511) and Pepin who eliminated their rivals. On Pepin's death his sons Charlemagne (742–814) and Carloman succeeded. When Carloman died in 771 Charlemagne seized full control [Key]. In 773 he answered the Papacy's call and defeated the Lombards. From 774 he ruled Italy by conquest and swore an oath of assistance with the pope.

## The reign of Charlemagne

The Papacy was now as frightened of the Franks as it had been of the Lombards and sought a way of restraining Charlemagne. The solution came in 800 when Leo III crowned Charlemagne [4], initiating the Holy Roman Empire and giving rise to the claim that the emperor held his power from God bestowed upon him by the pope.

Charlemagne was a warrior king. Wars were fought against the Lombards in Italy and against the Agilolfing dukes of Bavaria; in addition there was a constant succession of campaigns against the barbarians on the borders of the kingdom: Arabs, Avars, Slavs, Saxons and Danes. War was carried out not only for political reasons but also for plunder. Charlemagne was often poor in the early years of his reign and a Frankish king's power rested on his ability to reward his followers. Booty taken in war was his single most important revenue.

Charlemagne fought the Arabs in Spain in 778, a campaign that ended in the ignominious defeat of Count Roland at Roncesvalles at the hands of the Basques [7]. In the south he defeated the Lombards and overthrew Tassilo of Bavaria in 788, making Bavaria for the first time an integral part of the Frankish Empire [8]. From 772 to 804 he waged a bloody and almost continual war against the Saxons, led until 785 by Widukind, and he proceeded to conquer Bohemia in 805–6.

Charlemagne's military prowess recreated a centralized European government that needed an administration more complex than any known to the Franks. Charlemagne created a new court at Aachen [3], with a palace and cathedral built on an imperial model. He employed a circle of

1 A battle of crucial importance for the future of Europe was fought at Poitiers in 732 when Charles Martel and the Franks finally put a stop to the advance of the Arabs, who threatened to destroy the Christian West completely. The Franks had already been successful in defeating the German tribes east of the Rhine. Frankish expansion under Charlemagne was therefore based on 300 years of Frankish strength.

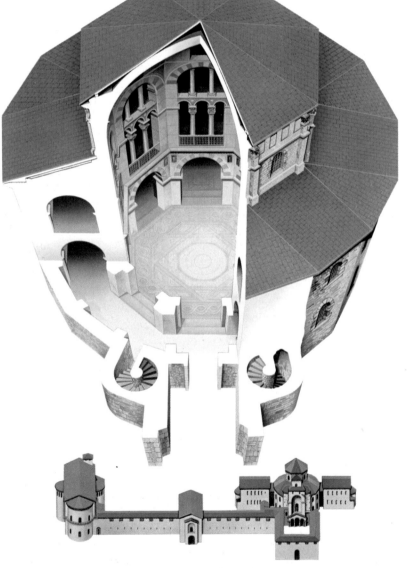

2 Charlemagne's military leadership was the basis of his power. Frankish custom, based on a tribal levy, made every freeman liable for military service and for equipping and feeding himself at war. Later, middle-class freemen gave up their lands to local lords and fought in the lords' retinues, saving the small man expense but destroying the unity of the Frankish army on which Charlemagne had built his power.

3 Charlemagne's Palace Chapel at Aachen was the architectural masterpiece of Carolingian Europe and a symbol of imperial power. It was based on the design of St Vitale in Ravenna, capital of the empire in Italy after the fall of Rome, and was designed as a chapel to house Charlemagne's throne.

scholars, including Alcuin from Northumbria and Theodulf from Spain, to educate a new literate class of administrator, to produce a new and legible script, to reform the practice and liturgy of the Church and to produce a theory of empire to accompany the reality of imperial power. Alcuin, above all, formulated the role and responsibilities of the Christian emperor, thus justifying the imperial side of the relationship with the Papacy.

## Organization of Frankish society

Charlemagne ruled his lands through local counts, of whom there were more than 200. Many were of royal blood, and their appointment by Charlemagne created the beginnings of an international aristocracy that long outlived the Carolingian Empire. He employed stewards to carry out the business of government and special travelling agents, the *missi dominici*, to keep the counts in line with imperial policy and to raise troops when necessary. The royal will was expressed in a series of imperial charters that were lucid and authoritative. The Church played a central role in administration both through the services of educated bishops and clerics and the unification of doctrine and practice.

Frankish society had earlier been based solely on personal loyalty to the king. Gradually Charlemagne insisted on a new oath of fidelity, initially only in times of crisis. These oaths were the beginning of a feudal monarchy based on the sworn allegiance of a landed nobility, a completely different concept from the personal loyalty of a tribe to its chief, for example.

Charlemagne intended to leave his empire divided between his sons, but Louis' reign, which began in 814, was a chapter of bitter family rivalry and the Church was increasing its control over secular affairs. A new wave of external attack from the Arabs, Bretons, Vikings and Normans further weakened the empire. Louis died in 840 and after three more years of feuding the Treaty of Verdun divided the empire in three.

Carolingian rule had disintegrated by the end of the ninth century but Europe had been given an imperial ideal, an international landed aristocracy and a series of significant social bonds that were soon to be revitalized.

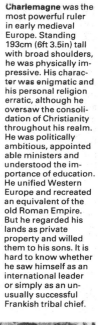
KEY

Charlemagne was the most powerful ruler in early medieval Europe. Standing 193cm (6ft 3.5in) tall with broad shoulders, he was physically impressive. His character was enigmatic and his personal religion erratic, although he oversaw the consolidation of Christianity throughout his realm. He was politically ambitious, appointed able ministers and understood the importance of education. He unified Western Europe and recreated an equivalent of the old Roman Empire. But he regarded his lands as private property and willed them to his sons. It is hard to know whether he saw himself as an international leader or simply as an unusually successful Frankish tribal chief.

**4 The coronation of Charlemagne** by Pope Leo III in St Peter's on Christmas Day 800 was depicted in a 15th-century miniature by Jean Fouquet. Charlemagne, who had just restored Rome to the pope after a revolt, needed a sacred seal on his *de facto* position as emperor. The coronation made him legally heir to the Western Roman emperors. It was more the culmination of Carolingian expansion than an expression of a papal claim to select temporal rule.

**5 The Lothar Crystal**, a solid piece of rock crystal delicately engraved with biblical scenes, made in the 9th century, was owned by Lothair II of Lorraine (r. 855–69). The quality of the carving demonstrates the continuing artistic achievements of the Carolingian Empire despite the political decline of the 9th century. The classical motifs show how Rome was being used as an example by the Franks.

**6 This page from the Sacramentary** of Charles the Bald (823–77) shows the coronation of a Frankish prince – possibly Charles himself. He is flanked by two clerics and appears to be being crowned by God in person, handing a crown down from heaven; the Church's role in supporting the throne and the royal sense of divine mission are thus illustrated together. The Sacramentary was written and illustrated in 869–70 and saw the height of achievement of the last great school of Carolingian illumination which had developed around the Court School at Aachen and spread to Reims and Tours before it reached St Denis.

**7 The death of Roland** at the Battle of Roncesvalles in 778 gave rise to one of the great epic poems, the *Song of Roland*. It epitomized Charlemagne's knights as chivalrous defenders of Christianity against the Saracens. In literature, as in politics, the Carolingians thus laid a foundation of medieval lore. On his immediate retreat across the Pyrenees to put down a Saxon rising in the north, the rearguard of his army was in fact annihilated by a Basque force at Roncesvalles.

8

Carolingian Empire 814
States tributary to Charlemagne
Byzantine Empire

Partition of Carolingian Empire at Treaty of Verdun 843:
(1) To Charles
(2) To Lothair
(3) To Louis

**8 The size of Charlemagne's empire** on his death in 814 makes a sharp contrast with the partitions ratified at Verdun in 843 after 30 years of squabbling among his successors. The poet Theodulf wrote: "The wall, so firm and artistically decorated in the days of my youth is showing cracks . . . . Everything sweet has fled from the ageing world and nothing is left of its former strength."

# The Anglo-Saxon monarchy

Between the seventh and eleventh centuries, Anglo-Saxon England became a strong and stable nation, organized around a solid and powerful monarchy. This institution developed from that of the warrior chieftain, and throughout the period it continued to rely on the personal relationship of a king with his thegns [1], to whom he gave lands in exchange for companionship in peace and war, and who had a role, uncertain and fluctuating according to the strength of the previous king, in electing and advising a new monarch. Gradually the king acquired institutional authority through the patronage of the Church and the organization of the currency [5] and, despite the informal nature of much of his authority, he was the hub of the stability and prosperity of the kingdom.

## The growth of a unified monarchy
In the eighth century kings of Mercia, in the Midlands, dominated England. The most famous of these was Offa (reigned 757–96) [2], the first king to have personal authority over most of southern England. He wrote a code of laws, set up a stable currency and was

a figure of international standing, dealing with Charlemagne on equal terms.

During the early ninth century power passed from Mercia to Wessex, but the first Viking raids [6], in 793 on the east coast, threatened the stability of England. Sporadic Viking attacks continued until 865, when the "Great Army" chose not to return with its loot to Scandinavia for the winter but instead divided up the land of East Anglia, the East Midlands and Yorkshire, and began to farm it. The English rallied under Alfred (reigned 871–99), king of Wessex, who defeated the Danish commander Guthrum [9] decisively at Edington in 878, and made a treaty confining the Danes to the region east of Watling Street, known as Danelaw [7]. Alfred's son, Edward the Elder (reigned 899–925), reconquered this district by 920, but the substantial numbers of Scandinavian settlers left a permanent mark on social institutions and placenames, notably in the suffix "-by", found, for instance, in "Derby". Alfred's daughter, Ethelfleda (died 918) Lady of the Mercians, led campaigns against a new enemy, Norwegian pirates, who attacked the

northwest coast, settled in Lancashire, and set up a kingdom in York in 919.

Alfred had organized his defence around burhs (forts), a practice continued in the tenth century. Some of the sites chosen were already towns. The burhs (later called boroughs) became the centres of trade and administration of taxation, and the site of mints [5], in the late Anglo-Saxon period.

## The revival of the monasteries
The Viking attacks had been particularly severe on the wealthy and unprotected monasteries, and had brought the Church to a low ebb by the beginning of the tenth century. A similar decline on the Continent was combated by the reform movement started at the monastery of Cluny in 910. Its ideas were brought to England, about 940, by some English monks who had spent time in the reformed monasteries. Notable among the monks were St Dunstan (c. 925–88) [11], who revitalized the monastery of Glastonbury, St Ethelwold (c. 908–84), Bishop of Winchester and St Oswald (died 992), Bishop of Worcester. Edgar (944–75), who

1 **The king and his witan** (council) were the ultimate source of justice. The witan comprised the leading churchmen and thegns, or nobles, who were bound to the king by ties of personal loyalty. These formal assemblies developed out of the king's council of the period of Mercian supremacy. They brought problems to the attention of the king and assented to his most important ecclesiastical appointments and land-grants.

2 **A standardized coinage,** based on the silver penny, was introduced by Offa of Mercia, whose name is shown on this coin. It was used for most transactions and was accepted on the Continent. Other coins of Offa copy Arabic models. Offa effectively ended the old heptarchy, or division of England into seven separate kingdoms, even though his immediate successors were unable to maintain the unity that he had created.

3 **Offa's Dyke,** running along much of the frontier between Mercia and Wales, testifies to the power of the 8th-century Mercian kings. It was intended more to mark the border than for defence.

4 **The Royal Hall of Cheddar** is typical of the halls that were the centre of royal power and were the first permanent royal residences. The witan enjoyed the king's hospitality and advised him in such halls.

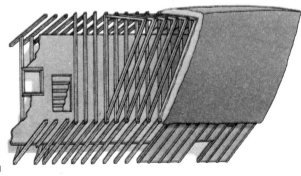

5 **Mints** were set up in many towns in the later Anglo-Saxon period. As many as 44 places issued coins during the ten-month reign of Harold in 1066 alone. The king kept strict control over the currency, maintaining the purity of the metal and regularly recalling the entire coinage for reissue, at one time every six years. Although the name of the mint appeared on the coins, the dies were centrally issued. Penalties for counterfeiting included mutilation and death.

• Mints
---- County boundaries

0          100km

6 **The Vikings** raided Lindisfarne monastery in 793, and raids on the east coast for loot continued for 50 years. Most of the surviving accounts of the raids were written by monks, so the Vikings have acquired an image of savagery that ignores the constructive side of their settlement.

became king in 959, was an ardent supporter of the monastic revival and was the first king to be crowned with a ceremony that underlined the religious associations of the monarchy [8]. The service, written by St Dunstan, remains the basis for coronation services. The alliance of monasticism with the king gave the ruler a new agency for asserting his authority in the country.

Edgar's son Ethelred II (reigned 978–1016), was again faced with attacks by aggressive Scandinavians. Large taxes, known as Danegeld, were collected to buy off these warbands, so that most of the late Saxon coins still in existence are in the collections of Scandinavian museums. The Danegeld did not prevent the eventual victory of the Danes under Sweyn Forkbeard (died 1014), whose son Canute (994–1035) [10] became king of England in 1016, and of his home country Denmark in 1018.

**The nature of Anglo-Saxon kingship**
The monarchy changed considerably in the course of the period 500–1050. There were, however, some constant themes. The impor-

tance of royal blood is emphasized in the early period by genealogies, whose chief function was to demonstrate the ancestry of the royal houses, and to relate them through mythical rulers to pagan gods and, in Christian times, through biblical characters to Adam and Eve. Later, with the growing regularization of rules of descent, the question of the right of the king to the throne took on a religious aspect.

The king did not rule absolutely, but was advised by his council of thegns, the witan [1] and observed accepted codes of law and custom. These might be issued by each king in accordance with established usage. There was a complex system of taxation; coinage was maintained at a high standard of purity and constantly changed. Local justice was organized through the courts of the shire and hundred, and the defence of each county by earls, appointed by the king. These institutions were strengthened, rather than weakened, by the desire to oppose the invasions of the Scandinavians. Norman administration was grafted onto an already existing complex and efficient system.

The *Anglo-Saxon Chronicle*, shown here in the version copied at Peterborough in 1122, is a vital source for knowledge of political history before the Norman Conquest. A collection of genealogies and chronicles prepared by monks, it appeared in a number of different versions. As a result, it is possible to see a regional view of events, as in the case of the crisis of 1051–2, when the authority of Edward the Confessor (*r.* 1042–66) was challenged by the sons of Earl Godwin (*d.* 1053). The *Chronicle* is said to have been founded by King Alfred as part of his encouragement of English culture.

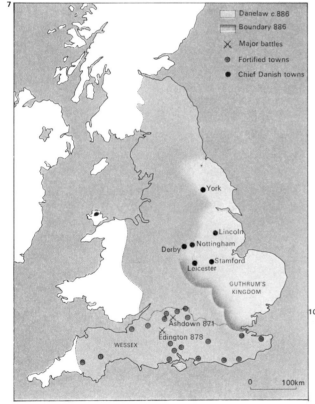

7 **The Danelaw** was recognized by King Alfred in the treaty of 886. In the east of the country the Danish traditions of independence and local autonomy continued well into the medieval period. A Viking kingdom was soon established in Lancashire which prevented the Danish expansion to the north.

8 **Edgar the Peaceable** was a powerful and efficient king who is said to have shown his political authority over the whole of England by being rowed on the River Dee by six subkings. He encouraged the monastic revival and this manuscript records his coronation, which took place in 973, two years before he died.

9 **Guthrum** (*d.* 890) is said to have been the first Scandinavian to settle in England. In the treaty of 878 with Alfred he agreed to convert the Danes to Christianity and took the name Athelstan after his own baptism.

10 **Canute, or Cnut,** set up an empire that took in much of the coastlands of the North Sea. As king of England he encouraged the established institutions (here he grants a charter to the New Minster at Winchester with his wife).

11 **St Dunstan,** shown here prostrate at the feet of Christ, was Archbishop of Canterbury from 959 to 988. He promoted the growth of the new monasticism. He founded abbeys at Peterborough and Ely.

# The Vikings

In the late eighth century the pagan Scandinavians, known as the Vikings, burst upon the rich kingdoms of Western Europe. Improvements in ship design, and overpopulation at home were two reasons behind Viking expansions at this time. They attacked rich and undefended monasteries, pillaging their treasures and killing and enslaving the priests. The attack in 793 on St Cuthbert's monastery at Lindisfarne in Northumberland [2] was the most shocking of these occurrences because it was the first.

## Colonization of Britain

Some of those who came from Scandinavia turned their attention to colonization. Graves in western Scotland, the Hebrides, Shetland, Orkney and Isle of Man, furnished after the pagan fashions of their Scandinavian homelands with weapons and household goods, tell of the gradual settlement of these areas [1]. In England, raids gave way to settlement in the 860s and, after a series of campaigns against the English kingdoms, the Scandinavians – by treaty with Alfred the Great in 878 – settled as conquerors to the east and north of a line from the River Lea to the Dee. Here they established at least one kingdom (based on York) as well as other political groupings in East Anglia and the Midlands (where their power was based on the "Five Boroughs" – Leicester, Stamford, Lincoln, Derby and Nottingham). By the middle of the tenth century the English had reconquered these areas, although in the early eleventh century the whole of England was again conquered by the Scandinavians, and a Dane, Canute (994–1035), became king of England for a short period.

The Scandinavian settlements in Scotland and the Isle of Man [8] continued until the thirteenth century (in Orkney and Shetland islands until the fifteenth century). The Scandinavians in Ireland did not attempt to conquer the whole country, but founded a series of towns (of which Dublin was the most important) through which they could influence the trade of the Western European seaboard. Goods from France and Spain were exchanged for slaves, furs, ivory and other products of the north.

In other Western European countries the Scandinavians were less successful as colonists or conquerors. Only in Normandy did they succeed. There in 911 a Scandinavian, Rollo, was given the right to settle and govern much of that corner of France.

The Scandinavians also moved into the North Atlantic looking for plunder and farmland. They settled the virtually unknown Faroe Islands and Iceland and reached Greenland, where they founded two major settlements. They also appear to have made landings on the coast of North America.

## Eastern Europe

The Scandinavians were also influential in Eastern Europe. From the Roman period onwards they traded spasmodically with the eastern Mediterranean, travelling by way of the Polish and Russian rivers. In the eighth century a larger and more organized commercial traffic developed. The Swedes founded trading stations and collected tribute from Finno-Ugric, Balt and Slav tribes in the east Baltic. In the ninth century the Scandinavians contributed to the growth of Russian trading towns at Staraja Ladoga,

**1 The Scandinavians of the Viking age** used these main routes in their search for wealth and land to settle. In the east are the riverside towns they established as centres, such as Kiev and Novgorod. From these, along rivers, the Scandinavians reached the rich trade and wealth of the Orient and the Byzantine Empire. In the west the chief areas of settlement were the northern and western islands of Britain, northern and eastern England, northern France and the Irish ports (which they also founded). By the western sea routes they reached America, but failed to establish any settlements there.

Vikings' homeland
Viking settlements
Sea routes
Land/river routes
Possible sea routes

0    1,500km

**2 These two views from a stone** on Lindisfarne commemorate the Viking invasion. An inscription from it reads: "793. In this year dire portents appeared over Northumbria . . . the ravages of heathen men destroyed God's church on Lindisfarne".

**3 This bronze figure** of the Buddha was imported from Afghanistan or India to Sweden in the early Viking age, presumably as a souvenir. Other objects imported into Scandinavia and found during excavation include Arabic, Byzantine, English, French and German coins, as well as silks and foreign animal skins, metalwork from Britain and pottery and glass from northern Germany.

**4 Thor, the Scandinavian god of thunder,** agriculture and war, is usually symbolized by a hammer. In this 6.7cm (2.5in) bronze, his beard develops into a hammer. The symbol was often used as an amulet to protect the wearer against evil.

House walls of turf
Pit with fire-scarred stones
Edge of terrace
Hearth
Post holes

0          10
metres

**5 This plan of a house** excavated at L'Anse-aux-Meadows in Newfoundland can be dated to the 11th century. It has many of the structural features of houses built by the Vikings in their colonial settlements in Iceland and Greenland.

Novgorod and Kiev. The river route along the Volchov and the Dnieper (which led from Lake Ladoga to the Black Sea and Constantinople, now called Istanbul) was largely controlled by the Scandinavians from the ninth to the eleventh centuries.

**Trade and economic organization**
The main exports of the Scandinavians were furs, honey and slaves; the main imports silver, spices and other luxury goods. The volume of this eastern trade is demonstrated by the fact that (at a conservative estimate) some 40,000 Arabic coins have been found in Viking age sites in Gotland and Sweden.

These eastern adventures are also reflected in long inscriptions carved, in runic characters, on Swedish stones. Some refer to merchant expeditions and imply a fairly peaceful Scandinavian presence in Russia. However some tell of more warlike episodes – a military expedition to Arabia, for example, or of Scandinavian mercenaries in Russia or Byzantium: Greek literary sources attest to the presence of Scandinavians serving in the bodyguard of the emperor.

The raids, colonization, trade and other activities of the Vikings, which have so firmly established them in European history, were based on a settled domestic economy. This economy had its foundation in agriculture but was expanded in the Viking age by the development of marginal land in Scandinavia itself and by the foundation of towns which functioned as major trading stations – towns such as Birka in Sweden and Hedeby in South Jutland [7]. The international contacts of the Scandinavians are clearly seen in these towns, both in excavated material and in the written descriptions of travellers. The Scandinavian of the Viking age was, however, basically a farmer – even traders and pirates were apt to travel extensively abroad, mainly in summer.

The image of the Vikings as marauders and pirates is influenced by the chronicles of priests who identified them with pillaged monasteries. The fact that the Scandinavians were pagan compounded any offence. But in the tenth century the Scandinavians were gradually converted to Christianity and so their image improved.

**This richly carved ship's prow** is part of a complete Viking longship found in a woman's grave of the 9th century at Oseberg in Norway. The ship itself, built of oak, was 23m (75ft) long, and was basically a coastal sailing vessel which could also be propelled by oars. One of the larger examples of Viking longships, it was probably used for raiding and longer voyages of discovery and colonization. Much smaller ships were used for coastal and river warfare and trading. The prow here is decorated with intertwining animals, and is shaped in the form of a serpent, a style that is characteristic of the final pre-Christian period of Viking art.

**6 The hull of a small cargo vessel** was raised from the bed of Roskilde fjord in Denmark and reconstructed. It is 13.5m (44ft) long. There is decking fore and aft with a hold in the centre. The mast is seated on the keel and the one large sail is supported by a single transverse spar. When not in use the spar could be lowered and stowed away. The vessel could also be rowed by means of sweeps inserted through the square holes that are clearly seen in the gunwale plank. Steering was by means of a paddle attached aft on the starboard quarter (starboard being an old Norse word for "steering side").

6

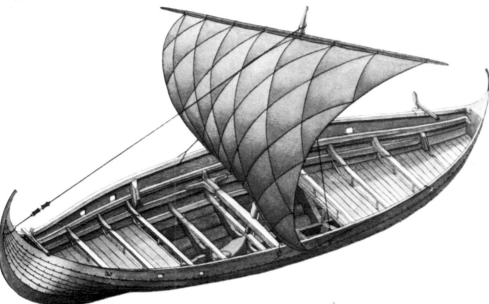

**7 The open fire** in the centre of this house, a reconstruction from the town of Hedeby in South Jutland, provided heat for the room and for cooking. The family would sit on the earth benches at the sides of the room and eat off low tables. The walls are of wattle and daub and may have been covered with hangings. There was a room at each end.

**8 The annual ceremony at Tynwald** on the Isle of Man comes from the assembly established there by the Scandinavians in the Viking age (the Norwegians finally surrendered Man in 1266). Such assemblies acted as a combination of town meeting, law court and fair, and were held in various places throughout the Viking world.

8

**9 The craftsmanship of the Vikings** is well demonstrated by this early 11th-century weather vane. Made of gilt bronze, it may originally have graced a Viking ship. The Scandinavians were fascinated by contorted animal ornament.

Throughout the Viking age, their craftsmen produced distinguished objects decorated with animal ornament largely free from the influence of contemporary European art. Objects like this vane demonstrate the brilliance of the ornamentation.

# Western European economy 800–1000

Western Europe in the ninth and tenth centuries was the poor relation of both the Arab and the Byzantine worlds. It was poor in the exploitation of its natural resources, in technical ability, in political cohesion and cultural achievement. Europe's social and economic backwardness was further threatened by Magyar hordes from the east and incessant raids by Vikings who swept southwards from the Scandinavian countries.

## The growth of self-sufficiency

The temporary political unity and economic regulations of the Carolingians (Charlemagne and his successors) throw little light on actual conditions of life in the ninth century. Charlemagne attempted to stabilize and centralize the coinage throughout his empire, centred on France, to avoid exploitation in times of scarcity by regulating prices, to facilitate trade by keeping down internal customs dues and to introduce a universal system of weights and measures. But the regularity with which his instructions were issued indicates their ineffectiveness; the actual unit of production and consumption

remained the great estate [1], a legacy of the Roman villa.

The economy of the Roman world in the invasion period was based on the great estates of the old landowning aristocracy. The decline of easy communications and trade forced these social units to become more self-sufficient. Alongside the estates, some of which passed into the hands of the invaders, there remained a free peasantry that still existed in the ninth century. But its decline was hastened by the centralization policies of Charlemagne and the obligations imposed by the government on all free men. It became preferable to surrender individual land rights to the local lord in order to escape the fiscal liabilities of freedom.

## The Church, trade and commerce

The decline in personal freedom benefited the great estates of the aristocracy and the Church. Most available records of ninth-century estates are monastic and show a pattern of organized growth indicating that the Church played a crucial role in maintaining economic stability in difficult times.

The growth of European towns was based both on the old Roman cities (especially in Italy and the south) and on the garrisons and royal residences of the Carolingians and the Merovingians, their predecessors, such as Aachen, Nijmegen, Worms, Frankfurt and Ratisbon. Other cities, and mercantile suburbs of older cities such as Paris, grew round the monasteries which were the major producers of surplus goods for sale.

The uncertainty of statistics of trade and commerce after the fall of the Western Empire has given rise to much theorizing by historians. It fostered especially the belief that the economy of the Western world survived the Germanic invasions, but was brought to a halt by the Islamic conquests of the seventh century. The loss of the Mediterranean, it was argued, destroyed the movement of merchandise both between East and West and also internally within the West, reducing trade to mere barter. In fact trade continued, although on a much reduced scale. The centres of commerce initially switched from Provence and Languedoc to the north of Europe – Frisia, the Low Coun-

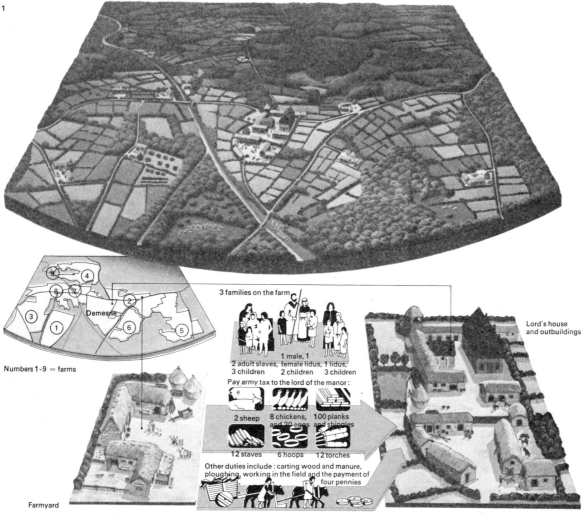

1

Numbers 1-9 = farms

Demesne

Farmyard

3 families on the farm

1 male, 1
2 adult slaves, female lidus, 1 lidus,
3 children    2 children    3 children

Pay army tax to the lord of the manor:

2 sheep    8 chickens    100 planks
           and 30 eggs   and shingles

12 staves   6 hoops     12 torches

Other duties include: carting wood and manure, ploughing, working in the field and the payment of four pennies

Lord's house and outbuildings

**1 A typical "villa"** or rural social unit in Carolingian Europe is here illustrated, and its population and composition shown. This organization was the result of the fusion of the old Roman "villa" with the customs of the invading

Germanic peoples. The status of the peasants varied: some were free, some owed various degrees and types of service to the lord. An estate was divided into the demesne land, the property of the landlord cultivated by forced labour, and

the land cultivated by his tenants as "mansi". The return for their tenancy was calculated in various burdens of service. These could be increased if the tenant exchanged his military obligations for service to the lord. Carolingian

peasants were divided into "coloni", free men still obliged to till their own land, "lidi", half-freemen owing certain legal obligations, and "servi" who had no legal rights at all. But although outside the law, "servi" did hold

property. The total population of the estate was known as the "familia" and was supervised by the landlord or his agent. Slaves in principle worked the demesne land for three days a week, while "coloni" and "lidi" performed set tasks throughout the year. Estates such as the one illustrated were centralized units of production on land redeemed from the surrounding forests. They were also early centres of rudimentary industrial

organization for weaving and cloth production. Finally, they were the basic unit of the rural feudal society that provided both the stability and the opportunity for oppression in early medieval society.

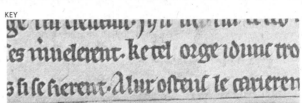

ties, northern France and the Rhineland. The old route to the north from Ostia (the port of Rome) to Provence and thence by land gave way to a land route over the Alps. Italian ports such as Amalfi [4] and Gaeta maintained a precarious commercial liaison with the East and in the tenth century the emergence of Venice [3] foreshadowed a new era in Mediterranean trade.

Charlemagne sought to create a stable coinage, but never succeeded in making the minting of money a royal monopoly which was one possible way of avoiding constant debasement. Charlemagne did understand the need for a coinage to be used as a medium of exchange, rather than barter, and his silver denarius, or penny, became one of the standard coins of the medieval West. But Carolingian coinage supplied only the small change of the West, whereas the international trading currency of the Middle Ages became the Byzantine gold nomisma and the Arab gold dinar [2].

The population of Western Europe expanded very slowly after the ravages of the invasion years. Stagnant economies could not support cities of 50,000 to 100,000 people such as those of the Arab world at Cairo, Antioch and in Spain at Córdoba. Under the manorial system, towns had lost their importance and many were abandoned.

## Industry and agriculture

Industry, such as mining and weaving, was only in its infancy in the ninth century and was mainly centred on monastic properties. Comprehensive rotational systems of agriculture barely survived on the old Roman estates. Agricultural technology gradually improved with the introduction of heavy wheeled ploughs for northern soils. The harrow and the flail were probably introduced at that time and the decline of slavery made the extended use of watermills for grinding corn an economic necessity. Yet production was too low to support any great increase in population and trade was too ill-organized to offset local effects of crop failure and plague [Key]. The technological knowledge of the Romans was never wholly lost, however, and new inventions were gradually developed.

**Early medieval life** was primarily agricultural. Harvest time was the crucial part of the year.

Cereals were the staple of life, meat being a luxury. Limited productivity and trade meant that

a successful harvest was the only insurance against famine and its constant attendant, plague.

**2 Medieval currency problems** were twofold: to preserve a coinage acceptable to all trading partners and also to enable transactions to be performed through a monetary medium rather than by barter. The Clovis II coin [A] shows the Merovingian attempt to maintain a prestige form of Roman coinage, but debased both in design and metallic content. Coins such as the gold solidus [B] of Louis the Pious (778–840) were minted in many towns, although under the control of the king. No Western economic system at this time could support such reliable coinages as the Byzantine nomisma [C] of Justinian II or the Arab gold dinar [D]. These coins were the basic tender of medieval international trade until the Florentine florin was minted in the 14th century.

2

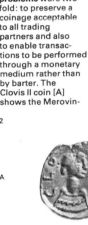

A

B

C

D

**3 Trade in the Mediterranean** was sharply curtailed by the pirates who followed in the wake of Arab conquests. Yet gradually the need for raw materials from the West and for luxury goods and spices from the East ensured that increasing numbers of vessels, as this one portrayed in a Venetian mosaic, plied the Mediterranean.

**4 Amalfi, with its natural harbour,** was one of the key commercial links between the Western world and Byzantium before the rise of Venice. The revival of western Mediterranean trade came from Italian towns such as Amalfi, Naples, Salerno and Ravenna that had the closest links with the Byzantine world.

# The Holy Roman Empire

The Holy Roman Empire sought to re-create a united Christian West such as had existed in theory during the last years of the Roman Empire. It was holy because it was based on the theory that the pope was supreme in ecclesiastical affairs, the emperor being the secular arm and the defender of the Church. It was Roman – despite the fact that the emperor was first a Frank and then a German – because Rome had for so long been the political centre of the world.

## Power struggle

The theory that the pope represented the spiritual authority of God on earth and the emperor temporal authority was rarely a reality. In practice there were strong emperors and strong popes, and power fluctuated. From the mid-eighth century the Papacy had looked increasingly to the Franks for protection against the Lombards, a dependence which culminated in 800 when Leo III crowned Charlemagne as emperor in Rome. Although the term was not used until the twelfth century, the papal recognition of Charlemagne may be seen as mark-ing the beginning of the Holy Roman Empire. The tenth century was dominated by the political success of the Ottonian emperors (962–1024), a Saxon royal house [Key 1, 2, 3]. Otto the Great (912–73) was enthroned as king of the Germans at Aachen in 936 and crowned as roman Emperor in 962 [4].

The Salian dynasty (1024–1125) saw the height of imperial power at a time when the Papacy was also powerful. The Salians were a Frankish family. Their empire under Conrad II (990–1039) included Germany, Burgundy and Italy, and Conrad saw himself as ruler of the city of Rome.

## The Investiture Contest

But a new reforming spirit within the Papacy made a major issue over the problems of investiture: who should appoint bishops, the pope or the secular ruler? The quarrel was essentially about the great wealth and power of the benefices at stake. No ruler could afford to relinquish control over appoint-ments to the wealthiest positions in the land. The so-called Investiture Contest culmi-nated in a complete breakdown of imperial-papal relations which damaged the theoret-ical justification and the effective power of the Holy Roman Empire. The contest reached its height in the reign of Henry IV (1050–1106), who found that there was no possible compromise on this issue with Pope Gregory VII. Accordingly he called an impe-rial synod at Worms in 1076 and deposed Gregory. Gregory retaliated, deposed and excommunicated Henry, and began to build up a strong anti-imperial coalition. Henry, realizing the seriousness of his position, spent three days in a hair shirt at Canossa [6] awaiting papal forgiveness. Gregory then withdrew the excommunication but not the deposition. Henry had his revenge in 1084 when he marched on Rome and drove Gre-gory to a bitter death in exile. The Investiture Contest was finally solved by a compromise in which the emperor was allowed to invest a bishop with his sceptre before consecration by the ecclesiastical authorities.

The religious and political pretensions of the empire reached their height under the Hohenstaufens (1138–1254). Frederick I

Empire of Otto I 962

Dependent state

Tributary province after 950

Invasion by Magyars until 955

**1 Expansion of the empire** followed the crowning in 936 of a Saxon, Otto I (912–73), as supreme leader of the five German tribal duchies – Saxony, Franconia, Bavaria, Swabia and Lotharin-gia. His attempts to increase his power led to constant strife and to his papal coronation as emperor in 962. He became King of the Lombards in 951 and in 955 his victory over the Magyars at Lechfeld began the westwards expan-sion of the empire.

**2 St Michael's** at Hildesheim in Sax-ony, destroyed in World War II, was built in the early 11th century under the supervision of Bishop Bernward. It was later decorated with fine bronze or-naments and a magni-ficent flat, painted ceiling entirely cov-ered with a represen-tation of the Tree of Jesse. The plan of the church re-ferred back both to early Christian and to Carolingian archi-tecture but its in-ternal rhythms were made subtler by two transepts and an apse.

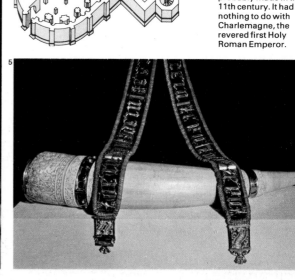

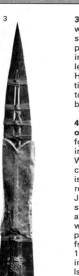

**3 The Holy Lance,** which pierced the side of Christ, was politically the most important relic. In legend given by St Helena to Constan-tine, it passed to Otto I, who bore it in battle.

**4 The imperial crown of Otto I** was made for his papal investiture in 962. With the Christian cross in front, it is octagonal to rep-resent the heavenly Jerusalem, with a semicircular strip above to represent world dominion. Two panels back and front each contain 12 stones represent-ing the tribes of Israel. On the sides are biblical kings. The crown symbolizes the functions of the wearer as temporal ruler and regent of Christ on earth.

**5 "Charlemagne's hunting horn",** one of the treasures of the emperors, was probably made in the 11th century. It had nothing to do with Charlemagne, the revered first Holy Roman Emperor.

"Barbarossa" (1123–90) and Henry VI (1165–97) saw themselves as the holy leaders of a God-given German Empire. Frederick I's power was based on an alliance with Henry the Lion of Saxony against the Normans and the Romans, and the opposition of the pope in 1159 led him to appoint his own pope, Victor IV. The Papacy thereafter backed the Lombard League – an association of north Italian cities that opposed Frederick and forced him to make peace after the Battle of Legano in 1176.

## A dream shattered

Henry VI claimed all the lands of the Normans, especially Sicily [9], and dreamed of capturing Tunis and even Constantinople. He built the first imperial fleet, and defeated a hostile coalition between northern Germany and Britain when he made Richard Coeur de Lion his prisoner. His son Frederick II (1194–1250) had been brought up in Sicily and was more Mediterranean than German. Ambitious but sceptical, he was the mortal enemy of the Papacy and achieved the greatest expansion of imperial influence [7].

Sicily under the Hohenstaufens was culturally a mixture of Italian, Arabic, Greek, Norman and Germanic influences, and was part of a larger culture that spread from Mesopotamia through Moorish Spain. Frederick saw politics as an art, government as a bureaucratic skill. He patronized the arts and sciences and founded the university of Naples to rival Bologna. He saw the empire as a German federation and in 1231 was prepared to recognize the territorial claims of the princes. In 1235, he published the Landfrieden of Mainz, the first German law written in German which defined the empire as a league of princes within a monarchic framework. His negotiations with the Muslims scandalized the Christian West but enabled him to be crowned at Jerusalem without fighting a crusade. At the Council of Lyons in 1245 he was condemned and deposed. When, on his death, the Papacy broke the power of his family, the future of the international empire of his dreams was shattered. The empire survived, but as a spectral organization, until Napoleon Bonaparte's arrival in Germany in 1806.

KEY

The imperial seal of Otto III (r. 980–1002) epitomized his ambition with the inscription *Otto Imperator Augustus Renovatio Imperii Romanorum* – Emperor Otto Augustus, the Renewal of the Empire of the Romans. The grandson of Otto I who founded the dynasty, Otto III was crowned aged three. His education was designed to produce an emperor who combined German strength and tradition with the new Arab, Greek and Latin learning. To identify himself with Charlemagne, Otto opened his tomb at Aachen and stole a tooth, nail clippings and clothes. On feast days his clothes were decorated with lions, eagles and dragons and hung with bells.

**6 Canossa** was the most humiliating episode in the history of the empire. Although the political results ultimately favoured Henry IV, the spectacle of a penitent emperor begging for the intercession of Abbot Hugh of Cluny and Matilda of Tuscany in seeking the pope's pardon was one that injured German pride so much that even Bismarck's 19th-century conflict with the Papacy was based on a desire "never to go to Canossa again".

**7 The territorial achievements** of Frederick II (1194–1250), culminating in the Battle of Bouvines (1214) at which he defeated his last remaining opponents, were the fulfilment of German imperial ambition. Frederick inherited his Sicilian kingdom and his southern ambitions from his father, and his lands completely surrounded the papal state. He achieved the federation of Germanic countries and an administration imbued with Mediterranean culture that had been the dream of Otto III.

Sole Hohenstaufen duchy 1152
Empire of Frederick I
Allied with Empire 1184
Tributary under Frederick I
Ruled by Henry VI and Frederick II
Papal states 1152
Papal states from 1213
Towns of Leagues of Lombardy and Verona

**8 The final humiliation of Henry IV**, portrayed in this contemporary illustration, came in 1105 when he was forced to surrender his imperial regalia to his son, Henry V. Some of Henry IV's family had disagreed with his deposition of Gregory VII and installation of a new pope. Henry V joined them after becoming co-ruler in 1099 and soon overthrew the emperor.

**9 Peter of Eboli's** illumination of the siege of Naples (1191) shows the army of Henry VI attempting to enforce his wife's claim to the south Italian Norman kingdom. Despite his early successes, Naples, aided by the failure of the imperial naval allies and by plague in the besieging army, did not fall. Henry VI was crowned King of Sicily only in 1194.

**10 Castel del Monte**, in southern Italy, is the finest of a chain of strategic fortifications designed in a novel and functional manner by Frederick II. He built up in Sicily and Apulia a system of defence and administration that was the most thorough and rational in Europe. As fortifications the castles protected Frederick from attack by the Papacy. As architecture, they were part of the flowering of the arts during Frederick's reign.

119

# European expansion to the east

In the centuries before AD 1000, while a lively, enterprising society was emerging in the villages and towns of Western Europe, Eastern Europe was a land of sparsely occupied forests, grasslands and low, easily crossed mountains through which passed at random a variety of peoples. The roaming shepherds of the Carpathians, the nomads from the south Russian steppe who settled in the Danube basin, and the forest peoples of the Vistula (ancestors respectively of the modern Romanians, Hungarians and Poles) travelled up and down the region between the Baltic and the Danube, the Pripet Marshes and the Elbe. They were untouched either by the political or the religious allegiances of the settled lands to the west and south and were impervious even to the cultures of each other.

The forest peoples, Polish and Czech Slavs, seem to have been divided into numerous tribes and many of the *grody* – fortified settlements on hills or marsh islands which were their capitals – have been uncovered. The grasslands of the middle Danube were the haunts of successive nomadic peoples who lived by raiding neighbouring lands. The last ones, the fierce Magyars of mixed Finnish and Turkish origin, reached the area by the late ninth century.

## The spread of German influence
To the west of these peoples were the Germans, whose national identity was also recent. Their relations with the Slavs were close, sometimes hostile but often peaceful; their society of well-organized communities and their Christian civilization, contained within the Holy Roman Empire, exercised a constant and fruitful pressure. Under the powerful Ottonian kings (919–1024; emperors from 962) the German advance was rapid and for the first time there is evidence that the tribes, in their turn, were beginning to unite: by 1000 the Magyars (whose raids were checked by the German victory at the Lechfeld in 955), the Bohemians and the Poles [1] had each united under single, independent dynasties. The earliest sign of the evolution was the advance of Christianity [7]. Already in the ninth century Byzantine missionaries converted the Moravians, whose mushroom empire was annihilated by the Magyars; in its place, under German influence, there grew up the Czech duchy of Bohemia, whose first ruler, St Wenceslas (*c.* 907–29), became a Christian and a tributary of the German king.

Bohemia under German auspices was the focus for the rapid development of all Eastern Europe. Duke Boleslav I (reigned 929–63) was the father-in-law of the first Polish duke, Mieszko I (reigned 963–92), who received Christianity at his hands; while the influence of St Adalbert, Bishop of Prague [3], caused the Hungarian Duke Stephen (reigned 997–1038) to be baptized. But German influence was ambivalent. In AD 1000 the Polish duke Boleslav the Mighty (*c.* 996–1025) received a crown from the emperor and Stephen, who ended the influence of Eastern Christianity in Hungary, received a crown from the pope.

## The emergence of national identities
In the eleventh century the Bohemians, Poles and Hungarians held their own and they acquired a sense of national identity under

**1 Boleslav the Mighty** was the founder of the first Polish monarchy. His reign resulted in 30 years of internal consolidation for his country, the building of a national Polish Christian Church and significant expansion abroad. All of these developments changed Poland from an alliance of Slav tribes into a powerful, centralized monarchy. Alliances with Bohemia, Hungary and Kiev enabled the king to make the Oder and the Vistula virtually Polish rivers and also allowed him to declare war on Emperor Henry II (973–1024) between 1004 and 1008. The emperor finally recognized the integrity of the Polish state and Boleslav was crowned in 1024.

**2 St Wenceslas**, Duke of Bohemia and an enthusiastic Christian convert, became the patron saint of Hungary, Poland and Bohemia. As duke he failed to resist the aggression of the German king Henry I (*r.* 919–36), who meant to subdue the Wends and Slavs as well as the Bohemians. Bohemia became a German fief (owing nominal allegiance to the emperor) and Wenceslas, who was blamed for the defeat, was murdered by his brother, Boleslav (who succeeded him as Boleslav I).

**3 The cathedral of Gniezno** (Gnesen) was the centre of the Christian religion of the new Polish state. It housed the relics of St Adalbert of Prague, one of the apostles of Eastern Europe. Gniezno, an ancient Polish centre, was the most important of the castle towns of Boleslav the Mighty. These towns were thriving garrisons which gradually fostered local trade and finally became centres for the export of corn to the West.

native dynasties. The Premyslids of Bohemia did not receive the royal title until 1198, but although they were included in the German Empire they retained intact their Slavonic language and customs.

The Polish dynasty of Piast was more aggressively anti-German and their court at Gniezno became the focus of resistance to the ambitions of the Salian emperors. But the unity of their vast territories was superficial and from 1079 to the end of the thirteenth century the country was ruled jointly by, and then divided among, several Piast princes. Throughout this period the unity and identity of the Poles was maintained only by a national Church and a common culture.

The Hungarian house of Arpad was more fortunate in maintaining its unity in close relation with the German emperors and Hungary flourished as a bridge between Byzantium, Russia and western Europe.

**Later German migration**
The eastward advance of the Germanic peoples had been checked after 1002 short of Pomerania, Poland and Hungary [Key]; after 1100 it resumed in force. Slavonic and Magyar rulers welcomed the Germans as cultivators of the sparsely inhabited soil. First came merchants, to swell the Wendish, Polish and Bohemian towns, especially Lübeck and Danzig on the Baltic. A massive migration of farmers followed in the twelfth century: they occupied the fertile lands of Silesia, spread throughout Bohemia and parts of Hungary and pioneered the opening up of Transylvania. Finally came the knights, ostensibly to convert the pagan Lithuanians to Christianity, but also to carve out new territories along the Baltic.

Several military orders were formed which in 1237 united as the Order of the Teutonic Knights of Livonia. This heralded German domination of the Baltic and the maritime communities soon founded an association, or Hansa [4]. The Hansa played the predominant role culturally and politically in northeastern Europe. But German rule did not accompany the migration; apart from Polish friction with the Teutonic Knights, relations with the new settlers were generally friendly and mutually profitable.

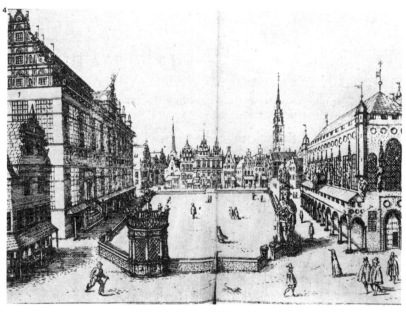

4 **Bremen**, on the Weser, is one of the great north German trading ports. Founded in the ninth century by Charlemagne, its merchants set up the city of Riga in 1158 and in 1358 joined the Hansa for protection.

5 **Marienberg, with its famous castle,** was the capital of the Teutonic Knights in Prussia. The knights, founded as a noble military, charitable and missionary organization in 1190, abandoned work in the Holy Land and settled on the Baltic coast to enforce the conversion of the pagan Prussians. In 1309 they established their headquarters at Marienburg.

6 **Pope Sylvester II** gave St Stephen the upper part of the crown of St. Stephen, symbol of Hungarian nationhood, in 1000. The circlet was given by the Byzantine emperor Michael VII 75 years later.

7 **The advance of Christianity** in Eastern Europe (1000–1250), and the conversion of the Slavs and Magyars, was quick on a superficial level, but thorough Christtianization took centuries. First came the German or Byzantine missionaries, whose real purpose was to convert the rulers and establish bishoprics; only later, in the twelfth century, did Christianity begin to reach the rural communities.

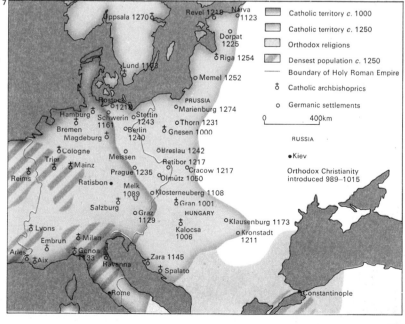

| | |
|---|---|
| | Catholic territory c. 1000 |
| | Catholic territory c. 1250 |
| | Orthodox religions |
| | Densest population c. 1250 |
| | Boundary of Holy Roman Empire |
| ⚲ | Catholic archbishoprics |
| o | Germanic settlements |

Orthodox Christianity introduced 989–1015

# The end of Anglo-Saxon England

Edward the Confessor (c. 1002–66) lived in exile in Normandy for 25 years during the reigns of Canute and his sons and succeeded to the English throne in 1042. His mother, Emma (died 1052), was a Norman and although there may not have been much love lost between Edward and Emma, he probably thought of himself as at least half Norman. He brought Norman followers with him to England, including Robert of Jumièges (died c. 1055) whom Edward made Archbishop of Canterbury in 1051 despite opposition from the earls. In a sense, therefore, Edward began the process, completed by William, of a transition from an English to a Norman society. Even royal castles, so much a part of of William's conquest, were introduced in a primitive form by Edward.

## The rise of Godwin and Harold
Edward's reign was constantly over-shadowed by the power of the family of Godwin (died 1053). Under Canute England had been divided into a few large earldoms, not unlike the old Saxon kingdoms. This consolidation produced a new and dangerous political situation, with a few earls controlling great territorial interests [2]. Much of the history of Edward's reign concerns quarrels between himself and these earls, and between members of the Godwin family, which controlled most of southern England.

Edward married Edith the daughter of Godwin, in 1045, and it seemed at first that Godwin controlled the country. But in 1051 the earl refused to obey Edward's order to subdue Dover, a town in Godwin's own earldom where disturbances had taken place. Open conflict was averted by Siward and Leofric, the other important earls, who supported the king. Edward exiled Godwin's entire family, but the following year Godwin returned, secure in his authority within his earldom, where his territorial control was much greater than that of the king. The mutual dependence of king and earl had been made apparent.

Towards the end of his reign Edward turned increasingly towards thoughts of piety and he left much of the detail of government to Harold (c. 1022–66), Godwin's son. At some time Harold visited France and fell into the power of William of Normandy (1027–87), who extracted from him an oath of support for his own claim to the English throne. Edward and Edith had no children (the king's reputation for piety derived from a legend that he never consummated his marriage), but towards the end of Edward's life an English candidate for the throne appeared, Edward the Aethling, son of the Confessor's brother. The Aethling died soon after his return from exile (c. 1059), leaving a son, Edgar (c. 1050–c. 1130), too young to be a serious candidate for kingship, and a daughter who later became St Margaret of Scotland (died 1093). So when Edward died in January 1066, Harold [4] proclaimed himself king and was crowned in Westminster, supported by Edward's council.

## The Norman invasion
Since the death of Canute, Norwegian and Danish rulers had been awaiting an opportunity to renew their claim to England. In 1066, after defeating the Danes, Harald Hardrada (1015–66) of Norway set sail for England, with the support of Tostig, the son of

1 Edward the Confessor was the last truly English king of England, because Harold was Danish by descent. The son of Ethelred II, he ruled over a court of Danes, Englishmen and Normans. This cultural mixture arose from the wealth and strength of the English throne in this period, which encouraged the ambitious Norsemen to invade the country. It was only the simultaneous attack on England on two fronts in 1066 that brought the downfall of the Anglo-Saxon kingdom. Although not such a great landowner as William became, Edward still commanded great authority through the veneration in which the monarchy was held.

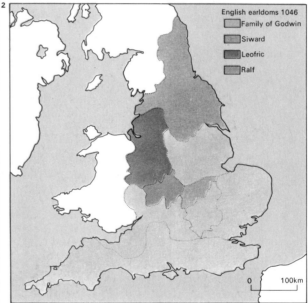

2 The great earldoms of Edward's reign were a result of Canute's policy of land distribution. Godwin himself had been an obscure soldier who rose to prominence in the service of the Danish king. In many areas, particularly Sussex and the west, he held considerably more land than the king, and the local thegns showed as much loyalty to him as to the king. Leofric and Siward, the other leading earls of Edward's reign, were unwilling to see their countryman Godwin acquiring unlimited power over the king. The distribution of earldoms on the map shows the power of the House of Godwin at its peak in 1051.

English earldoms 1046
- Family of Godwin
- Siward
- Leofric
- Ralf

0 — 100km

3 Edward (centre) quarrelled with Godwin (right foreground) in 1051 over the latter's apparent disregard for his son Sweyn's irresponsibility in 1046–9. But in 1052, the Earl Godwin was able to return virtually unopposed because Edward's policy of encouraging Normans at his court was unpopular (it was at this time that Edward is said to have promised the throne to William of Normandy). Although Godwin died in 1053, Harold was able to take advantage of this sympathy and take virtual control of the country until the death of Edward.

4 Harold, the son of Godwin, was accepted as king on Edward's death, although Edward had probably offered the throne to William of Normandy, and Harold had sworn to support him.

5 Stigand, an infamous pluralist, was Archbishop of Canterbury in 1066, but William, an ardent supporter of Cluniac reform, replaced him with Lanfranc, who introduced feudalism to the Church.

STIGANT ARCHIEPS

Godwin. The English king decisively defeated his northern enemies at Stamford Bridge but then had to march from York to Hastings to meet the second enemy, William, who had landed at Pevensey on 28 September to assert his own claim to the throne. William brought new military skills to England, using ranks of lancers on horseback against the traditional English foot-soldiers fighting with axe and sword. Nevertheless, the Norman victory at the Battle of Hastings, fought on 14 October, was not a foregone conclusion and owed much to the exhaustion of the English.

### England after the Conquest

The Battle of Hastings is depicted on the Bayeux tapestry [Key, 5, 7], a long embroidery completed *c.* 1080, perhaps commissioned by Bishop Odo of Bayeux (*c.* 1036–97). William refused to be crowned by Stigand, Archbishop of Canterbury (died 1072), whom he replaced in 1070 with Lanfranc (*c.* 1005–89), an Italian monk. After a rebellion in Exeter in 1067, and in the north in 1069, drastic measures were taken to bring

the country under control [7]. There were a few pockets of resistance [8] but much of the English nobility had died in battle; their heiresses often married Norman barons.

A uniform system of land tenure was imposed, all land being distributed in return for specific military services, which facilitated long-term garrisoning of the castles that defended Norman rule [6]. In order to establish precisely the obligations of his tenants, William ordered a survey to be made of his new possessions – the Domesday Survey, completed in 1086.

Much of the Anglo-Saxon way of life disappeared with the ending of free land tenure for the thegn and ceorl. Some legal institutions continued in a debased form, but art and literature, which had been flourishing at that time, died out. Fifty years after the Conquest, the distinction between English and Norman had been lost. The Conquest gave new vitality to the towns, reorganized the Church in 1070 and brought England closer to the culture of Europe; in many ways it can therefore be considered the beginning, as much as the end, of an era of English history.

**Harold was killed at Hastings** either by an arrow in his eye or, as is more likely, by being cut down by a Norman horseman. His army of about 7,000 men consisted of both the traditional Anglo-Saxon king's band of followers, and the fyrd, or local militia comprising less well-trained soldiers who were called out to deal with emergencies. After the battle, William advanced swiftly to London before any significant new opposition could be organized around the last remaining member of the English royal family, Edgar the Aethling. William founded a monastery on the site of the battle, a symbol of the unity of political power and religious duties for a Norman.

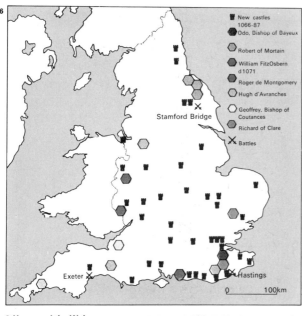

**6 William allocated the land of England** in such a way as to allow his invading forces to control the country. He built castles in the towns, and gave estates to his followers, who were spread throughout the kingdom to prevent any of them from gaining local power as Godwin had done. The south of England, the most strategically vital area, remained in the hands of a few trusted friends. But he gave the lands of more than 2,000 thegns to fewer than 200 Norman barons, and so radically centralized the power structure of England. William kept large estates for his own use. The introduction of feudalism was perhaps the most dramatic effect of his rule.

Map legend:
- New castles 1066-87
- Odo, Bishop of Bayeux
- Robert of Mortain
- William FitzOsbern d 1071
- Roger de Montgomery
- Hugh d'Avranches
- Geoffrey, Bishop of Coutances
- Richard of Clare
- Battles

Stamford Bridge
Exeter
Hastings
0    100km

**7 The revolt of the north,** in 1069, was punished by William with such severity that the Domesday Survey, of 20 years later, shows the most affected areas – Yorkshire and Lancashire – as still far less prosperous in agriculture than the rest of the country. Such brutality, and the force with which the Normans cleared the centres of towns to build castles to overawe the populace, meant that many Englishmen hated the invaders. Although the Normans ended the Anglo-Saxon institution of slavery, they reduced freemen to the level of serfs and cut the authority of the common law.

**8 Hereward the Wake** was a semi-legendary English thegn who carried on opposition to William from a hideout in the Fens of East Anglia. Before the Conquest he had held significant estates in Lincolnshire. But opposition to the Normans as violent as shown in this 19th-century illustration was not common; most English accepted the new king and by the early 12th century it was common for a man of English descent to become a royal official such as a sheriff. At the end of the story of Hereward, it is said that he was pardoned by the king. Only two Englishmen survived the Conquest as important landowners; others became managers of their old estates.

**9 The late Anglo-Saxon stone carving** at Kilpeck Church, Herefordshire, is one of the few examples of an English cultural survival after the Conquest. In most other respects, a sharp change occurred after 1066. Norman-French and Latin became the official languages, and vernacular literature died out, as learning became more completely the province of the Church, and secular literacy became less common. But the *Anglo-Saxon Chronicle* was still written until the early 12th century. The Church itself was revitalized from the torpor into which it had fallen since 1020. Stone architecture on a massive Romanesque scale became common for churches and castles.

# Norman and Angevin England

Between 1050 and 1100 Europe was transformed by the conquests of a warrior people from a section of the north French coastlands: the Normans. They overran England and southern Italy, and settled in Scotland, Wales, the Byzantine Empire and (after the first Crusade) the Levant. These extraordinarily successful people were a closely interrelated group of families, several of them related to the Viking-descended dukes of Normandy. They took the art of cavalry warfare further than any of their contemporaries and crystallized as a distinct group under the leadership of Duke William I (1027–87), the foremost general of his age.

## The conquest of England

The Normans' greatest achievement was the conquest of England, which because of its distinctive civilization, advanced organization and great wealth was the richest prize in Europe for soldiers of fortune. Normans had begun to settle there before 1066; but the transformation of England into a Norman kingdom required the ambition of William, an adventurer like the rest. The invasion of 1066 was a corporate enterprise, ostensibly to establish William as the heir of King Edward the Confessor, but really to win the Normans new fortunes. The narrow victory of Hastings, the slow advance from Canterbury to York, and the rewarding of his companions with wide estates was only just successful, for his success created in the midst of a living society an uneasy circle of adventurers [1], in some ways less civilized than the surrounding people.

Although William hoped to rule like an Anglo-Saxon king, his enemies – King Philip of France, Malcolm of Scotland, Canute of Denmark, in league with dissident Englishmen and rebellious Normans – imposed a state of virtual siege on his dominions and forced him to original expedients, critical for the future. These included the elaborate system of military service in return for land, out of which the striking solidarity of the Anglo-Norman state was born [4], the series of mighty castles – at the Tower of London, Wallingford and Colchester, in which the grandeur of Norman ambitions can still be seen [5] – and the detailed survey of English wealth made by his order in 1086: the Domesday Book [2]. The Normans transformed England, not least by reordering the diocesan structure of the Church.

## Under the Norman Empire

When William died, in 1087, England and Normandy were ruled separately by his sons William Rufus (r. 1087–1100) and Robert of Normandy, but so strongly were their societies united that within a few years they were again governed by a single ruler.

The Norman Empire, ruled by Rufus's successor and Robert's supplanter Henry I (1068–1135) and his descendants, held together until 1204. For the great Norman families, England was a colonial El Dorado but Normandy was "home". Rarely have English and continental history been so intertwined, with marked effect on English civilization: Englishmen such as Adelard of Bath and John of Salisbury contributed to the European revival of learning and science; the great English cathedrals, from Durham at the beginning of the twelfth century to Canterbury at the end, were designed by the most

**1 The Conqueror** and his companions, as portrayed in the Bayeux tapestry, demonstrate the *esprit de corps* of the Norman leaders, which was one of the secrets of their success. Bishop Odo of Bayeux (on the Conqueror's right), half-brother to William, was probably highlighted because he commissioned the tapestry.

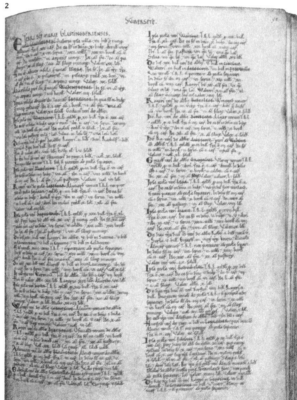

**2 The Domesday Book** was an astonishing monument to masterful and inventive rule. The survey was ordered by William in 1085 and completed in six months. Its precise purpose is uncertain, but it constituted a record of the wealth of the king and his principal subjects, of stock, of the land and the condition of the peasants who cultivated it. Teams of commissioners gathered the necessary information from jurors. This particular page describes a manor in Somerset.

**3 The Norman Empire** spread farthest under Henry II, partly because of the union, via Matilda, of Norman and Angevin domains, but largely through his marriage to Eleanor of Aquitaine.

**4 The network of Norman power** was gradually extended by linking powerful families in marriage alliances, although civil war was needed to bring the Angevins to the English throne. England alone was acquired through conquest.

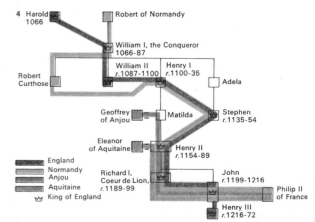

advanced French builders; an English scholar, Nicholas Breakspear, was the first and last Englishman to become pope (as Adrian IV from 1154 to 1159); and Norman French remained for three centuries the language of the English courts and society.

**England's growing prosperity**
It was also a period of unprecedented prosperity for England, apparently based on sheep: England was the main supplier of wool to the Flemish textile industry. Many landlords, especially the monasteries, owned vast estates. They were progressive farmers, opening up the fens and the Yorkshire uplands. English towns [6] such as Norwich, Oxford and Salisbury developed rapidly, usually around existing episcopal seats and castles. Flourishing markets for agricultural products needed special protection and for the first time there was a definite movement towards self-governing guilds.

Norman England was also remarkably advanced in the arts of government and a series of careful monarchs (broken only by the disputed succession between Henry I's daughter Matilda and his nephew Stephen of Blois) sought to marshal England's resources rationally. On Stephen's death, Matilda's son Henry II of Anjou (reigned 1154–89) governed with professional skill, using men who were prepared to experiment with legal forms, establish precedents for consistent action and keep records as a matter of routine. The exchequer, the jury and the common law courts are institutions that began their organized life in his reign [7].

Their significance, however, lay in the future. At the time there were many signs that the now unwieldy empire was breaking up [3]. Its French inhabitants increasingly looked to the king of France, and the last years of Henry II's reign were disrupted by rebellions, in which his sons joined. After his death the empire was held together by the sheer military genius of his son Richard I (reigned 1189–99); but Richard's brother John, who was no general, lost it forever in only five years [8]. By 1204, England had once more become a separate kingdom, enriched and transformed by a century and a half of Norman and Angevin rule.

KEY

**Orford Castle** in Suffolk, built by Henry II, was typical of the many stone castles that were constructed in every part of England. Control of these castles was the first requirement of effective authority; they could be captured only with the expenditure of much time and effort. The earliest was the Conqueror's wooden prefabricated castle set up on the beach at Hastings before the battle. Henry II showed characteristic inventiveness in the design of Orford, built between 1166 and 1172 to control the Alde estuary and the Suffolk hinterland. Its keep is polygonal outside and cylindrical within; its services are in the outer shell.

5

**6 Old Sarum,** an intact medieval town site, is dominated by the ruins of its castle. Sarum is an example of a town flourishing under royal patrons: Norman kings often resided there and William I made it a bishopric. It declined from 1222 when the bishop moved to nearby Salisbury.

6

**5 The Abbey Church of St Albans** is one of the greatest Norman buildings. Its immensely long nave and elaborate east end, which was later rebuilt, are characteristic of the Anglo-Norman style. The Norman part (the central tower and most of the nave) was built, 1077–93, under the direction of Abbot Paul. Although Norman in inspiration, many of the details are Anglo-Saxon since rebuilding had been planned before the Conquest.

7

8

**8 King John** was buried at Worcester Cathedral after a reign that provoked hatred and distrust among most of his subjects, principally because he presided over the dissolution of the Angevin Empire. After 1204, when he lost most of his continental possessions, he devoted himself to their recovery. Most of the troubles of his reign were caused by the need for heavy taxation when prices were rising sharply. Abortive campaigns ended with the rebellion of the barons and the imposition on him of the Great Charter at Runnymede in 1215. After the sealing of the charter the Norman Empire had to make way for the emergent English nation.

**7 The Great Seal of Henry II,** despite its use in the orderly life of the realm, bears a warlike image. With the aid of capable ministers, Henry transformed the existing customs into a systematic body of law and an efficient administrative procedure.

# Islam in Europe

The overthrow of the Visigothic state of Iberia in AD 711 by Berber forces recently converted to Islam (further penetration into France was stopped by Charles Martel in 732) was an event unforeseen by the Arabs of the East. The distance of Spain from Damascus was such that these forces could not have expected to enjoy the full fruits of their conquest.

## Independence from the East

In the early years the governors of Al-Andalus, as the Muslim-controlled area of the Iberian Peninsula was called, were nominated, however, by the caliphs in the East and revenue from taxation did find its way across the Mediterranean. No such benefits were forthcoming after AD 756 when the Umayyad family achieved pre-eminence among the small number of Arabs (probably fewer than 20,000) who had settled in the peninsula. This family retained supremacy in Córdoba [2] for nearly 300 years, maintaining from the outset political independence from the East.

Although there was an increasing inci-dence of conversion to Islam among the indigenous population during that period, the Umayyads of Córdoba could seldom command the loyalty of all Muslims in the peninsula. It was only in the tenth century, under Abd ar-Rahman III, who declared himself caliph in AD 929, that hitherto semi-autonomous regions acknowledged, sometimes after protracted conflicts, the supremacy of the Umayyads. The ensuing unity gave Al-Andalus a strength that enabled the state to brush aside sporadic forays by the kingdoms of the north and even, on occasions, to arbitrate in the dynastic disputes of these kingdoms. Profitable treaties were struck with some of the small North African dynasties and trade was established with the German and Byzantine empires.

## Importance of Córdoba

Córdoba became the undisputed capital of western Islam and a magnet for scholars [9], poets and craftsmen who assembled there from throughout the Islamic world. A palace was built in the cooler foothills of the nearby Sierra Nevada where the caliph resided and conducted affairs of state, while in Córdoba itself successive additions imparted increasing splendour to the Great Mosque.

Unity in Al-Andalus proved, however, to be difficult to maintain and as a result the caliphate was formally dissolved in AD 1031. The subsequent fragmentation of Al-Andalus into some 30 city states, all jealous of their own independence and covetous of the territories of their neighbours, occurred in the eleventh century when Christians from beyond the Pyrenees, actively encouraged by the pope, became involved in the internal affairs of the northern Spanish kingdoms.

## The reconquest of Muslim Spain

The reconquest of Muslim Spain may be considered in two phases, before and after the capture of Toledo in 1085 [6]. Before this date there is scant evidence from Latin or Arabic chronicles that the gradual occupation of territories to their south by the Christian states was either premeditated or concerted. This settling of sparsely populated areas indicated a colonial intention rather than any attempt to wrest territory away from

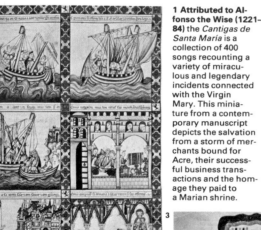

**1 Attributed to Alfonso the Wise (1221–84)** the *Cantigas de Santa María* is a collection of 400 songs recounting a variety of miraculous and legendary incidents connected with the Virgin Mary. This miniature from a contemporary manuscript depicts the salvation from a storm of merchants bound for Acre, their successful business transactions and the homage they paid to a Marian shrine.

**2 The Great Mosque of Córdoba,** begun in the 8th century, was later enlarged and embellished and is a lasting testimony to the magnificence of Islamic civilization in Spain. By 1031 the city had been devastated by civil strife and lost its place of eminence. The mosque survived, was consecrated to Christianity after the reconquest (1236) and had a church built in its centre in the 16th century.

**3 A commentary on the Apocalypse** of St John the Apostle by Beatus of Liebana shows one remarkable side of the culture of Islamic Spain. Christian manuscripts were still copied and studied in monasteries, but their style shows an enormous Islamic influence. Thus in this illumination to the text (which was done at Gerona in about 975) Jerusalem becomes a Mozarabic (Spanish-Muslim) city with the horseshoe arches to the first-floor windows that are the hallmark of the style.

**4 Rodrigo Diaz de Vivar** (*c.* 1043–99) *left,* known as "El Cid", was a Castilian knight estranged from the king, Alfonso VI. His exploits were widely celebrated and resemble those of a present-day mercenary. Supported by a force of faithful Castilians he moved freely in Muslim-held territory. His crowning achievement was the capture of Valencia in 1094, which effected his reconciliation with the Castilian king.

**5 El Cid was born** at Vivar, Burgos, where these monuments mark the site of his ancestral home. The Spanish epic *Poema de Mío Cid* portrays him as a noble Christian hero, loyal to his king despite being banished from Castile. Arabic sources emphasize his cruelty. Many ballads celebrate his achievements as an invincible knight and it has become difficult to distinguish the Cid of history from the Cid of legend.

Muslim control and it achieved very little.

Lack of any effective political cohesion among the Christian states was the main obstacle to territorial expansion at the expense of the Muslims. The Duero and Ebro valleys remained the approximate boundaries until Alfonso VI's definitive occupation of Toledo in 1085 altered the map of the peninsula by placing a permanent Christian wedge in Al-Andalus. From this time the reconquest gathered momentum and the religious factor, hitherto largely dormant, now emerged. The confrontation between Santiago and the Bible for the Christians and Mohammed and the Koran for the Muslims was evident in the clashes between the Almoravids and Almohads, Berber tribes from northern Africa, on the one hand, and the forces of Castile and Aragon on the other.

After suffering reverses, notably at the battle of Alarcos in 1195, the forces of Castile, Aragon and Portugal, usually acting independently of each other, reduced the power of Al-Andalus to some 400km (250 miles) of coastline from Gibraltar eastwards. The Nasrid kingdom with its capital at Granada lasted 250 years by dint of shrewd diplomacy, judicious alliances contracted from time to time with both Castilians and Muslims from North Africa, trading links with Genoese and Catalan merchants and geographical barriers, such as the Sierra Nevada, that discouraged assaults. The Alhambra, built in the fourteenth century, is the major monument of this bastion of Islamic civilization in a Spain whose political orientation was by then the same as that of the other Western European powers.

Hostility towards the Muslims and reverence for the Islamic cultural tradition were not incompatible in the new Spanish state. While wars were being waged in frontier zones, Toledo, like Norman Sicily [8], became a centre from which Greek and Arabic learning was transmitted to Western scholars. Churches in ornate styles were built by Muslim craftsmen; kings were familiar with Arabic and yet the power of Islam in Spain and Sicily was on the wane. The reconquest was a major political achievement, but the vestiges of nearly 700 years of Islamic presence in Spain were indelible.

**The castle of Manzanares el Real,** to the north of Madrid, was constructed near the site of an earlier fortress during the second half of the 15th century in the elaborate Mudejar and late Gothic styles. It was the residence of the Mendoza family, whose members were granted the marquisate of Santillana and the dukedom of Infantado for distinguished political and military service. This brought them material enrichment and increasing prominence in Castile's affairs.

Christian territory
Muslim territory
....... Internal boundaries

**6 The boundaries** between Christian and Muslim Spain altered little until the capture of Toledo (1085). The reconquest achieved its greatest momentum in the 12th and 13th centuries, when the crusading zeal was at its height. The small kingdom of Granada, however, survived until 1492.

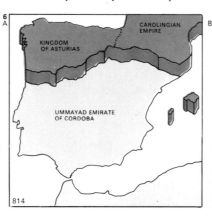

6 A
CAROLINGIAN EMPIRE
KINGDOM OF ASTURIAS
UMMAYAD EMIRATE OF CORDOBA
814

B
KINGDOM OF LEON
KINGDOM OF NAVARRE
COUNTY OF BARCELONA
EMIRATE OF CORDOBA
912

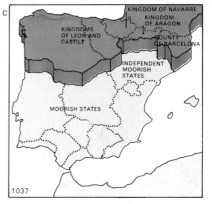

C
KINGDOM OF NAVARRE
KINGDOM OF ARAGON
KINGDOMS OF LEON AND CASTILE
COUNTY OF BARCELONA
INDEPENDENT MOORISH STATES
MOORISH STATES
1037

D
KINGDOM OF NAVARRE
KINGDOM OF LEON AND CASTILE
KINGDOM OF ARAGON
KINGDOM OF PORTUGAL
DOMINION OF THE ALMOHADS
1150

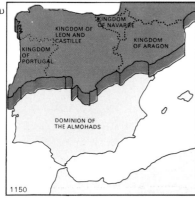
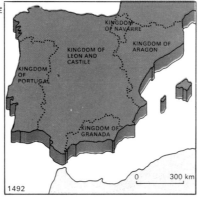

E
KINGDOM OF NAVARRE
KINGDOM OF LEON AND CASTILE
KINGDOM OF ARAGON
KINGDOM OF PORTUGAL
KINGDOM OF GRANADA
1492
0    300 km

**7 St James the Elder** (died c. 44) is the patron saint of Spain. His body was miraculously discovered in the 9th century in the remote province of Galicia where the city of Santiago de Compostela now stands. The shrine became a centre of pilgrimage for Christians, thus opening Spain to European influences, and the Spanish Christians acquired a warrior saint who would lead them into battle against the Muslims.

7

8

**8 Byzantine and Arabic features** are prominent in Monreale Cathedral, built by the Norman William II (1154–89) who challenged Muslim political and religious supremacy in the Mediterranean.

9
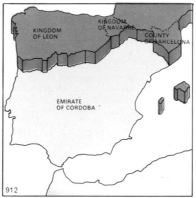

**9 During Raymond of Toledo's** archbishopric (1125–51), large numbers of Arabic works were translated into Latin by scholars from all over Europe. Scientific and philosophical treatises were thus introduced to western Christendom.

127

# The Crusades

The immediate cause of the First Crusade – and the starting-point for a major stage of European expansion – was the threat to the Byzantine Empire created by the Seljuks. These Muslim tribesmen had conquered the empire's richest province, Anatolia, and farther east had dispossessed the caliphs of Antioch, Tripoli and Jerusalem. An attack on Constantinople seemed inevitable.

In 1095 the emperor, Alexius I Comnenus (reigned 1081–1118), an able soldier and diplomat, therefore asked Pope Urban II (1042–99) for assistance, baiting his request for a contingent of mercenaries to retake Anatolia with the suggestion that they could then travel on to liberate Jerusalem. Urban responded [1] and for the first time the Papacy sanctioned a "holy war". It promised that whoever undertook this pilgrimage would be freed from all penances due.

## The First and Second Crusades
The four separate armies of the First Crusade [3] converged on Constantinople in the winter of 1096–7: men from Lorraine, the Norman kingdom of Apulia, Provence, Brit-tany, Normandy and Flanders. The Franks took Nicaea and Dorylaeum; Antioch fell after a lengthy siege, and the Crusaders stormed Jerusalem in July 1099 [2].

With the holy places conquered, territorial motive now became paramount. Four Frankish states [5], defended by the castles and garrisons of the Templars and Hospitallers [6], survived increasing Muslim pressure until 1144, when Edessa fell. A crusade was called for by Pope Eugenius III (died 1153). Emperor Conrad III (1093–1152) and King Louis VII of France (1121–80) incompetently led the armies of the Second Crusade (1147–9) to starvation and disaster in Anatolia.

## Jerusalem falls to the Turks
A further revival of Islam and the empire's final loss of Anatolia to the Seljuks in 1176 left the Latin states in danger. Saladin (Salah ad-Din, 1137–93), the brilliant Kurdish vizier of Egypt, united Islam from the Nile to the Tigris and in 1187 invaded the Latin Kingdom of Jerusalem, and overran the Frankish states.

The armies of the Third Crusade (1189–91) came to their aid and Frederick I (Barbarossa) (1123–90), the Holy Roman Emperor, took the Seljuk capital of Iconium. Phillip II Augustus of France (1165–1223) and Richard I of England (1157–99) joined the ex-King of Jerusalem, Guy of Lusignan (1140–94), in besieging Acre, which surrendered after a two-year siege. Richard then set out for Jaffa, the port of Jerusalem, and although he won the coast from Tyre to Jaffa for the Christians, was prevented from attacking Jerusalem.

The Fourth Crusade (1202–04), supported by Pope Innocent III (c. 1160–1216) to restore the kingdom of Jerusalem, resulted in the debasement of the ideal: war was now made against fellow-Christians for gain. Venice, which largely controlled the eastern Mediterranean, forced the army to accept a price for transport to Egypt which it could not pay. The Doge of Venice agreed to remit the debt only if the troops were diverted to repossess Zara on the Adriatic, a former Venetian city taken by the Magyars in 1186. The army was then persuaded to intervene in

**1 Pope Urban II's appeal** to the Council of Clermont (1095) launched the First Crusade and was an attempt to reconcile Church and state. The reply to his call, a shout of *"Deus vult"* (God wills it), later became the battle-cry of Crusader-knights in the Holy Land. His appeal led to the spontaneous and ill-disciplined People's Crusade (1096). The Pope's appeal to biblical images of Jeru-salem, the heavenly city, made the idea of freeing the earthly city one of great splendour and power. The Pope reinforced his appeal with calculated references to Western over-crowding and famine.

**2 Crusaders besieging Jerusalem** in June and July 1099, faced fortifications more complex than any in northern Europe. A quick assault was necessary as the defenders had poisoned the wells for 10km (6 miles) around the city. Wood had to be fetched by sea for the scaling ladders, mangonels (beams that hurled boulders), giant catapults and trebuchets (slings worked by counterweights). Three wooden "castles" on wheels, to make possible attacks on the upper levels of the walls, were hung with hides to ward off arrows and "Greek fire" (a blazing naphtha-based mixture extinguishable only by vinegar). The knights cared for their horses before they looked after themselves: heavy warhorses, trained to charge home against infantry and able to carry a man wearing a third of his own weight again in armour, were irreplaceable in the East. Loss of his horse reduced the knight to the ranks of the foot soldiers. The heat claimed many lives.

First Crusade 1096-9
Second Crusade 1147-9
Third Crusade 1189-91

0  400km

**3 The recovery of the holy places** and the protection of the subsequently established Frankish states were the aims of the early Crusaders. The separate armies of the First Crusade (1096–9), from France, Provence, Normandy, Flanders and Apulia, joined at meeting-points throughout Europe, marched through Magyar territory to Constantinople and fought their way across Asia Minor. Those of the Second Crusade (1147–9), led by the kings of France and Germany, also went overland, but their refusal to adapt to conditions of Eastern warfare led to their destruction by the Seljuks of Asia Minor. By the Third Crusade Western naval strength had improved and Richard I chose a sea route to Acre.

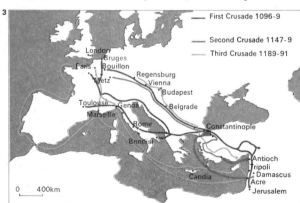

Fourth Crusade 1202-04 Venice-Constantinople
Fifth Crusade 1218-21
Sixth and Seventh Crusades 1228-9 and 1248-50

0  400km

**4 Directly concerned with saving Jerusalem,** the 4th–7th Crusades, aroused far less enthusiasm in the West than had their predecessors. Greed and hatred for fellow-Christians in the East made the army of the Fourth Crusade easy prey for the manipulations of Venice. Personal magnetism and negotiating skill brought about what successes were later achieved by Emperor Frederick II and King Louis IX of France.

a Byzantine dynastic quarrel and besiege Constantinople itself. The presence of a Frankish army brought to a head hatred between Greek and Latin Christians, long fostered by mutual blame for successive crusading disasters. In April 1204 the Crusaders seized and looted the city.

## The Crusaders finally defeated

After the failure of the Fifth Crusade, 1218–21, the last in which the Papacy was actively involved, the Pope's Hohenstaufen enemy in southern Italy, the Holy Roman Emperor Frederick II (1194–1250), conquered Jerusalem by political means. He claimed its throne through his wife and sailed on the Sixth Crusade (1228–9) while actually excommunicate. Supported by the Teutonic Knights, he negotiated a ten-year truce that restored Jerusalem (except for the Temple and Muslim holy places) to the Franks. In 1229 Frederick crowned himself King of Jerusalem but, after the truce, quarrels over territory between Templars and Hospitallers so weakened the kingdom that it fell in 1244 to the onslaught of mercenary Turks.

Louis IX of France (St Louis, 1215–70) made another attack on Cairo in the Seventh Crusade of 1248–50, but was taken prisoner. Freed by ransom, he rebuilt Jaffa and Acre and conciliated Muslim leaders. His return to France, however, left the kingdom of Jerusalem crumbling because of the renewed rivalry of the military orders. Baibars, Mameluke Sultan of Egypt from 1260 to 1277, took advantage of this division; in 1268 he seized Jaffa and Antioch, and in 1271 the castle of Krak des Chevaliers [Key]. Louis IX, mortally ill, set out again on the Eighth Crusade (1270) but died in Tunis; Prince Edward (later Edward I of England, 1239–1307) reached Acre in 1271 and negotiated an 11-year truce, but in 1289 Tripoli fell to the Mamelukes and in 1291 they captured the last stronghold, Acre.

The territorial and spiritual triumphs of the Crusades were short-lived. Urban's vision of a united Christendom degenerated into papal autocracy; the division between Latin and Orthodox Christians became absolute. The West's chief defence against Islam, the Byzantine Empire, was fatally weakened.

**Krak des Chevaliers,** best-preserved of Crusader castles, guarded the north-west flank of the County of Tripoli. Begun in 1142 by the early Crusaders, it defied 12 sieges, falling to Baibars in 1271 when its garrison of 2,000 was reduced to under 200. Frankish forts were first built by the Templars to protect the pilgrim route to Jerusalem and later grew into chains of castles guarding the frontier and ports.

5
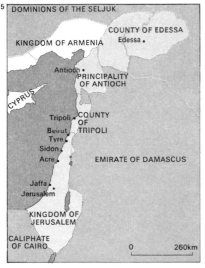

DOMINIONS OF THE SELJUK

KINGDOM OF ARMENIA

COUNTY OF EDESSA
Edessa

Antioch
PRINCIPALITY OF ANTIOCH

CYPRUS

Tripoli
COUNTY OF TRIPOLI
Beirut
Tyre
Sidon
Acre

EMIRATE OF DAMASCUS

Jaffa
Jerusalem

KINGDOM OF JERUSALEM

CALIPHATE OF CAIRO

0        260km

Muslim territory
Extent of Crusader States, about 1140

**5 The four Crusader states** comprised the County of Edessa (founded 1098), the Principality of Antioch (1098), the Kingdom of Jerusalem (1099), which claimed the overlordship, and the County of Tripoli (1109). The last, the smallest and weakest, had an unexpected ally in the Assassins, an heretical Muslim sect which supported the Franks against Damascus for 200 years. The states were feudal, had their own coinage and traded widely with Europe and the Levant.

6

Hospitaller          Teutonic Knight          Templar

**6 The military orders'** offer of a life of religion and battle brought recruits from England, France, Portugal, Spain, and Italy. The Hospitallers began in the 11th century as guardians of the pilgrim hospice of St John in Jerusalem. The first Templars, given their rule by Bernard of Clairvaux in 1128, lived in the palace of the King of Jerusalem, the "Temple". In contrast the Order of Teutonic Knights, founded in 1198, was confined to German nationals only. The orders were answerable only to the pope and held the only standing armies in the East.

7

**7 The fortified cathedral of Albi** in southern France, founded in 1277, was a deliberate symbol of the Church Militant's triumph over the Cathar heresy, which denied the reality of Christ's incarnation. The Cathars were brutally supressed by Simon de Montfort l'Amaury (1160–1218) in a crusade of 1209, inspired by Innocent III, who introduced the idea of mounting crusades to crush Christian heretics and enemies of the Papacy.

8

**8 The sixth-century Quadriga of Lysippus,** four splendid bronze horses taken during the sack of Constantinople (1204), still stand over the portal of St Mark's, Venice. A less tangible result of the Fourth Crusade was the flow into Western Europe of Greek scholars seeking refuge from the Turks, which gave impetus to the Renaissance. Earlier Crusades imported to the West new goods: damask, muslin carpets, rice, sugar, lemons, spices, dyes; and the Arabic numerals which revolutionized mathematics.

9

**9 Saladin, a chivalrous and courteous enemy,** was taken as an ideal by many Frankish knights. This 13th-century drawing from the *Chronica Majora* of Matthew Paris shows him wresting a relic of the True Cross from Guy de Lusignan, King of Jerusalem, at the battle of Hattin (1187).

10

**10 Crusaders' tombs** in English churches usually show a knight lying peacefully, his legs crossed. But in Dorchester Abbey Sir John Holcombe, who died on the Third Crusade, is shown in effigy struggling to draw his sword.

# The king and the barons

The institutions of English government were born between 1100 and 1400; only the monarchy itself is older. Kings before Henry I had taxed and dispensed justice, but the permanent institutions of the Exchequer and the King's Court on Justice took shape in his reign. They were the foundations of the vast structure of government that developed in the twelfth century: the Chancery, the Privy Seal, the courts of King's Bench and Common Pleas. The workings of this great machine penetrated into every corner of the kingdom, and its powers and limits were the underlying political question of the age.

## The growth of the leading families

Naturally, those with most to gain or lose from the king's government were his greatest subjects, whom medieval chronicles and documents such as Magna Carta call the "barons". During the twelfth century, the English nobility constituted a formidable order. Until then, the members of great noble families had been adventurers, and few survived more than two generations. From Henry I's reign onwards the natural life of a baronial family was much longer, as political co-operation and the development of landed estates became more attractive.

In defence of the principle of inheritance, the families made a determined front, and subsequent kings could not ignore the power and the steadily accumulating wealth of successive generations of Lacys, Clares, Bigods and Mortimers. Far from being opponents of central government, they usually wished to participate in it, and the "common law" administered in the king's courts, with its sensitivity to questions of land and inheritance, was developed to meet their needs.

The twelfth century was the period of formation for both the baronage and the king's government. Henry I (reigned 1100–35) [Key] raised many new families from obscurity, which threatened old-established barons, but it was reasonably possible in his reign for a landed family to hold on to its property and to prosper. But the civil wars of Stephen's reign (1135–54) [1], which followed Henry's death, was the critical time for all landed families, old or new. The succession dispute, far from providing opportunities for them, made their tenures radically insecure. The Treaty of Winchester (1153), which assured the succession of Henry II, also ensured the survival of the great landed estates, and most of the barons gave Henry their loyal support in return for the profitable "incidents" (wardships, or marriage to heiresses in the king's protection) or offices (such as the shrievalty of a county) created by renewed royal power.

## Magna Carta and after

The loss of the European dominions by King John (reigned 1199–1216) [2], and his attempt to regain them forced him to exploit his authority and patronage, and "amerce" or take a fine from the barons for every favour he did them and every real or imagined offence he "overlooked".

Many were brought to the point of ruin. The inevitable reaction resulted in Magna Carta (1215) [4], in which the barons tried to enumerate and forbid the various abuses of royal power. Its reassertion of fundamental rights was not a revolutionary idea, but it marked the resumption of the leadership

1 **Henry II crossed to England from France** in 1153, as this contemporary miniature shows. By 1150 it was clear that King Stephen could not eject the Empress Matilda or her son Henry from Normandy, nor could they expel the king from England. Henry's invasion threatened another bloody stalemate, but Stephen was made to disinherit his son. Henry II and his magnates co-operated in restoring order, devising a more just and effective law, and introducing trial by jury and assize courts. These courts, which relied on travelling judges dispensing royal justice, impinged to some extent on the barons' rights to hold feudal courts on their own estates.

2 **The Great Seal of King John** (c. 1210) symbolized the beginnings of a momentous change in methods of government. In John's reign the Chancery formalized its procedure and began to keep systematic records of the grants and royal acts made under the Great Seal. The two series of Patent Rolls (open letters) and Close Rolls (written to individuals) show the birth of a professional civil service with its own interests.

3 **John gives the traditional kiss of peace** to Philip II Augustus, King of France (r. 1180–1223), his feudal superior. John, who as the brother of Richard I (r. 1189–99), had occasionally been an accomplice of Richard's enemy, King Philip, was far less successful at holding together the Angevin Empire than Richard. By 1204, the French king's armies had swept through the fortresses of Normandy; the attempt to regain them put a strain on English resources until the Treaty of Paris in 1259. The loss of Normandy brought to an end long wars in France, but in the subsequent recriminations it also had the effect of tarnishing John's image, and from then on he was regarded as an incompetent king.

4 **A copy of Magna Carta** (one of only four official copies to survive) symbolizes the acknowledgment of the fact that the monarchy is subject to the law of the land. This recognition was extracted from an unwilling King John at Runnymede by a league of barons, churchmen and townspeople. Magna Carta is a detailed schedule of specific articles that guaranteed many kinds of inherited rights and privileges and limited the king's prerogatives.

5 **The Battle of Evesham** (1265), which ended the "Barons' Wars", saw the defeat and death of Simon de Montfort. Despite this, his reforms of government, which reflected the growing authority of the classes below the baronial one, were largely accepted.

of the community, by the united baronage.

Most of the subsequent conflicts between king and barons were the result of the Plantagenets' foreign ambitions and the strain this put upon their subjects. In each case the barons acted merely as the spokesmen of a now entrenched and articulate landed class. The ambition of Henry III (reigned 1216–72) to intervene in Italian politics led to a spirited contest with Simon de Montfort (c. 1208–65) at the head of a strong popular movement. The baronial programme, enshrined in the Provisions of Oxford of 1258, put control of the administration into the joint hands of the king and the barons to prevent the Crown developing interests against those of the nobility and, by implication, those of the country. De Montfort's cause was finally overthrown [5], but he had sufficiently shown the impossibility of foreign wars without a broad consent.

**The barons and external wars**
Edward I (reigned 1272–1307) was more masterful than his father, Henry III: but the strain put on the economy by his Scottish

wars – taxation, the king's right to "purveyance" (seizure of supplies for his campaigns), and the hard military service – alienated his barons in the absence of decisive victory. They vented their frustration on his weaker son Edward II (reigned 1307–27). At first only his favourite, Piers Gaveston (died 1312), was under attack, but the barons demanded in the "Ordinances" of 1311 control over the king's household and his powers of patronage.

Edward III (reigned 1327–77), however, showed that confrontation could be avoided. He reconciled the baronial factions in the great national enterprise of the French wars and opened up for them prospects of new wealth at French expense, at a time of falling profits from land. Richard II (reigned 1377–99) [10], because of his reliance on a private army and household government and Henry VI (reigned 1422–61; 1470–1), because of his insanity, were both driven from their thrones; but a fundamentally stronger national government came into existence in the fourteenth century through the combined efforts of kings and barons.

KEY

**The nightmare of Henry I** was narrated in an illustrated 12th-century chronicle by John of Worcester. According to this, Henry dreamed that he was confronted first with a mob of infuriated peasants, then with a group of armed knights brandishing their swords, and finally with a company of aggrieved prelates. The dream symbolizes the contemporary idea that society was divided, as King Alfred said, into "Men who fight, men who work, and men who pray". Henry's extortions from the propertied classes had given him a reputation as a rapacious ruler. He also encouraged centralization of power, a concept that aroused opposition from the entrenched nobles and their followers.

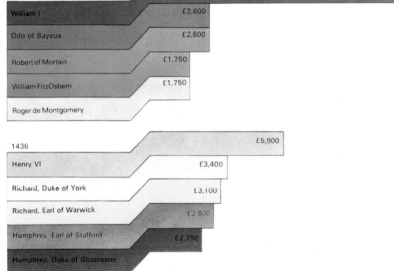

6
1086

| | | | £11,000 |
|---|---|---|---|
| William I | | £2,600 | |
| Odo of Bayeux | | £2,600 | |
| Robert of Mortain | £1,750 | | |
| William FitzOsbern | £1,750 | | |
| Roger de Montgomery | | | |

1436

| | | | £5,900 |
|---|---|---|---|
| Henry VI | | £3,400 | |
| Richard, Duke of York | £3,100 | | |
| Richard, Earl of Warwick | £2,800 | | |
| Humphrey, Earl of Stafford | £2,250 | | |
| Humphrey, Duke of Gloucester | | | |

**6 The king's income** in 1086 and 1436, compared well with that of noblemen for the same period. The king's land in 1436 was mostly Lancaster (ie private) estates but his income was greatly boosted by taxes and customs (which are not shown here). By 1436 the king's advantage in landed wealth had obviously diminished.

7

**7 The Court of King's Bench** in about 1250 administered laws and functioned by means of already established procedure. The judges, clerks and attorneys were all professional lawyers. The court was one of the most valuable institutions to the Crown in terms of prestige in the country and income from fines.

8

**8 The wheel of fortune** was a popular symbol in the 1300s and 1400s. It testified to the preoccupation with the acquisition of wealth and advancement via patronage. Many medieval illustrations stressed the impermanence of authority, and new balances of power had constantly to be made. The opportunities open to able, ambitious but poor young men increased in the 1300s. Fortunes could be made from war, and time spent in the service of the king or a great nobleman could also be profitable.

**9 John of Gaunt** (1340–99), the greatest noble of the reigns of Edward III and Richard II, kept a small armed retinue even in peacetime; it derived from the army he collected for the wars in France.

**10 Richard II handed over his sceptre** when challenged by his exiled cousin, Henry Bolingbroke (Henry IV). The unreliable Richard had made too many of his subjects feel insecure to attract their permanent loyalty.

9

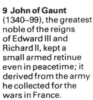

10

131

# Medieval Ireland

The continual feuding of the petty Irish kings during and after the Viking period eventually brought about English intervention in 1169, and the Norman barons who settled in the country soon controlled the greater part of it. Throughout the period there remained in the west a distinctly Gaelic culture, by which the Anglo-Irish lords of the Midlands in the fourteenth century came to be affected; the east maintained its ties with England. The great Midland families gradually increased their power and independence from the English king and the eastern English colony, and because of internal strife the English kings were in no position to reassert their control until the end of the fifteenth century.

## The Vikings and the English

By 900 the Vikings had already gained footholds along the Irish coast [1, 2], and Dublin had been founded as a trading colony as early as 841. But the Vikings had not shaken the rule of the Irish kings in the interior. The strongest of these proved to be the northern Ui Néill dynasty who defeated the Eóganacht kings of Munster in 908. The Eóganacht power in Munster then gradually passed not to the Vikings in Waterford and Limerick but to the Dál Cais of north Munster. The most famous personality of this *sept* (Irish clan) was Brian Boru (941–1014), who succeeded in becoming king of all Ireland by 1002, and finally destroyed the Viking threat at the Battle of Clontarf in 1014 [3].

Despite the reputation the Vikings had earned as ruthless plunderers, they contributed much to Irish life. Many of the country's most important maritime towns were founded by them, and from the Vikings the Irish learnt seafaring, and commerce based on coinage and market-places.

By the eleventh century the great Irish monasteries were in decline, and at a number of synods, culminating in the synod of Kells in 1152, reforms were introduced to bring them into conformity with the rest of Europe. Many older monasteries were not revived by the new division of Ireland into dioceses, but others gained new purpose by adopting Augustinian rule. The foundation of Mellifont by the Cistercians in 1142 kindled a new enthusiasm for monastic life, which was maintained and fostered by the Dominicans and, particularly in the fifteenth century, by the Franciscans.

## Invasion and resurgence

With the extinction of Viking power and the death of Brian Boru, the Irish chieftains were free to pursue unresolved wars for 150 years. In 1166 the ruler of Connaught, Rory O'Connor (1116–98), became the first king of all Ireland since 1014, but his glory was brief. Dermot McMurrough (1110–71), whom he had ousted from Leinster, sought English aid and the English king, Henry II, sent over from Wales a contingent of Norman barons. But the conflict of interests soon ended any arrangement between the Irish and the invaders, despite the brief peace of 1171 and a second compromise, the Treaty of Windsor of 1175. The Irish kings were outraged by Henry's repeatedly granting land to his vassals, but what the English king made over on parchment, the barons were determined to conquer by the sword. One region after another – although not the

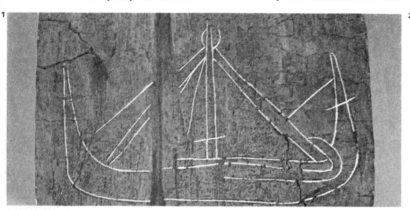

**1 A ship drawn on wood,** dating from about 1100, was discovered during excavations in Dublin. Showing clear Viking influence, it offers a rare insight into the type of vessel used by traders of the period.

**2 The many Viking descents upon Ireland** began in the fateful year of 795. During the next 50 years, Norwegian Vikings made sporadic raids down the west and east coasts, plundering as they went. They also sailed up the Shannon from Limerick in an attempt to gain a foothold in the area of Clonmacnoise and Lough Ree. They established a permanent settlement with the founding of Dublin in 841. In the century after the Danes appeared (c. 850), Viking settlement was extended south of Dublin along the east and south coasts, and towns with Viking names such as Wicklow, Waterford and Wexford were founded.

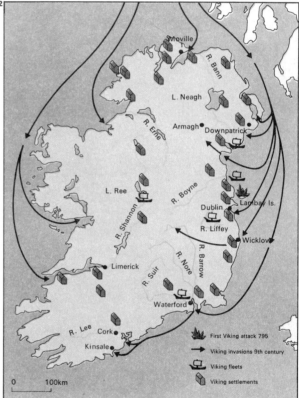

First Viking attack 795
Viking invasions 9th century
Viking fleets
Viking settlements

**3 "Brian Boru's harp",** traditionally said to have belonged to the Irish high-king, was in fact made about three centuries after his death in 1014. It was Brian who finally subjugated the Viking invaders in Ireland. In 978 Brian inherited his brother's kingdom of Munster and began his avowed conquest of all Ireland. By 984 he controlled Leinster and was supreme over southern Ireland; in 1005 Brian became the first King of Ireland. In 1013 the opposition to his rule – the men of Leinster and the Vikings with support from the Orkneys – united in armed revolt. Brian Boru's army met them at Clontarf in 1014 and emerged victorious, although Brian was slain by the fleeing enemy.

**4 Dunguaire Castle,** on Galway Bay, is one of many surviving tower-houses built by native Irish chieftains between 1450 and 1650. The fortifications of these structures were much smaller than those of the 13th-century Norman castles.

northwest – fell to the Normans [6], who were better equipped and better disciplined than the Irish. The invasion of Connaught in 1235 marked the greatest extent of Norman power. The Normans consolidated their newly won territories by building castles- [Key], and settlers founded and fortified many inland towns.

Despite the Norman Conquest, Gaelic Ireland survived. It not only retained its laws, language, traditional institutions and culture, but from 1260 began to fight back. The English presence in Ireland was severely shaken by the invasion in 1315 of the brother of the king of Scotland, Edward Bruce (c. 1275–1318), who saw himself as a liberator, and lost only his final battle in 1318. The colonists were further reduced by the onset of the Black Death in 1348. It was in the west, the stronghold of Gaelic power and culture, that the de Burgo family in Connaught began the trend among the Anglo-Irish lords of adopting Irish customs and even language. In 1361 Lionel, Duke of Clarence, the second son of Edward III, having failed to reduce the whole country to his rule, enacted the famous and divisive Statutes of Kilkenny (1366). These in effect outlawed all who adopted "the manners, fashion and language of the Irish enemies".

### Virtual independence

Two visits by Richard II in the 1390s were no more than superficially successful [7]. The "Pale", the area remaining English and loyal, became smaller in the fifteenth century, while the virtually independent Anglo-Irish lords of the Midlands expanded their power. In the west, Gaelic chieftains had wrested the land from absentee landlords. First the earls of Ormond, then the earls of Desmond and finally the earls of Kildare were the greatest power in the land; and the greatest of these was Garret More Fitzgerald, the Great Earl of Kildare, who when he died in 1513 was the uncrowned king of Ireland. A parliament at Drogheda in 1460 had declared that Ireland, should be bound only by laws passed by itself. The 1494 parliament under Edward Poynings (1459–1521), the viceroy of Henry VII, revoked this and heralded the Tudor reconquest [8].

**Trim Castle** is the largest stone castle in Ireland. Completed by a Norman baron named De Lacey (c. 1200), Trim consists of a central tower in the middle of a free-standing area defended by a curtain wall, originally surrounded by water. Shortly after the Normans first landed in Ireland, in 1169–70, they built strong fortifications to enforce their claims. At first they built mottes – earth mounds shaped like plum puddings – with a wooden tower on top. The massive stone castles were built later.

**5 The Normans** defeated the native Irish armies, at first, both by superior tactics and by better weapons and armour. This superiority is epitomized in the splendid effigy of a knight at Kilfane, County Kilkenny, shown here. He is clad from head to toe in mail with his body covered by a surcoat (a sleeveless outer garment, worn on top of chain mail). A sheathed sword hangs from a loosely buckled belt slung round his waist, and he wears the early type of rowel spurs, which helps to date the effigy at around 1320. The coat of arms on his triangular shield proclaims him to be a Cantwell, probably "Long Cantwell", who described himself as old in 1319. This was a period when Norman power had already begun to decline in Ireland, and shortly before the Normans changed over to the use of plate armour.

**6 The Normans arrived in Ireland** in 1169–70, and by 1172 were masters not only in Dublin, Wexford and Waterford, but also of much of Leinster. By submitting to King Henry II of England, many Irish rulers opened the way for Norman colonization and the founding of towns in their lands. Subsequently, Norman barons conquered Meath, eastern Ulster and large parts of Munster. By the early 13th century, they had overrun most of the areas east of the Shannon. In 1235 they established their dominion over the western province of Connaught, and 15 years later over Co Clare. By 1250, the greater part of Ireland was in their hands, the northwest alone succeeded in retaining its independence. But by 1400, the Gaelic chieftains had regained many of their lost territories, so that by the 15th century, Anglo-Norman domination was largely confined to the provinces of Leinster and Munster.

Map labels: Mottes ▲ | Major castles ♛ | Walled towns; Greencastle, Carrickfergus, Ballymote, Dundrum, Dundalk, Greencastle, Carlingford, Drogheda, Roscommon, Randown, Trim, Maynooth, Athlone, Drummagh, Dublin, Galway, Athenry, Clonmacnoise, Kildare, Newcastle, Roscrea, Blackcastle, Arklow, Nenagh, Carlow, Ferns, Limerick, Kilkenny, Adare, Enniscorthy, Wexford, Carrick, New Ross, Ballyteigne, Waterford, Cork; 0 100km

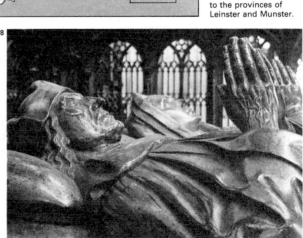

**7 Art McMurrough Kavanagh (right)**, King of Leinster confronts the Earl of Gloucester. The Earl had been sent by Richard II to demand McMurrough's submission. But he averred that he was Ireland's king.

**8 Henry VII** (r. 1485–1509), seen here in effigy in Westminster Abbey imprisoned his viceroy in Ireland, Garret More Fitzgerald, in London for a year while the Irish parliament passed Poyning's Law, in 1494, reasserting English control.

# Scotland to the Battle of Bannockburn

The Romans attempted to protect their British province by extending their power amongst the Pictish tribes beyond the frontier. For a while, in the second century AD, they occupied the south of what was later called Scotland and built the defensive Antonine Wall across the narrow waist between the Forth and the Clyde [1].

## The foundation of Scotland
In the sixth century "Scots" from Ireland crossed the narrow sea and began to settle among the scattered tribal communities of Picts, founding the kingdom of Dalriada in what is now Argyll. Eventually in the ninth century, by a mixture of royal intermarriage and conquest, the Scottish king Kenneth mac Alpin (died 858) became king of both Scots and Picts, and his successors extended this kingdom to include the area of Strathclyde, occupied by Britons, and of Lothian, where there were also Anglo-Saxon settlements. The Picts disappeared from history and the Scots spread their language, Gaelic, over most of their new kingdom, from then on to be called Scotland.

The kingdom was Christian, for the Scots had come from Christian Ireland and the Picts had been converted, partly by the mission of St Columba (521–97) [3]. It did not include all of modern Scotland, for the northern and western islands, Caithness and parts of the southwest were held by a new group of invaders, the Vikings from Scandinavia. These men had started raiding in the late eighth century, and made settlements in the ninth. Their mark in Scotland survives in placenames, and ruined buildings. It was not until the mid-1200s that a Scottish king, Alexander III (reigned 1249–86), defeated a king of Norway and took over the western isles. The northern isles remained under Scandinavian rule until the fifteenth century.

## The monarchy and feudalism
The monarchy gradually developed its own institutions. For a time the succession moved between two related lines of kings, but with the succession of Duncan I (died 1040) in 1034 an attempt was made to confine it to a single direct line. Duncan was defeated by his rival, Macbeth in 1040, but his son Malcolm III (c. 1031–93) regained the throne in 1058 and established direct succession. Malcolm married Margaret (c. 1045–93), an English princess, initiating two centuries of frequent royal marriages between the two countries. Their youngest son, David (1084–1153) [4], who became king in 1124, had spent much of his youth in England and held the earldom of Huntingdon. As King of Scotland he brought some Norman barons and friends from England and settled them in fiefs in southern Scotland. His long reign is important not only for this but also for the start of medieval monasticism in the country.

Succession was still not entirely assured, so to ensure peaceful inheritance David, when his only son died, took his 11-year-old grandson Malcolm round the kingdom to be proclaimed as his heir [Key]. Malcolm IV (reigned 1153–65) and, following him, his brother William the Lion (reigned 1165–1214) took David's policy of feudalization further, and William spread it to central and northern Scotland. Feudalism provided the kings with mounted knights in time of war and established clearly defined

1 **The Antonine Wall,** the northernmost boundary of Roman rule in Britain, was built in the 2nd century AD. But even before the end of the century it had been abandoned by Roman forces under pressure from invading Pictish tribes. This monument, from where the wall meets the North Sea, shows a Roman horseman riding down four naked tribesmen armed with spears, swords and shields.

2 **This defensive tower or broch,** built of flat stones without cement, still stands more than 12m (40ft) high on the island of Mousa in the Shetland Isles. Its thick walls offered a safe refuge from raiders and contained dwelling rooms and galleries. There are more than 500 known examples of brochs scattered along the coast of north Scotland, some dating back to the 1st century AD.

3 **Iona church** stands on the former site of St Columba's monastery (founded in 563). It was from here that Christianity was first carried by Columba to the Scottish mainland.

4 **The impulse** that David's founding of burghs gave to Scottish economic life is symbolized by the fact that his were the first coins to be minted by a Scottish king. Under his administration, trade and commerce flourished.

obligations. The new office of sheriff gave them administrators for a wide number of tasks. The founding of monasteries brought Scotland into the important religious movement of the twelfth century.

In spite of close marriage ties and cultural links with England, and the fact that some Scottish barons held land in England too, peace between England and Scotland was not firmly established. The border between the two long remained unstable; under David I, Scotland controlled Northumberland, Cumberland and Westmorland. Its claim to these countries was formally abandoned only in 1237. Successive kings on one side or the other of the border attempted to enlarge their kingdoms by conquest.

**Rebellions and the War of Independence**
The male Scottish royal line ended with the sudden death of Alexander III in 1286. It was arranged that his Norwegian granddaughter should succeed and be married to the son of King Edward I of England (reigned 1272–1307). On her death in 1290, the Scots left the decision about the succession to Edward. He chose John Balliol (reigned 1292–96), the best claimant by feudal law, but attempted to dictate to the new king. This led to an unsuccessful rebellion in 1296 [5], invasion by Edward [6], the resignation of Balliol and the removal of the Stone of Scone – on which Scottish kings were enthroned – to Westminster. For a time Scotland appeared to be conquered. But in 1297 a knight, William Wallace (c. 1270–1305), launched another and more serious national rebellion, which was not suppressed for several years. In 1306 came a third rising, ultimately successful, by Robert Bruce (1306–29) [7], whose grandfather had been a claimant against Balliol in 1291. In the long War of Independence Bruce taught the Scots how to avoid pitched battles, dismantle castles and rely on the inability of the English to sustain an army for long so far from home. Finally he defeated Edward II (reigned 1307–27) in the Battle of Bannockburn in June 1314 [8]. English claims to Scotland were not ended, and the two countries were often at war during the next three centuries, but Scottish independence was proved at Bannockburn.

KEY

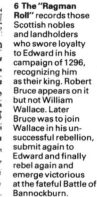

David I (left) and his grandson Malcolm IV, who succeeded him as a young boy, are shown on this 12th-century abbey charter. With David's death the country had been transformed through the widespread introduction of feudal, Anglo-Norman ways of life, a policy continued under Malcolm. David had to have Malcolm proclaimed as his rightful heir because there were other claimants to the throne by earlier rules of succession.

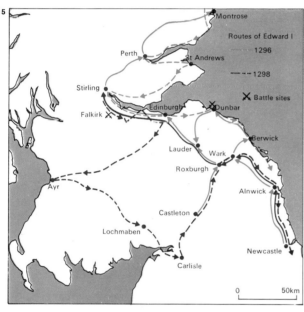

5 In 1296, Edward I invaded Scotland to put down Balliol's rebellion. After sacking Berwick and Dunbar he easily took other castles and towns, but resistance continued to the end of his reign in 1307.

6 The "Ragman Roll" records those Scottish nobles and landholders who swore loyalty to Edward in his campaign of 1296, recognizing him as their king. Robert Bruce appears on it but not William Wallace. Later Bruce was to join Wallace in his unsuccessful rebellion, submit again to Edward and finally rebel again and emerge victorious at the fateful Battle of Bannockburn.

7 Robert Bruce was crowned King of the Scots in 1306, but within three months he had been defeated by an army sent by Edward I. It was not until 1309 that Bruce had gained enough power to hold a parliament – then his guerrilla tactics were gaining the upper hand against the English forces.

8 The Battle of Bannockburn was a resounding victory for the Scottish forces under Robert Bruce. The two sides met as the English troops attempted to relieve Stirling Castle. But Edward II, unlike his father, was neither a good general nor a man of determination, and the Scots, outnumbered three to one outmanoeuvred the English.

# Wales to the Act of Union

The Welsh language and nation came into recognizable being with the expulsion of the Goidelic (Irish) Celts in the fifth century AD. The Welsh were slow to establish stable political and social order, but by the tenth century there had emerged uniquely Welsh institutions, codified by Hywel Dda or Hywel the Good (died 950) [3]. Threatened by the Saxons, encroached upon by the Normans and finally conquered by Edward I, Welsh nationalism smouldered and flared, notably in the rebellion of Owain Glyn Dŵr, or Owen Glendower (1359–1416).

## The creation of a Welsh kingdom

Evidence from Goat's Hole at Paviland in Gower proves that Wales was inhabited in Palaeolithic times by cave-dwelling hunters. After 8000 BC and until about 1000 BC Iberian migrants settled along the coast. Between 1000 and 500 BC the Celts penetrated Wales, bringing with them Druidism and the basis of the Welsh language.

The Celts remained the power in Wales until the arrival of the Romans in AD 43. Roman rule was largely military [1], and their chief interest lay in the Welsh mineral deposits, but they established a number of urban communities which exerted a civilizing influence [2]. With the withdrawal of the Romans at the end of the fourth century, Wales was rent by the struggle for power between the Brythonic (native) Celts and incoming Goidelic (Irish) Celts. Largely through the efforts of Cunedda (flourished early fifth century), who founded a number of dynasties and the new kingdom of Gwynedd [Key], the Irish were expelled. In the fifth and sixth centuries Christianity came to Wales, brought by such men as St Illtyd and St David.

Anglo-Saxon incursions during the seventh and eighth centuries greatly hindered attempts to achieve political unity in Wales. The limits of Saxon colonization of the Welsh borders are marked by Offa's Dyke, constructed in the mid-eighth century. The reigns of Rhodri the Great (died 877) and Hywel Dda established a sound political and social framework, but the greatest measure of success was achieved by Gruffydd ap Llywelyn (died 1063) who fleetingly held sway over the whole of Wales.

Towards the end of the eleventh century, Norman invaders seized control of large parts of Wales and consolidated their conquest with powerful castles [4] built at strategic points in the March of Wales (central and eastern Wales). But the princes of Gwynedd resisted their incursions and in the twelfth century presented a strong challenge to the English Crown. Llywelyn the Great (died 1240) began to weld the Welsh territories into a feudal state, and his grandson Llywelyn II ap Gruffydd (died 1282) [5] was able to assume the title Prince of Wales and was recognized in it by Henry III of England in 1267. Henry's successor, Edward I, was less easily defied. He conquered Gwynedd in 1277, humbling Llywelyn and restricting his domain to west of Conway. Following Llywelyn's death in 1282 Welsh political independence came to an end.

## English rule and Welsh discontent

The Edwardian conquest destroyed the social system of five orders established by Hywel Dda. The *brenin*, or king, with the

**1 Caerleon-upon-Usk (Roman Isca) was,** with Chester (Deva), the largest legionary base in or near Wales. The view shows the stone amphitheatre at which soldiers of the 2nd Augustan legion might watch entertainments or military demonstrations. The amphitheatre stands outside the fortress, built in AD 73.

**2 The tiny 4th-century Christian chapel,** here shown reconstructed, at Caerwent (Roman Venta Silurum) is the sole archaeological evidence of Christianity in Roman Wales. Venta Silurum was a tribal capital situated in the better developed southeast, and it was in urban communities of this kind that Romano-British Christianity had modest popularity.

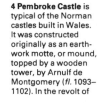

**4 Pembroke Castle is** typical of the Norman castles built in Wales. It was constructed originally as an earthwork motte, or mound, topped by a wooden tower, by Arnulf de Montgomery (*fl.* 1093–1102). In the revolt of 1094, when the Welsh severely defeated the Normans, it survived two sieges, and was almost the only castle in Wales not to fall. It subsequently became an important base for the reconquest of the country. It was rebuilt with a round keep of stone by the powerful William Marshal, 1st Earl of Pembroke (*d.* 1219). Extended in the 13th century, it was much damaged in the English Civil War and greatly restored in the late 19th century.

**5 The head of the last independent Prince of Wales,** Llywelyn II ap Gruffydd, King of Gwynedd, was borne through the streets of London after he was killed in a skirmish in 1282. Llywelyn was a first-rate soldier and a clever diplomat; he had behaved and been treated as a sovereign both by Henry III and by Edward I. The revolt in which he died was not his doing, but he was bound to support it for reasons of kinship and pride. At his death "Wales was cast to the ground", as one chronicler wrote, and swiftly subdued.

**3 This silver penny** was minted by Hywel Dda, the first Welsh king to issue his own coinage. His coins, like this one, bore the words "Hopael Rex", or King Hywel, thus asserting his claim to rule all Wales and, by its Latin, demonstrating his civilizing intention.

Hywel Dda earned his sobriquet "the Good" by codifying Welsh law; his system was to govern Welsh society until the imposition of English rule. He tried to organize Wales to conform with the rest of Christendom, and c. 930 had undertaken a pilgrimage to Rome.

*uchelwyr* (nobles) and *priodorion* (freemen) had owned and ruled the land; subservient to them had been the *taeog*, serfs with some privileges, and the *caethion*, bondsmen with none. Kinship was the primary social tie, and because inheritances were divided between all the sons, smallholdings were the norm. Fast-moving social and economic changes after 1284 swept the traditional way of life away and produced a pattern of substantial landed estates and farms consolidated under a single ownership.

With these agrarian changes, and plague, slump and, not least, alien rule, there was discontent. From 1284 to 1536 Wales was divided into the English Principality (comprising the old Welsh kingdoms) and the Welsh March [6]. In the Principality, English administration was harsh, Welsh law was disregarded, and commercial privileges were conferred mostly on English burgesses. There was at this time opposition throughout Britain to the Lancastrian regime, and, aggravated by local conditions, there were a number of rebellions in Wales, the most important being the Glyn Dŵr revolt of 1400.

Triggered by a dispute between Owain Glyn Dŵr, Lord of Glyn Dyfrdwy [8] and his neighbour Reginald Grey of Ruthin, the revolt soon spread nationally. Although it brought no political amelioration, the revolt stands high in Welsh national sentiment.

### Henry Tudor raises hopes

The collapse of the rebellion brought in its train penal laws reducing Welshmen to second-class citizens, but hostility to the English rule could find an outlet in the fifteenth century only in prophetic poetry. Prophetic bards assured Welshmen that a son of destiny would arrive to reassert Welsh supremacy in their land. During the Wars of the Roses the bards threw in their lot variously with the House of York or the House of Lancaster until, when the Lancastrian claim passed to Henry Tudor, they urged his support unanimously. Henry's victory at Bosworth in 1485 was hailed as a Welsh triumph. But the new king was an opportunist, and the call by the Welsh gentry for improved law and order and for equal rights with the English was not yet answered.

KEY

..... Kingdom boundaries 7th & 8th centuries
—— Offa's Dyke
----- Wat's Dyke

**The map shows the Welsh kingdoms** in the 7th and 8th centuries AD. The largest of them, Gwynedd, was roughly the area that Cunedda had seized in the 5th century. It was to be the last outpost of Welsh independence. Powys was the kingdom next in importance and in the south Dyfed was sometimes united with Seisyllwg. The southeastern kingdoms were frailer, so that Rhodri the Great and Hywel Dda managed more easily to subdue them in their attempts to unite Wales in the 9th and 10th centuries. In the east the boundary of Wales was defined for all time by Offa's Dyke, constructed to mark the limits of the Kingdom of Mercia *c.* 790. Wat's Dyke was built to defend Mercia against Welsh raiders 80 or 90 years earlier.

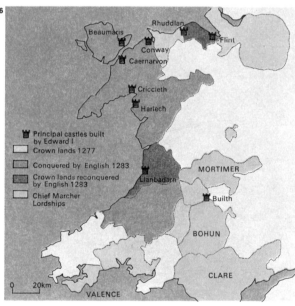

**6 There was a new dispensation** after the Edwardian conquest. The Welsh kingdom of Gwynedd was entirely dismembered and now became the shires of Anglesey, Merioneth and Caernarvonshire. With these, Cardiganshire, Carmarthenshire and Flint were held under the direct rule of the Crown, and these six shires were known as the Principality. The rest of the country, of which the possession had long been Norman, passing only occasionally into Welsh hands, was held as before by Marcher lords. The statute of Rhuddlan, enacted in 1284, provided the judicial and administrative framework by which the Principality was to be governed until 1536. But it made little difference to Welsh culture.

**7 Harlech Castle** was considered at the time to be the best fortified of all the powerful castles constructed by Edward I. It was built on a rocky site with a series of concentric defences. Its mighty gatehouse was buttressed by several strong doors and portcullises, and it had no equal in Wales. The work, which cost over £8,000, was undertaken in 1283 by about 900 labourers, carpenters and stonemasons, and was completed within six years. The master mason was James of St George, who had gained his experience of castle-building in Savoy. His wage is recorded as three shillings a day, more than any other builder in the realm could command.

**8 Owain Glyn Dŵr** is a national Welsh hero (this statue stands in Cardiff City Hall), but ill-recorded as a man. His rebellion in 1400 drew enormous support from the peasantry but was mainly sustained by gentlemen and squires. Once he was established as a self-styled Prince of Wales, Glyn Dŵr had the enterprise to form a constructive policy; he established an alliance with France, and proposed to create two universities and an episcopacy independent of Canterbury. He governed through the Welsh parliament he had summoned. When the tide turned against him after 1409, Glyn Dŵr went in and out of hiding; he was active in 1415 for the last time. With this mysterious end, he was an inspiration to the bards who kept nationalism alive.

**9 Henry Tudor** was acclaimed in Wales as **the first Welshman to** be ensconced on the English throne. The bards jubilantly greeted Henry's triumph in late August 1485 as a victory for Wales and fulfilment of the hoary prophecy that a descendant of the Ancient Britons would oust the Saxon oppressors of their land. When he landed at Dale in Pembrokeshire with 2,000 Frenchmen in August 1485 and promised to deliver the Welsh from their "miserable servitudes", he did indeed attract a great many recruits. But although Henry rewarded his supporters and made some attempt to render the Welsh equal subjects with the English, he disappointed many expectations. In 1489 he revived the title of Prince of Wales for his young son Arthur.

# Triumph of the Church

The years from the accession of Gregory VII in 1073 to the removal of the Papacy to Avignon in 1309 saw the highest achievements of the medieval Christian Church in all its spheres of activity. Western Christendom could genuinely be seen as a unity with about 500 bishoprics all working as part of an international papal system that became ever more organized and powerful. Roman Christianity laid the ground rules for everyone in European society, rules from which only the Jews were exempt. The twelfth and thirteenth centuries also saw the triumph of Gothic architecture and decoration, an achievement paralleled by the complete codification of law, knowledge and philosophy in a Christian theological context by the scholastic philosophers, St Thomas Aquinas (1225–74) in particular.

## The power of the Papacy

The eleventh-century Papacy had been inspired by the example of Cluniac reform, demonstrated best in the Lenten Synod at Rome in 1074 which laid down strict rules for the appointment and behaviour of the clergy.

The following year Gregory VII formally prohibited lay investiture (the appointment of bishops by a secular ruler), which not only antagonized Emperor Henry IV (reigned 1056–1106), but generally incurred violent hostility throughout Germany, France and England [8]. The resulting battle made it necessary for the Papacy to indulge in extensive legal justification of its position and led eventually to an institutionalized Papacy that would have been abhorrent to the original Cluniac reform.

The pope claimed to be the supreme judge and moral arbiter in temporal disputes. Only in this period could Emperor Henry IV have been humbled at Canossa by Gregory VII; could so powerful an English king as Henry II have appeared at Canterbury in a hair shirt to atone for the murder of Thomas à Becket; could King John (reigned 1199–1216) have been forced to submit himself (and the English crown) as a vassal of Pope Innocent III [Key]; or could Innocent IV have been able to annihilate the Hohenstaufen line of emperors in 1250.

The most imposing instrument of papal government was the Ecumenical Council, a decision-making body of all the bishops of Western Christendom summoned to attend at the request and direction of the pope. There were no fewer than seven such councils during the years 1123 to 1312.

## Papal administration

The growth of the Curia, the administrative focal point of the Vatican, also led to its increasing use as an international court of law. By the thirteenth century the ecclesiastical nature of the Papacy was at times overshadowed and popes such as Innocent IV (reigned 1243–54) were lawyers and administrators rather than religious leaders. The Papacy became increasingly embroiled in international politics, a development which culminated in its forcible transference to Avignon by the French monarchy from 1309 to 1377 [10].

In contrast to the growing complexity of papal administration there was a wave of reforms within the religious orders, all of which were based on piety, simplicity and austerity. Despite the Cluniac reforms, the

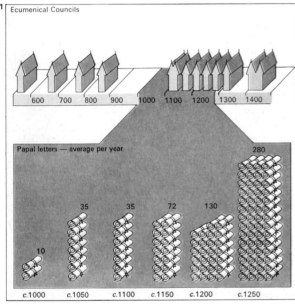

**2 This miniature of St Bernard of Clairvaux** (1090–1153) being nourished by milk from the breast of the Virgin Mary is taken from a 15th-century Venetian Cistercian breviary. It exemplifies one of the chief tenets of St Bernard's teaching, an almost sentimental devotion to the mother of God. The reverence of Mary was one of the striking elements of popular piety in the 12th century.

**3 The *Decretals* of Gregory IX,** the manuscript from which this miniature is taken, show the importance attached in the 13th century to the doctrine of transubstantiation. This was made the official teaching of the Church by the 4th Lateran Council (1215) which also prescribed annual confession. Gregory IX patronized the new monastic orders and canonized Dominic, Francis and Anthony.

**1 Ecumenical councils,** meetings of representatives of the whole Church, reached a peak in the 1100s and 1200s. As the Roman Church established its role as religious authority and arbiter of political events its administrative function developed: the ecumenical council grew and litigation at the Roman courts increased, as did the correspondence of the Curia, the juridical, legislative and administrative offices of the Papacy. Papal correspondence, a record of ecclesiasical intervention, grew from 130 letters during Adrian IV's Papacy (1154–9) to 3,646 during John XXII's (1316–34).

**4 The pilgrimage** was the "package tour" of the Middle Ages; pious Muslims went to Mecca just as devout Christians sought to go to Rome, Compostela or Canterbury. The pilgrimage was at once the fulfilment of an active religion and also the experience of a lifetime. In the early Middle Ages the focus of Christian pilgrimages was Rome; but the gradual appearance of famous relics around the Western world led to a proliferation of provincial shrines, the most famous of which was that of the body of the apostle James at Compostela in Spain. The pilgrimage route to Compostela became a thoroughfare along which many famous Romanesque churches were constructed.

**5 The Dance of Death** or *danse macabre* shows death in the role in which he appeared in late medieval popular mythology. He was seen to be an immediate tangible threat, a maleficent joker. Although many of the precepts of Christianity which are emphasized today appear to have been ignored in the early Middle Ages, it was the common religion of all in the West, and death for the Christian was the consummation of life. Death was therefore prominent in contemporary hagiography and was personified in the popular religious mystery plays. Awareness of death was intensified by the various catastrophes of the 14th century, especially the Great Plague of 1348 which depopulated Europe.

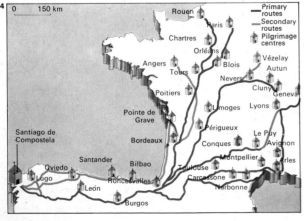

Benedictine Order had lost its pious intensity by the early twelfth century. The constitution of the Cistercians, the *Charter of Love*, written by St Stephen Harding in 1119, was an adaptation of the Benedictine Rule based on a denial of ostentation and an austere life located away from centres of population. The response to this rigorous life of prayer was overwhelming and 530 Cistercian houses had been established by 1200. Another offshoot of the Benedictine system were the Carthusians, founded by St Bruno at the monastery of the Grande Chartreuse in 1084.

There were many other new orders in the twelfth century – Augustinian canons, hermits, Hospitallers, crusading orders, Templars and organizations for the visitation of the sick and the imprisoned. The ultimate in clerical reform was the foundation of the Friars [7]. St Francis of Assisi (1181–1226) and St Dominic (c. 1170–1221) both stressed that their followers should take vows of complete poverty, and that neither individuals nor the order as a whole should possess any property. Friars were by definition to live by the work of their hands and, if necessary, by begging.

They were to preach and exhort and to set a visible example of self-denial. By the fourteenth century, however, the orders denied their founders' intentions, held communal property and became part of the structure of the Church.

The twelfth and thirteenth centuries were ages of secular piety and involvement with the Church as well as clerical reform. The Crusades were central to religious activity as were pilgrimages to Rome. Compostela in Spain [4], Canterbury and local shrines.

**Persecution of heretics**
The ugly side of the universality of papal pretensions and the increasing extremes of the religious life was the persecution of heretics [6]. The Jews, as non-believers, were largely left alone at this time, but heretics, as deserters from the true faith, had to be reconverted, by force if necessary. Among those heretics were the Albigensians, who held all material things and social life to be evil, thus presenting a challenge both to the Church and to the stability of society. The Albigensians were destroyed in the 1200s.

**Pope Innocent III**
(c. 1160–1216), a brilliant jurist, was trained at the universities of Paris and Bologna. His ambition and administrative gifts brought the medieval Papacy to the height of its powers. Through the legislative power of the papal Curia, his tight control of ecclesiastical affairs throughout Europe and his influence in imperial elections, Innocent fulfilled for a time the papal ambition of directing the affairs of the entire secular European world.

6 Some followers of Amalric of Chartres were burnt at the stake in the early 12th century for believing that those in love with God partake in His perfection and are proof against sin. Traditionally it was the business of the Church to preserve orthodoxy; the ecclesiastical authorities, the Dominicans and Franciscans in particular, investigated heresy, the secular powers punished it.

7 The religious orders increased greatly in number as a result of popular piety and the growing complexity of Church organization. The Cluniac reformers of the 10th century merely tightened the Benedictine Rule. The Carthusians [A], founded by St Bruno in 1084, and the Cistercians, the "white monks" [B], lived according to new rules that emphasized the virtues of self-denial and the strictest religious observance. The orders of friars, the Dominicans [C] and Franciscans [D], were a new kind of wandering priest who travelled Europe preaching, possessing neither property nor money and relying on begging for a livelihood. The original appeal of St Francis, both ascetic and poetic, was unacceptable to the Papacy, because a large body fulfilling an important religious function needed corporate property if it was not to become socially subversive. Despite opposition from loyal followers, the friars soon obtained property and became an integral part of the Church.

8 The question of who should invest bishops caused a rift between popes and secular rulers. Great local wealth and political power went with the office of bishop, the sort of wealth with which any ruler would want to reward or bribe a useful servant. This bronze depicting Emperor Otto I investing Bishop Adalbert of Magdeburg in 962 demonstrates the imperial position at its strongest. The new bishop is seen receiving his authority from the secular ruler, not the pope.

9 This fresco illustrates the triumph of the Church as seen through the eyes of the late 14th-century Florentine artist Andrea di Buonaiuto. It is in the Spanish Chapel of the church of Sta Maria Novella in Florence and is a contemporary commentary on the development of the structure of the Church into a vast international organization with a role in administration and religious teaching. Sta Maria Novella is a Dominican church and the picture emphasizes the role of the Dominican friars, many of whom had been made permanent commissioners for the extermination of heresy, the origins of the Holy Inquisition, under Gregory IX. Dominican friars are here shown as the *domini canes*, "hounds of the Lord".

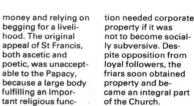

10 The Papal Palace in Avignon was a more efficient centre of papal government than Rome, and it is testimony to the wealth, success and culture of the papal court in captivity. After two centuries of great power, the Papacy entered a period of submission to temporal rulers when from 1309 to 1377 it was forcibly removed to Avignon. Ostensibly the move was to resolve the conflicts it had suffered in Rome; but the influence of the French monarchy over the Papacy increased.

139

# Western European economy 1000–1250

Between 1000 and 1250 the economic foundation of Europe shifted to the north. The new wealth came from a rapidly developing agriculture in the northern European plain [2] between the Loire and the Elbe. Under the Romans this had been a sparsely populated forest area; now as a result of expansion, it was the Mediterranean that became a frontier zone.

## An era of expansion

In this new world all the energy and enterprise of the pioneer was yoked to clearing the forests, establishing villages and marking out the routes, largely independent of the Roman system, that bound the plain together. Here and there the directing force of some powerful family or monastic community could be detected, but almost certainly most of the work was done by small family groups and peasant communities. In the progressive draining of the marshes of Lincolnshire, Flanders and the Po basin – among the most remarkable achievements of these centuries – the lead may have been given by abbeys such as Ramsey or Les Dunes, but the fiercely

independent spirit of the subsequent peasant proprietors suggests that many took matters into their own hands and proceeded to drain the land themselves.

Intensive settlement of the soil implies an increasing population. In this period, without records of taxation, there is no direct evidence to measure population growth; but an indication that numbers increased rapidly comes from the twelfth-century migrations of both peasants and knights from France, Germany and Flanders to Eastern Europe, Spain, Sicily and Palestine.

Within the bounds of Western Europe the few surviving monastic estate documents give glimpses of the slow development of a farming expertise geared specifically to northern climates, such as the use of the heavy-wheeled plough (carruca), the harnessing of draught animals in columns and the development of the watermill for grinding corn, which gradually came into use between 1000 and 1250. By 1200, horses were shod and harnessed with a shoulder collar. More had, by then, been learnt about spring and autumn crops: wheat and rye for standard

autumn-sown cereals, but other varieties for the more rigorous climates. The use of spring-sown oats and barley for poorer soils was understood by progressive estate managers of the thirteenth century, such as the agricultural writer Walter of Henley.

## Social and economic organization

The social structure of this developing agrarian society is difficult to determine and probably varied dramatically from area to area. Where seigneurial and monastic landlords took an interest in developing their lands (and many did, especially the new order of Cistercian monks), it was common to attract landless labourers with the promise of heritable tenures, on condition that they bound themselves and their heirs to the soil. Serfdom was one way of organizing labour for co-operative work, but it is a mistake to see it as universal. The peasant "communes" of the open-field system in France and England, with their periodic redistribution of holdings, the independent holdings (allods) of Aquitaine and the farmsteads (casalia) of Italy all resulted from peculiarities of local

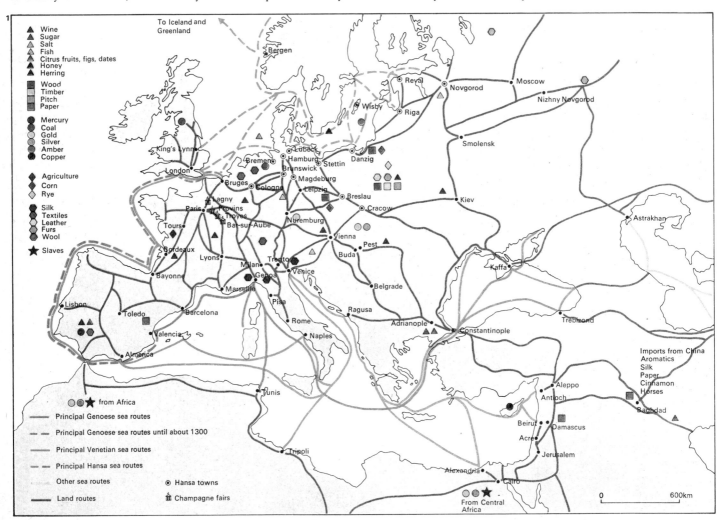

1

Wine
Sugar
Salt
Fish
Citrus fruits, figs, dates
Honey
Herring

Wood
Timber
Pitch
Paper

Mercury
Coal
Gold
Silver
Amber
Copper

Agriculture
Corn
Rye

Silk
Textiles
Leather
Furs
Wool

★ Slaves

◐◐★ from Africa

—— Principal Genoese sea routes

-- -- Principal Genoese sea routes until about 1300

—— Principal Venetian sea routes

-- -- Principal Hansa sea routes

—— Other sea routes

—— Land routes

◉ Hansa towns

🏛 Champagne fairs

Imports from China
Aromatics
Silk
Paper
Cinnamon
Horses

From Central Africa

0        600km

**1 The number of trade routes,** by both land and sea, increased during the High Middle Ages. The most popular form of bulk transport in the early Middle Ages was by river. In the 11th and 12th centuries land transport be-

came much easier, partly because the routes were safer, partly because of the increased use of pack animals. The trade of the carrier, often a native of the high Alps, had by 1250 become an integral link in Italian

commerce with northern Europe. The routes primarily linked importing centres such as the Italian and Hansa towns with the centres of production and exchange – the fairs of northern Europe and Flemish towns. But

links were also forged through Poland and Hungary with the ancient Asiatic routes. Sea routes developed dramatically during the 12th century. Mediterranean ships of the period were small, rarely more than 100 tonnes.

They usually sailed in convoy and with enterprising crews from Venice, Pisa and Genoa to most Mediterranean ports. Some Levant towns had Italian quarters as early as 1110. Subsequently the Venetians established

themselves at Alexandria and their attempts to control the trade of Constantinople culminated in their conquest of that city in 1204. The northern seas had their own Viking tradition of seamanship. The trade in furs

originally carried by Scandinavians from Novgorod to the Baltic fell into the hands of merchants from the north German towns in the 12th century. The merchants soon organized themselves into a protective league or *Hansa*.

custom and circumstance. What is reasonably certain is that the number of such communities increased sharply during the eleventh and twelfth centuries.

## The rise of towns

The other consequence of population increase was the growing importance of towns as centres both of exchange and production. The origins of towns varied, but most of them grew up to serve local needs, as strongpoints (the *burg*) to which agricultural markets were attached, or as ports importing and exporting goods. The more intensive the settlement of the land, the larger and more numerous were the towns. The number of cities in Flanders and northeastern France – Bruges, Arras, Valenciennes, and others – reflects a high agricultural population. The burgeoning cloth production of Bruges in the twelfth century, in part depended on the farming of sheep in the Flemish salt marshes. The towns' specialized way of life needed independent institutions: the earliest guild of merchants known, that of Tiel in Holland, existed earlier than 1000, but the merchant guild as an instrument of communal government became common only in the twelfth century. The towns flourished, however, because of the vast consumer market that had developed by 1200.

By 1000 Western Europe was in sporadic but persistent contact with the East through the Baltic and Russia, and with the decline of Saracen piracy in the Mediterranean the Italian ports developed strong links with Egypt and (after 1098) the Crusading states, which enabled Oriental silks and spices to reach the West. Mediterranean trade [1], necessarily large-scale and risky since goods bought abroad were never pre-sold, gradually led Venetian merchants to develop a "capitalist" system of investment [3].

The High Middle Ages was a period of almost universal expansion in Western Europe, an underdeveloped continent ready for sustained exploitation. As conditions changed, however, the warning signs of overpopulation and overuse of the land went unnoticed until persistent famine and plague swept over the region brought a general recession in the fourteenth century.

**Horizontal treadle looms,** introduced in the 13th century, stimulated textile manufacture, the medieval industry that employed most urban craftsmen. The less efficient vertical loom was replaced by a machine using treadles [1] to raise or lower the lengthwise threads as the shuttle [2] passed through them. Cloth was wound on to the cloth beam [3] as thread was released from the warp beam [4] by depressing a lever [5]. About two-thirds of all trade was in cloth or raw materials required for it. Most weaving was done in the Low Countries, partly by urban industry and partly by cottage labour.

**2 Drainage and land reclamation** was one of the most spectacular aspects of the clearing of the northern European plain in the 11th and 12th centuries. An area near St Omer in France shows how, in the early Middle Ages, polders were diked, marshy land made fit for grazing and a system of waterways constructed. Cultivation of new lands both fed a larger population and gave greater freedom to farmers, who paid for pioneer lands in fees rather than in services: two vital factors for the commercial and industrial expansion of the Low Countries during this period.

**3 The Fondaco dei Turchi** (Turkish warehouse) on the Grand Canal in Venice was built in the late Romanesque style in the 13th century. Although it takes its name from a later period of the city's mercantile development, the building exemplifies Venetian power in the first era of its commercial success. From the 11th century, Venice dominated European trade with the East and its arsenal and dockyard comprised the biggest industrial unit of the age.

**4 Illustrated calendars** of seasonal activities provide the best visual evidence of medieval costume and methods of agriculture. Shown here are May: a shepherd and his flock [A]; June: cutting wood [B] and July: haymaking [C].

**5 The grape harvest** depicted in an Italian calendar shows the method of pressing the grapes with the feet, a tradition that survived in parts of rural Italy until after 1945. Wine was produced in quantity throughout southern Europe, in most of France and in the Rhine and Moselle areas of Germany. Production methods had changed little since the days of the great Roman villas and viticulture was, throughout the Middle Ages, still the economic prerogative of the big landowner or entrepreneur. By the 13th century a genuinely international wine trade had developed along a north-south axis with large quantities of wine being shipped in barrels by water transport.

# 4000-2000 BC The first civilizations

## Principal events

**Assisted by the invention of writing and the wheel, the world's first urban civilizations grew up and flourished in Mesopotamia, and later in Egypt in the fourth millennium BC. Mesopotamian city states emerged from ancient agricultural and religious settlements, encouraged by the immigration of the Sumerian people into the area, and grew rich from agriculture and long-distance trade. With growth, however, came conflicts between cities, though none achieved permanent supremacy. In Egypt early unification and centralization led to the Pyramid Age with its celebration of the pharaoh's authority. In both areas hereditary monarchies were set up c.3000 BC, with a bureaucracy that placed emphasis on public works, especially canal building. Towards 2000 BC, Sumeria was threatened by barbarian invasions, while Egypt declined from internal stresses, as Minoan civilization emerged.**

### 4000-3800 BC

**Farming settlements** found in the lower Mesopotamian plain since 5000 BC probably included the sites of the future royal cities of Eridu, Uruk, Nippur and Girsu by 4000 BC.
**The need for irrigation** led to a more concentrated population and complex social systems.
**The site of Babylon** was settled by Sumerians c.4000.
**The Nile cultures** were based on farming villages c.4000.

### 3800-3600 BC

**The Creation,** in Jewish tradition, dates from 3761 BC.

### 3600-3400 BC

**Uruk** (modern Warka), the greatest Sumerian city, already possessed many features of the city state by 3500 BC. At least twelve autonomous cities, including Ur, Lagash, Umma and Kish, developed over the next millennium.
**The pastoral Sumerians** moved into the Mesopotamian plains and encouraged the growth of this civilization, c.3500, building a network of canals for irrigation.

### 3400-3200 BC

**The Nile Valley provinces** (nomes) had been merged into two separate kingdoms – Upper and Lower Egypt – by 3300 BC.
**City states** began to develop in Syria and Palestine c.3300.
**The Proto-literate period,** when writing was first used in Sumer c.3500-3000 BC, coincides with the semi-legendary rule of the First Dynasty of Kish.
**Mesopotamian influence** is thought to have stimulated Egyptian cultural development c.3400 BC.

## National events

**Neolithic society emerged from Mesolithic hunting communities in Britain after 4000 BC, producing a megalithic (large stone) culture similar to those emerging, apparently independently, throughout Europe. An advanced civilization using bronze developed in Wessex and built Stonehenge c.2000 BC**

**Mesolithic man** was a hunter-gatherer and had lived in Britain since 10000 BC, using flints and boats for hunting and fishing.

**The first traces of farming** found in Britain date from c.3700 BC.

**Neolithic man** domesticated his animals and cultivated crops, building causewayed camps and barrows in Wessex on the Salisbury Plain c.3500 BC

**Megalithic tombs** and standing stones were built in Maeshowe and Nympsfield c.3300 BC. Similar monuments were also built in Denmark and Brittany.

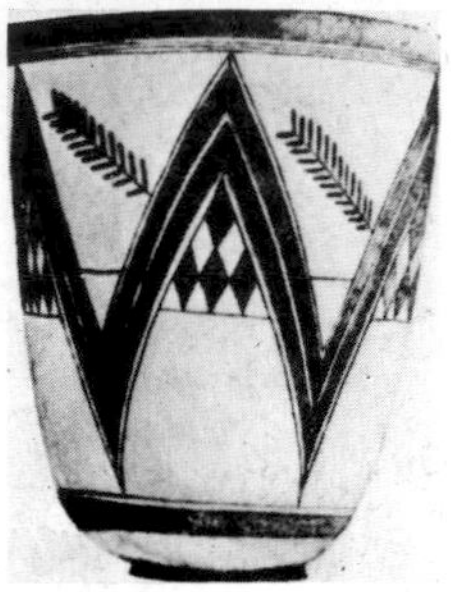
Susa ware, 4thc. BC

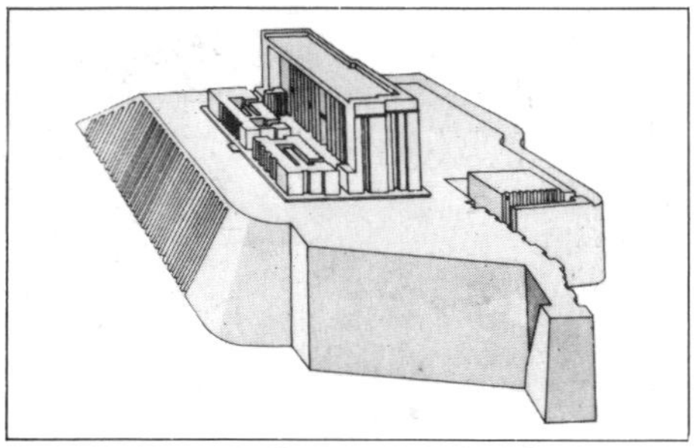
White Temple, Uruk, Mesopotamia 4thc. BC

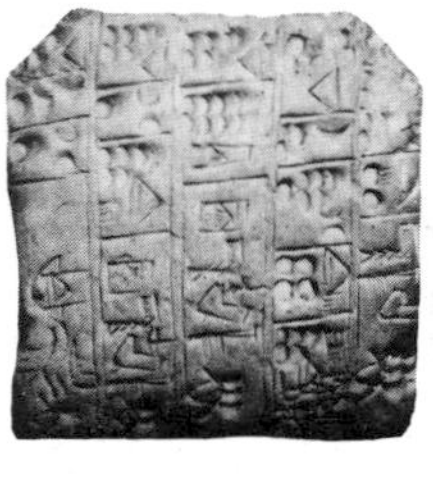
Sumerian cuneiform, 4thc.

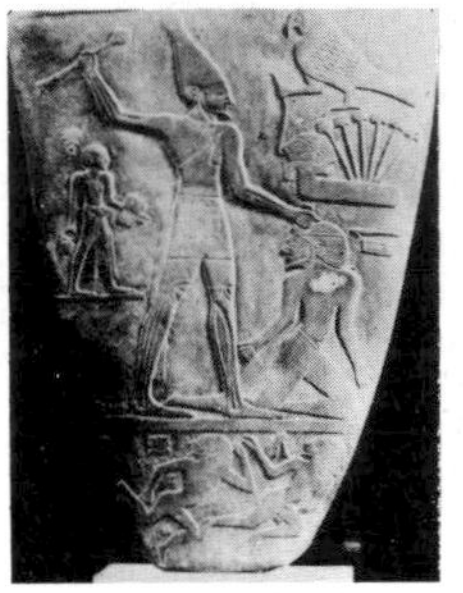
Palette of Narmer

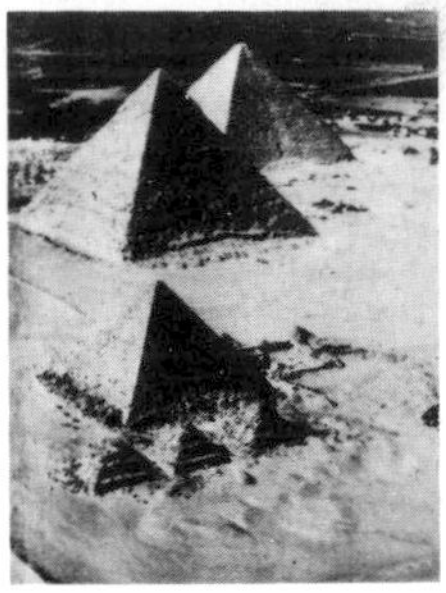
Pyramids of Giza

## Religion

**The development of religious ideas in early history was closely related to the rise of settled agriculture and the emergence of the first states and empires.**

**The change from a hunting economy to one based on arable agriculture was reflected, first of all, in the rise of fertility cults in which the central figure was a mother or earth goddess.**

**With the growth of urban civilizations in the fertile valleys of the Nile and the Euphrates, a priest-dominated society grew up with a system of gods, each related to a particular city or region. As the authority of the state and the priesthood became more centralized this was reflected in the changing importance of particular gods, and in Egypt in the rise of the doctrine of divine kingship and the construction of increasingly elaborate temples and royal tombs culminating in the Age of the Pyramids.**

**Fertility cults** arose with settled farming. Sacramental concepts and techniques centred on fertility of the soil, its products and seasons. These cults in the Near East, were associated with the cycle of death and rebirth and took as their chief divinity a sexual mother goddess or a non-sexual creator – the earth goddess, known as Ninna in Mesopotamia.

**Burial cults** had existed since early prehistory. A specific site was often marked by a mound and sacrifice and ritual eating of the dead were frequently involved. The placing of artefacts in the graves indicated a desire to ensure the continuity of life. Cave paintings at Lascaux and Trois Frères, France, dating from c.20000 BC, show witch doctor-like figures among animals hunted by Cro-Magnon man.

**Before the third millennium BC** peoples of Mesopotamia worshipped nature gods in human form, each god being associated with a city temple and the temples themselves occupying a central place in city life. The gods were organized as a democratic council which reflected the political relations between the various city states.

**The religion of Egypt before the foundation of the dynasties** was based on totemism, the idea that there is a relation between kinship groups and specific animals and plants. Independent principalities each had their own totem: **Horus** the falcon was that of Bedhet in the north, while the god **Seth,** represented by a he-goat, protected Naqadah in the south. Above these local gods was the sun god, Re, the source of all life.

## Literature

**Writing developed in Mesopotamia as the Sumerians tried to simplify and regularize earlier picture writing and ideograms; a system for depicting sounds rather than ideas was probably invented by temple clerks in response to the need to record tribute payments and wages in the Mesopotamian city temples. With the development of the regular cuneiform style of script, writing became a skill for every aspiring man to acquire.**

**Literature had its origins in oral chronicles such as the *Gilgamesh* epic in Sumeria and in written prayers in Egypt, where a hieroglyphic script developed after 3400 BC and poetry emerged during the Pyramid Age. By 2000 BC, China was creating independently an elaborate system of word signs.**

**The Sumerian language** was in use by 5000 BC and a pictographic script developed by 4000 BC. Although this communicated ideas by the use of pictures, it gradually began to take on a more formal appearance with agreed symbols standing for ideas. This simplified the task of the Sumerian picture writer.

**The first use of writing** is attributed to the Sumerian city of Uruk. Simplification of the characters in earlier pictographic script led them to the idea of using conventional symbols to represent the sound of a word rather than the idea it conveyed. Motifs on painted pottery indicate that a script incorporating phonetic elements was in use in Uruk by 3700 BC.

**Temple clerks** recording wages, tribute and stores had developed after 3500 BC some 2,000 signs, which were engraved on clay tablets. The linking of these signs with sounds made it easier to write names and abstract ideas as well as lists of objects. As Sumerian words were largely of one syllable, the system is called a *syllabary.*

**An Egyptian hieroglyphic script** developed after 3400 BC, possibly influenced by trading contacts with Sumeria. A hieroglyph could represent either a sound, an idea, or an identifying mark attached to another sign. The syllabic signs did not indicate differences in vowel sounds, as did the Sumerian script.

## Art and architecture

**In Egypt and Mesopotamia, the development of pottery and small domestic articles, cosmetic implements and jewellery occurred in the Neolithic period, but with the growth of states and technological advance sophisticated metal crafts and stone sculpture developed. In the absence of stone, builders in Mesopotamia used as their basic medium the baked mud brick which they later decorated with ceramics and copper reliefs, while the finest sculpture and much beautiful jewellery was produced in metal. In Egypt, stone was used for a series of monuments, culminating in the pyramids, as well as for a highly sophisticated tradition of sculpture with its own rules of proportion that persisted for over 1,000 years.**

**Throughout this period in China and after c.3000 BC in the Aegean, the manufacture of fine decorated ceramic ware anticipated the artistic achievements of subsequent centuries.**

**The appearance of painted pottery** coincided with the late Neolithic/early Chalcolithic period – a transition period between the late Stone Age and the early uses of copper. Richly decorated pottery dating from c. 4000 BC has been found in Anatolia at Hacilar and in Assyria at Arpachiyah.

**In Egypt black-topped polished bowls (Badarian ware)** and terracotta figurines were produced. Ivory combs and cosmetic articles also date from this period.

**The Sumerians in Susa,** capital of Elam (SW Iran), became associated with a variety of remarkably fine pottery vessels, on which sharp geometric devices were brilliantly interwoven with stylized figures of birds, animals and men.
**Egyptian Amratian culture,** c.3600 BC, showed technical advances on the Badarian period. Decorated ivory and bone combs were found and figures of animals such as hippopotamuses appear on pottery.

**Undecorated stone vases from Egypt's Gerzean period** superceded vessels of the Amratian culture. Spherical and cylindrical jars were light and skilfully hewn out of solid blocks of hard stone by means of flint borers. Votive objects, tomb paintings and palettes depict battles, ships, animals and vase bearers.

## Music

**Music probably originated in man's desire to express himself more richly and formally than he could in speech alone; ritual chants rapidly developed into musical forms with special meanings. Widely separated cultures produced similar kinds of instruments, adapting natural objects to musical uses: bone flutes and whistles found in Hungary and Russia date from c.25,000 BC**

**The harp,** in prehistory, probably developed from the archer's bow, played over a covered pit to add resonance. In Mesopotamia musicians played flutes, as well as drums and rattles.

**Drum and reed pipe music** bloomed in Mesopotamia. Called bull and reed music, it symbolized strength and weakness with the use of drums for a vigorous beat and pipes for the melody.

**Religious music** was performed by musicians chanting and playing on reed pipes, flutes, drums and tambourines as part of the liturgy of temple worship in the Sumerian city states.

## Science and technology

**The elaborate civilizations of Mesopotamia and Egypt depended for their development on the settled agriculture practised by Neolithic peoples in these regions since c.8000. Without it they could not have sustained either the increased population or the specialization of urban life. Once secure these societies spawned a remarkable series of technological advances. The 4th millennium BC saw the invention of the plough, the wheel, the sailing boat and methods of writing. Stone tools gave way to those of copper and bronze, a hard alloy that came into use c.2500 BC.**

**Scientific method as we know it – the systematic testing of theories about the material world – did not develop until much later but the technical knowledge of these early societies was very sophisticated. The pyramids remain one of the finest engineering feats of all time and in west Asia, as later in China and Mesoamerica, the mathematics used by priests provided the basis for the development of other sciences.**

**Neolithic, New Stone Age, settlements** prospered in Egypt, Mesopotamia between the rivers Tigris and Euphrates, and in other parts of the East, between 8000 and 3500 BC. Stone tools included polished stone axes and a type of flint sickle mounted in an animal's lower jawbone. The flints were mined. Buildings were reed and wattle huts or made of hand-moulded clay bricks dried in the sun.
**Clay seals** were used c.4000 in the Middle East, to place the owner's name on pots.

**Land transport vehicles** in Sumeria included sledges.
**The wheel** was invented in Mesopotamia during the period of the establishment of city states. It took two forms: a stone potters' wheel, and a cartwheel, made from a single, solid piece of wood.

**Copper,** fashioned into beads as early as 6000 BC in northern Europe, was smelted from ores or melted as the native metal over wood fires from 4000 BC in Sumeria.
**Kilns** were introduced c.3400 in Sumeria. Many pots were fired at once, and raised above the fire, thus protecting the painted designs from wood ash. Shadow clocks originated in Sumeria c.3500 BC

**Ploughs** take their first form, that of a forked branch, in Mesopotamia and Egypt, the forks being held by the ploughman and the sharpened end, or share, being drawn through the soil by oxen. Horses were not used. Such ploughs were shown c.3000 BC in Egyptian picture writing, although used earlier.
**The Egyptian Copper Age** began in the Upper and Lower Kingdoms c.3200, and lasted until 2000 BC, after which iron and bronze artefacts were made.

## 3200-3000 BC

**The Delta Kingdom of Lower Egypt** was conquered by Menes (Narmer) *c.* 3100, who came from the south and unified Egypt into a single monarchy. He is attributed with the founding of the First Dynasty which he ruled from his new capital at Memphis.
**The Phoenicians,** a Semitic-speaking people, began to settle the coast of Syria *c.* 3000 BC.
**Copper** was widely used throughout the Near East *c.* 3000 BC.

## 3000-2800 BC

**Cretan Neolithic culture** gave way to bronze-based culture *c.* 3000 BC.
**Sumerian cities** came to be ruled by hereditary kings from 2900 onwards. The Archaic Tablets of Ur came from this Early Dynastic or Classical Sumerian age.
**Public works in Egypt,** especially canal construction, led to the growth of the Egyptian bureaucracy in the Early Dynastic Period, when a national government first developed.

## 2800-2600 BC

**Gilgamesh,** the legendary king of Uruk, *r. c.* 2750 BC. **Records of Sumerian kings** began with Mebaragesi of Kish *c.* 2700.
**The Old Kingdom Of Egypt,** a 500-year period of stability and cultural splendour, began *c.* 2700 with the reign of Zoser. Egypt also expanded towards Nubia, *c.* 2600.
**Akkadians** came to dominate the northern Mesopotamian plain in the Early Dynastic II period.

## 2600-2400 BC

**Conflict between Sumerian cities** such as Ur, Kish and Lagash reached a climax *c.* 2500.
**A prosperous culture** emerged at Yang-shao in China *c.* 2500.
**Royal power reached its zenith** in the Egyptian Old Kingdom *c.* 2500 under the pharaohs Khufu and Khaphre.
**A sea-going Minoan civilization** developed in Crete *c.* 2500.

## 2400-2200 BC

**Sargon the Great** built Akkad in northern Mesopotamia, conquered Sumer and created an empire stretching from the Persian Gulf to the Mediterranean *c.* 2350. His soldiers settled at Ashur, the future Assyria.
**Urukagina,** King of Lagash, introduced reforms but was ousted by Lugalzaggisi of Umma.
The Indus Valley civilization around the cities of Harappa and Mohenjo-daro emerged *c.* 2300.
**The Gutians** destroyed the Akkadian Empire *c.* 2230.

## 2200-2000 BC

**Gudea of Lagash** restored disrupted Sumerian commercial prosperity in southern Mesopotamia.
**Ur-Nammu of Ur** drove out the Gutians and established a brief Sumerian renaissance.
After Egypt had expanded into Nubia and west Asia on a large scale, its Old Kingdom ended in anarchy with the collapse of the central government, 2181.
**King Mentuhotep of Thebes** re-united Egypt *c.* 2060.
**The first Minoan palaces** were probably built on Crete *c.* 2000.

---

**Stone temples** were built at Ggantija and Haġar Qim on Malta *c.* 3000 BC by a Neolithic culture.

**Silbury Hill,** a man-made earth mound near Avebury, Wiltshire, was built *c.* 2500 BC.
**Chieftains** probably emerged in Wessex at this time.

**Stonehenge** was built *c.* 2000, testifying to the astronomical knowledge and social organization of Wessex. Gold and bronze objects were placed in tombs.

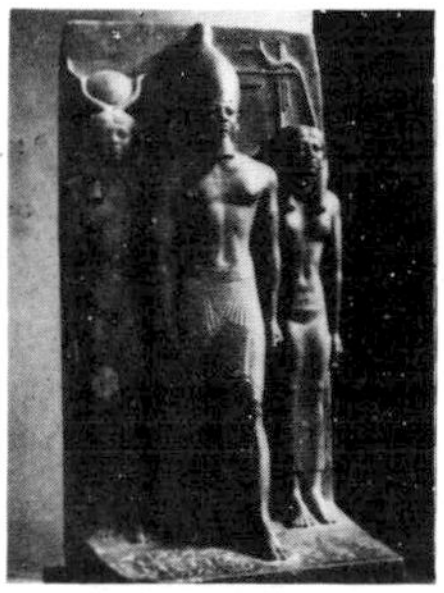

Egyptian sculpture, *c.* 2500

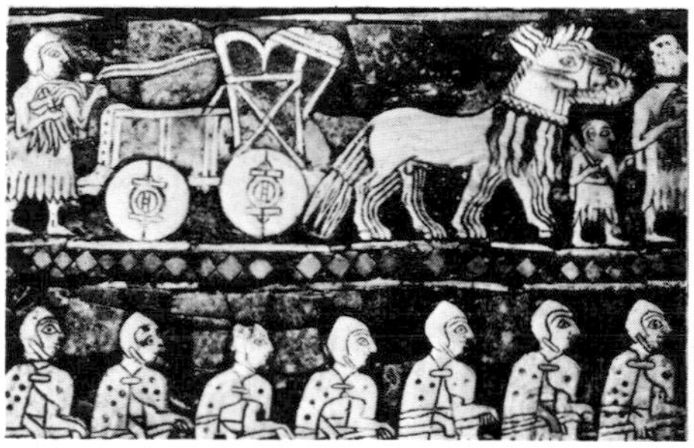

Royal standard of Ur, Mesopotamia

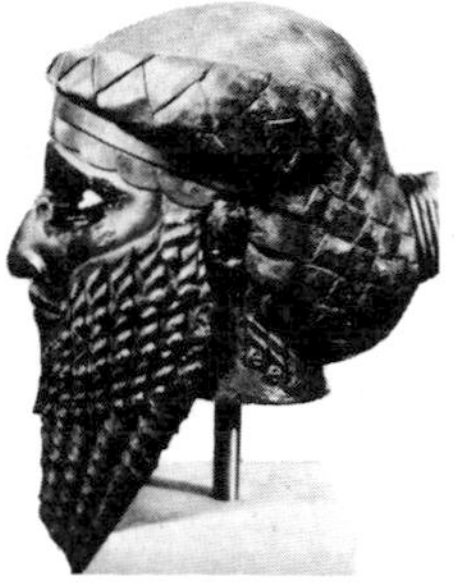

Bronze bust of Sargon 1

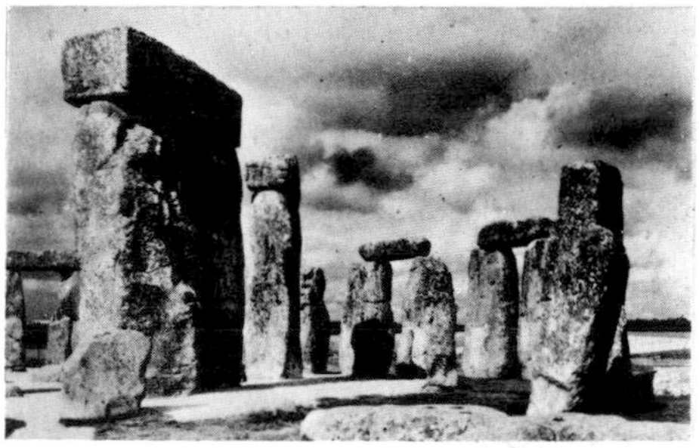

Stonehenge, Wessex, *c.* 2000 BC

---

**The religion of Mesopotamia reached its classical form** with the rise of more centralized political units in the early dynastic period. There were four main gods: **Anu**, god of heaven; **Enlil**, god of the winds; **Ninhursag**, goddess of birth; and **Enki** (Ea), god of water. Hierarchical relationships between the gods reflected the growing separation between the strata of Mesopotamian society. Divination of dreams and interpretation of entrails were practised.

**The priests at Memphis** in Lower Egypt established the Memphite theology after the unification of Upper and Lower Egypt. Their god **Ptah** was believed to have created the world and was known as the patron of craftsmen. The creation myth associated with him is more abstract than those of the pre-dynastic period, and testifies to the sophistication of the Memphite priesthood.

**In the Egyptian early dynastic period** the king became associated with **Horus** the falcon, deity of Hierakonpolis in Bedhet.
**Classical Egyptian religion** described an optimistic vision of an ordered cosmos, itself an expression of the predictability of life in Egypt governed by the regular flooding of the River Nile.
**The first pyramid tombs** were built in Egypt *c.* 2700 BC.

**The concept of divine kingship** was well established by 2500, as was the existence of a specialized priesthood. Both contributed to the force of royal authority. The king became identified with the god **Horus**, who by this time was associated with the whole land of Egypt.

**With the decline of the Old Kingdom,** the idea of survival after death was extended to include people other than royalty for the first time. This may have been a reflection of the growing power of the nobility.

---

**A cuneiform script** was in use in Sumeria by 3200 BC. It consisted of vertical, horizontal and oblique strokes made with a sharpened wooden stylus on a wet, hand-sized clay tablet. The name comes from the Latin *cuneus* (wedge) and refers to the wedge-shaped strokes of the stylus.

**As cuneiform spread,** writing began to serve a wide range of social needs, although there is no indication that it was used for anything but practical purposes. The Babylonians and Assyrians kept lists and inventories for business and legal purposes. There is an Egyptian record of farming procedures.

**Literature had yet to emerge** but writing was becoming an important tool of social advancement and literary form was evolving in the oral tradition of the Sumerian-Babylonian epic of *Gilgamesh*, mankind's first great poem.

**Another script** was evolving on the Indian continent, not yet settled by Aryans – the Indus (or proto-Indian) script, found on seals dating back to *c.* 2500 BC in which each sign seems to have had a single phonetic value.
**In Sumeria,** the Akkadians produced a simplified script of only 550 symbols, seen in the legal code of Urukagina *c.* 2400.

**The first literature** dates from *c.* 2300 BC in the prayers of Egyptian pyramid texts. Also preserved in papyri is the "Pessimistic Literature", which includes the *Prophecy of Neferty* and *Admonitions of an Egyptian sage*, the *Tale of an Eloquent Peasant* and *A Dialogue of a Desperate Man with his Soul.*

**A Chinese script** emerged though it was not standardized and no examples survive. A "concept script" in which each idea had a corresponding sign, it replaced a system of knotted cords and was used to record commands and perhaps chronicles and poetry.
**In Babylon,** the first known library, composed of clay tablets, existed by 2000 BC.

---

**Mesopotamian cylinder seals** dating from the **Protoliterate period** were used in the business of temple administration and bear the miniature prototypes of the relief friezes that were to become important in Sumerian art, and reached a high degree of craftsmanship by the Akkadian period.
**The Palette of Narmer,** *c.* 3100 BC, a carved slate tablet from Hierakonpolis in Egypt, shows the king wearing the crowns of both kingdoms.

**Complex tombs for Egyptian notables** were constructed. These *mastaba* consisted of underground funerary chambers with stone or brick structures above.

**In Mesopotamia,** a typical temple of the Ubaid period, 2900–2800 BC, had a façade decorated with niches dedicated to the cult of the god Enki. Sculpture of the period consisted of terracotta statuettes of both men and women.

**The outstanding advance of Egyptian Old Kingdom architecture** was the building, under the direction of royal architect Imhotep, of Zoser's step pyramid at Sakkara *c.* 2700. The Great Pyramid at Giza and the Great Sphinx of Kafre were built *c.* 2500 BC.

**Egyptian royal sculpture** concentrated on idealized figures with an emphasis on set proportions.

**Early Minoan art** was characterized by marble statuettes of goddesses (Cycladic idols) *c.* 2500 BC and vases made from Cretan and imported stone.
**Mesopotamian decorative arts** – in particular the use of gold and copper, lapis lazuli and other fine inlays – achieved a high degree of craftsmanship.
**In China** the painted ceramics of the late Neolithic Yang-shoa culture, *c.* 2500, have geometric patterns painted in black and red pigments.

**Narrative reliefs and stelae** proclaimed the achievements of Mesopotamian culture in the Akkadian period, while **King Sargon's bronze bust** is one of the greatest examples of ancient portrait sculpture.
**The earliest Indus Valley cities** of Harappa and Mohenjo-daro were constructed of fire-baked bricks and utilized such features as corbelled arches. Among the few known vestiges of Indian art are seals with animal motifs and figurines.

**A group of diorite statues of Gudea,** the famous ruler of Lagash, *c.* 2130, are the finest works of Sumerian artistic revival.
**The temple of Ur** – a ziggurat dedicated to the moon goddess Nanna – was built by the Sumerian King Ur-Nammu.
**Minoan pottery** *c.* 2200-2000 BC is represented by ceramics with a creamy white glaze over a dark ground.

---

**Egyptian pottery** depicts instruments like those used in Mesopotamia, including harps, drums, sistra (metal rattles on a U-shaped frame) and reed pipes of various lengths.

**Vertical (end-blown) flutes,** sistra and tambourines were played in processional music, suggesting the possible use of music in courtly ritual in Mesopotamia and Egypt *c.* 3000 BC

**A harp** from ancient Egypt has been unearthed, dating *c.* 2500 BC. It has a lower sound chest to improve its resonance. About the same time, doubled reed flutes were played, probably in unison.

**Two kinds of harp,** dating from *c.* 2400 BC, were uncovered during the excavation of the royal tombs at Ur, in Mesopotamia. One had a lower sound chest and the other an upper sound chest.

**Antiphonal forms,** in which two choirs or a priest and choir chant responses, appeared in the ritual music of Sumerian temples under the Akkadian ruler Naram-Sin *c.* 2200 BC.

---

**Boats,** as depicted on Egyptian pre-dynastic pottery, had square sails and many oars. Boats of bundles of reeds navigated the Nile *c.* 3000 BC.
**Metal-moulding** was practised in Sumeria by 3200 to make copper and bronze axes with moulded sockets for holding the shafts. Previous models had weaker sockets of folded metal.

**Horse-drawn chariots** were recorded in Mesopotamia *c.* 3000 BC.

**Bronze alloys** were widely made in Mesopotamia by 2800 BC; they were a mixture of copper and tin ores and were fashioned into ornaments, tools and weapons. Copper ores were plentiful and widespread in Syria; the chief ore, tin, being found as an alluvial deposit in rivers and lakes. Some Sumerian bronzes are very hard as they accidently contain silicon.
**Cotton** was grown in India *c.* 3000 BC.

**Populations in Mesopotamia and Egypt** had grown by 2800 BC owing to improved agricultural methods. Despite its primitive appearance and action the fork-branch plough brought greatly increased crop yields.
**The first calendar** of 365 days was invented by the Egyptians.
**The first pyramid,** of King Zoser, was built *c.* 2700. Its construction involved a practical knowledge of geometry which was not formulated in theory for many centuries.

**Mesopotamian metallurgy** advanced significantly by 2600, for example in the development of soldering techniques, used to make the ornaments found in the royal tombs at Ur.
**The Great Pyramid** of Khufu was finished *c.* 2500. It is 146.6m (481ft) high and covers 5 hectares and yet is accurate to within a fraction of an inch.
**Egyptian wooden boats,** are shown on tomb walls from 2500.

**Weaving with looms** was practised well before 3000 BC in west Asia and Egypt. By 2300, horizontal looms, with the warp thread pegged on the ground, were usual in the Near East.
**Weight standards** and accurate scales were used in Egypt from 2200 BC. For example, the dried fish eaten by miners in Egypt was measured by their masters using stone weights.
**Sewage and drainage systems** were built in Harappan cities.

**Ziggurats** became most refined *c.* 2000 BC. These Mesopotamian buildings served both as storehouses for grain and as platforms for astrological and astronomical observations.
**The Bronze Age** reached the Neolithic settlements and nomadic cultures of western Europe *c.* 3000-2000 BC.

# 2000-1200 BC Hittites and Assyrians

## Principal events

**An influx of Aryan tribes, at the beginning of the second millennium BC, disrupted the civilizations of Sumeria, the Indus, and to a lesser extent Egypt, while adapting well to the existing cultures, especially in Babylon. After 1600 the Egyptians, the Hittites in Anatolia and the Assyrians all developed large-scale military organizations to sustain their growing imperial ambitions. In the eastern Mediterranean new civilizations began to emerge in this period. The Cretan Minoans created a sea-based empire and a flourishing, peaceful civilization based on Knossos, and Mycenae began to establish itself as a power in southern Greece where olive and vine farming formed the basis of future economic development.**

**After the fall of the Minoan civilization Mycenae took over much of its maritime power and culture, but with further invasions from the north *c.* 1200 BC she too declined.**

### 2000-1920 BC

**The brief Sumerian renaissance** centred on Ur continued until *c.* 1950 BC when Semitic Amorites overran much of Sumeria. This was the beginning of a long period of instability in Mesopotamia.

**In Egypt** the Middle Kingdom reached its height with the 12th dynasty, 1991-1785, after Amenemhat I had subdued the nobility and restored prosperity. Building, art and international commerce flourished.

### 1920-1840 BC

**Senusret III,** 1887-1849 BC, further consolidated royal authority in Egypt by suppressing provincial rulers (nomarchs) and assisted the rise of a bureaucratic and trading middle class.

**Unrest in Sumeria** centred on conflict between the cities of Isin and Larsa, during which the area broke down once more into independent city states.

**The Semitic language** of the Amorites gradually superseded Sumerian in Mesopotamia, between 2000 and 1700 BC.

### 1840-1760 BC

**Hammurabi the Great of Babylon,** *c.* 1792-1750 BC, an Amorite, subdued the other cities of Mesopotamia and built an empire from the north Euphrates to the Persian Gulf, ruling with a code of laws based on principles absorbed from Sumerian culture.

**The Middle Kingdom of Egypt** ended *c.* 1786 BC, weakened by an influx of the "Hyksos", a Semitic people from Syria.

**The Indus civilization,** already in decline, was destroyed by invading Aryans *c.* 1760 BC.

### 1760-1680 BC

**The Hyksos** became firmly established in the Delta region of Egypt and adopted Egyptian culture. By 1700 BC a dynasty of Hyksos pharaohs was established.

**The Babylonian Empire** slowly crumbled under Hammurabi's son *c.* 1700 while culture and religion flourished.

**A natural disaster on Crete** caused the Minoan palaces to be rebuilt *c.* 1700 BC.

**The Hittites,** an Aryan people, grew powerful in Anatolia.

## National events

**The Bronze Age in Europe, which stretched from 3000 BC to 750 BC in three main phases, became more widespread in western Europe in the third millennium. Copper and bronze working entered Spain *c.* 2000 and came to flourish in southern England, apparently as a result of trading contacts with Europe.**

**The so-called "Bell-Beaker" folk,** originating in the middle Rhine area, made contact with the Wessex culture *c.* 2000 and introduced metallurgical skills.

**During the Early Bronze Age,** *c.* 2000-1700, Wessex flourished because of its control of the trade routes taking British gold and copper to the rest of Europe.

At this stage most of the bronze used in England was imported, already worked as cups and other useful objects.

**In the Middle Bronze Age,** *c.* 1700-1300, a highly skilled indigenous metal industry emerged but the objects made were mainly luxury articles.

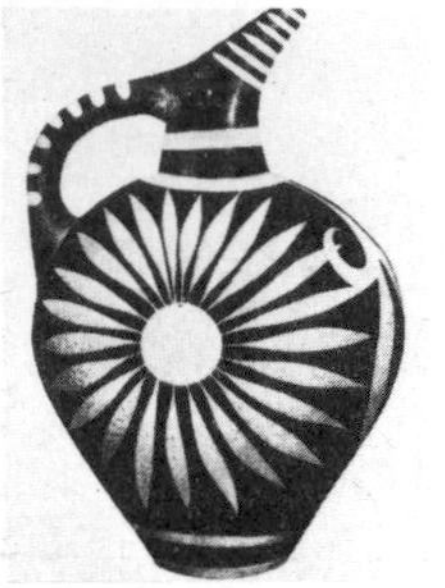

Minoan jug, *c.* 1800 BC

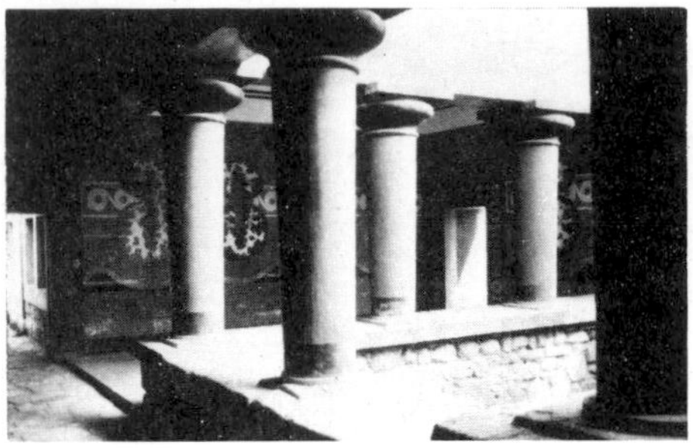

State apartments of the Palace of Knossos, Crete

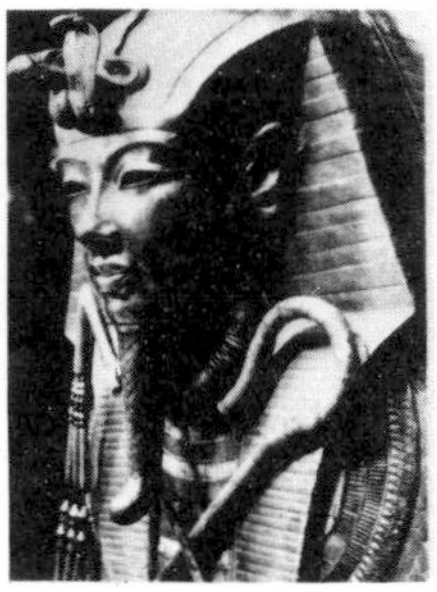

Mask of Tutankhamen

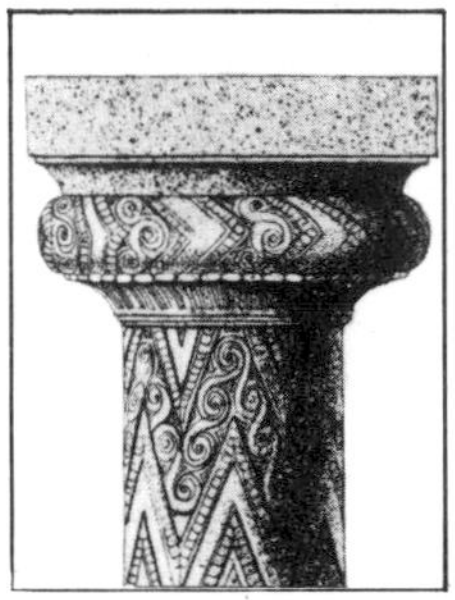

Mycenaean capital, 14thc.

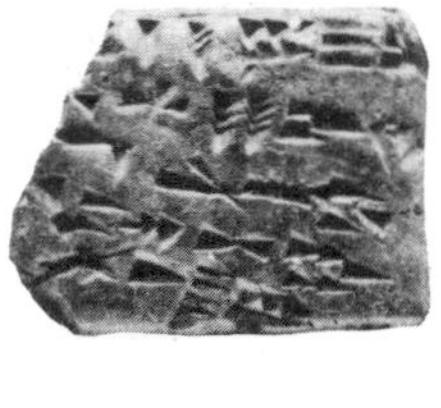

Early Ugaritic script, 14thc.

## Religion and philosophy

**The incursions of Aryans and other invading peoples into the main centres of civilization in the Near East disrupted the established religious traditions, dispersed some of their elements and introduced new ones. The gods of the newcomers reflected their warlike nature, and the worship of their gods evolved into ecstatic sacrificial cults. Their impact upon Egypt, however, was transitory, and the traditional religious system continued and developed, interrupted by a brief but interesting monotheistic interlude under Pharaoh Akhenaton in the early 1300s BC. Once the more turbulent areas of Mesopotamia had settled to orderly lives of commerce and agriculture in city-centred communities, the first codes of law and concepts of citizenship were devised. In this period the basis of the Judaic tradition, with its emphasis on ethical monotheism, was laid among the Israelite tribes.**

**Amenemhat I,** the founder of the Egyptian 12th Dynasty, claimed descent from **Amun,** a local god of his native Thebes. From this time Amun, a father of the gods, and the Heliopolitan god Re were identified as **Amun-Re,** emphasizing the change in the royal family and confirming the divine right of the king to rule all of Egypt.

**The Canaanite religion** emerged in Palestine with **El** as supreme god, and **Baal**, god of rain, vegetation and fertility sharing the central position. The Canaanite religion was an important influence, both negatively and positively, on Israelite culture. It is possible that **Yahweh,** the sole god of Israel, was an Israelite name for the Canaanite El.

**The migrations of Aryans** and other peoples from the Black Sea area helped to disperse religious ideas and practices. The Hurrians who invaded Upper Mesopotamia at this time transmitted elements of Sumerian beliefs northwards to Hittite areas.

**The complex law code devised by Hammurabi the Great** of Babylon *c.* 1792-*c.* 1750, was created in response to the needs of increasing trade, usury and commerce. It sought to end blood feud and personal retribution and replace these with a secular state code based on the idea of citizenship. For example, one of the articles of the code stated that if a man's home fell down and someone was injured, then the owner was to be held responsible.

## Literature

**Cuneiform became more sophisticated after 2000 BC but a more important development was the emergence of the first consonantal (BCD) script, far simpler to master than earlier syllabic systems of writing, none of which have remained in use. The Syrian Ugaritic script, however, which developed in the mid 2nd millennium BC also had three vowel signs although the five-vowel alphabet would not be elaborated until after 1000 BC by the Greeks who would draw on a variety of Semitic scripts.**

**Literature of the period ranged from narrative and love poetry in Egypt to historical narrative among the Hittites, the religious *Vedas* in India and the ethical and divinatory *I Ching* and philosophy in China.**

**The Egyptian Coffin Texts** 2040-1786, found on coffins and papyri, include spells, ritual texts and mythological stories. Their purpose was to give the dead person power in the afterlife, and after 1570 they would evolve into a more unified text, the Egyptian ***Book of the Dead.***

**The Babylonian ritual poem, the *Epic of Creation*,** first written about 2000 BC, had reached a classic form as part of the ceremonies associated with the new year. It told how the god Marduk slew the sea monster Tiamat, and created men as servants of the gods. Babylonian literature of the period is infused with a sense of metaphysical pessimism.

**The ancient Greek script, Linear B,** was deciphered only in AD 1952 by Michael Ventris (1922-56). It was used by the Mycenaeans from *c.* 1450 BC to *c.* 1150 BC. It derives from Linear A, an undeciphered script which was used by the Minoan civilization of Crete from *c.* 2000 BC to *c.* 1450 BC. Linear A dates from 1700 BC and is a syllabic script.

## Art and architecture

**The brilliant civilization which emerged in Crete reached its peak of cultural achievement between 1900 and 1500 BC with palaces of a highly functional design and decorative arts whose grace and vitality reflected a long period of peaceful development. Minoan fresco painting, sculpture and painted pottery were characterized by a humane outlook and a love of nature and movement. The influence of Minoan art extended to Mycenae.**

**Temple architecture revived in Egypt with the Middle Kingdom and enjoyed its golden age in the 14th and 13th centuries. The New Kingdom ruler, Akhenaton, who made sun worship the sole cult during his reign, built some of the finest of these and introduced a revolutionary naturalism into royal portrait sculpture.**

**Chinese bronze workmanship was the most advanced in the world and calligraphic art was beginning to develop.**

**In Egypt**, the establishment of the Middle Kingdom in 1991 BC was marked by an economic and artistic revival. The Great Temple of Karnak, built during the 12th dynasty, *c.* 1991-*c.* 1785, showed a high level of craftsmanship in tomb reliefs, gold ornamentation and paintings. Middle Kingdom sculpture adheres rigidly to rules dictating proportion and posture devised in the Old Kingdom, despite a new element of naturalism in royal portraiture.

**The Bell-Beaker culture** in central and western Europe made good-quality red ceramic beakers decorated with horizontal bands of geometric patterns. **In China**, wheel-turned **Lungshan** black pottery (named after a site in Shantung) replaced the Yang-shao type at the end of the Neolithic period. With thin walls and a metallic, burnished finish, it marked a great technical advance and was commonly used for ritual purposes and funerary ware.

**The Minoan palaces** at Knossos, Phaestos and other Cretan sites were rebuilt on a grander scale in the Middle Minoan period, 1900-1600, with more varied architectural features such as light shafts and efficient sanitation. By about 1760 BC, Minoan potters were producing fine Kamares ware pottery in graceful and varied shapes with a profusion of floral and geometric motifs. Craftsmen specialized in small works such as faience figurines.

**A major revival of Mesopotamian art** marked the rule of **Hammurabi,** *c.* 1792-*c.* 1750. Old palaces and buildings were strengthened and new ziggurats constructed. To the north, the city of Mari, partly built under the ruler **Zimrilim**, *c.* 1779-*c.* 1761 BC, is remarkable for its size. Its 200 rooms cover four hectares (10 acres) and the fine painted decorations include narrative pictures such as the Investiture of Zimrilim.

## Music

**The development of a metal-working technology in ancient civilization enabled craftsmen to make metal instruments based on older instruments made from organic materials and stone. Bells of bronze replaced stone chimes, and bronze, copper or silver trumpets replaced hollowed horns. A metal tube with a more cylindrical bore than animal horn gave a brilliant tone.**

**The yellow bell**, or huang chung, was the name given to an absolute (fixed) pitch produced by a bamboo pipe of set length. It is attributed to a mythical Chinese emperor of *c.* 2000 BC.

## Science and technology

**Trade and warfare were the main stimuli of technological advance in the 2nd millennium BC. Larger sailing ships were used to bring tin from the Mediterranean countries to Mesopotamia and to carry away bronze objects made using the tin; radical improvements took place in chariot design, but the greatest technological event was the mastery of iron by Hittite smiths. Although they lacked heat enough to melt the metal, the Hittites made iron implements by hammering them out of the heated ore. The resultant metal, albeit flawed by slag, could be tougher and harder than bronze. Weapons, sword blades in particular, benefited while metalwork for decorative purposes in iron, bronze, gold or silver became highly refined, as the objects found in the tomb of Tutankhamen show. Bronze vessels of superlative craftsmanship were made in China too under the Shang dynasty.**

**The shaduf**, a device for raising water from one level to another with a bucket, appears on Mesopotamian seals *c.* 2000. This is an Egyptian invention still used in the Nile region.

**Early Chinese technology** is suggested by the finding of jade plaques, which could only have been worked effectively with metal tools.

**Iron weapons** and ornaments, dating from 2000 BC, have been found in the Near and Middle East.

**Early iron technology** involved repeated hammering of the ore until most of the slag was beaten out. Wood or charcoal fires are not hot enough to melt iron. This can only be accomplished in some kind of blast furnace, which was not developed until the Middle Ages.

**Cosmetics**, in Egypt, already used in the 4th millennium included perfumery oils extracted from fruits by pressing them through a cylindrical cloth bag, held upright with sticks. Filter pressing methods of this kind are still used in the food and chemical industries.

**Bronze-casting** in Mesopotamia followed the *cire perdue* method, a one-off process necessarily reserved for valuable items. Objects were modelled or sculptured in wax, covered with clay, and the wax melted out to make a mould for the molten metal. Hollow objects were made by moulding the wax around a clay centre.

### 1680-1600 BC

**The Minoans** established a sea-based empire in the eastern Mediterranean under their semi-legendary King Minos *c.* 1650 BC, creating the Minoan golden age centred on Knossos.

**The Babylonian Empire** was increasingly threatened by the influx of Aryan Kassites from the north *c.* 1600 BC.

**The Shang dynasty,** which introduced writing to China, developed an urban civilization *c.* 1600 BC.

### 1600-1520 BC

**The Hittites** plundered Babylon in *c.* 1550 under King Mursilis I. In their wake the Kassites ruled there for 400 years.

**The Hyksos** were driven from Egypt in *c.* 1570 BC by the Theban kings Kamose and Amosis, who established the New Kingdom, sparking off a growth of nationalist feeling.

**Mycenaean civilization** was growing on mainland Greece, and has left rich "shaft-graves".

**Minoan civilization** reached its height *c.* 1550 BC.

### 1520-1440 BC

**Mitanni,** a kingdom of Aryan Hurrians in northern Mesopotamia, the **Hittites** and **Assyria** all grew as military powers *c.* 1500 BC.

**Thutmose I** of Egypt established an empire in the Near East between 1520 and 1510, and began the construction of the valley of the tombs of the kings at Thebes.

**Minoan civilization** was destroyed *c.* 1450, probably by an earthquake at Thera.

### 1440-1360 BC

**After the volcanic eruption** at Thera, *c.* 1450, Cretan civilization revived and continued to spread to mainland Greece.

**Mitanni** conquered Assyria *c.* 1440 BC to become a military power equal to Egypt.

**Amenhotep III,** 1417-1379 BC, extended the Egyptian Empire and brought peace and prosperity at home, which was threatened by the attempted religious reforms of his successor, Akhenaton, and by internecine murders.

### 1360-1280 BC

**Under Ashur-uballit I,** Assyria again became a military power.

**Tutankhamen** ruled as pharaoh in Egypt, *c.* 1348-1340 BC.

**Hittites** destroyed the empires of Mitanni *c.* 1360 BC, conquered north Syria and Aleppo and built a major empire in the Near East.

**Mycenaean** civilization reached its height *c.* 1320 BC.

**Rameses I** re-established the Egyptian Empire in the Near East *c.* 1319 BC. Rameses II fought the Hittites at the battle of Kadesh *c.* 1299 BC.

### 1280-1200 BC

**A truce was agreed** between Egypt and the Hittites *c.* 1270 as both came under pressure from migrations of "Sea Peoples".

**The Trojan War** reflected stresses in Mycenaean culture from Dorian invasions, *c.* 1200.

**Shalmaneser I** of Assyria, *r.* 1274-1245, took Babylon from the Cassites and defeated the Hittites and the Hurrians.

**Moses led the Jews from Egypt** *c.* 1250 BC.

**Olec civilization** emerged in Mexico *c.* 1200 BC.

---

**Amber-bead spacers** originating in Wessex have been found in Mycenaean shaft-graves of this period, suggesting considerable long-distance trading contacts.

**The number of bronze objects** found in British tombs suggest an increase in British wealth and trade.

**The Late Bronze Age,** *c.* 1300-700, saw an increase in the use of metal for everyday objects.

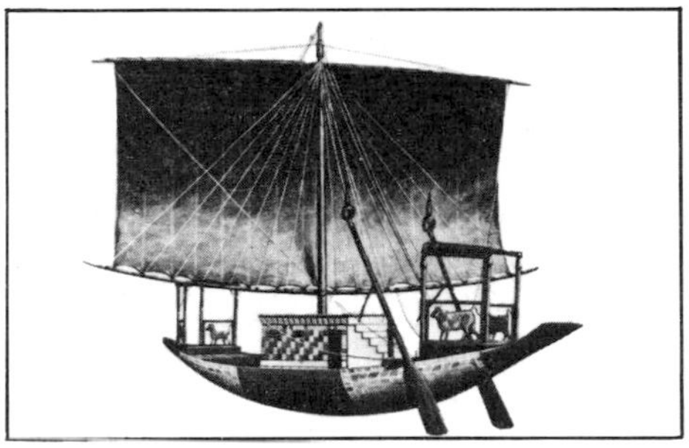

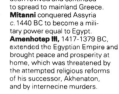

Egyptian ship, *c.* 1300 BC

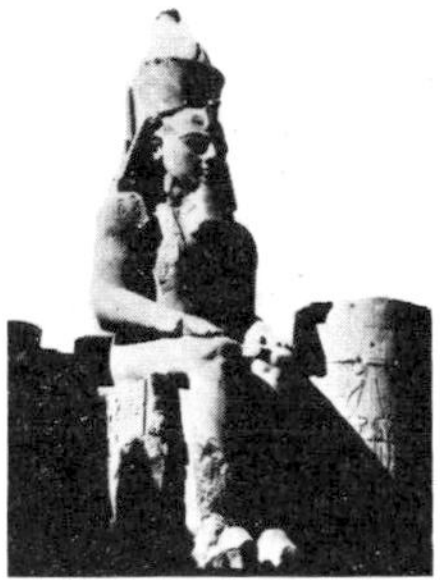

Rameses II at Luxor

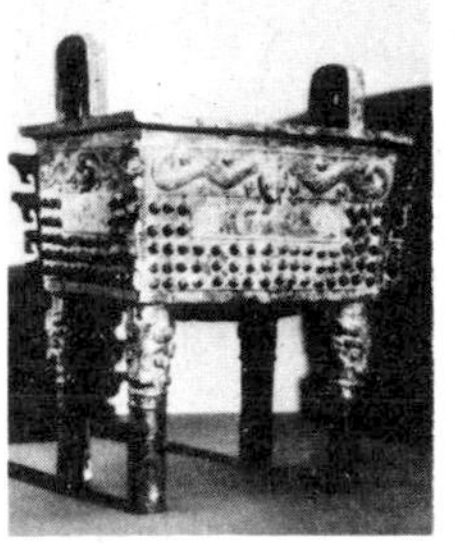

Shang bronze ritual vessel

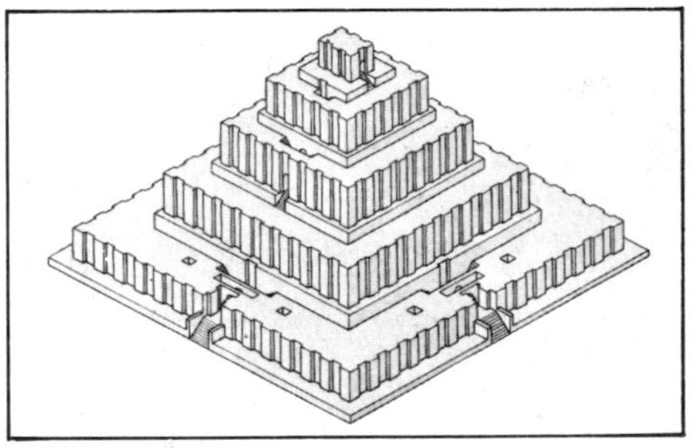

Ziggurat at Elam, 13thc. BC

---

**The royal palace at Knossos** was a centre for the worship of nature-gods with human and animal characteristics. These deities included a fertility goddess associated with snake worship and possibly a bull-god. The extant palace is decorated with a bull's horn motif and is thought to have provided the model for the Labyrinth in the Greek myth of the Minotaur.

**The religion of the Hittites,** who overthrew Babylon in the mid-1500s, derived from many sources. Several of their gods were attributed characteristics that varied locally, and they indiscriminately absorbed the gods of other tribes. However, the mother goddess and the weather god were always retained, the dominance of the latter reflecting the importance of rain to fertility.

**Egyptian religion** went through a short-lived phase in which only one god was worshipped in the reign of **Akhenaton,** *c.* 1379-1362. He suppressed the older gods including Amun-Re and instituted **Aton**, represented by the solar disc, as the only god. During his reign the only other god acknowledged was King Akhenaton himself, who was thought to be eternally revitalized by Aton's rays. After Akhenaton's death, however, Egypt reverted to its traditional gods.

**The Aryan invaders of India** brought with them a religion which came to be embodied in the ***Vedas***, a set of sacred hymns codified by the end of the 2nd millennium BC. The Vedic pantheon of nature gods included **Indra**, the storm god, **Agni**, the fire god, and **Soma**, the intoxicating ritual juice; these and many other gods were involved in a complex mythology and an elaborate system of ritual.

**The Israelites fled Egypt** *c.* 1250 BC under the leadership of Moses, who instituted worship of a single god, **Yahweh**, to whom the tribes were bound by a covenant promising them possession of Canaan (Palestine). The Israelites quickly conquered much of Canaan and their monotheistic religion became common to the "twelve tribes" of Israel.

---

**The first known Phoenician inscriptions**, found at the city of Byblos, date from *c.* 1600 BC. From Byblos, a main trading centre for papyrus, the Greeks took their word for books, *biblia*. The Phoenicians developed the simplest of all the consonantal scripts, reducing the number of symbols used to represent sounds to 22.

**Egyptian love songs** had evolved into a sophisticated literary form by 1200 BC. Although the surviving songs date from the New Kingdom (*c.* 1570–1085) many are clearly from older sources. They are vigorous, direct and lyrical in their appeal to the senses: "When the wind comes it desires the sycamore tree; When you come near to me, you will desire me".

**Hittite literature** would flourish between 1600 and 1200 BC. It was written in cuneiform or, for private communication, in an older pictographic script. There are royal decrees, treaties, a law code, religious instructions and some Sumerian and Babylonian tales. The literary style is distinguished by laconic vigour and lack of verbosity.

**Cuneiform** had become entirely syllabic with fewer and more simplified characters, each having a phonetic value. This development culminated in the **Syrian Ugaritic script**, one of the first scripts with vowel signs. The earliest examples of writing in this Semitic language date from 1400 BC and describe Canaanite mythology.

**The origin of the Greek alphabet** is attributed in mythology to the Phoenician Cadmus (son of Agenor, king of Tyre), who is said to have brought 16 letters to Boeotia *c.* 1313 BC. Evidence from Mycenae indicates that this legend may have some basis in fact. The Phoenician consonant signs certainly provided a model for the Greeks, who later added vowel signs.

**The *Vedas*,** verse hymns dealing with sacrificial and magical formulae, were written in Sanskrit between 1500 and 1200 BC in India. The foremost is the *Rigveda*. The hymns include incantations and spells for good health and long life. Indian literature of this period was primarily religious in inspiration.

---

**Minoan culture** was approaching its golden age. Wheel-thrown pottery decorated with figures, a wide range of gold jewellery and fine quality seals were made, together with miniature sculpture in bronze, terracotta figurines and ivory carvings. Carved vases of stone and marble appeared *c.* 1600 BC with relief decoration, some in the shape of bulls' heads, reflecting the Minoan passion for bull sports and the religious significance of this animal.

**Egyptian art** experienced its classical flowering under the New Kingdom, *c.* 1570-1085. A standard temple plan, often on a monumental scale, was established, with floral motifs as characteristic decoration on the columns. A spirit of freedom produced lighter and more elegant sculpture, coupled with precise rendering of detail, but formal rules were preserved. Fine quality work in precious materials reflected the influence of new trade links.

**The peak of Minoan culture** was reached, its influence extending to Greece, particularly in Mycenae. The Minoan's love of depicting nature in their art is exemplified in the lively frescoes of the palaces, in works such as the unique painted limestone coffin, *c.* 1450, from Hagia Triada, Crete, and in the richly decorated pottery which flourished *c.* 1500-1450, depicting marine creatures of many varieties, as in the Octopus Jar from Heracleon.

**A more naturalistic style of Egyptian royal portraiture** was encouraged by **Akhenaton,** *r.* *c.* 1379-1362, who built a new palace and temple to the sun god at Tell el Amarna. A head of his consort **Nefertiti** is one of the most beautiful works of this short-lived Amarna style. The temple of Amun and Colossi of Memnon were built under **Amenhotep III**, 1417-1379. Examples from **Ras Shamra** (Ugarit) show a high standard of Phoenician decorative art.

**The tomb of Tutankhamen** with its rich furnishings included a sarcophagus with a gold and lapis lazuli funerary mask.

**Under China's Shang dynasty** at An-yang, mastery of bronze casting produced distinctive vessels, drums and bells, some with calligraphic ornamentation.

**Tholoi (beehive tombs)**, including the Treasury of Atreus, with great vaulted ceilings, were built at Mycenae, in the 14th century.

**Ramesses II**, *c.* 1304-1237 completed the colonnaded hypostyle hall at Abydos, with fine funerary reliefs. His rock temple at Abu Simbel was one of the most grandiose achievements of Egypt's New Kingdom. Hewn from a pink sandstone cliff with an entrance 32m (105ft) high, it extended 61m (200ft) into the mountain and was flanked by four massive statues of the king. He also added to the Temple of Luxor and erected a colossus of himself in the forecourt.

---

**A lute-like instrument** with fretted fingerboard appears in a wall painting in an Ancient Egyptian tomb dating from about 1520 BC. Earlier types are found in Mesopotamian pottery *c.* 2000.

**The oldest known Chinese instruments** are suspended stone chimes and globular bone flutes, dating from about 1500 BC. They were played in the early part of the Shang dynasty.

**Bamboo culture** in South-East Asia produced an unusual music, mixing the sounds of blown pipes, such as flutes, and struck pipes in the form of bamboo xylophones.

**Copper and silver trumpets** found in the tomb of Tutankhamen date from about 1320 BC. The brilliance of their tone would have contrasted with other instruments in use at the time.

**Vedic chant**, a sung form of ancient Hindu scriptures, was established by 1200 BC and is the world's oldest continuous musical tradition. It was based on a three-note scale system.

---

**Ships** underwent improvement in the second millennium BC. A major impetus for sea trade came from the Mesopotamians, who had probably become cut off from their major sources of tin in Syria and so imported the metal to make bronze. Many vessels sailing the eastern Mediterranean were built from planks and could be made up to 12m (40ft) long. Minoan ship design was particularly influential.

**Sea battles** took place towards the end of this millennium.

**Ploughs** were improved *c.* 1600 in Mesopotamia, by the invention of a share and sole that dug deeper furrows.

**Cementation steel** was made by the Chalybes, a subject people of the Hittites. This, the earliest form of steel, is made by repeatedly hammering red-hot iron together with charcoal until carbon enters the iron.

**Fine metalwork** in iron, copper bronze, gold and silver, with filigree and inlay work reached a new peak in Egypt.

**Chinese bronze** urns and vases appeared suddenly *c.* 1500 BC, under the Shang dynasty with no previous evidence of a metal technology (except for jade carving). Shang bronzes were moulded in sections to extremely complex designs.

**Glass bottles** appeared in Egypt *c.* 1500 BC. Glazed beads and glass imitations of precious stones have been found dating from a thousand years earlier, but this is the first evidence of work with molten glass.

**An Egyptian water clock,** *c.* 1400 BC, had bucket-shaped vessels from which water drained by way of small holes in the bases. Hours were marked inside the vessels.

**Mathematics** may have developed from linear measurement used in the division of land in Egypt and Mesopotamia. Measurements were often made in units based on parts of the body, such as the Egyptian cubit, from the elbow to the fingertip.

**Currency**, in Egypt, took the form of copper ingots in the shape of a stretched ox-hide. These ox-hide ingots were often transported by ship, as we know from Egyptian wrecks.

**Egyptian chariots** were improved by increasing the number of wheel spokes from four to six, and the movement of the axle rearwards so that the rider's weight was more evenly distributed. This prevented see-sawing movements over rough ground, giving a smoother ride.

**Cavalry** soon challenged the charioteer in war. Saddles and reins were developed in south Turkey, but stirrups were not used for 1,000 years and did not reach Europe until 8th c. AD.

**Hittite ironsmiths** scattered with the destruction of the Hittite Empire, *c.* 1200 BC, with far-reaching consequences. The smiths had kept their techniques secret for hundreds of years, but knowledge of them now began to spread, reaching eastern Europe by 1000.

# 1200-700 BC Iron swords and the alphabet

## Principal events

**Barbarian invasions continued to strike the Near East, obliterating the power of the Hittites and Mycenaeans and limiting Egyptian and Assyrian military ambition. In the same period, however, the smaller trading societies, particularly the Jews and Phoenicians, flourished. The Phoenicians built colonies throughout the Mediterranean and the Jews established their distinctive identity and claim to the region west of the river Jordan. After 900 the military power of Egypt and Assyria recovered, financed by tribute from their subject peoples, but the focus for cultural development moved to Greece where the adaptation of the Phoenician alphabet marked the end of the Dorian-imposed dark ages.**

**In India, the Aryans overran the Ganges area and established a caste system based on the Vedic religion. In China the Shang dynasty fell to their former subjects, the Chou, but this had little cultural effect.**

### 1200-1150 BC

**The Sea Peoples** invaded the eastern Mediterranean from the Caspian Sea area and destroyed the Hittites *c.* 1200 BC. Some settled on the Canaanite coast to become the Philistines. **Ramesses III** *c.* 1198-1166, repelled their invasion of Egyptian soil *c.* 1190 BC, after which Egypt withdrew into cultural and political isolation. **The Canaanites**, a Semitic race, settled in Syria and developed a flourishing culture based on the production of purple cloth.

### 1150-1100 BC

**Nebuchadrezzar I**, *r.* 1124-1103, of Babylon restored stability in Mesopotamia, facilitating the recovery of Assyrian trade disturbed by the Hyksos. **The Egyptian monarchy** fell under the growing influence of the priesthood of the sun god Re, the Amun, causing political and economic stagnation *c.* 1100. **The Shang dynasty in China** consisted of 30 kings in fraternal succession but declined through internal unrest *c.* 1100 BC.

### 1100-1050 BC

**Tiglath-Pileser I** of Assyria conquered Mesopotamia and the eastern Mediterranean, defeating Babylon and exacting tribute from the Phoenician city states. After his death in *c.* 1077, **the Aramaeans** took Babylon and destroyed Assyrian power, driving the Canaanites south. **The Philistines**, a trading people, conquered **the Jews** who had settled in Palestine after leaving Egypt and were at this time a loose confederation of tribes ruled by the Judges.

### 1050-1000 BC

**Aramaean rule** in Assyria produced little military or cultural activity. **In Greece**, monarchical city states including Athens, Thebes and Sparta, developed *c.* 1000 based on wealth derived from trade and agriculture. **Saul** became the first king of the Jews *c.* 1020 BC with powers limited by religious tradition. **Aryan rule** was established in north India by 1000 BC. **The Chou dynasty** was set up in China in 1027 BC.

## National events

**The Bronze Age was a period of relatively peaceful evolution. Bronze tools became commonplace in Britain from the 12th century onwards and villages were organized with divisions of land for arable farming purposes. The introduction of the plough in the 12th century led to an increase in population.**

The expansion of the **"Urnfield" people** westwards from central Europe *c.* 1200 onwards led to close contacts between England and Europe.

**Cremation in urnfields** was normal in Britain by 1100 BC. **Iron metallurgy** spread through Europe after the fall of the Hittite kingdom *c.* 1200.

A fairly simple **subsistence economy** developed in southern England based on barley and livestock agriculture using oblong field patterns.

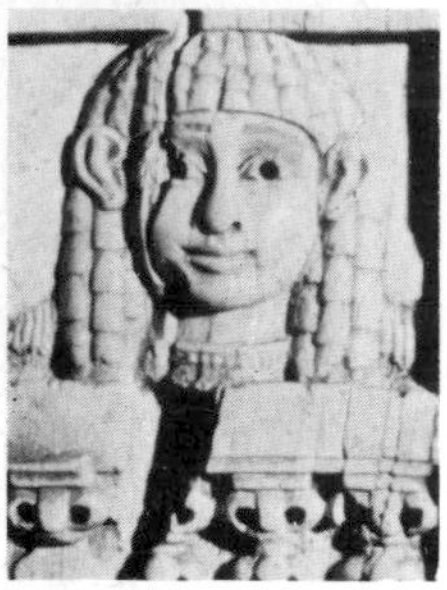

Phoenician ivory, Nimrud

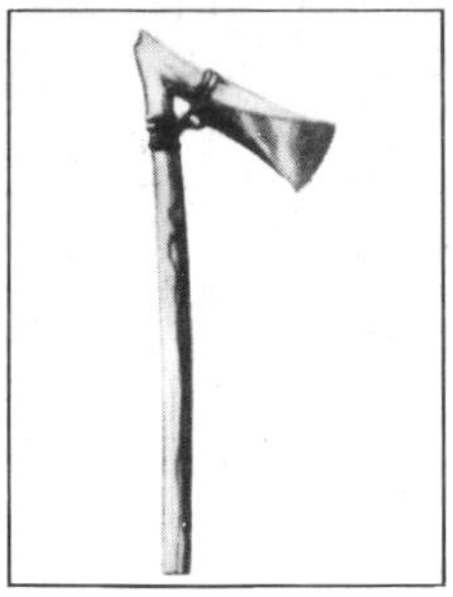

Bronze axe, *c.* 1000 BC

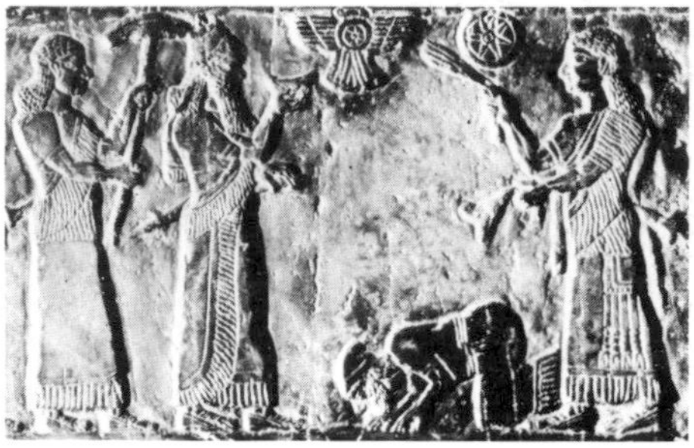

Black obelisk of Shalmaneser III

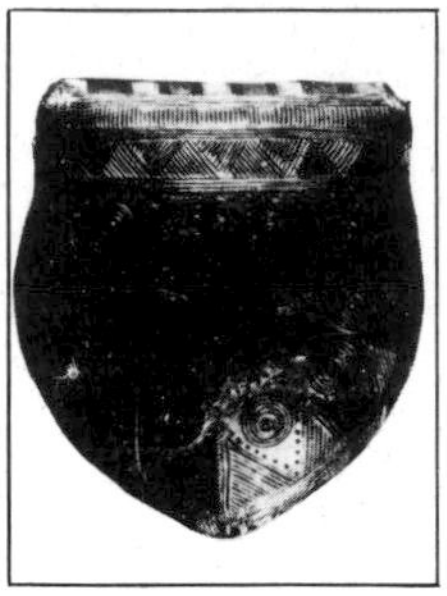

Hallstatt art: pendant

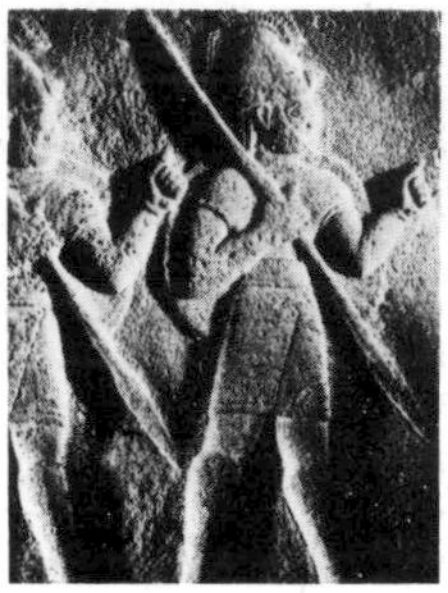

Hittite relief, *c.* 800 BC

## Religion and philosophy

**Beginning with the period of the Judges, Israelite history shows a continual effort by certain individuals and nomadic groups to defend the purity of the religion of Yahweh against its dilution by the pagan affiliations of her central rulers. This unceasing resistance to the addition of other gods of their faith reinforced the distinctive features of the Judaic tradition.**

**In China the emergence of a secular philosophy foreshadowed the development of later religious sytems, with their characteristic lack of emphasis on the supernatural.**

**The invasion of Greece by a succession of northern tribes led to a joining of new Olympian gods with older deities. This varied religious atmosphere, contrasting sharply with the rigid, priest-dominated society of Egypt, would play an important part in the emergence of the brilliant culture of 5th-century Greece.**

**Successive invasions** of Greece culminating in that of the Dorians, *c.* 1200, brought Aryan gods such as Zeus, Apollo and Hermes, who largely replaced the more nature-oriented gods of the Minoan-influenced Mycenaeans. These gods, who in Greek mythology became associated with Mount Olympus, bore a far more arbitrary relation to human affairs than the original Mycenaean deities.

**Chinese philosophy** emerged during the Chou dynasty, 1027-221 BC, as increasing control over nature and the growth of social stability led to a demystification of thought. Irrigation replaced prayers for rain, and heaven (*T'ien*) was seen as rewarding virtue, thus giving man the power to control his own destiny through being virtuous.

**The Israelites** began to assimilate Canaanite ideas during the period of the Judges, which ended *c.* 1050 BC. The Yahweh of Moses and his nomadic followers absorbed features of the Canaanite deities as Israelite society became more settled and structured. Religious purists such as **Rechabites** and **Nazarites** opposed this degeneration of the monotheistic ideal.

**Religion** in Iran before Zoroaster (6th century BC) bore similarities to the early Vedic religion of India. Many of the Iranian pantheon of gods coincided with Vedic ones, including **Mithras**, the cult of fire, and **Haoma**, the sacred liquor.

## Literature

**The Greek alphabet, in which letters were used to represent vowels for the first time, had developed from Phoenician forms by the 8th century BC. It provided the most flexible and economical way of writing yet devised. At about the same time the ballads of the Trojan wars, which had emerged in oral form in the 10th century, were compiled and written down by Homer in the *Iliad* and the *Odyssey*. It is not entirely clear whether Homer was a single man or the name for a group of poets. But the later Greeks, who drew strongly on Homeric traditions, regarded him as an individual, the father of Greek poetry. Similarly, in Mesopotamia, the *Gilgamesh* epic neared its final form, and a Chinese poetic tradition grew up.**

**Ten thousand Hittite cuneiform tablets** constituting the state archives at Boğazköy, the capital, survived the destruction of the empire *c.* 1200 BC. These represent the main source of information on Hittite history and culture.

**The collection of myths and folklore** that coalesced into the *Gilgamesh* epic in Mesopotamia was now approaching its final form. It combined religious elements with story themes that were to become widely popular throughout the Middle East, including references to a flood, the quest for immortality and the friendship of two great warriors.

**Traces of the *Gilgamesh* epic** can be found in the Trojan ballads, which culminated in the poetry of Homer, as well as in Hebrew and other classical literature. The adventures of Gilgamesh, king of Uruk, and his friendship with Enkidu, a wild man sent to destroy him, were the centre of a pessimistic poetic cycle that combined realism with myth.

**The Greek alphabet** is thought to have begun evolving after 1050 BC as the Greeks modified symbols they had borrowed from the Phoenicians to suit the sounds of their own language. The name alphabet comes from the first two symbols, *alpha* and *beta*. By using signs for vowels as well as for consonants the Greeks made a crucial advance, enabling any word to be written.

## Art and architecture

**The trading societies that emerged during this period helped to spread artistic styles and techniques in the eastern Mediterranean. In Greece foreign influences imported especially by the Phoenicians led to the adoption of complex figurative images in pottery where previously only geometric patterns had been used. The influence of the Phoenicians was similarly felt in the Hebrew kingdom of King Solomon, who employed their craftsmen to build his Great Temple at Jerusalem.**

**Monumental architecture ceased to be built in Egypt but in Assyria the political resurgence of the 9th and 8th centuries led to the restoration of Nimrud and the building of Sargon's palace at Khorsabad.**

**In Central America the isolated Olmec civilization produced colossal sculpture without the aid of metal tools.**

**With the decline of the Egyptian New Kingdom** major architectural programmes ended and the sarcophagus of **Ramesses III**, *d.* 1166, is one of the last major works in the classical New Kingdom style. **The earliest form of Greek art** was the Proto-Geometric style of pottery decoration painted with zigzags and wavy lines. This pottery probably originated in Athens, the leading city at the end of the Bronze Age.

**San Lorenzo**, the earliest Olmec site, was established *c.* 1150. The chief Olmec art forms were large stone monuments,including colossal heads, some weighing over 40 tonnes.

**In China** the artistic traditions of the Shang dynasty were perpetuated by the Chou, *c.* 1122-221. Jade and ritual bronze vessels became increasingly elaborate, palace architecture developed and roof-tiling and bricks were introduced. Wall painting probably began during this period.

**Egypt's Late Dynastic period** was dominated by the High Priests of Amun, and primarily religious artefacts were made. Metal was increasingly used to make figurines and larger statuary was often made in the harder stones such as schist and basalt.

## Music

**Noticing that there was a mathematical relationship between the length of a pipe or a string and the pitch it produced, musicians in the ancient civilizations linked this relationship with the underlying order of the universe and phenomena of the natural world. This aspect of musical theory would later be expressed in Pythagoras' concept of the harmony of the spheres.**

**Secular music** was established as an important part of the life of the Assyrian court *c.* 1200. Minstrels were highly regarded and music held a recognized place in court entertainment.

**Pentatonic scales** became prevalent in the East. The five notes of these scales, still characteristic of Eastern music, were often related to north, south, east, west and centre.

**The reed mouth organ** or shêng developed in China. It has several bamboo pipes rising from a wind chest into which air is blown through a mouthpiece.

## Science and technology

**The major technological advance of the 2nd millennium BC – a radical improvement in the quality of wrought iron – was a major factor in the expansion of the later Assyrian Empire. Assyrian ironsmiths were able to make a sharp edge using a process of tempering which involved repeated hammering and quenching in water. For the first time, effective iron swords and axes could be made; these weapons, together with siege towers and the use of cavalry, greatly contributed to the image of Assyrian indomitability. Sharpened iron was first used effectively in agriculture with the introduction of iron ploughshares in Mesopotamia. Iron blades withstood wear far better than bronze-shared ploughs and could cut deeper furrows, which led in turn to greater crop yields.**

**In South America the Chavin produced beautiful objects in hammered gold, and Chinese bronze and ceramic technology was further refined.**

**Phoenician sea trade**, by 1200 BC, supplanted that of Minoan Crete and would later focus on the docks of Tyre and Sidon. The Phoenicians are thought to have developed the bireme *c.* 1100. **Early food technology** included the preservation of fish by drying, smoking and salting, thus allowing it to be stored. Such methods were used widely in the Bronze Age, but in particular by the Greeks and Phoenicians who were great eaters of fish.

**Vitreous enamelling** was an achievement of the later Mycenaeans. This process involves fusing glass materials on to a metallic base and first appeared in Cyprus in the form of glass decorated gold rings.

**Iron ploughshares**, developed in Mesopotamia *c.* 1100 BC, constituted a further leap forward in agricultural technology. The new wrought iron was sufficiently hard to take a sharp cutting edge.

**The mass production of iron tools** was a major feature of the Assyrian Empire. The Assyrians were not great innovators, but they used techniques developed by Hittite and other subject artisans. **Early South American farming** settlements appeared on the coasts of Ecuador and Peru *c.* 1000 BC. The simple technology of these Neolithic peoples included building in mud, brick and stone, cultivation of the potato and maize which was first grown there *c.* 3000 BC.

## 1000-950 BC

**David, king of the Jews**, 1000-961 BC, defeated the Philistines. His successor, Solomon, 961-922, built the temple at Jerusalem and a trading fleet in the Indian Ocean. **Hiram I**, king of Byblos, 969-36, consolidated the Sidonian states and assisted Phoenician trade by building a harbour at Tyre, his new capital. **Damascus and Geshu** were founded by the Aramaeans.

## 950-900 BC

**Assurdan II**, *r.* 935-913, briefly restored Assyrian military authority *c.* 935 BC. But by 912 Assyria was at its smallest size. **Egypt re-emerged** as a military power reconquering Palestine in 918, after Shoshenk, *c.* 935-914, had reunited Egypt by making his son high priest. **The Jewish kingdom** was divided on Solomon's death into the kingdom of the Israelites in the north and Judah in the south, following religious and political opposition to his rule in the north.

## 900-850 BC

**The Phoenician city of Byblos** grew up *c.*900 BC and became the centre of the cult of Baal. **Egypt and Assyria** fought in Syria-Palestine 900-830 BC. At the **battle of Qarqar**, 854, the Aramaeans and Israelites, inspired by Elijah, defeated Shalmaneser III of Assyria. **In Greece** there was a gradual shift from monarchies to oligarchies in most of the city states with the exception of Sparta. The Chavin culture flourished in Peru *c.*900- *c.*200 BC.

## 850-800 BC

**Shalmaneser III** of Assyria, *r.* 858-824, defeated the forces of Damascus and Israel and exacted tribute from the Phoenician cities. **Damascus** came to dominate the Aramaean states and subdued the Israelites *c.* 820 BC. **The Medes**, an eastern people noted for their horse rearing, were first mentioned in Babylonian records *c.* 835 BC. **The Phoenicians** colonized the eastern Mediterranean, and established Carthage *c.* 814 BC.

## 800-750 BC

**Assyrian military power** declined under a succession of weak monarchs *c.* 800 BC and with it Assyrian wealth. **A Greek renaissance** occurred under the stimulus of trading contact with the Phoenicians. **Judah** played an important role in a military alliance against the Assyrians *c.* 769 BC. **Jeroboam**, 780-740, brought prosperity to the Israelites. **The caste system** was now firmly established in India. **Rome** was founded in 753 BC.

The increase in **luxury bronze goods** used in England and found in graves marks a rise in trading contacts with the Continent of Europe.

## 750-700 BC

**Tiglath-Pileser III**, *r.* 744-727, Shalmaneser V, *r.* 726-722, and Sargon II, *r.* 721-705, restored Assyrian military power, founding a standing army and often moving subject peoples. Babylon was conquered and Damascus paid tribute to Assyria. **Greek cities** founded colonies in Sicily and southern Italy *c.* 750. **The Kushite kingdom** in Nubia was founded *c.* 800 BC with its capital at Napata. In 725 BC, it overran Egypt and a Kushite dynasty, 725-656, was founded.

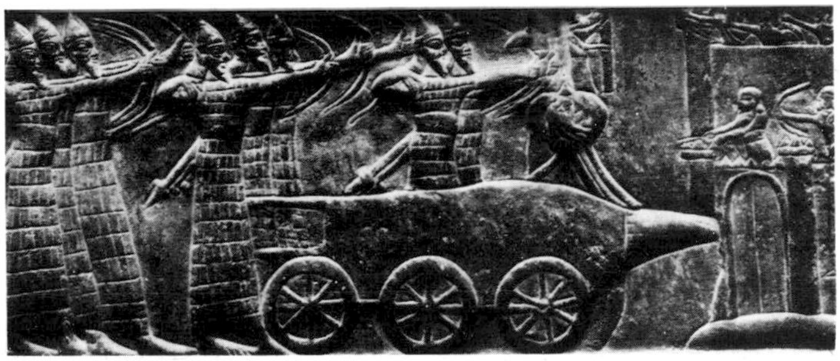

Gates of Shalmaneser III: Assyrian war machines

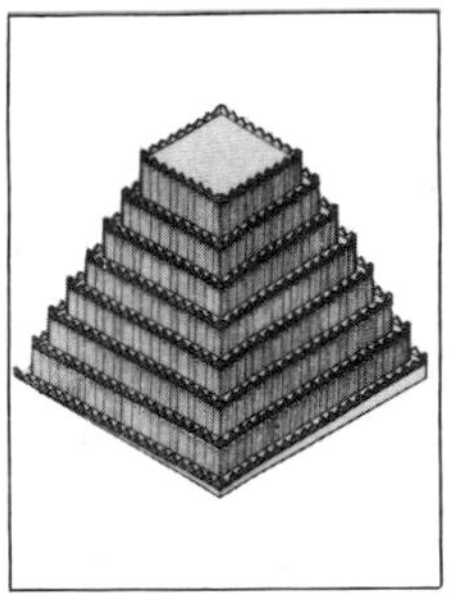

The Ziggurat at Khorsabad

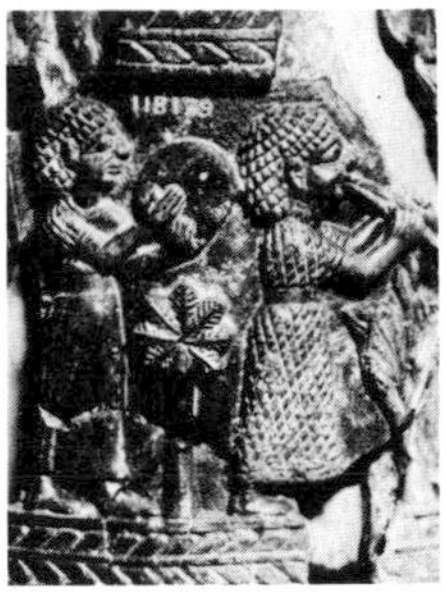

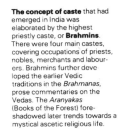

Phoenician musicians, 8thc.

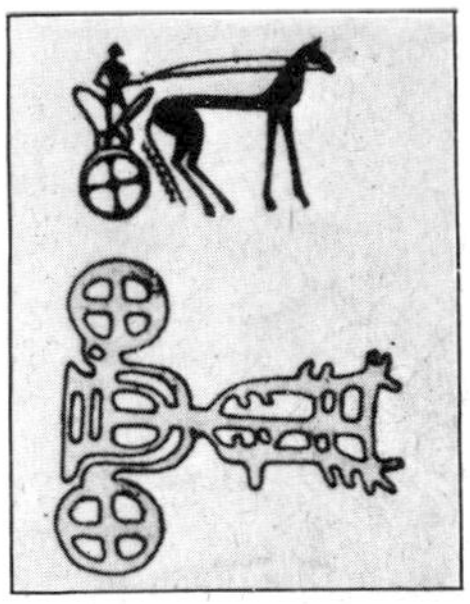

Chariot from Greek amphora

**The foremost Vedic writings** were the *Rigveda*, a collection of hymns and sacred formulae of "mantras" that formed the liturgical basis for a priesthood. Cremation of the dead came to replace burial, and there was a differentiation of priestly functions into those relating to actual sacrificial procedures and those relating to the ritual chanting of the sacred hymns.

**Primitive Japanese religion**, Shinto, was based on a love of nature. The powers of nature, **Kami**, were seen as beneficent rather than awesome, and pollution was "biological" rather than moral. Pollution from contact with death or menstruation had to be removed by ritual cleansing. The art of divination by burning bones was practised.

**Jezebel**, wife of the King of Israel Ahab, *r.* 874-853 BC, built a temple to the Canaanite god Baal. This aroused opposition among the zealous followers of Yahweh led by Elijah, *fl. c.* 875. Elijah's disciple **Elisha** inspired the slaying of Jezebel and the complete overthrow of the royal family.

The orgiastic cult of the nature divinity **Dionysus, or Bacchus**, reached Greece from Thrace and Phrygia. His followers, mostly women known as **Maenads** (mad ones), would take to the hills in ecstasy under the god's inspiration and wander about in *thiasori*, or revel bands. Dionysus was god of fruitfulness and vegetation, and was especially known as the god of wine.

**The concept of caste** that had emerged in India was elaborated by the highest priestly caste, or **Brahmins**. There were four main castes, covering occupations of priests, nobles, merchants and labourers. Brahmins further developed the earlier Vedic traditions in the *Brahmanas*, prose commentaries on the Vedas. The *Aranyakas* (Books of the Forest) foreshadowed later trends towards a mystical ascetic religious life.

The 8th-century prophets of the Old Testament, **Amos, Hosea and Isaiah**, castigated the moral turpitude of the Israelite rulers and their syncretist tendencies. The prophets rejected contemporary and foreign standards and urged other worldly ideals, prophesying that the dilution of the old religion would lead to the fall of the kingdom of Israel. This prediction was fulfilled when the Assyrians conquered Israel in 721 BC.

**Hebrew literature** flourished in the tenth century with the composition of the mystical *Song of Songs*, a poetic drama full of lyrical beauty celebrating nature and love. It is attributed in the Bible to Solomon, king of Israel, but its origins may be even older.

**The Trojan cycle of ballads** which Homer would immortalize in his *Iliad* and *Odyssey*, had probably begun to evolve in the 10th century although they may well not have been written down. The cycle told of the twelfth-century war between Greece and Troy, the wrath of Achilles and the wanderings of another Greek hero, Odysseus.

**The Moabite Stone**, or Mesha Stele, was erected at Dibon *c.* 850 BC by King Mesha, who composed the inscription on it to commemorate his successful revolt against Israel in the ancient land of the Moabites. It approximates Hebrew but the script is the Phoenician one from which the Greeks derived the alphabet.

**The *Upanishads*** in India summed up much of the wisdom of earlier Hindu scriptural writing and expressed it in the form of a dialogue between teacher and pupil which would provide the basis for the major philosophical branches of Hinduism. The dialogues bring out the essential unity of Brahman (god) and Atman (soul).

***The Iliad*** and ***Odyssey***, Greek poems of 24 books each, belong in style to the 8th century BC but little is known of their authorship. They combine ancient legends with a vivid evocation of scene and event and masterly delineation of character. Their literary magic is generally attributed to a single poet, Homer, who may have lived in Asia Minor.

**The first surviving Greek inscription**, the Dipylon vase from Athens, is dated *c.* 710: "Who now of all dancers performs most gracefully, he shall receive this". **Hesiod**, *c.* 750-700 BC, a didactic poet from Boeotia, wrote the *Theogony* and *Works and Days*, providing indispensable information on Greek myths, religion and agriculture.

**The Scandinavian Iron Age** developed a high level of metal craftsmanship in grave goods. The most outstanding example is the Sun Chariot from Trundholm, Denmark, *c.* 1000. It shows a horse and six-wheeled chariot, with a bronze-gilt solar disc.

**The first Temple of Jerusalem** was completed *c.* 950. Built by Phoenician craftsmen under the direction of King Solomon, it was based on Canaanite and Phoenician models. The main building, decorated with massive carvings in ivory, wood and gold, was flanked by three-storey chambers. **The 'Megaron B'** temple at Thermon, one of the earliest major examples of Greek architecture, has the characteristic form of later Greek temples.

**Nimrud in Mesopotamia** was restored and enlarged by Ashurnasirpal II, 883-859, who built at least two temples and four palaces, decorated with winged human-headed lions in carved stone and reliefs showing the king himself. Ivories from the northwest palace show the widespread assimilation of Phoenician craftsmanship.

**The Black Obelisk**, known as "Jehu's stele", describes the campaigns of Shalmaneser III, *r.* 858-824. The frieze shows King Jehu of Israel making obeisance to him – the earliest representation of a Semite in traditional costume.

**Pottery in Greece** flourished between *c.* 900 and 750 BC, decorated with a wide range of human and animal figures, which prefigured the classical narrative style. Bronze work, and the small terracotta figurines made for the new sanctuaries at Delphi and Olympia, herald the emergence of Greek sculpture. New motifs such as floral designs were included in geometric pottery decoration as a result of increased trade with Cyprus and the Near East.

**The art of the late Assyrian Empire** flowered under **Tiglath-Pileser III**, *r.* 744-727, and **Sargon II**, *r.* 721-705. Tiglath-Pileser's palace at **Nimrud** was decorated with reliefs in the epic tradition, but freer in style. Sargon's palace at **Khorsabad**, was a sophisticated structure covering 9 hectares with its own drainage system. Man-headed winged bulls guarded the entrance and 2m (7ft) reliefs depicted members of the court.

**Bronze trumpets** or lurs date from about 1000 BC. Found in Danish bogs, lurs were made with conical bores ending in flat discs. They are usually found in pairs.

**Psalms** were the central feature of the music of the first temple of the Jews. Responses between priests and congregation established the pattern of many later forms of Christian music.

**Lyres and harps** were used to accompany Jewish temple songs. Trumpets and cymbals were played to signal special moments or interludes in the liturgy.

**The lyre** was popular in Greece. A large form with from three to twelve strings called the kithara was plucked with a plectrum while the player's other hand dampened the strings' vibrations.

**Professional bards** in Greece recited or sang epic poems to their own lyre accompaniment, while shepherds played pan-pipes made of reeds of various lengths bound together side by side.

**Assyrian military technology**, 1000-700 BC, was stimulated by constant warfare. The Assyrian Ashurnasirpal II, was the first to use cavalry units to any extent in addition to infantry and war chariots. The Assyrians also developed siege weapons for attacking the mud walls of enemy cities. Battering rams that rocked to and fro were not very successful, but iron-shod beams, which were raised and allowed to fall, were extremely effective.

**Chinese chariots** had wheels with many more spokes than the chariots of the Middle East, but otherwise differed very little from them. The Chinese, however, who had acquired chariot design from nomads who lived to their west, still placed the axle centrally beneath the platform. **Peruvian gold ornaments** of the Chavin culture date from *c.* 900 BC. Goldsmiths used stone hammers to beat gold into stone moulds, probably without attempting to melt it.

**Iron mines in Italy** were worked from *c.* 900 BC, and would later be taken over by the Etruscans.

**Leather manufacture** originated with the animal skins taken by men of the Old Stone Age. Leather technology, however, developed slowly and few of the dates are certain. The Egyptians treated hides with fat, to increase durability, before 1500 BC. Tanning, or soaking the hides in a solution containing vegetable material to make leather, probably evolved much later, as did a method for hardening leather with alum, but all these techniques were in use *c.* 800 BC.

**Trade in glassware** became widespread, extending as far as the Atlantic coasts. Simple glass technology, such as the manufacture of glass beads, followed this trade and was practised in Britain *c.* 800 BC. **Crops grown in the Middle East** included wheat, barley, flax and, latterly, cotton.

**Siege towers** were a later development of Assyrian military inventiveness. These wooden towers on wheels, often armour-plated and fitted with battering-rams, were used to attack the walls of besieged cities. Although clumsy, they were undoubtedly effective; defenders could retaliate only with spears and arrows, grappling at the battering-rams with iron hooks. **Biremes**, ships with double banks of oars, are pictured in Assyrian reliefs of 700 BC.

# 700-300 BC The birth of philosophy

## Principal events

**Middle Eastern civilization entered a phase of turmoil between the 6th and 4th centuries BC with a series of short-lived empires established by the Babylonians, Persians and Greeks, while the Magadha Empire grew up in India.**

**The most striking feature of the period, however, was cultural – a massive shift towards the systematization of thought which took place in literature and the sciences and was manifested above all in the founding of many of the Eastern religions and the principal schools of Western philosophy.**

**Athens, where culture and democracy flourished in the context of a prosperous city state, stood at the centre of the first brilliant flowering of European urban culture, and although her power even in Greece was limited by Spartan and Macedonian militarism, the conquests of Alexander would carry this culture throughout the Middle East.**

### 700-660 BC

**Sennacherib II**, 704-681, of Assyria made Nineveh his capital after destroying the rebellious Babylon. Esarhaddon, his successor, *r.* 681-669, rebuilt Babylon and attacked Egypt, captured Memphis and drove the pharaohs back to Kush in 671.
**Tyrants** (non-hereditary rulers, mostly of the merchant classes) appeared in many Greek cities and in Athens in 683 BC, assuring growth and prosperity.
**Twelve Etruscan cities** flourished in Central Italy *c.* 675.

### 660-620 BC

**Sparta** became dominant in the Peloponnese after subduing the Messenians in 630 BC.
After the reign of **Ashurbanipal**, 668- *c.* 627 BC, a time of military activity in Egypt and artistic splendour, Assyrian fortunes declined suddenly. The **Chaldean Nabopolassar** led a successful revolt in Babylon.
**Josiah**, 640-609, inspired a successful political and religious uprising in Judah, and **Phoenicia** won her independence from Assyria in 627 BC.

### 620-580 BC

**Nabopolassar** of Babylon destroyed Assyria with Median help in 612 and took Nineveh.
**Sparta** introduced barrack life and military education *c.* 610.
**Nebuchadrezzar II**, *r.* 604-562, built a Babylonian empire in Syria-Palestine, taking the Jews to Babylon as prisoners in 586 BC, and ending Pharaoh Neko II's imperial aspirations.
**Solon**, who became the archon in Athens in 594, smoothed the growing tensions between the aristocracy and the merchants.

### 580-540 BC

**Babylonian power** waned after Nebuchadrezzar died in 562.
**The Peloponnesian League** was founded on Spartan military strength in 560 BC.
**Pisistratus**, *c.* 600-527, the tyrant, secured Athenian authority in eastern Greece.
**Cyrus the Great**, *d.* 529, founded the Persian Empire, defeating Media in 549 and Ionia in 547.
**The Kushite kingdom** reached southwards to Khartoum *c.* 550.
**The Magadha Empire** was established in Bihar *c.* 542.

## National events

**The Iron Age reached Britain and, as elsewhere in northern and eastern Europe, stimulated the development of a tribal Celtic culture, made homogeneous by the supremacy of the druids. A rising population and pressure on the land ended the tranquillity of the Bronze Age.**

**The so-called Hallstatt culture**, developing in Bavaria *c.* 720, reached Britain *c.* 675 introducing iron weapons, mainly through trading contacts.

**Urnfields** were gradually replaced by barrow tombs, of which many rich examples from this period have been found in southern England.

**The use of iron** made land-clearance easier and thus facilitated population growth.

**Trading contact** with Europe apparently declined. The earliest hill-forts date from this period, for instance Beacon Hill in Buckinghamshire.

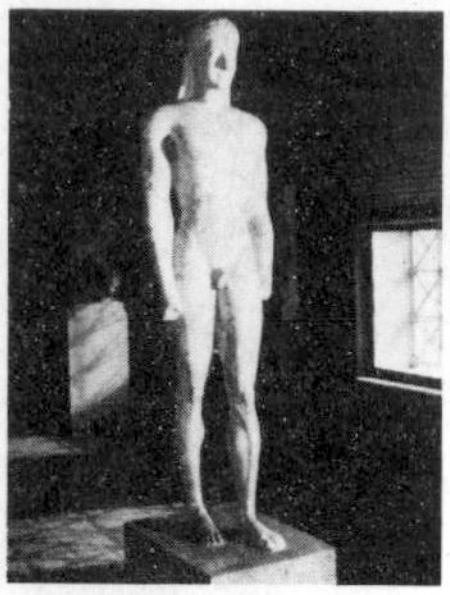
Greek *Kouros* figures, 6thc.

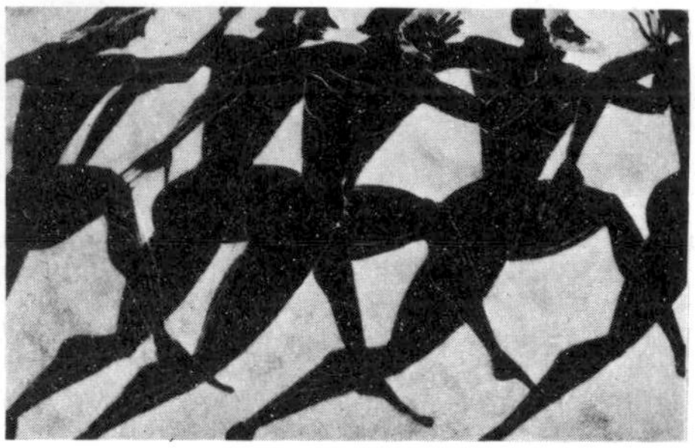
Greek black-figure vase decoration

Ming portrait of Confucius

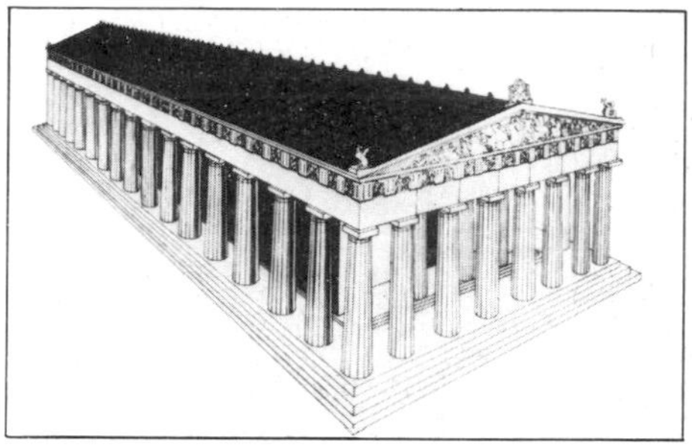
The Parthenon on the Acropolis, Athens

## Religion and philosophy

**Within a remarkably short time, a number of diverse and highly sophisticated religions of world significance arose. Buddhism and Jainism in India marked a break with Brahmanic ritualism. Zoroastrianism in Persia established religious themes which were to spread westwards with far-reaching consequences. In China, both Taoism and Confucianism established the doctrine of harmony as their central idea.**

**The flowering of Greek philosophy is one of the most extraordinary episodes in the history of thought. A questioning of accepted ideas, including the tenets of religion, and an emphasis on rational argument resulted in Greek thinkers from Thales to Aristotle raising most of the issues which have occupied Western philosophy up to the present time. Central concerns were the nature of reality and the basis of virtuous conduct.**

**Thales of Miletus**, *c.* 640-*c.* 546, believed that the essence of all matter was water. His attempt to find simple material causes was seminal to Greek thought.
**Zoroastrianism**, proclaimed in Iran by **Zoroaster**, *c.* 600, proposed a dualistic cosmology of the spirit of good, Ohrmazd, and of evil, Ahriman, between whom man is free to choose. The core of Zoroastrian scriptures, the *Avesta*, was the *Gatha* hymns.

**Taoism** is thought to stem from the work of the Chinese philosopher Lao Tze, *c.* 604- *c.* 531, to whom the *Tao-te Ching* anthology is attributed. The Tao is an imperceptible state of void and undifferentiated being exemplified in the childlike innocence in man. Taoism led to quietism and a retreat from worldly affairs for both rulers and subjects. This was in accordance with the notion of Tao as the all-embracing void, the oneness of all things.

**Jainism** was developed in India by **Mahavira**, *c.* 560- *c.* 468, a member of the Kshatriya noble caste. It emphasized self-denial and non-violence, and rejected **Vedic** authority in reaction to the dominance of Brahmin ritual.
Within the mainstream of Vedism **the first *Upanishads*** were written epitomizing the doctrines of samsara (rebirth) and karma (inescapable consequences). Unity with the cosmos through contemplation provided the only escape from suffering.

## Literature

**From religious mysteries and epic poems, literature began to develop secular forms of many kinds. The most varied and accomplished writing emerged in Athens where theatre became a medium into which most poetic energy flowed, whether tragic, epic, comic or lyrical. Poetry flourished and prose writing developed in the fields of history and philosophy, although Plato's use of the Socratic dialogue indicated the all-pervading influence of the dramatic form.**

**Systematization of previous literary developments occurred in all the major cultures of the world. For the first time, the *Gilgamesh* epic was collected, as were the Indian epics, while in China the teaching of philosophers was written down.**

**Etruscan inscriptions**, mostly liturgical or funerary, dating from *c.* 700 BC, have been found at Magliano, Italy, and elsewhere – indicating the existence of a literature that has been lost. The language is incomprehensible and of unknown origin but the alphabet is Greek-based and led to the development of a Latin alphabet.

**A library** of 20,000 tablets was established at Nineveh by **King Ashurbanipal**, *r.* 668-*c.* 627, who collected Assyrian, Babylonian and Sumerian writings, among them the *Gilgamesh* epic and religious and scientific works.

**In the *Bhagavad Gita***, or Song of the Beloved, Hindu sacred literature took the form of poetic dialogues on the soul.
In Greece, the period saw the rise of **burlesque plays** with religious themes in which the chorus consisted of satyrs.
The **earliest existing Latin inscriptions** – on the Black Stone of the Roman forum and the Manios clasp – date *c.* 600.

The poetic style of **Sappho** was echoed in the simpler lyrics of **Anacreon of Teos**, *c.* 570-485, but he had no successors in Greece where literature served a public function linked to religion.
**Aesop**, a slave from Thrace who died *c.* 564, wrote popular animal fables to illustrate moral points, some possibly derived from Oriental sources.

## Art and architecture

**Although the Assyrians and Babylonians produced much striking monumental art in the 7th and 6th centuries BC the most significant artistic development of the period was the evolution of Classical Greek art in which a new realism superseded the stylization common to the ancient Near Eastern art.**

**A narrative style grew up in pottery decoration drawn with a fluid hand in black- and red-figure work. In sculpture the traditional *kouros* figure gradually took on a more relaxed pose and a representational style developed – the single most vital step in the emergence of European art.**

**Greek architects, especially in Athens, designed simple but subtle buildings using austerely ornamented lintels and columns as their basic units and counteracting the effects of foreshortening with the help of mathematics.**

**Assyrian wall reliefs** of the 7th century were incised on stone instead of moulded, giving finer detail to scenes of savage conquest of the expanding Assyrian Empire.
**Saite artists** of the early 7th century attempted to revive the brilliance of the Old Kingdom. Sculpture and bas-relief were elegant, and the new use of hard stone made for a studied and severe style.

**Olmec sculptures** at La Venta between 800 and 400 BC produced basalt monuments carved in elaborate relief, depicting scenes of historical and contemporary events.
**A gold scabard from Litoi**, *c.* 650 showed typical Scythian designs of ceremonial weaponry characterized by the designs combining different animals to make a mythical beast.

**Babylon** was rebuilt by Nebuchadrezzar between 612 and 538. The decorated glazed bricks of the **Ishtar Gate**, and the famous **Hanging Gardens** were intended to outshine the brilliance of Assyrian palaces.
**Etruscan tomb frescoes** began in the mid 6th century. Those at Tarquinii depicted scenes from the life of the dead man in a realistic style.

**Attic black-figure pottery** achieved technical excellence by the mid-6th century and came to predominate in Greek vase painting. Mythological scenes were depicted in black glaze against a red background.

## Music

**Music theories developed in the East and the West, and especially in China, as complex scales were devised, but little is known of the style of music produced at this period.**

**The seven-note scale, later to become the basis of most European music, entered Europe from the Near East through Greece *c.* 550 BC. In India, the basis for the râga was evolving.**

**Terpander**, the Greek composer, *fl. c.*675 BC, was a founder of classical Greek music. He is sometimes credited with having completed the octave.

**Scale theory** was developed in Babylonia in the Chaldean period (626-538 BC). Mathematical division of strings produced a four-note scale, which was associated with the four seasons.

**The kettledrum** appears as a bowl-shaped drum beaten with sticks in a relief dating from *c.* 600 BC found in Persia.

**Pythagoras** introduced Chaldean scale theory into Greece *c.* 550 BC. He based a system of tuning on the fact that a string stopped at two-thirds its length sounds a fifth higher than its full length.

## Science and technology

**By the 5th century BC the Athenian Greeks had established a rich and complex pattern of manufactures, particularly in pottery and textiles with trading contacts from the Black Sea to the Rhine. They did not introduce many advances in technology, which they preferred to regard as the preserve of slaves. Their theoretical writings, however, have provided the basis for much Western European science even where, as in the case of Aristotle, this consisted in the systematization of earlier thinking or the elaboration of untested hypotheses.**

**Greek mathematics began in the 6th century with Pythagoras but by the 4th century the focus of the science had moved to Alexandria where scientific study flourished.**

**In China, where military technology may have received a spur from constant attacks by nomadic invaders, the crossbow was invented and a way was found to melt and cast iron.**

**Greek silver coins**, stamped with an owl design, came into usage in 700 BC. Early coins from Lydia, in Asia Minor, were made of electrum, a gold and silver alloy. Coinage was developed, because the barter system was inadequate to deal with the growing trade between the countries of the Middle East and the Mediterranean.
**Greek silver mines** at Laurion were heavily worked by the Athenians, using prisoner or slave labour.

**Central European technology** thrived at Hallstatt, Austria, with the mining, manufacture and export of iron and salt

**Anaximander**, *fl.* 6th c. who believed the Earth to be cylindrical in shape, is thought to have produced the first map of the known world.
The **potter's kick wheel** may have been invented at this time, although pottery designs still showed potters using the old two-man turntable method.
**Indian mathematical texts** of the 6th-3rd centuries BC deal with simple geometric forms, and calculations involving large numbers.

**Thales**, *fl.* 580 BC, "Father of Greek philosophy", made detailed observations on methods of triangulation navigation.
**Pythagoras**, *c.* 580-500 BC, and his school, studied medicine, astronomy and musical scales and mathematics, particularly the theory of numbers.
It is debatable whether Pythagoras invented the theorem that bears his name.

## 540-500 BC

**Cyrus took Babylon** in 538 BC, thereby assisting the Jews' return to Jerusalem, and Egypt in 525 BC. Darius I, 548-486, benevolently ruled a centralized empire from the Indus to the Mediterranean, divided into regions (satrapies) for administrative purposes.
**Rome expelled her Etruscan kings** in 509 BC and became an independent republic.
**Cleisthenes** reorganized Athenian local government, and laid the basis for democracy in 508.

**Celtic La Tène culture**, which emerged in Switzerland c. 500 and spread quickly throughout northern Europe, had close ties with Etruscan civilization.

**Confucius**, or K'ung Fu-tzu, 551-479, taught social ethics in China. His doctrine was taken up by the rulers and governed the Chinese way of life for over 2,000 years. It embraced elements of traditional Chinese religion and emphasized aristocratic social virtues and conduct harmonious with the heavenly order. It stressed awareness of fate and the decrees of heaven.
In Greece **Pythagoras' theory of numbers and music** quickly developed into a mystical cult.

**Classical Greek tragedy** began with **Aeschylus**, c. 525-456. He developed drama from choral cult songs by introducing dialogue between the actors when tragedy became a regular feature of the spring Dionysiac festivals. His greatest work is the *Oresteia* trilogy.
**The Boeotian Pindar**, c. 522-c. 440, wrote patriotic poems often celebrating athletic prowess.

**Painted grey ware** of the urban Ganges cultures, c. 500, was a hard wheel-turned pottery decorated with linear and dotted patterns.
**Bronze and ceramic vessels** and ornamental and ritual jade carvings were the primary Chinese art forms under the Chou dynasty, 1000-200 BC.
**Cyrus' funerary monument** at Parsagadae, 529 BC, anticipated Achaemenid success with its artistic traditions of Greece and Mesopotamia.

**The ancient Greeks** developed modes (patterns of sounds in descending order, a basis for tunes) with distinct moods, and named them after Greek tribes, such as the Lydian and Phrygian.

**Anacharsis the Scythian** and **Theodorus of Samos**, *fl.* 6th century, are thought to have developed the key, a metal anchor, with grappling flukes, a lathe and an improved bellows.
**Iron welding**, by hammering the red-hot metal, is associated with the name of Glaukos of Chios. Before his time iron sections were joined by elaborate lappings and flanges.
**Heraclitus**, c. 540-c. 480, held that fire is the fundamental principle of the universe.

## 500-400 BC

**Athens** checked Darius' invasion of Greece at Marathon, 490. A second Persian invasion by **Xerxes**, c. 519-465, in 480 was stopped by the Athenian fleet at Salamis, 480, and by the Spartan army at Plataea, 479.
**The Delian League** was founded in 478 BC, reflecting Athenian ascendancy in eastern Greece.
**Celtic culture** spread in Europe c. 500 BC.
**The Greeks defeated Carthage**, 480, and the Etruscans, 474, and thus won control of the sea.

**Wheat** became an important crop in England c. 500.
**Salt**, useful both for preserving meat and as a medicine, and **wool** were traded in Britain c. 500.

**Buddhism** was founded in India when **Siddhartha Gautama**, c. 563-c. 483 BC, began propagating the insights he achieved through long periods of contemplation. He taught that suffering can be avoided only by following an eight-fold path of moral conduct, non-violence and meditation, leading to a state of perfect enlightenment, nirvana.
**Zeno of Elea**, c. 495-c. 430, a Greek philosopher, originated the dialectic and supported his argument with paradoxes.

**Sophocles**, c. 496-406 BC, and Aeschylus continued the tradition of classical tragedy. In his plays like *Oedipus Rex* Sophocles retained a functional chorus but shifted the centre of interest to the actors.
**During the time of Confucius**, 551-479, the five classic *Ching* books reached their final form.

**Early Celtic bronze** wine flagons from the Moselle region, c. 460 BC, show how classical and eastern elements were assimilated to produce a new and purely Celtic art form. The human mask was a typical motif.
**The Palace of Darius**, 522-486, records Persia's victory over the Median kings in the bas-relief friezes on the gigantic columns.

**The rise of drama in Greece** linked dance, music and poetry. The chorus performed in an area called the orchestra in front of the stage, after which the modern orchestra is named.

**Athenian culture**, reflected in the volume and variety of their trade and industry, was well advanced; producing large quantities of metals, oil and cloth. Pottery, too, was of the highest quality in design and manufacture and was in great demand abroad.
**Anaxagoras**, c. 500-c. 428, who came to Athens from Ionia in c. 480, gave the first scientific explanations of celestial events, especially eclipses. He influenced much of Aristotle's scientific works.

## 460-420 BC

**Athenian power and culture** was at its height under Pericles, c. 490-429, who assisted Egypt in an abortive revolt against the declining Persian Empire, 456-454.
**Rome expanded** into central Italy and the plebeians won new constitutional rights 445 BC.
**Buddhism** became popular in India, especially among the merchant classes.
**The Peloponnesian war** between Athens and Sparta began in 431 resulting from political and cultural tensions between them.

**Increasing population** led to new pressure on available land c. 450, and increased warfare between rival tribes in Britain.

**The Greek Sophists**, led by **Protagoras**, c. 485-c. 410, were agnostic towards the gods.
**Socrates**, c. 469-399, argued that no one can possibly do that which he knows to be wrong. He followed this principle to the point of political dissent for which he was tried and condemned to death.
In China, **Mo Ti**, c. 470-391, taught pacifism and universal love; he also established a dialectical method of argument.

**Euripides**, c. 480-406 BC, last of the great writers of tragedy, dealt with social issues as well as myths, reflecting a growing humanism in Greek drama.
**Herodotus**, c. 485-425, emerged as the first major historian with a lively account of the Persian Wars, while **Thucydides**, 460-400 BC, took a more rigorous approach to the history of the Peloponnesian War.

**Greek art** became increasingly independent of foreign influences and more humanistic in style, reaching its High Classical period between 450 and 400. The *Cretan boy*, c. 460, from the Acropolis showed a relaxation of the 6th-century *kouros* pose. Pottery after 530 was dominated by the red-figure technique. Doric architecture became less severe in style. The **Parthenon**, 447-432, built entirely of marble, was the least conventional of this style.

**A Chinese text** showed how the chromatic scale (of 12 half tones) can be derived from the cycle of fifths but in practice they used it only to transpose pentatonic scales into various "keys".

**Democritus**, c. 460-370, held the theory that matter was composed of atoms.
**Quarries on Mount Pentelicon** provided the Athenians with fine milky-white marble, with which they built the Parthenon.
**Hippocrates** of Cos, c. 460–c. 377, called the Father of Medicine, explained mind and body conditions in terms of "humours", glandular secretions whose imbalance caused disease. He emphasized dietary and hygienic factors in the maintenance of good health.

## 420-380 BC

**The Peloponnesian war** ended in naval defeat for Athens at Aegospotami in 405 BC.
**The Romans** captured Veii, an Etruscan city, in 396, but Rome herself was sacked by marauding Celts in 390 BC, who also hastened the Etruscan decline.
**Socrates**, c. 469-399, was put to death in Athens in 399 BC.
**The Chou dynasty** in China declined in the long "Warring States period", 475-221.

**Many hill-forts** such as Badbury Rings were built and fortified, and a warrior class emerged. Swords became more common than daggers.

**Plato**, *fl.* 4th century BC, founded the Academy in Athens, where philosophy was taught to young members of the Athenian aristocracy, in, c. 387 BC. He advocated subordination of the individual to the all-powerful republic, and also maintained that phenomena perceived by the senses are merely impure copies of the perfect reality of eternal Ideas.

**Aristophanes**, c. 448-c. 388, was the best comic dramatist and topical satirist at the Athenian drama contests. His *Lysistrata*, 411 BC, deals with a strike by women aiming to end war.
**The philosopher Socrates**, 469-399, invented the cross-questioning (dialogue) teaching method but his sceptical approach to religion brought him a death sentence.

**The Greek Late Classical period** was between 400 and 323. The more complex Ionic capitals superseded the Doric style, with the richly ornate designs of the **Erechtheum**, c. 430. The monumental gate building of the Acropolis, the **Propylae**, was begun c. 430. A new naturalism dominated sculpture, as seen with the transformation of the archaic kore in the figure of *Victory* from Olympia c. 420.

**The *Ramayana***, a book of Hindu myths, recorded nine basic moods associated with scales in Indian music c. 400 BC. Similar to Greek modes, this music anticipated the râga.

**Chinese cast iron** appeared c. 400 BC. The Chinese, unlike early Western ironsmiths, were able to melt iron to cast it, helped by the high phosphorous content of their iron, which lowered the melting point; however, it also made the iron brittle. Two centuries passed before the Chinese could produce a satisfactory cast iron.

## 380-340 BC

**Athens defeated Sparta** in 371 in alliance with Thebes, which became leader of the opposition to Sparta.
**Philip of Macedon**, *r.* 359-336, built up his military strength in northern Greece.
Many of the Persian satrapies had become semi-autonomous.
**The Persian Artaxerxes III**, *r.* 359-338, restored royal authority and re-established Persian rule in Egypt in 343 BC, thus ending the last native pharaoh dynasty.

**The druidic religion**, based on fertility cults, became firmly established c. 350 BC.

**The Cynics** in Greece, such as **Diogenes**, c. 412-323, believed that happiness needed the repudiation of human values and the adoption of a simple animal-like existence.
**Aristotle**, 384-322, rejected Plato's idealism, urging a more detailed empirical examination of natural and social phenomena and the doctrine that good consists in individuals achieving the states appropriate to their natures.

**Plato**, c. 427-347, continued the Socratic method in a masterly series of prose dialogues, including the *Republic*, which achieve the quality of a drama of ideas. His pupil **Aristotle**, 384-322 BC, made important contributions to literary criticism, although his books are mainly lecture notes, in *Rhetoric* and *Poetics*, which analysed classical drama.

**Idealized grace and beauty** was characteristic of Late Classical Greek sculpture. The sensual possibilities of carved marble were explored by **Praxiteles** in *Hermes with young Dionysus*, 350, at Olympia. The nude female form was introduced, and Praxiteles' *Aphrodite from Cnidus*, 350, initiated a feminine ideal of narrow shoulders and broad hips.

**Aristoxenus**, a pupil of Aristotle, tabulated Greek modes c. 320 BC, after the fall of Athens had resulted in a decline in the status of music and the use of modes in practice.

**Aristotle** systematized knowledge in the realm of science, logic, politics and ethics. His scientific thinking, although often merely speculative, was enormously influential. For example, his belief that heavenly bodies move in perfect circles governed Western thinking until the 17th century AD.
**Eudoxus**, c. 408-355 BC, studied mathematical proportions and developed a method of successive addition to determine irregular areas; this theory was the forerunner of calculus.

## 340-300 BC

**Alexander of Macedon**, having assured his authority in Greece, defeated Darius, of Persia *d.* 330, at Issus in 333, and crossed the Indus in 327. He died at Babylon in 323 after turning back to consolidate his authority. His empire had fallen apart by 306.
**Chandragupta**, *r.* c. 321-c. 297 created the Maurya dynasty at Magadha in India.
**Rome** had effectively destroyed Etruscan power by 300 BC.

**The druids** acted as priest-kings, providing an overall cohesion and cultural unity to the tribes of Celtic society.

**Zeno**, 334-262, of Citium, founded Stoicism, claiming virtue to be the only good and wealth, illness and death of no human concern.
**Epicurus**, 342-270, of Samos, believed pleasure to be the essence of a happy life.
**Mencius**, 372-289 BC, a Confucian philosopher, saw man as inherently good and urged filial piety.

**The New Comedy** flourished in Athens from c. 330. This was a comedy of manners, using stock characterization and avoiding touchy subjects. **Menander**, c. 342-292 BC, was its best exponent but was less popular than **Philemon**, c. 365-265 BC. Greek prose style was meanwhile brought to its zenith by the Athenian orator Demosthenes, c. 383-322 BC.

**Corinthian columns** were first used on the exterior of Greek architecture with the monument at Athens, built c. 335 to celebrate a victory.
**La Tène art** from a 4th-century grave at Waldagesheim shows how classical motifs decorating neck torques and bracelets had superseded earlier Celtic styles.
**The Appian Way** between Rome and Capua was begun c. 312.

**Alexander the Great's invasion** of India brought with it new instruments and a developed theory. The introduction of the lute c. 300 BC and new theories affected Indian music deeply.

The elements of Aristotle, **earth, air, water and fire** in fact proposed by earlier Greeks, represent an early attempt to systematize nature. These elements could be used to produce each other; for example, smoke (air) and ash (earth) could be made by burning wood (fire).
**Epicurus**, 342-270, advanced an atomic theory, similar to that of Democritus.

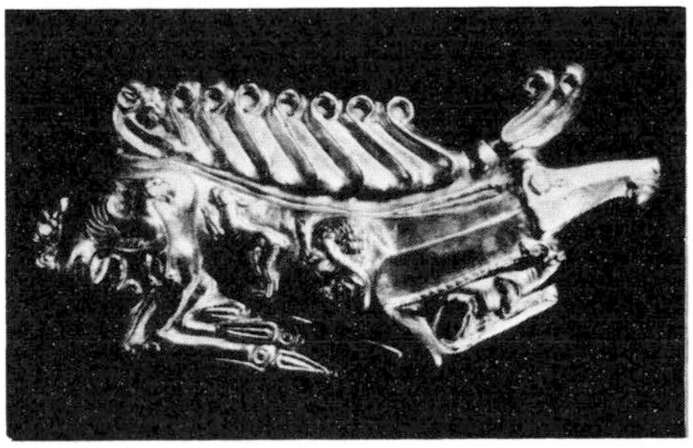
Scythian gold plaque, 5thc.

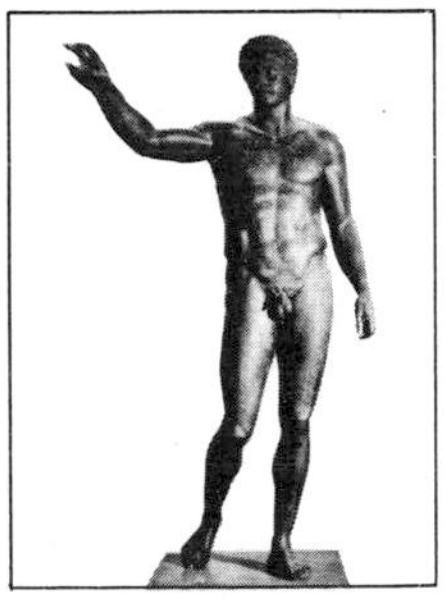
Classical Greek sculpture

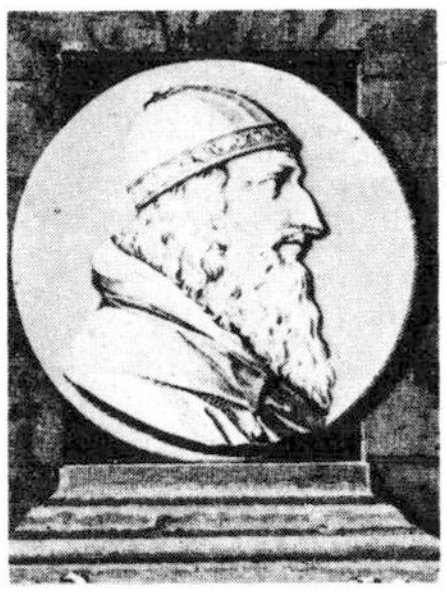
18thc. Portrait of Aristotle

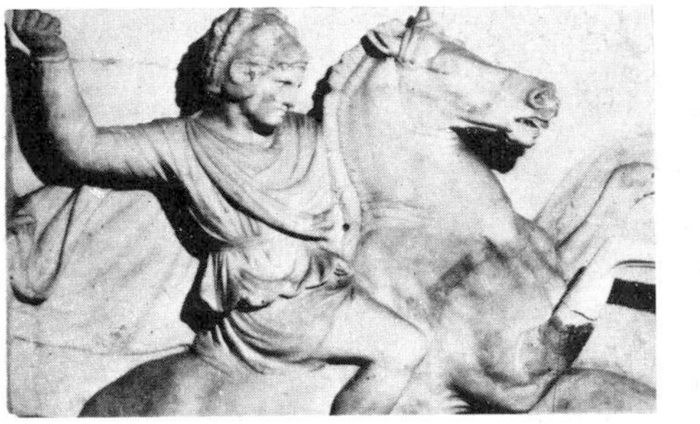
Alexander the Great in battle

# 300BC-AD100 Rome conquers the West

## Principal events

**Despite the constant political unrest that followed Alexander's fall, a cosmopolitan Hellenistic culture spread throughout the Middle East. This was absorbed by Rome, which now emerged as a great power, creating eight provinces by 146 BC, including Macedonia and Spain. Conquest, however, brought with it chronic social conflict in Italy which finally helped to destroy the Roman Republic and led to the establishment of the empire in 28-27 BC, a constitutional solution which left the problems of expansion untouched. By AD 100 the empire stretched from Egypt to Britain, bringing to Rome new manpower, art forms and the many religious cults she incorporated, among them Christianity.**

**In the East Buddhism and Confucianism grew influential; the former spread by Ashoka in southern India, the latter becoming an integral part of society in China where it would remain so for 2,000 years.**

### 300-260 BC

**Alexander's empire** had broken into four parts by 297 BC: the Hellenistic kingdoms of Macedonia and Thrace, the Seleucid dynasty in Syria and the Ptolemaic in Egypt (whose invasion of Palestine in 301 BC revived old tensions with Syria). **Rome** gained control of southern Italy and with the defeat of Tarentum in 272 BC came into conflict with Carthage in Sicily. **Ashoka**, c. 274-c. 236 BC, expanded the Mauryan Empire and promulgated Buddhist principles.

### 260-220 BC

**In the first Punic War**, 264-241, Rome built her first fleet, took Sicily and the Lipari Islands and defeated Carthage, which expanded into Spain.
Conflict continued between the flourishing **Hellenistic kingdoms**. **Ptolemy II**, *r.* 285-246, extended Alexandria in Egypt.
**Bactria** left the Seleucid kingdom, and developed a combination of Greek and Buddhist social philosophy, *c.* 250.
**Olmec civilization** in Peru began to decline *c.* 250 BC.

### 220-180 BC

In the **second Punic War**, **Hannibal**, 247-183, invaded Italy across the Alps in 218 but retreated after Roman aggression in Spain *c.* 206. His alliance with Macedon, 215, involved Rome in eastern Mediterranean politics.
**The Roman nobility** took control of the wealth from the new provinces while smallholders suffered from military service in the new standing army.
**Huang-Ti**, *r.* 221-210, completed the Great Wall of China in 214.

### 180-140 BC

**Rome** invaded and defeated Macedon, and after further unrest annexed Greece in 147.
**Carthage** was totally destroyed by a Roman army in the third Punic War, 149-146.
**The Arsacid dynasty** ruled in Parthia, stretching from the Euphrates to the Indus *c.* 150.
Under **Menander**, *r.* 155-130, the Indo-Greek kingdoms reached over much of northern India.
**The Han dynasty** in China consolidated imperial authority over the provinces.

## National events

**The Roman Empire came closer to Britain, which was torn by conflicts between Celtic tribes. Contact with Europe, and especially Gaul, increased. After Julius Caesar's abortive expedition in 55-54 BC, the divided Britons were able to put up only minimal resistance to the Roman conquest.**

**La Tène culture** flourished in England, producing highly decorated military equipment.

**Italian silver coins** have been found in Cornwall dating from this period, when Britain was exporting hides, gold, tin and slaves to Europe.

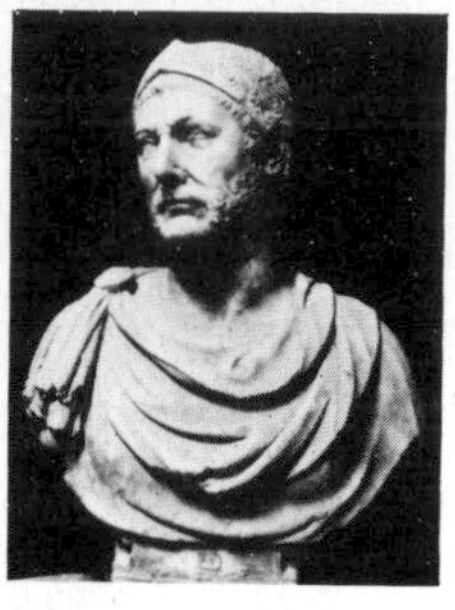

Roman bust of Hannibal

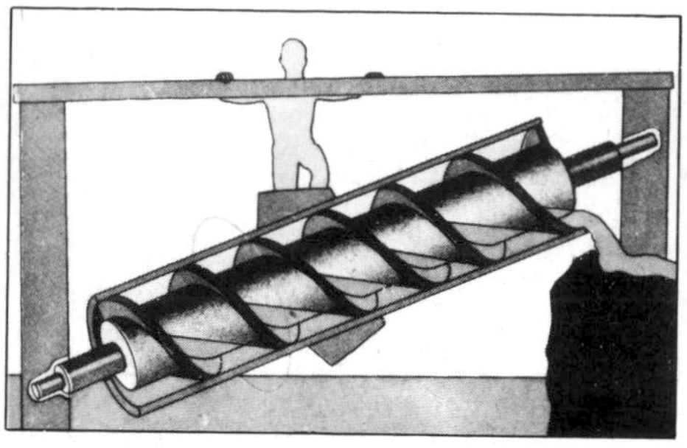

Archimedean screw

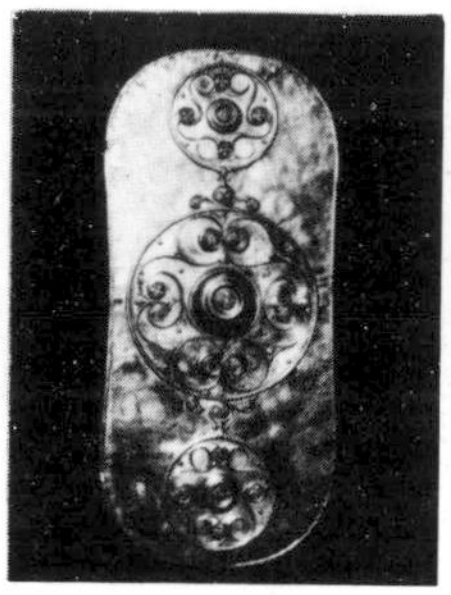

La Tène art: shield

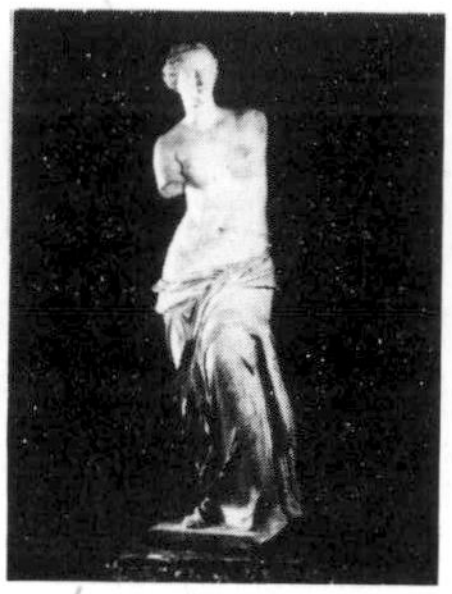

The Aphrodite of Melos

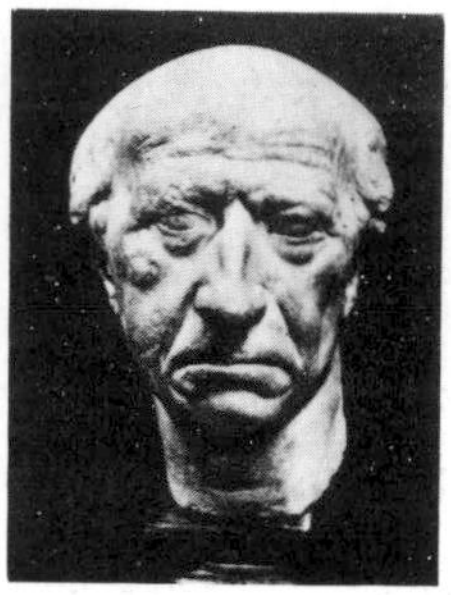

Roman bust: old Republican

## Religion and philosophy

**Christianity grew from being one of several Jewish nationalist sects into a more universally significant religion, as Paul spread it throughout the Roman Empire and introduced Hellenic ideas. The Christian emphasis on the individual conscience and on love brought persecution in Rome where religion was primarily a public or political concern.**

**In India a proliferation of Hindu sects provided more popular forms of worship than the traditional Brahminical cult and important additions to the sacred literature expressed further compromises with the everyday needs of worshippers.**

**New schools of thought grew up in China, while Confucianism became adopted as the official state religion under the Han dynasty *c.* 140 BC.**

**The Yin-Yang** school of Chinese philosophy and cosmology, the leading exponent of which was **Tsou Yen**, 340-*c.* 260 BC, considered the universe to comprise five elements, metal, wood, water, fire and earth. The Yin-Yang school thought the universe was governed by the two complementary forces of yin, female and passive, and yang, male and active.

**Ashoka**, *r. c.* 274-*c.* 236 BC, established Buddhism as the state religion in the Mauryan Empire.
**The developing Shinto religion in Japan** had a hierarchy of deities presided over by the sun goddess **Amaterasu** and her descendants, the imperial family. Past heroes became mythological figures and each clan venerated its own deity.
**In China Hsun Tzu**, 313-238 BC, taught that human nature was fundamentally evil. Goodness required training.

**Mystery religions** and Eastern astrology took hold in Rome in response to the stress of the second Punic War, 218-201 BC. Novel gods, such as the Great Mother of Asia Minor, **Cybele**, and **Dionysus** superseded the traditional deities of Greek origin.
**The introduction of the Stoic philosophy** to Rome at this time with its emphasis on Fate, encouraged the development of mystical and astrological thought.

**Within the Vedic tradition yogic thought** was codified by **Patanjali**, *c.* 150 BC, into the four volumes of the *yoga sutras*, rules dealing with transcendental trance states and mystical liberation. **Bhakti** (popular devotional cults) emerged as well as cults centred on the gods Vishnu, Shiva and Krishna. The *Bhagavad Gita* was added to the earlier epic poem of the *Mahabharata*, and in it a new emphasis on salvation through the performance of duty emerged.

## Literature

**Although Greek literature itself declined its influence spread first in the wake of Alexander and then through Rome, which built its culture to a large extent on that of Greece.**

**A Latin literature arose in the third century BC based on Greek models in poetry, drama and history although under the late republic a number of writers, among them Caesar, Livy and Virgil, set out to glorify specifically Roman culture and history. The New Testament was written in Greek, still at the end of the first century the lingua franca of the eastern Mediterranean.**

**The Chinese classical literature flourished while in India the epics and Buddhist scripture were finalized.**

**The last classical writer, Chü Yüan**, 343-277, is traditionally described as the author of the celebrated *Ch'u Elegies*, the most famous of which is the *Heavenly Questions*.
Bucolic and pastoral poetry by **Theocritus**, *c.* 300-260 was imitated by his fellow Greeks **Moschus**, *fl.* 150, and **Bion**

**A Latin literature** emerged, based largely on Greek poetry, drama and history.
**Naevius**, *c.* 270-*c.* 201, was the first Latin epic poet. A freed Greek slave, **Livius Andronicus**, *c.* 284-*c.* 204, wrote plays and translated the *Odyssey*. **Ennius**, 239-169, historian and playwright, was important for his efforts to adapt to Latin the methods of writers such as Euripides.

**The Chinese Classical period** came to a dramatic end with the reign of Ts'in, 221-210. He burnt many Confucian texts.
**Latin drama** emerged with **Plautus**, *c.* 255-184, who used Greek metres and plots from the New Comedy. *Miles Gloriosus*, *c.* 205, was his best play.
**Terence**, *c.* 190-159, was less popular but more influential with work such as *Adelphi*.

**The Indian epic *Ramayana***, with between 20,000 and 40,000 couplets in its various versions, is attributed to the 2nd century BC. Although incorporating much religious material, it is primarily the story of the Aryan victory over the indigenous Indians. It was the forerunner of court poetry and had much influence on literary developments throughout southern Asia.

## Art and architecture

**Throughout the Hellenistic world private patronage helped artistic production and collectors' demands were so great that copying and pastiche developed, although many artists explored new ideas. Styles like that of the Pergamon school, marked by a new and masterful handling of emotion, were still for the most part associated with places rather than individuals. The Roman Empire absorbed the art of both the Hellenistic world and Italy. Etruscan iconography was copied, and the basic design for Roman architecture came from Etruscan models. Roman municipal architecture reflected both a strong civic pride and the varied leisure pursuits of her urban elite. Baths, theatres and basilicae, constructed with careful attention to practical requirements, also served to create a dramatic framework for public life. Monuments were erected to commemorate the victories of the late republic and early empire.**

**The Colossus of Rhodes**, one of the Seven Wonders of the ancient world, was a huge bronze representation of the sun god Helios which was built astride the harbour at Rhodes between 292 and 280 BC.

**The Temple of Horus** at Edfu in Egypt, begun by **Ptolemy III** in 237, was planned with one main axis, typical of Egyptian temple architecture.
**The Hellenistic period** in Greek art, *c.* 323-1st century BC, developed the sensuous possibilities of marble sculpture. The naturalistic poses of the bronze "Eros" from Tunisia and the "Sleeping Hermaphrodite" are typical of three-dimensional realism of 3rd-century Greek sculpture.

**Town planning** played an important role in Greek architecture. The chaotic market places of Ephesus and Miletus were replaced by public squares.

**The "Venus de Milo"**, *c.* 150, was a Pergamene pastiche of preceding sculptural styles. The classical features coldly echoed 5th-century tradition, while the slight twist of the torso accommodated the new taste for multiple-view figures. This Hellenistic Aphrodite became the classic source for the Roman models.
**The Great Altar of Zeus** at Pergamon was begun *c.* 170. The exterior frieze depicts the battle of gods and giants.

## Music

**Music stagnated in the West under the Roman Empire, but the Jews maintained their vocal tradition from which the Christian Church borrowed heavily later. In the Arab world, music was still a lively art. The progress of music in the East had little influence on Western musicians, but Western incursions affected Eastern music to some degree.**

**The Indian vina**, from which the sitar later developed, was a lute-like plucked instrument thought to have evolved from the instruments carried by Alexander's invading soldiers.

**The first keyboard instrument** was the hydraulis, a water-powered organ. It was built by Ctesibius, who was working in Alexandria from 246-221 BC.

**The Imperial Court** of the Han dynasty in China employed more than 800 musicians to impart a rich panoply of sound to the rituals of state occasions.

**A Greek hymn** to Apollo composed at Delphi survives from this date.

## Science and technology

**In the Hellenistic world Alexandria became the focus of scientific work particularly in mapping, astronomy and mathematics. At the same time Greek technology found its greatest mathematician and experimental physicist in Archimedes.**

**As Rome expanded she developed the use of concrete and the arch in the building of bridges, roads and aqueducts, creating a series of civil and military engineering projects that surpassed in scale any since those of the Assyrians and Egyptians. Nevertheless, whether because of the widespread use of slave labour or the stifling effects of a powerful bureaucracy the Romans, like the Athenians, failed to exploit many inventions of their time.**

**In China, iron metallurgy improved still further, surpassing any in the West. Chinese astronomy was also active, and the preparation of many useful drugs, from plants, became a speciality of Chinese medicine.**

**Euclid** wrote his *Elements of Geometry* at Alexandria *c.* 300. Alexandria became a centre of learning in the century that followed Alexander's death, acquiring a great library and museum. Alexandrian inventions were based on the known principles of the siphon, gear-wheel, spring, screw, lever, pulley, cam and valve. The lighthouse of Pharos, a Greek achievement, stood 76m (250ft) high, with a 56km (35-mile) beam.

**Aristarchus**, 310-230 BC, was the first to maintain that the Earth moved around the Sun.

**Archimedes of Syracuse**, *c.* 287-212 BC, discovered fundamental laws of floating bodies, made advances in mathematics and was the greatest of Greek inventors: the "Archimedean" screw is still used in Egypt to raise water.
**The crossbow** was invented in the 3rd century BC in China. This weapon had a cocking and trigger mechanism similar to that of children's toys today.

**A map of the world** produced by Eratosthenes, *c.* 276-*c.* 194, a librarian at Alexandria in the 3rd century BC, was a great improvement on its predecessors. He calculated the diameter of the Earth to within a few hundred kilometres, and did work in number theory.
**Glass-blowing** spread to Alexandria from Syria via the Romans and for two centuries was the most active of the technologies. Larger vessels and dishes were now made, by blowing the molten glass at the end of an iron blowpipe.

**A piston bellows** with a double action was among Chinese inventions of the 2nd century BC. It provided a regular, steady air draught for the production of higher quality cast iron.

## 140-100 BC

**Han emperor, Wu Ti**, *r.* 140-87, established Confucianism as the basis of Chinese civil administration, 136 BC.
**The Gracchus brothers** proposed radical land reform to relieve Roman unemployment and poverty 133 BC. Gaius Gracchus, 157-86, introduced state control of grain imports and allowed landless men into the army in 112.
**The Senate** feared the destruction of both the constitution and the nobility's power, and so opposed these measures.

**Chariots** were introduced to Britain *c.* 100 BC.

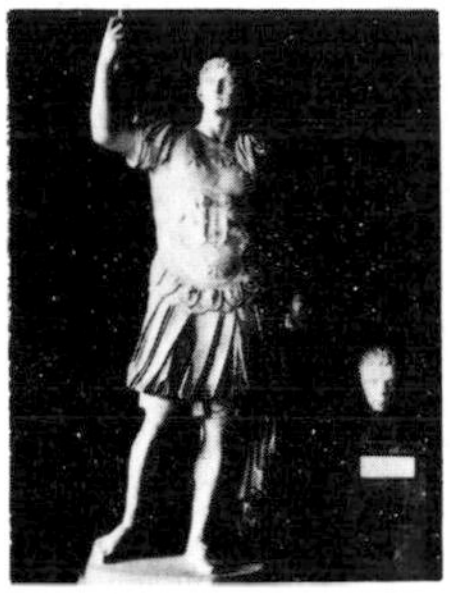

Julius Caesar

**Tung Chung Su** established Confucianism in China as the state cult *c.* 140 BC, combining elements of the Yin-Yang school and Confucianism. He taught that Heaven, Earth and Man formed a triad that the emperor, ruling by decree of Heaven, must maintain in harmony. This idea was important throughout Chinese imperial history, being associated with the stable order of Chinese society which lasted for 2,000 years.

**Fu poetry**, influenced by Chü Yüan, was brought to perfection *c.* 100 BC. Used mainly for description, it combined elements of prose and poetry in a form that was freer than that of the more personal **sao poetry** which continued to develop. **Ssu-ma Chien**, *c.* 145-86, wrote the first dynastic history of China. His *Historical Record* is notable for its objectivity.

**Roman sculpture** at first reproduced and imitated the styles of the past. The "Dying Gaul", *c.* 100, was an accurate copy of the Pergamene original. **The steam baths of Stebiae**, *c.* 120, were an early example of domed Roman architecture.

**Music notation** had been devised in China, according to Symaa Chian, 163-85 BC, a chronicler who tells of a music master who wrote down a zither tune.

**Peruvian technology** during the last three centuries BC developed the moulding of elaborate pottery and metal casting. **Hipparchus**, 190-120 BC, was the greatest Greek astronomer of his time. He estimated the Sun to be millions of miles away, instead of hundreds as previously thought. He also made a catalogue of stars.

## 100-60 BC

After Marius' death in 86, **Sulla**, 138-78, rescinded his reforms. **Cicero**, 106-43, prosecuted Verres, *d.* 43, for corruption while he was governor of Sicily in 70, and denounced Cataline's attempt to gain a consulship by force in 63 BC, defending the constitutional basis of the republic which depended upon no one man gaining supreme power. **Pompey**, 106-48, and **Julius Caesar**, 100-44, rose to power after Pompey's victories had led to the annexation of Syria.

**Celtic Britain** was divided between many warring tribes. **Close trading contact** was established with Gaul followed by population movements.

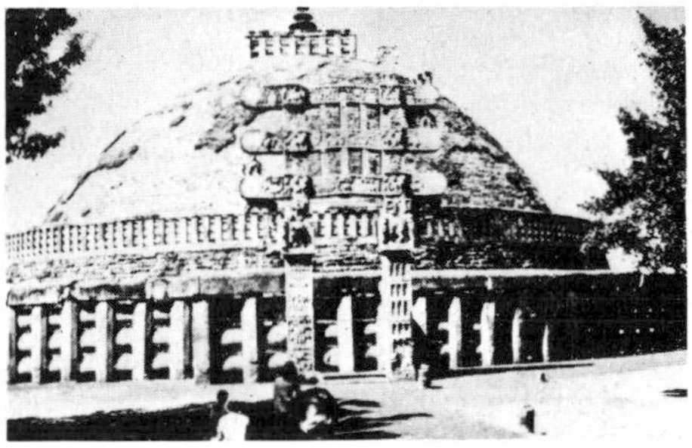

The Great Stupa of Sanchi

**The Pharisees in Israel**, opposed the adoption of Hellenistic culture by their conservative Sadducean rulers and were accused of arid formalistic legalism because of their emphasis on the regulation of all aspects of life in accordance with Jewish law. However, they enjoyed the allegiance of much of the population because of their personal austerity and asceticism.

**Cicero**, a politician and philosopher, brought Latin oratory to a peak. His letters are a model of literary style. Latin poetry flourished with **Lucretius**, *c.* 99-55, who gave emotional body to Epicurean philosophy in *De rerum natura*, and **Catullus**, 84-54 BC, who showed a mastery of technique and lyrical intensity.

**Roman arches** were used for tenement houses and theatres in the highly populated cities of the 1st century BC. **Silverware** brought to Rome following the sack of Corinth began a new taste for luxury articles in Roman circles. "The Old Republican", a portrait bust *c.* 75 BC, captures Roman realism in a grim projection of asceticism and authority.

**An Imperial Office of Music** was founded in China *c.* 100 BC. The office supervised such activities as standardizing pitch and the building and administration of music archives.

**Only two furnaces** both using charcoal and a draught could produce iron in a malleable (workable) form in which it could be forged with carbon to produce steel. These were the **Catalan iron furnace** with two bellows and the **two-storey shaft furnace**. Neither, however, produced sufficient heat to melt the iron completely. **Lucretius**, *c.* 95-55 BC, a Roman poet, wrote *De rerum natura*, a scientific treatise praising Epicurus and his ideas.

## 60-20 BC

**The Han dynasty** in China, 206 BC-AD 220, expanded into central Asia *c.* 60 BC. **Julius Caesar** subdued Gaul, 58-51 BC, and after defeating Pompey became "dictator" in 45. Civil war followed his assassination in 44 by a pro-senatorial conspiracy. **Octavian (Augustus)**, 63 BC-AD 14, took Imperial authority, 27 BC, to centralize power and prevent the unrest recurring. **Egypt** became a Roman province in 30 BC.

**Julius Caesar invaded** Britain in 55-54 BC, but retreated. **Druids** organized the opposition to the Roman invasion.

**In Rome Marcus Cicero**, 106-43 BC, and **Lucius Seneca**, *c.* 55 BC-*c.* AD 40, developed an **Eclectic philosophy**, drawing on Platonist, Stoic, Epicurean and Aristotelian sources. **Titus Lucretius**, *c.* 99-55 BC, composed a long poem, *De rerum natura* (On the nature of things), in which he elaborated the Epicurean theory of physical atomism – a doctrine derived from Democritus that the world is composed entirely of microscopic particles.

**Julius Caesar**, *c.* 100-44 BC, wrote his history *Commentaries on the Gallic War* in a style of exemplary clarity. **Roman history** was idealized in the *Aeneid*, by **Virgil**, 70-19 BC, second only to Homer as a model for Western poetry. He also wrote fine pastoral poetry, the *Eclogues* and *Georgics*. **Horace**, 65-8 BC, combined elegance with humanity in his *Odes*.

**Wall paintings** at the Pompeian **Villa of Mysteries**, *c.* 40 BC, portrayed Dionysiac themes. Roman villas of the 1st century BC increasingly introduced walled gardens and Greek peristyles. The "Augustus" from **Prima Porta**, *c.* 20 BC, displays a naturalistic classicism characteristic of Augustan portrait sculpture.

**The Julian calendar** of 45 BC, introduced under Julius Caesar, took a base year of 365.25 days. It was designed by the astronomer Sosigenes of Alexandria, and was inaccurate by a mere 11 minutes per year. This calendar was not supplanted until the 16th century AD, by which time it was inaccurate by ten days. **Water mills** were a feature of Roman technology, as early as the 1st century BC, but were only fully described a century later, by Vitruvius.

## 20 BC-AD 20

**Augustus** strengthened the Roman Empire in the north and east and brought peace to Rome. **Tiberius**, *r.* AD 14-37, did the same although imperial power became increasingly dependent on the approval of the Praetorian Guard (the emperor's bodyguard). **Judea** became a Roman province in AD 6. **The Kushite kingdom** in Nubia was in decline *c.* AD 10. **Mexican lake houses** were built.

**Large-scale tribal kingdoms** developed with conflicts between the Catavellauni to the north and Atresates south of the Thames.

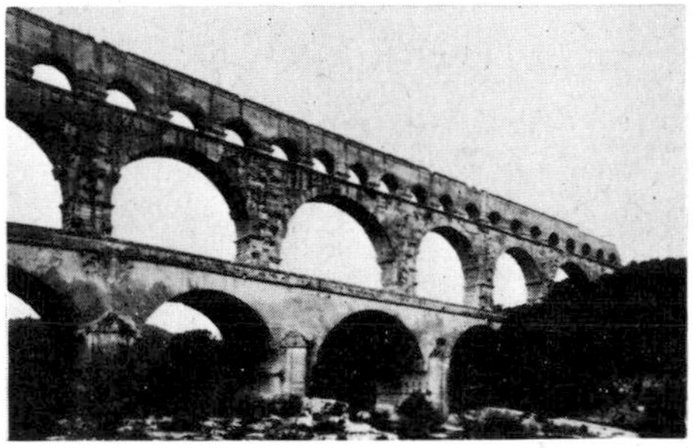

Roman civil engineering: the Pont du Gard, Nîmes

**Jesus Christ** was born in Bethlehem in Judea in 4 BC and crucified in Jerusalem in AD 30.

**Ovid**, 43 BC-AD 17, the supreme Roman poet of love, and one of the most influential of classical writers, developed erotic verse into a major form in his long poem *Metamorphoses*. It was completed in AD 8, the year of Ovid's banishment, partly for his witty but irreverent *Art of Love*. His later poetry is sceptical, often elegaic.

**Roman temples** derived their typical high podia and deep porches from Etruscan architecture, while the **Maison Carrée** at Nîmes, *c.* 16 BC, has colonnades built in imitation of a Greek façade. **Roman bas-reliefs** like that on the **Ara Pacis**, 9 BC, often used a combination of real and mythological figures to evoke contemporary Roman history. **Thermae**, magnificent municipal buildings, were developed at Rome *c.* 20 AD.

**Strabo**, *b.c.* 64 BC, a Greek historian and geographer, wrote on the uses of materials. **A roller bearing** for a cart wheel is another example of sophisticated engineering of the 1st century BC; made entirely from wood it was found in Denmark but probably made in Germany or France.

## AD 20-60

**Tiberius and Claudius**, *r.* 41-54 AD, expanded the empire, instituted social reforms and consolidated imperial power, although the danger of palace revolutions increased. **Jesus of Nazareth** was crucified in Jerusalem *c.* AD 30. The **Christian cult** was taken to Asia Minor, Greece and Rome by Paul, *fl.* 1st century AD. **Buddhism** was accepted as the official religion of China by **Emperor Ming**, *r.* AD 58-75.

**Emperor Claudius** established a Roman province in the prosperous southeast of Britain. **The Fosse Way** made a frontier with the Celtic world AD 45.

**After the Crucifixion** in AD 30, the early Jewish/Christian sect developed a unique emphasis on the resurrection of a Messiah and the imminent transformation of the world at the dawning of a millennium of universal love. **Paul of Tarsus**, *fl.* 1st century AD, who saw the death of Jesus as a universal sign reflecting cosmic forces, spread Christian ideals through the Roman Empire. Contact with Hellenic thought turned Christianity into a world religion.

**Seneca the Younger**, 4 BC-AD 65, made nine melodramatic adaptations of such Greek tragedies as *Oedipus*. They influenced Spanish literature and the revenge tragedies of Jacobean England. A noted orator and philosopher, Seneca exercised power in Rome in AD 54-62 but was finally ordered to commit suicide.

**Roman columns** acquired a new function in the support of arches and when used as a free form. The Tuscan and Composite orders developed as more ornate variants of the Doric and Ionic. **Roman villas** of the 1st century AD were often decorated with wall paintings which, like that at the **Villa Albani**, made use of idyllic scenes to evoke the peace of the countryside.

**Buddhist monks** arrived in China *c.* AD 50 from India, bringing with them chant and decorative melodic features that were incorporated into Chinese music of later periods.

**Metallurgical developments of the Romans** include the manufacture of brass and the amalgamation of mercury with gold in the extraction of gold from its ores. **Roman civil engineering** left an impressive record, including a 5.6km (3.5 miles) mountain tunnel, many aqueducts and 85,000km (53,000m) of roads. **The city of imperial Rome** received a million cubic metres of water each day through lead piping, which in turn went to cisterns and centrally heated baths.

## AD 60-100

**Nero**, *r.* AD 54-68, rebuilt Rome after a fire in AD 64, which was blamed on the Jews and Christians, who were unpopular because they refused to recognize the emperor's divinity. **Peter and Paul** were executed in the ensuing persecution *c.* 64. **Vespasian**, *r.* AD 69-79, became emperor after a civil war which followed Nero's death. **Jewish religious revolt**, 66-70, was defeated by the Romans. **Mongol invaders** brought iron and rice to Japan by 100 AD.

After the defeat of **Boadicea**, *d.* AD 62, Roman power reached Scotland. By AD 90, several legions were withdrawn and a town-based administration set up.

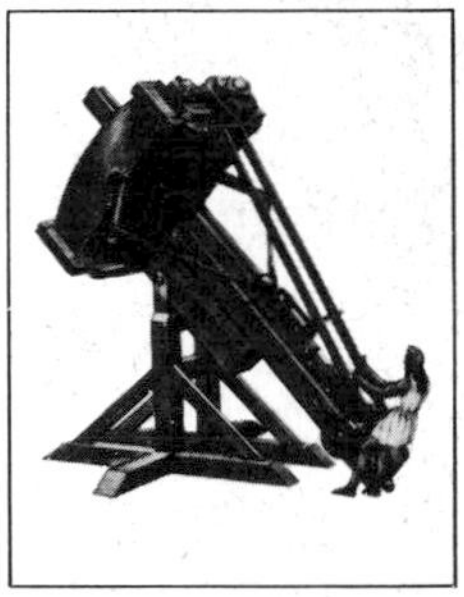

Graeco-Roman ballista

**After the death of Paul**, AD 64, and the destruction of Jerusalem in AD 70, the **Pauline version of Christianity**, with its more transcendental significance, became completely dominant. A few Christians who still upheld Jewish law became a small sect without links with either synagogue or Gentile Church. The oral tradition of early Christianity was gradually replaced by composed narratives, the first of which was the Gospel of St Mark.

**Plutarch**, *c.* AD 46-120, the Greek biographer, wrote *Parallel Lives of Illustrious Greeks and Romans*, a work that approached history from the viewpoint of the characters of the men and women who made it. Shakespeare and many other European writers drew from its vivid portraits of life in Rome and Greece.

**The Arch of Titus**, a triumphal arch of the kind developed in the 2nd century BC, portrayed Roman victories in the Judean War, AD 70. **Stupas**, typical Buddhist edifices, derived their dome shape from Vedic tombs. Stupa I at Sanchi, *c.* AD 100, was embellished with a square base, balconies and ornamental gateways.

**Destruction of the Second Temple**, AD 70, led to the dispersal of the Jews. To keep their identity, secular music was discouraged and only singing permitted.

**Chinese science** was very active under the Han dynasty. Astronomers recorded eclipses and observed planetary motions. Mathematicians constructed "magic squares" of numbers that add up to the same answer in any direction and influenced arithmetic and algebra. **Paper** was invented in China *c.* 100 AD. Chinese inventions of this time include a camera obscura, and convex and concave mirrors.

# 100-400 Early Christianity

## Principal events

The Roman Empire reached its greatest extent under Trajan but further expansion became impossible due largely to pressure from barbarian migrations in the north and east, which brought increased economic and social instability to Rome. Various defensive measures were adopted, such as allying with the barbarians, but Rome remained weak because of the dependence of most emperors on the support of the army. The reign of Theodosius saw the beginning of the close identification of the interests of the Christian Church and the empire in the east.

Cultured and prosperous civilizations arose in India, where the Guptas set up a northern empire and the strong southern Chola kingdom traded with Rome. In Central America the Mayas entered their classic period, while China suffered from instability and lack of central authority.

### 100-30

**Emperor Trajan**, *r.* 98-117, expanded into Dacia. His heir **Hadrian**, *r.* 117-38, pursued an essentially defensive policy, suing for peace in order to limit the eastern boundaries of the empire. He established his personal authority in Rome and travelled widely, but his eastern policy was unpopular because it caused a drop in the import of slaves.
**The Western Satrap dynasty** in Malwa, India, made Ujjain a centre of Sanskrit learning.

### 130-60

**Emperor Antoninus Pius**, *r.* 138-61, continued Hadrian's peaceful policies and quelled opposition from the Roman Senate.
**The dispersion of the Jews** followed the ruthless suppression of a Zealot revolt in Jerusalem in 135.
**Migrating Goths** settled on the northern Black Sea coast.
**Taoism** became popular in China, stimulated by military and social instability during the decline of the **Han dynasty** and the introduction of **Buddhism**.

### 160-90

**Plague** brought back by troops returning from the wars with Pathia depopulated the Roman Empire in 166-7.
**Marcus Aurelius' reign**, 161-80, marked the high point of **Stoicism** as the dominant philosophy, with its emphasis on the empire as a "common weal". Marcomanni from Bohemia crossed the Danube, 167, and were settled by the Romans in areas depopulated by the plague.
**The persecution of Christians** in Rome increased *c.* 170.

### 190-220

**Praetorian scheming** prevented the establishment of a strong emperor, 192-3, until **Severus**, *r.* 193-211, reformed the army and reinforced provincial administration.
**Caracalla**, *r.* 211-17, expelled the Goths and Alamanni and in 212 bestowed citizenship on most free inhabitants of the empire, a token of Rome's reliance on provincial talent.
**The Han dynasty in China** fell in 220 and was replaced by three separate kingdoms.

## National events

Under Roman rule Britain was prosperous. Celtic civilization assimilated Roman culture and urban life flourished. Hadrian's Wall established a permanent frontier in the north and British produce, particularly woollens, brought trading contacts with the rest of the empire in Europe.

**Hadrian**, *r.* 117-38, consolidated the conquest of Britain, building a wall from Solway to Tyne, 122-7. His large garrisons brought prosperity to England.

**Urbicus**, the governor, built the Antonine Wall from Clyde to Forth, 140-42. **The St Albans theatre** was built, 140, as a place of recreation.

**After Caledonians took the Antonine Wall**, 180, the Romans concentrated on defending Hadrian's Wall.

**The Roman governor Albinus** rebelled against **Severus** in 196, who then divided Britain into two provinces with York as the northern capital, *c.* 208.

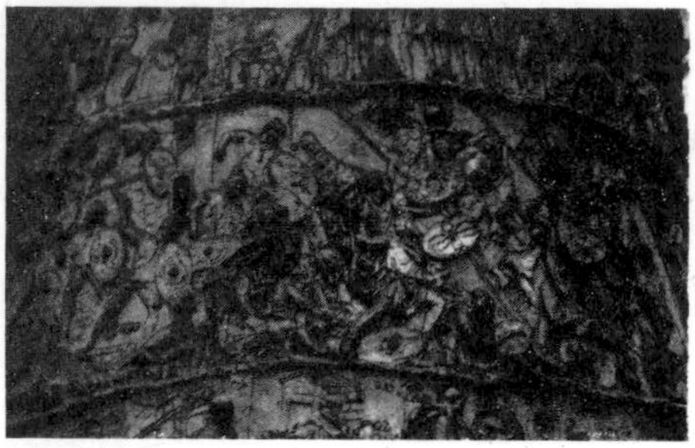

Trajan's Column: Romans fighting the Dacians

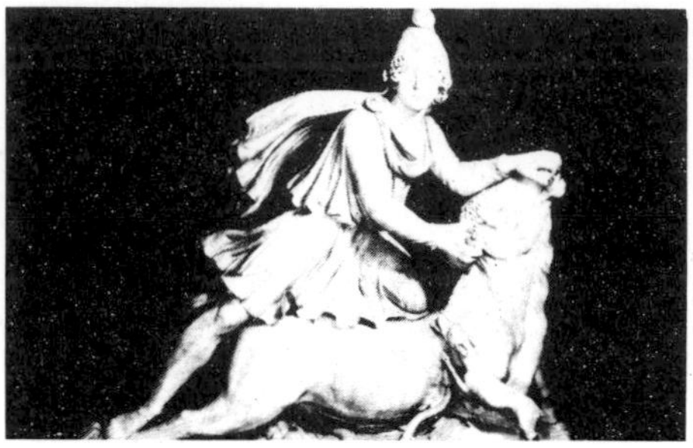

Late Roman sculpture: "Mithras slaying the Bull"

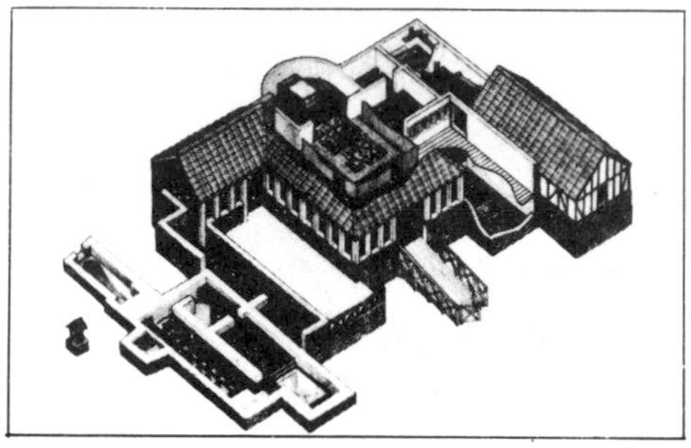

Roman villa at Lullingstone, 1stc. – 4thc.

## Religion and philosophy

The early Church clarified and developed a sophisticated theology in response to attacks from religions whose origins lay outside the Judaeo-Christian tradition, including Gnosticism, Manicheanism, Montanism and Mithraism. By 400, Theodosius the Great had finally established Christianity as the religion of the empire but with the barbarian invasions began a long struggle against paganism. Missions were sent out to the Germanic tribes, and those who were converted largely adopted the Arian form of the Christian faith. Under Pope Damasus the Roman see claimed primacy over the five patriarchates of Rome, Constantinople, Antioch, Jerusalem and Alexandria, basing its claim on the "Petrine" text.

Buddhism began to influence the development of Hinduism in India and similarly affected religion and society in China.

**Gnosticism**, a diffuse movement based on a variety of religions, some earlier than Christianity, absorbed Christian ideas, giving the Gospels equal weight with Greek and Oriental texts. Many Gnostic sects were proclaimed heretical by the early Church and Gnostic interpretations of the scriptures forced the Church to establish authoritative versions of the Gospels and to consolidate the basis of a universal Church.

**The Mahayana school of Buddhism** was founded by **Nagarjuna**, *c.* 150-*c.* 250, in India. This school, often known as "The Great Vehicle", departed from the traditional Hinayana or Theravada, "Little Vehicle", doctrines in holding that laymen as well as monks could achieve nirvana through the intervention of saints. This development resulted from the impact of the Brahmin religion on Buddhism.

**Montanus**, who appeared in Phrygia *c.* 172, preached that prophecy and revelation had not ended with the death of Jesus. This belief and the expectation of the Second Coming of Christ threatened the stability of the Church, and many Montanists were excommunicated *c.* 177.
**Buddhism reached China** in the 1st century AD and began to exert an influence there in the 2nd century, when it received official patronage.

**Origen**, 185-254, became head of the Christian Catechetical school at Alexandria *c.* 212. This was the most famous of the Christian schools and offered a wide curriculum, including Greek, philosophy and science. Origen, a Platonist, furthered the synthesis of the Christian Gospels and Greek philosophy, emphasized the study of the Bible as essential to a proper understanding of Christianity.

## Literature

With the diffusion of Christianity the scriptures began to spread in translation, notably in Latin, although fragments exist of translations into Gothic (mainly from the New Testament) made by Bishop Wulfila. The influence of the Gospels was literary as well as religious, setting the stage for the Christian allegorical treatment of pagan literature that was to dominate European literature until the 17th century. Homer, Virgil and Ovid were all interpreted in this way. Classical Latin literature petered out after AD 200.

In China, paper (chih) was invented but took nearly a millennium to reach Europe, where papyrus gradually gave way to stitched parchment or vellum.

**The Latin satirical tradition** had begun with **Lucilius**, *c.* 180-102 BC, but culminated with **Juvenal**, *c.* AD 55- *c.* 140, whose verse *Satires* on folly and Roman corruption profoundly influenced Western satirists. Tacitus, *c.* 55-*c.* 120, like Juvenal, vividly recounted the cruelties of the period up to the death of Domitian in 96, in his *Histories*, 104-9, and *Annals*, 117.

**Asvaghosa**, *c.* 80-150, was the first known poet and dramatist to write in classical Sanskrit. He was a Brahmin convert to Buddhism who wrote two epic poems, *Saundaranada* and *Buddhacarita* (The Life of Buddha), a philosophical work that became the source for later studies of Buddha's life.

**The prose romance** became a popular literary form in both Latin and Greek. *Satyricon*, a romance of Nero's Rome written by **Petronius** *c.* 60, gained popularity during this time.
**Elements of science fiction** were introduced into a parody of traveller's tales by a Greek writer, **Lucian**, *c.* 115-200, living in Syria. His *True History* describes a trip to the moon.

**Apuleius**, *b. c.* 125, wrote the only Latin prose romance that survives in full. His *Metamorphoses*, now known as *The Golden Ass*, relates the hilarious adventures of a man magically transformed into a donkey.

## Art and architecture

The Imperial and Hellenistic styles of Rome gradually lost ground, to be replaced in western Europe by the more mysterious and magic art of the Christian period. A recognizable Christian style in art and architecture had developed by the 4th century, by which time the empire was divided into east and west, presaging the lasting division between the Byzantine and Western Christian traditions in art. Into this world of changing imagery the barbarian invaders brought new decorative abilities and tastes which were also assimilated into the art of Rome.

The Persian culture of the Sassanids and the Indian culture of the Ghandara region were influenced in part by Rome and this influence penetrated China during the late Han period, producing the basis for a recognizable style. Indian art flourished under the Guptas, during whose dynasty the Ajanta cave paintings were done.

The ascending spiral bas-relief narrative on **Trajan's column**, 113, relates and glorifies the emperor's military victories during the Dacian campaign.
**The Pantheon**, *c.* 118, is an architectural realization of the climax of imperial grandeur.
**Monumental stone tomb sculpture** appeared in China during the Han dynasty, probably due to foreign influence. The tomb of **Ho Ch'uping**, *c.* 117, includes a figure of a horse trampling a barbarian.

**The Temple of Mithras**, 2nd century, in London, is a typical architectural design of the period with its small size, basilican plan and central apse. Temples were common throughout the periphery of the empire.

One example of **Roman imperial sculpture** is the bronze equestrian portrait of Emperor Marcus Aurelius, *c.* 173, which still dominates the Campidoglio in Rome.
**Sculpture from Gandhara** in northwest India of the 2nd to 4th centuries exemplifies the meeting point of Graeco-Roman and Buddhist canons of beauty. Delicate reliefs depict the life of the Buddha – the first time he is represented figuratively.

**Early Christian painting** remained stylistically in the tradition of Roman decoration as can be seen in the fresco "The Celestial Refreshment", *c.* 200, in the catacomb of St Calixtus in Rome.
**The Synagogue of Dura Europus** in northern Mesopotamia is decorated with symbolic frescoes on the subject of Ezekiel in the valley of the bones, typical of the art resulting from the development of mystical religions in the Middle East.

## Music

Plainsong, a form of religious chant, developed in Europe. St Augustine, 354-430, warned of the "peril of pleasure" in this music, whose austere unaccompanied line would be the basis of later European developments in polyphony (two or more related melodies played together) and harmony (chord progressions). Eastern music, with its sensuous sonorities, reached its peak.

**The Chinese zither**, adopted by Buddhist monks from *c.* AD 100, brought more instrumental colour to their music. Zither players produced sliding runs and delicate harmonic overtones.

**Greek modes** lived on in the **plainsong chants** of the Christian Church in an adapted form, ascending rather than descending as the Greek modes did.

**Buddhism** became a vital force in China from *c.* AD 200. Its chants were accompanied by the music of elaborate percussion orchestras of bells, gongs, triangles, drums and cymbals.

## Science and technology

In the Graeco-Roman world, there was a decline in science and technology, although a brief revival started in the reign of Constantine the Great. The "occult sciences", astrology and alchemy, were held in great esteem, forming the basis for much technological innovation.

Most Western scientists of the 4th century were engaged in translating, collecting and commentating on the works of earlier thinkers, rather than making observations or doing experiments of their own.

In China, however, in spite of unsettled times, scientific thought progressed as advances were made in mathematics, astronomy and medicine, while materials technology remained active and productive.

In Central America Mayan culture began its classic period. This would produce remarkable advances in mathematics and astronomy and massive stone buildings constructed without the aid of metalworking.

**Menelaus**, a Greek mathematician, *fl.* 100, wrote the first work on non-Euclidean geometry.
**Hadrian's Wall** was built in Britain, 122-7. It was 118.3km (73.5 miles) long, with many forts.
**Surgical instruments** were well developed in Rome, as described by Celsus in the 1st century; but no pain-killing drugs were available to sufferers.
There is evidence that the **wheelbarrow** was invented in China at the beginning of the 2nd century.

**Ptolemy**, the Hellenic astronomer and geographer, wrote the *Almagest c.* 150. This became the "bible" of astronomers for the next 1,400 years, although it contained few new discoveries. Like Hipparchus and other Greek astronomers, Ptolemy accounted for the erratic paths of planets by suggesting that they moved in epicycles (small circles centred on the rim of a planet's orbit). Ptolemy's *Geography*, which included Africa and Asia, had great subsequent influence.

**Galen**, *c.* 130-*c.* 200, a surgeon and philosopher of Alexandria, wrote over 500 works on medical subjects. His experiments on animals led to the science of physiology. Galen's knowledge of the body was influenced by the works of Aristotle and Hippocrates, who believed in vital substances or essences at work in the body. Despite practical knowledge of the circulatory system, he postulated that blood vessels carried the blood to the skin where it was transformed into flesh.

**Alchemists** of the first two centuries include **Dioscorides of Cilicia** *fl. c.* 60, who described the processes of crystallization, sublimation and distillation of substances. He also described the use of minerals for medical purposes.
**Alchemy**, a pseudo-science of obscure origins, sought a philosopher's stone thought capable of changing base metals into gold, and the elixir of life which would preserve youth indefinitely.
**The abacus** is recorded in use in China *c.* 190.

## 220-50

The murder of **Alexander Severus**, *r.* 222-35, instigated a period of military control over the Roman emperor and factional warfare among the troops. **Official persecution of Christians** began under **Decius**, *r.* 249-51, as the worship of living rulers became proof of loyalty. **The new Sassanid Empire** in Persia, founded by **Ardashir I**, *r.* 224-41, took Armenia from Rome in 232. **The first written records** in Japan date from *c.* 230.

## 250-80

**The Goths** took Dacia in 257. A series of capable emperors from Illyria began with **Claudius II "Gothicus"**, *r.* 268-70, who defeated the Gothic invasion of the Balkans and settled the Goths in the Danubian provinces. In 271, **Aurelian**, *r.* 270-75, drove out the Alemanni who had invaded Italy but abandoned the Roman province of Dacia. **China** was nominally reunited under the **Western Ch'in dynasty** in 265.

## 280-310

**Diocletian**, *r.* 284-305, divided the empire into eastern and western spheres in 285 with two equal emperors. In 285 the western capital moved to Milan to defend the northern frontiers more easily. **Rome** recaptured Armenia and Mesopotamia in 297. **The Mediterranean economy** continued to collapse under heavy Roman taxation, *c.* 300. **The Franks, Alemanni and Burgundians** crossed the Rhine.

## 310-40

**Constantine**, *c.* 285-337, became interested in Christianity and granted religious freedom to all religions in 313. He founded Constantinople as his eastern capital in 330 and gave Christian bishops a major administrative role in the empire. **The Gupta dynasty** united much of northern India under **Chandragupta**, *c.* 320, and introduced a classic period of urban culture in north India.

## 340-70

**Julian**, 331-63, tried unsuccessfully to organize a pagan Church, and campaigned against the Franks. **The Persians** recaptured Mesopotamia in 364. **Samudra Gupta**, the Indian emperor, conquered Bengal and Nepal and broke the power of the tribal republics in northwest India. This marked a victory for caste over tribe. **The Pallava dynasty** was set up in southern India *c.* 350. **Japan** conquered Korea *c.* 360.

## 370-400

**Roman absorption** of the Germanic tribes was reaching its limits. **The Visigoths** crossed the Danube in 376 and were settled as military allies by **Theodosius the Great**, *r.* 370-95. **Stilicho**, *c.* 368-408, a Vandal Roman commander, defeated a Visigoth invasion under Alaric. **Christianity** received official support from the emperor **Theodosius**. **Persian power** was at its zenith under **Shapur II**, *r.* 309-79.

**Many towns** whose public architecture reflected their prosperity and importance as administrative centres were fortified *c.* 250, including Colchester.

**Roman villa-based estates** provided the foundation for a more efficient agricultural system than the former Celtic villages.

**Carausius' control of channel shipping** enabled him to declare Britain independent in 285, but **Constantius** restored imperial authority in 297.

**British woollen cloth** was popular throughout the empire.

**Theodosius** expelled an invasion of Picts, Irish and Saxons, 369. **Luxury products** found in Britain attest to the wealth of this period.

**The Romans** began to withdraw from Britain in 383 after repelling a second barbarian invasion. Christianity was popular among the upper classes.

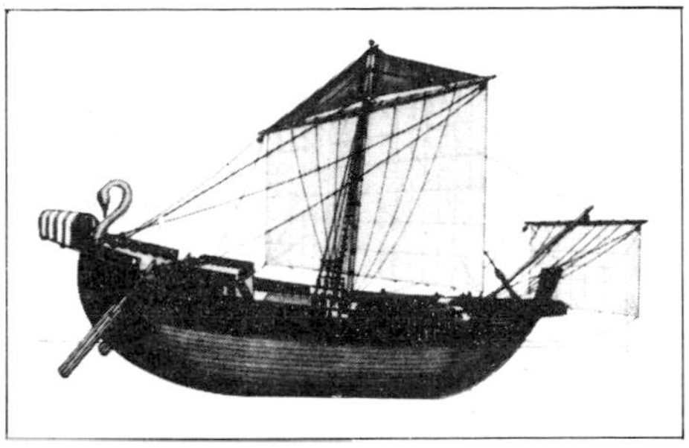

Roman grain ship

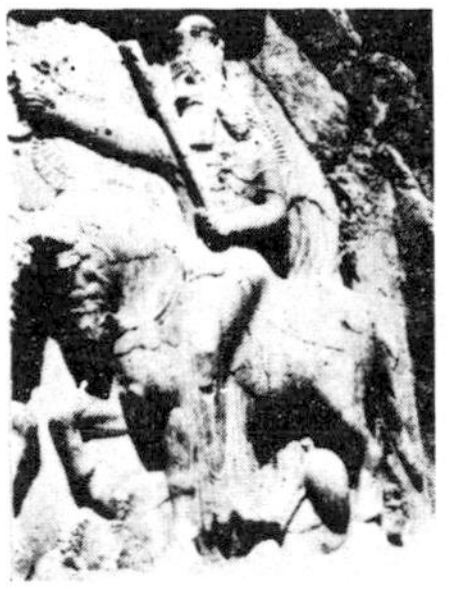

Relief at Naqsh-e-Rustan

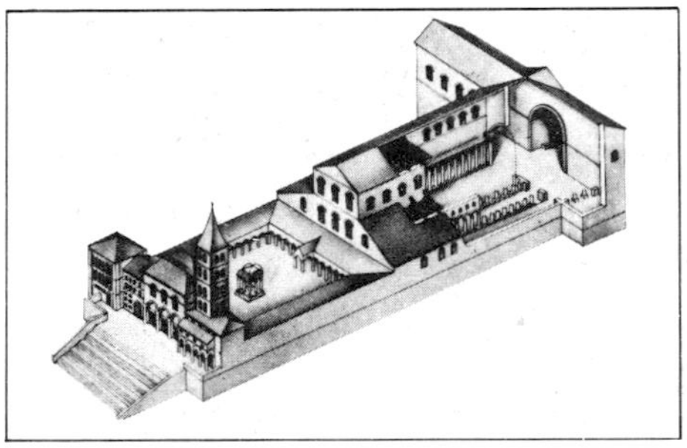

Early Christian churches: St. Peter's, Rome

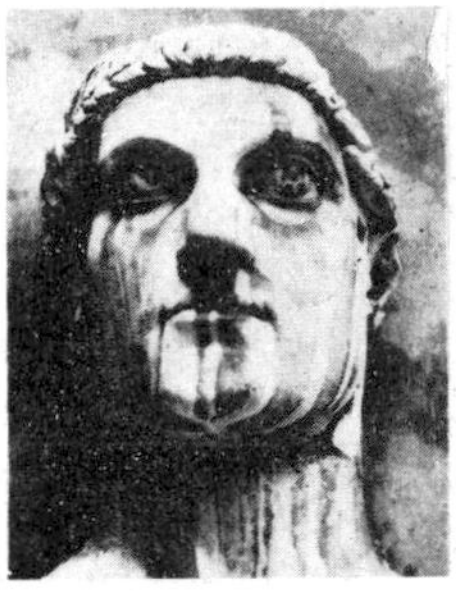

Constantine the Great

**Neo-Platonism** was founded by **Plotinus**, 205-70; his belief in the superiority of ideas over mundane reality fostered the Christian conception of heaven, widely influencing Christian and Islamic thought. **Mithraism**, a cult based on the recognition of the two powers of good and evil, became popular with Roman legionaries and received official patronage.

**Manicheanism**, founded by **Mani**, *c.* 216-76, a dualistic religion combining the teachings of Zoroaster, Buddha, Jesus and Gnosticism became widespread from Europe to China. Mani held that knowledge of oneself and God guaranteed salvation (light) and liberation from one's present fallen condition (darkness). The soul had to be kept pure and in communion with God, both of which could be achieved by an abstemious life.

**The Desert Fathers** in Egypt formed the earliest Christian monastic orders. They included **St Anthony**, 250-355, who organized a group of hermits in 305, and **St Pachomius**, *c.* 290-346, who founded many communal monasteries, in which monks lived and worked together. **Neo-Taoism** was created in China by **Kuo Hsing**, *d.* 312, and **Wang Pi**, 226-49, who believed in controlling the emotions and in an ultimate all-uniting principle of non-being.

**At the Council of Nicaea**, in 325, called by Constantine the Great, a group of bishops from all over the Christian world issued a creed stating that God and Christ are of one identical substance. **The Arian ist heresy**, stating that only God was divine and that Christ was created as other men, was condemned by the Council. Constantine continued to support Arianism in spite of this.

**The Latin Fathers** of the Church, **Jerome**, *c.* 347-420, and **Ambrose**, 340-97, began their life's work of theological writing and furtherance of monasticism in the West. Jerome was baptized in 366, after he had studied Latin literature. His Latin translation of the Bible, the Vulgate, is still important today.

**The Nestorian Church** continued to develop, but separately, in Asia Minor. **The spread of Buddhism** in China was greatly speeded by **Kumarajiva**, 344-413, who translated Mahayana Buddhist texts from Indian into Chinese. **Theodosius the Great**, *r.* 379-95, extirpated Arianism and linked the Christian Church with the Roman state.

**Early Tamil literature**, associated with the kingdoms of southern India, dealt with the themes of courtly love and kingship. Its earliest works are the *Eight Anthologies* and possibly the *Ten Songs*, both written *c.* 100-500 by the third of the legendary Sangam literary academies which are said to have lasted for thousands of years.

**Valluvar**, *c.* 200-*c.* 300, was the author of the classic Tamil poem the *Tirukkural* (sacred couplets). The work is a collection of aphorisms dealing with government, society, virtue and love, and has proved almost impossible to translate. The outlook of the poet is so varied that several religious groups in the Tamil region have claimed him as their own.

**A more uninhibited** and individualistic writing sytle evolved in China with Taoist and Buddhist thought. The poet **Lu Chi**, *fl.* *c.* 300 was the first to express this movement towards original creativity. Simple language styles and folk-songs were used by the poet **Ts'ao Chih**, *c.* 300, and later developed in the poetry of **Tao Ch'ien**, 365-427.

**Runes** were the early Germanic script, used for magical charms and riddles. One of the earliest surviving examples, dating from the 4th century, is the *Mojbro Stone* from Upland, which says that a man was slain on his horse.

**The golden age of classical Sanskrit** began with the rule of the Guptas, 320-535. The poet and dramatist **Kalidasa**, 388-455, excelled in the epic genre of the *kavya* school. **The childhood** and licentious youth of **Saint Augustine**, 354-430, before the time when he became a Christian convert in 387, is described in his *Confessions*, 397-401.

**Realistic portraiture** flourished throughout the Roman Empire. Paintings recalled Egyptian mummy portraits in both style and technique. Most exquisite were the delicate miniatures on gold glass medallions, among them the "Family of Vennerius Keramis", *c.* 250. **Sassanid Persia** reached its cultural zenith during the reign of **Shapur I**. The rock carvings at Naqsh-i Rustam, 242-73, record the humiliation of the Roman emperor Valerian.

**Mohican art** flourished on the coast of Peru, *c.* 200-500, and was notable for its naturalistic ceramics, particularly of warrior figures. **Mayan culture** grew in Central America from about the first century AD and lasted for the next 900 years. The architectural monuments of this civilization and the cities of Palnque, Copan, Uaxactan and Yaxchilan were built from the 3rd century onwards.

**Roman architecture** was at its most massive in the early 4th century with the Palace of Diocletian at Split and the Baths of Diocletian and Basilica of Maxentius in Rome. **The fixed hieratic expression** on the colossal head of Constantine in the Forum marked a break from Hellenistic realism and heralded the formalized style of Byzantine art.

**The old church of Saint Peter** in Rome was built in 330, but destroyed during the Renaissance. The first religious building designed specifically for the needs of Christian worship, its basilican shape determined the layout of the majority of Western churches. **Sta Costanza**, 323-37, also in Rome, is an early example of the alternative centrally planned style of Christian architecture.

**Hsieh Ho's** *Six Canons of Painting* is the earliest work on the theory of art, written in the mid-4th century. The Taoist **Ku K'ai Chih**, *c.* 344-406, produced masterly landscapes and genre paintings, conforming to Ho's artistic definitions. **Gupta art** flowered with some of the greatest paintings at the Ajanta caves in the north Deccan. Massive Buddhist stupas were built, with a marked stylistic influence from central Asia and China.

**Roman art** became increasingly stiff and formalized, as with the ivory diptych of **Stilicho** (a Vandal leader in the Roman army) and his wife Serena, *c.* 396. The Jonah Sarcophagus in the Lateran in Rome shows the merging of late Roman classical style with Christian motifs.

**Heroic poems** were sung among the German tribes by bards who accompanied themselves on harps. The songs were narrative lays of couplets set to music.

**The harp**, Europe's main musical instrument, was regarded as a precious possession. Later versions of the instrument became the national emblems of Ireland and Wales.

**Psalms** used by the Christian Church in its liturgy were among the first Christian chants. They were sung as responses by two choirs, or a priest and congregation sang alternate verses.

**Persia** under the Sassanid dynasty, 224-642, was rich in musicians and well developed instruments. Azâdâ's songs were celebrated in poems. Trumpet, lute and mouth organ flourished.

**Chinese music** was further enriched by foreign influences. After the conquest of Kutcha in Turkestan, 384, drums, cymbals and Persian harps with upper sound chests were imported.

**In China** the use of paper became widespread during the period of the Three Kingdoms, 220-64. **Diophantus of Alexandria**, *fl.* 250, wrote the *Arithmetica*, of which six volumes survive in Greek manuscripts. He was the first to introduce symbols into Greek algebra. His numerical equations, together with the Hindu system of numbering, influenced the development of Arabian algebra.

**In China Huang Fu** wrote a treatise on acupuncture, in use since 2500 BC. **Chinese mathematical books** describe the Pythagorean theorem, solve problems involving square roots; and give the value of $\pi$ as 3.1547. **Shafts on chariots and carts** first appeared in Europe in the 3rd century although they had been used in China for many hundreds of years.

**Hippology** – the science of breeding and managing horses – flourished under the Romans. **Clinker-built boats**, made from overlapping wooden planks fastened with iron rivets, were developed in northern Europe in the 3rd century. **By order of Diocletian**, Roman emperor from 284 to 305, all books on the working of gold, silver and copper were burnt to prevent counterfeiting. The effect was to increase interest in alchemy and magic as a method of turning base metal into gold.

**Mathematics** – developed by the Central American civilization of the Mayas, between the 4th and 10th centuries – was the first to make use of a symbol for zero. Mayan arithmetic was based on the number 20 and is notable for calculations involving very large numbers. One reason for this may have been the smallness and cheapness of the Mayan unit of money, the cocoa bean. **Yu Hsi** studied the equinoxes *c.* 330 and was one of the first astronomers to describe the precession of the equinoxes.

**Mayan calendars**, superior to those of early Christianity, were developed in order to calculate the year more accurately for religious purposes. **Mayan astronomy** was in some ways very advanced, owing to the Mayan concern with time. Thus the Mayas calculated the length of a year on Venus and used it partly to work out the dates of religious festivals. **Pappus of Alexandria**, *c.* 300-50, rewrote and commented on the works of earlier mathematicians such as Euclid and Diodorus.

**Chinese astronomers** of the 4th century believed, fairly correctly, that the blue of the sky was an illusion and that the Sun, Moon and stars float freely in space.

# 400-700 The new barbarian kingdoms

## Principal events

**After the fall of Rome in 476, the Western Roman Empire divided into a galaxy of unstable "barbarian" kingdoms which adapted Roman institutions, while the Byzantine Empire became cut off from the west despite Justinian's brief expansion c. 550. The growing independence of the papacy and the new monastic movement made Christianity a powerful political weapon among the barbarian kingdoms, so that national conversion and the suppression of heresy had a more than religious significance.**

**The teachings of Mohammed brought a new unity and aggression to the Arabs, who threatened Constantinople and expanded towards India.**

**The T'ang dynasty completed the development of the Chinese imperial system, on which Japan modelled its own, while India split into smaller kingdoms with the fall of the Guptas, although the classical era they initiated outlasted them.**

### 400-30

**The western capital** of the Roman Empire retreated to Ravenna in 402.

**The Visigoths** under **Alaric** sacked Rome, 410, and invaded Spain in 415 under **Ataulf**, displacing the Vandals, who then moved to Africa.

**The Franks** and Burgundians, who created the first barbarian kingdom inside the empire, occupied Flanders and the Rhineland in 406.

### 430-60

**The Huns'** attack on Gaul led by **Attila**, *c.* 406-53, was defeated by a Roman/Visigothic alliance in 452, and their invasion of Italy stopped on Attila's death.

**The Vandals** attacked Rome in 455 from North Africa and annexed the Mediterranean islands.

**After St Patrick's conversion of Ireland** the Irish monasteries developed into centres of Christian learning.

### 460-90

**The Western Roman Empire** ended in 476 when **Odoacer**, *d.* 493, set up a barbarian kingdom in Italy. But **Theodoric the Ostrogoth**, *r.* 489-526, invaded Italy in his turn in 488.

**The Frankish king Clovis I**, *r.* 481-511, defeated the Roman governor in Gaul in 486 and set up the Merovingian dynasty.

**In China** political fragmentation prevented the development of Chinese culture, while Buddhism won many converts.

### 490-520

**Odoacer** surrendered in 493 to Theodoric, who set up an Ostrogothic kingdom that was initially recognized by Byzantium, 497. He built his capital at Ravenna.

**Clovis** was baptized in 497, becoming the first non-heretical barbarian king and thus winning the support of the papacy and the emperor against the heretical Germanic tribes. In 507 he drove the Visigoths into Spain.

## National events

**Anglo-Saxon invaders replaced Roman culture with their own and set up seven predominantly agricultural kingdoms. Christianity was reintroduced from both Ireland and Rome, and was popular particularly with the warrior aristocracy, acting as a unifying force on the disparate kingdoms.**

**Roman troops** were evacuated in 410, and Angles, Jutes and Saxons brought to England by the Romano-British civilians to repel the Picts *c.* 429.

**Widespread Angle and Saxon invasions** from the Rhineland destroyed Roman town life and Christianity. The invaders settled along the eastern rivers.

**The Anglo-Saxon invasion** continued westwards. The invaders stayed mainly in lowland areas.

**The kingdom of Wessex** was founded *c.* 495 and **King Arthur** is said to have organized the Celtic defence against the Anglo-Saxon advance *c.* 520.

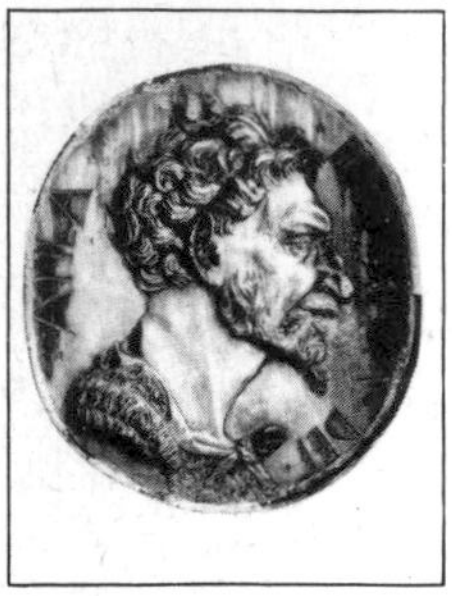

Attila the Hun

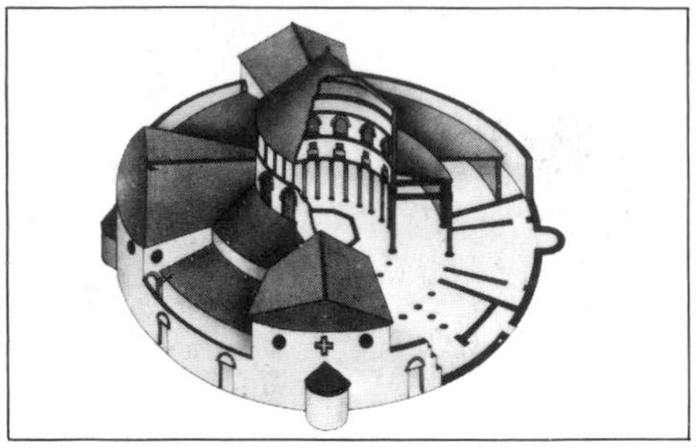

Early Christian churches: S. Stefano Rotundo, Rome

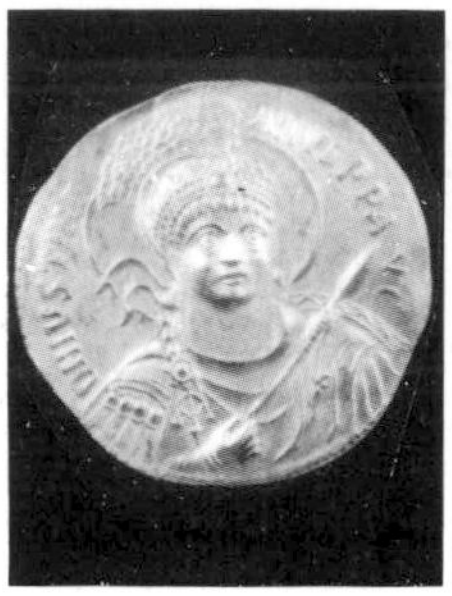

Coin of Justinian the Great

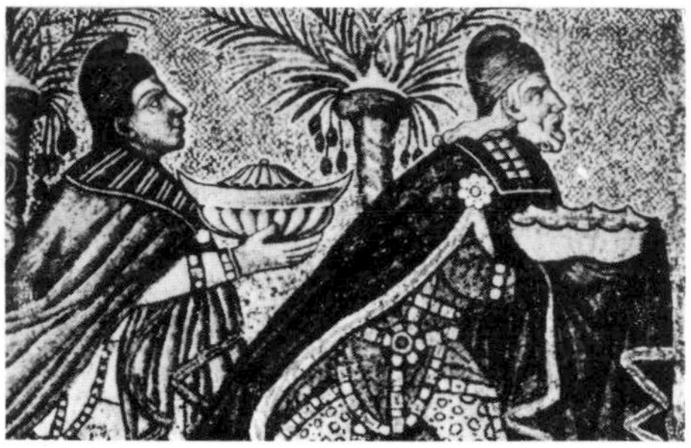

Mosaics from S. Apollinare, Ravenna, 6thc.–7thc.

## Religion and philosophy

**With its consolidation and the removal of the threat of alien ideas, the Christian Church turned in upon itself and became engaged in a series of fierce internal doctrinal disputes centring on the many interpretations of the nature of Christ. At the same time Western monasticism emerged with the founding of the Benedictine rule.**

**Islam arose as a small sect in the early 7th century and quickly became a powerful cohesive movement with an aggressive evangelical mission. By 700 it had spread throughout the Middle East. After the death of the prophet Mohammed, however, it became subject to internal schismatic tendencies deriving from the conflicts between the temporal and spiritual aspects of the Islamic religion.**

**Buddhism advanced beyond the borders of the Indian subcontinent; by 700 it had become firmly established in both China and Japan.**

**Nestorius**, consecrated Bishop of Constantinople in 428, maintained that Christ was both divine and human.

**The Council of Ephesus**, 431, asserted the unity of Christ and declared this view heretical.

**St Augustine of Hippo**, the greatest theologian of Christian antiquity, combined the New Testament with Platonism. In *The City of God*, *c.* 410, he put forward the doctrine of predestination.

**The Council of Chalcedon**, 451, in response to the claim of **Pope Leo I** to universal supremacy, declared the Patriarch of Constantinople to be of equal authority. This council also emphasized that Christ had both a human and a divine nature, countering the doctrine of **Monophysitism**, which stated the essential unity of Christ.

**St Patrick**, entrusted by Pope Celestine I to convert the Irish people, landed in County Wicklow, Ireland, in 432.

**The Shakta and Tantra cults** became important in India, emphasizing mystical speculations on divine fertility and energy. These doctrines were regarded as unorthodox by religious teachers. Tantrism was also an important trend in the Buddhist tradition.

**Under the Guptas, Vaishnaism** flourished as a separate cult distinct from **Shivaism**.

The **Yogacara** school of meditative techniques flourished within Buddhism.

**Buddhism grew in China** at the expense of the more elite cult of **Confucianism**. There were two schools of Buddhism, the **T'ien-T'ai sect**, rationalists who sought to integrate Hinayana and Mahayana Buddhism, and the **Mahayana Amitabha sect**, who believed that salvation required reflection on the **Amitabha Buddha** as well as general meditation.

## Literature

**The classical tradition of literature largely disappeared with the fall of Rome in 476 but survived in Byzantium and in Christian monasteries where a few late Latin works were influential. Western European literature centred around the heroic myths of the Germanic invaders and the Celts, sung by bardic poets whose verse forms Christian writers later adapted to religious poetry. With the founding of Islam in the Arab world the Koran was collected but the re-emergence of Arabic poetry would await the prosperous dynasties of the 8th century.**

**In India and in China under the T'ang dynasty lyric poetry flourished, both religious and secular, while a Japanese writing and literature emerged.**

**Buddhist sacred literature**, in its earliest complete forms, appeared in the 5th century Pali texts that collected together the *Jataka Tales* (birth stories). These 547 tales consisted of prose and verse fables about the former births of the Buddha, often in animal forms. Similar tales are found in Aesop and in non-Buddhist Indian literature.

**Japan** assimilated Chinese civilization in the first four centuries AD and evolved a writing system of extreme complexity by adapting the script of the monosyllabic Chinese language to convey the phonetics of Japanese. The earliest texts are the 8th-century histories *Kojiki* and *Nihon Shoki*, but include songs and myths probably from the 5th century.

**The Jewish Haggadah texts** in Palestine and Babylonia used legends, stories and anecdotes to illustrate ethical and theological matters dealt with in the Talmud. This material, with its lively embellishment of such Old Testament stories as that of Noah, influenced the similar treatment of biblical tales in the miracle plays of medieval Western Europe.

**An oral literature** of heroic verse known as **Heldenlieder** developed among the tribes of western Germany. From these songs and from pagan hymns and laments emerged later epic narratives, notably the story of Siegfried and Brunhild which was incorporated into Germanic epics like the 13th-century *Song of the Nibelungs* and into the heroic lays of Iceland.

## Art and architecture

**The fall of the Western Empire in 476 enabled new art forms combining Celtic, Scandinavian, German and Roman styles to develop in northern Europe, reaching their high point in the exquisite illuminated manuscripts produced by the Irish and Northumbrian monasteries.**

**Byzantine art, a sacred and stylized offspring of late Roman art, spread from Greece to Italy, blossoming in the 6th century with the building of Hagia Sophia in Constantinople and S. Vitale at Ravenna – the main cultural centre in Italy after the fall of Rome.**

**Middle-Eastern culture, divided until the 7th century between Byzantine and Persian influences, later collapsed before the onslaught of Islam, which absorbed certain elements of church design but forbade the use of representational imagery.**

**Japanese art during the Asuka period developed a style of its own distinct from that of China and Korea.**

**The Mausoleum of Galla Placidia** in Ravenna, *c.* 425, shows a Byzantine influence in its plan and its decorations. The mosaics were made over a period of one hundred years and illustrate the shift from the light, decorative qualities of Rome to the sombre and awe-inspiring images of a wholly Byzantine style.

**The hieratic** and stylized form of Roman art can be seen in the ivory carvings "Scenes from the Passion", dating from the early 5th century. Classical ideals of proportion and anatomy were no longer considered important.

**Christian architecture** was a blend of Roman and indigenous styles, AD 400-600. In Egypt monasteries with frescoes were built at Bawit and Sakkara and the basilica of St Mena was constructed near Alexandria.

**The church of St. Stefano Rotondo** in Rome, 468-83, is exceptional for its entirely circular plan, although the centrally planned style continued a tradition which reached back to the Pantheon.

**Chinese art** during the Six Dynasties period, 220-589, developed the Han tradition of monumental stone sculpture. In 460 a series of rock-cut shrines were begun in the caves of Yunkang, which contain a 13.7m (45ft) figure of a standing Buddha.

**Manuscript illumination** was an important art form of the early Christian period. Only four religious texts survive, including the *Vienna Genesis*, a luxurious work on purple ground, and the *Rossano Gospels*, the earliest illustrated version of the New Testament. Both texts date from the early 6th century.

## Music

**In India, râgas were well established by the fifth century, having evolved from traditional melodies and scale theory that utilized many seven-note scales and complex rhythms to evoke various moods. In the West, by 600, Christian monks had developed plainsong to a level of accomplishment, codified by Pope Gregory I, that placed it lastingly in the liturgy.**

**The marimba**, played today by the Bantu in Africa, developed from a xylophone introduced to Africa by Indonesian immigrants in the 5th century.

**Japan adopted music and dance** that were to die in their countries of origin. Supple Indian and Chinese forms were considered female, and Korean and Manchurian forms male in character.

**Irish song**, carried through Europe by minstrels and monks, revitalized musical composition. Unlike classical verse, which might be sung to a melody repeated as often as the poem required, Irish poetry – with its lines of irregular length but equal accents – demanded specific settings. This inspired musicians to greater feats of ingenuity and expression.

## Science and technology

**Chinese science and technology was by far the most active and inventive of this time. Under the T'ang dynasty the sciences and arts were encouraged and science was no longer hampered in any way by religious dogmas or prohibitions. Chinese attitudes to medicine were particularly enlightened: even before the 5th century medical treatment was regarded as a public service and was administered by the state. In astronomy, practical chemistry and mathematical calculation China also led the world.**

**By contrast Western science had dwindled to commentaries, and even these often met with discouragement of an extreme kind. Boethius, one of the last major Western commentators on science and philosophy, was executed in 524 by Theodoric the Ostrogoth for advocating a return to political and intellectual liberty. Although overshadowed by China, Indian mathematical, astronomical and medical sciences also advanced.**

**The university of Constantinople** was founded in 425 by **Theodosius II**, 401-50, the Roman emperor of the East, who later (438) produced the **Theodosian Code**, a systematization and simplification of the Roman legal code.

**Chinese scientific instruments** of the 5th century included water-driven armillary spheres, which revolved in phase with the stars, and a compass, originating in the 2nd century, whose pointer was a metal spoon balanced on its bowl. From the 9th century these spoons were replaced by magnetic needles.

**Boethius**, 480-524, wrote on the four advanced "arts", geometry, arithmetic, music and astronomy. Two of these manuscripts survive, *De Institutione Musica*, and *De Institutione Arithmetica*.

**Indian astronomical literature** shows an upsurge which lasted a century, beginning with the publication in the late 5th century of the work of the astronomer **Aryabhata**, 476-550. This mentions rotation of the Earth and the epicyclic movements of planets. He also obtained an extremely accurate calculation for $\pi$.

**Metal stirrups**, invented in 5th-century Korea and used by the Avars on their incursions from Asia, were first seen in southern Europe *c.* 500.

## 520-50

**The Byzantine emperor Justinian the Great**, *r.* 527-65, temporarily reconquered North Africa in 534 and Italy in 554, and codified Roman law. His alliance with the papacy led to the suppression of heresy in the empire.
**Chosroes I**, *r.* 531-79, brought Persia to its greatest strength in a protracted war with Byzantium.
**The Gupta dynasty** in north India fell in 535.

## 550-80

**Byzantium** had reconquered most of the Mediterranean seaboard by 560, but by 571 the Lombards had taken Italy and settled in the North.
**The Frankish kingdom** stayed divided because of the Merovingian custom of equal division of inheritance between the king's sons.
**Persia** took southern Arabia from the Abyssinians in 576.
**The introduction of Buddhism** to Japan in 552 marked the start of a period of Chinese influence.

## 580-610

**Pope Gregory I**, *r.* 590-604, assisted papal authority by defending Rome against the Lombards.
**Persia and Byzantium** were at war in Syria-Palestine, 602-28.
**The Sui dynasty** reunified China in 589 by conquering the southern Chen dynasty.
**In Japan**, the Soga clan rose to power in 587, introducing a paternalist, Chinese-style constitution.
**Irish missionaries** worked in Scotland and Germany *c.* 600.

## 610-40

**The Muslim era** began with the flight of Mohammed, *c.* 570-632, from Mecca to Medina in 622. His ideas brought a new unity, sense of responsibility and aggression to the diverse Arab traders and tribesmen. After Mohammed's death **Caliph Omar**, 581-644 (the head of Islam), expanded the Islamic realm in the Near East.
**The T'ang dynasty** was founded in China in 618, ruling with a large and powerful imperial bureaucracy.

## 640-70

**Disputes** about the authority and succession of the caliphate under **Othman**, *d.* 656, and **Ali**, *d.* 661, led to civil war, which destroyed the unity of the Ummah and led to the establishment of the **Umayyad dynasty** at Jerusalem in 638. The Muslims then took Iran and Egypt, 642, Armenia, 653, and Afghanistan, 664, ruling as an autocratic but tolerant minority.
**Japan** entered a period of reform in 646, imitating Chinese society.

## 670-700

**The Islamic world** was divided by disputes which led to the emergence of the Sunni, Shi'ite and Khawarij sects, reflecting the problems of succession and the growing discontent at the prosperity of the Meccans, which was increasing at the expense of other Muslims.
**A 30-year truce** was concluded between the Byzantine and Muslim empires after the failure of the Muslim blockade of Constantinople in 673-8.

**The kingdom of Bernicia** was founded from Anglo-Saxon settlements in the north *c.* 547. It ultimately reached the Firth of Forth.

**St Columba**, 521-97, set up an Irish monastery at Iona, 563. The seven Anglo-Saxon kingdoms (**the heptarchy**) were established by 550.

**St Augustine** arrived to preach Roman Christianity, 597, in Kent, which was the chief of the seven kingdoms *c.* 600.

**St Aidan**, *d.* 651, introduced Irish Christianity to Northumbria, 635. Its king, **Edwin**, had won the overlordship of the heptarchy except Kent in 626.

**The Synod of Whitby**, 664, secured the victory of Roman Christianity in Northumbria.
**The Sutton Hoo ship burial** took place in East Anglia *c.* 650.

**Anglo-Saxon society** comprised king, thanes, freemen and slaves. The Northumbrian monastic culture produced the **Lindisfarne Gospels**.

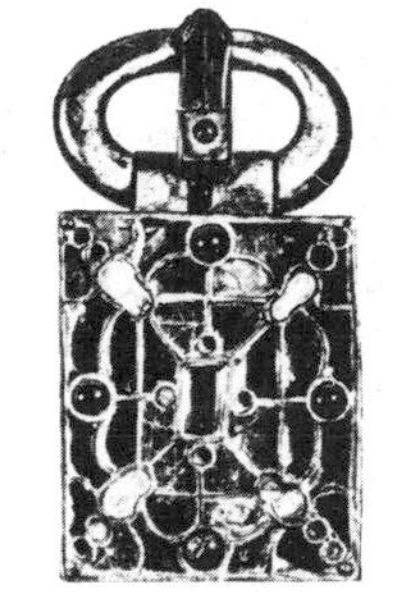

Merovingian buckle, 6thc.

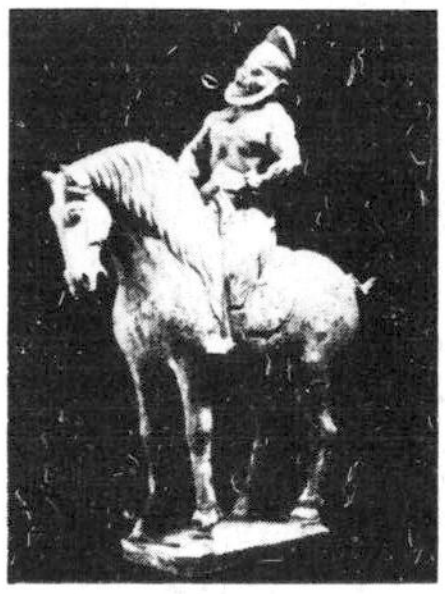

T'ang pottery figure

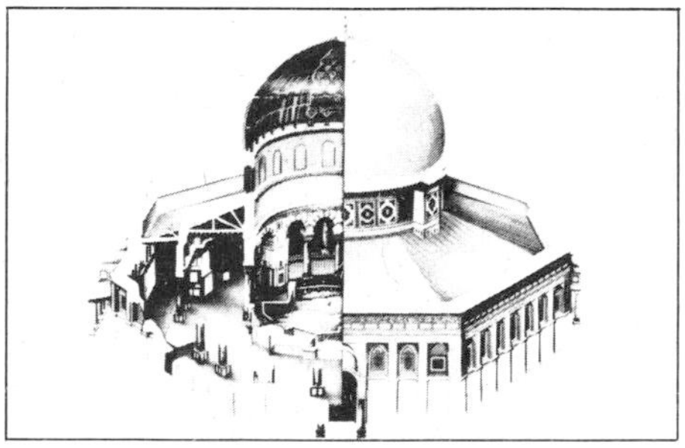

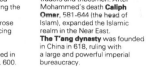

Early Islamic architecture: the Dome of the Rock

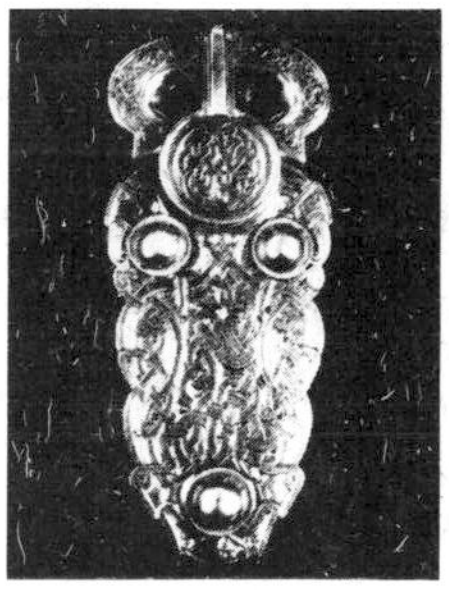

Gold buckle, Sutton Hoo

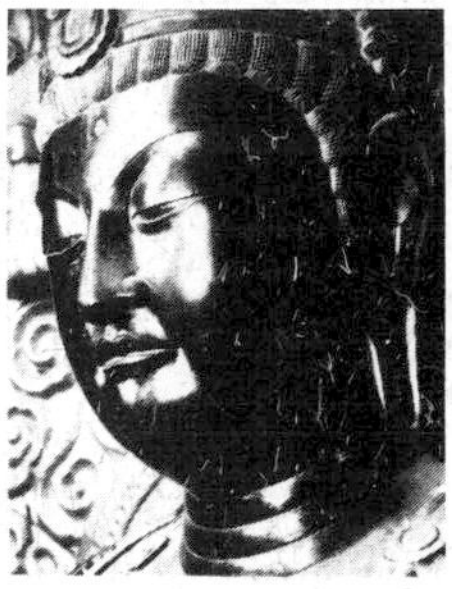

Japanese Buddha, 7thc.

**St Benedict**, *c.* 480-547, founded the first Benedictine monastery *c.* 529. He laid down a complete set of rules for monastic life, including a period of probation before full membership of the monastic community, prohibition of ownership and, most important of all, rules for obediency, celibacy and humility. His monastic ideal was of a self-contained and self-sufficient community.

**Buddhism**, supported by the **Soga clan**, was officially introduced into Japan in 552.
**Mazdakism**, founded by **Mazdak**, *fl.* 560, in Iran was an offshoot of **Manicheanism**. Mazdak held that good (light) acted by free-will and evil (darkness) by chance. Light could only be released into the world by asceticism, vegetarianism and non-violence.
**The prophet Mohammed**, was born in *c.* 570 in Mecca.

**Mohammed, founder of Islam**, received his first prophetic call in 610. Thereafter he began to proclaim his message publicly. His revelation was of a majestic being, the one God, Allah, whose command was that Mohammed was to be his prophet. This and subsequent revelations form the content of the *Koran* which emphasizes generosity, the goodness and power of God and retribution on the Day of Judgment.

**In 622 Mohammed** and a small following emigrated to Medina after opposition and harassment in their native Mecca. The **Ummah**, or Muslim community, claimed supremacy over tribal or familial loyalties, regarding all Muslims as brothers. In so doing it helped to make Arab society more cohesive. The crucial concept of **jihad** (holy war) was instituted at this time by Mohammed and led to the conquest of Mecca in 630. Mohammed died in 632.

**Divisions appeared in the Ummah** over the succession after the death of Mohammed. The supporters of his son-in-law **Ali** were the forerunners of the major **Shi'ite** division of Islam. The puritanical **Kharijites** who opposed Ali withdrew from the main body of the Ummah. The Shi'ites stressed leadership, the Kharijites community and permanent religious aggression.

**The Monothelites** were condemned as heretics at the Ecumenical council at Constantinople in 681. The heresy concerned the divinity and humanity of Christ. The Monothelites, following the decision reached at Chalcedon, claimed that although Christ had two natures He had a single will. The Council insisted on Christ's duality by asserting that both a divine and a human will were in Christ's person.

**Aristotelean logic** was translated into Latin by **Boethius**, 480-524, the last great Roman writer. A Christian who served as a minister under Theodoric the Ostrogoth, he was condemned to death and in prison wrote *De consolatione philosophiae*, 523, a treatise in verse and prose on free will, good and evil which helped spread Greek thought in the Germanic world.

**Alliterative bardic verse** romanticizing the heroism of Celtic warriors had become an established literary form by the middle of the 6th century.
**Nennius**, *c.* 800, attributed to a Welsh bard, **Taliesen** (possibly a mythical figure), odes and lays in praise of **King Urien**, *fl.* 547–59. These were later collected with others in the 14th-century *Book of Taliesen*.

**An Irish bard, Dallan Forgaill**, *d.* 597, is credited with the *Eulogy of St Columba*. Its vigorous alliterative style is also found in Irish sagas about the hero **Cú Chulainn**, possibly 7th century, known as the Ulaid cycle. Ireland had a class of professional poets, the filiad.
**A Welsh poet, Aneirin**, *c.* 600, celebrated northern British heroes in *Y Gododdin*.

**In India**, classical Sanskrit literature, which had thrived under the rule of the Guptas, 320-535, reached its late flowering in the poetry of **Bhartrhari**, *c.* 570-651, a philosopher who wrote three collections of verses, the *Sátaka*, on the sensual pleasures of love, the nature of justice and the means of liberation from earthly existence.

**The *Koran*** reached its final form, 651-2. Written partly in rhymed prose reflecting the mood of Mohammed during his life as a solitary visionary preacher, it was regarded by Muslims as the perfect word of God. Its style and thought permeated the literature of Islam, an expansionist force that took many Persian stories to Europe.

**The first named English poet, Caedmon**, *fl.* 670, used the metre and diction of Old English pagan verse to compose poems on biblical and religious themes at the monastery of Whitby. A nine-line *Hymn on the Creation* is the most generally accepted of several works attributed to him in a 10th-century MS. He was an untutored herdsman, according to the Venerable Bede.

**The age of Justinian** saw the flowering of Byzantine architecture. The architecture and mosaics of **S. Vitale**, Ravenna, 526-48, were the splendour of Italy. The great cathedral of **Hagia Sophia** in Constantinople, 532-7, was an architectural and engineering triumph.
**King Theodoric's mausoleum** in Ravenna, *c.* 530, is surmounted by a colossal domed monolith, a fitting tribute to the half-barbarian, half-civilized king.

**The distinctive Japanese art style of the Asuka period**, 552-645, culminated with the temple complex of Hōryūji, Nara. The courtyard with its Pagoda, Konda (Golden Hall) and Kodo (for meetings) was based on the traditional Chinese and Korean layout.
**The solid ivory throne** of Maximian, archbishop of Ravenna, was carved in Constantinople and was a gift from Emperor Justinian *c.* 550.

**The Basilica at Turmanin** in Syria is a typical eastern variation of Roman Christian architecture, which was common throughout Syria and Palestine before the rise of Islam.
**The art of Sassanid Persia** of the 5th and 6th centuries shows a combination of Byzantine and Irano-Buddhist styles. Metalwork was highly developed and decorated with complex motifs and intricate filigree work.

**The Great Chalice of Antioch** is typical of Christian metalwork from the Roman provinces. It probably dates from the early 7th century, when there was an enormous output of silverware and fine gold jewellery.
**The Ashburnham *Pentateuch*** is a masterpiece of vivid narrative illumination dating from the late 6th or early 7th century. It is not known where it was made, nor whether by a Jewish or Christian illuminator.

**The Sutton Hoo treasure** comes from the grave of an East Anglian king who died in 654. It includes superb examples of Anglo-Saxon decorative metalwork.
**Christian scholars and artists** who took refuge in Ireland during the period of the Anglo-Saxon invasions produced an abstract and extremely ornate style of illumination, the 7th-century *Book of Durrow* being one of the best surviving examples.

**The Dome of the Rock** in Jerusalem is the first great Islamic architectural monument. Construction began in 688 in the reign of Abd al-Malik, but the design was a creative adaptation of Christian church buildings.
**Book illumination** reached great heights in Northumberland. The *Lindisfarne Gospels*, *c.* 700, combine the Roman narrative tradition with the decorative skill of the Celts.

**Confucian ceremonies** in China closely integrated music, dance and poetry. Chinese court music and dance expressed the form and calligraphy of poems around which they were created.

**Harps** of six to twelve strings were played by European musicians. The instrument became a symbol of their calling. A six-string example, found at Sutton Hoo, dates from about 640.

**Pope Gregory I** supervised the compiling and codifying of plainsong *c.* 600, giving his name to Gregorian chant, an unaccompanied and unharmonized style that has persisted to the present day.

**Under the T'ang dynasty**, 618-907, orchestral suites and programmatic works, some describing battles, were composed in China. Music-dramas incorporating folk-song developed.

**Classical Arab music** evolved richly under the Umayyad caliphs, 661-750, in Damascus. **Ibn Misjah**, died *c.* 715, codified its theory, embracing eight modes for lute music. Arab modes were nearly identical to Greek modes, but were performed with rich embellishments characteristic of the sinuous ornamentation of much Arab visual art and architecture.

**Justinian**, Byzantine emperor, *r.* 527-65, closed the Athenian university because the teachers were not Christians.
**John Philoponus**, *fl. c.* 530, speculated that a projectile would gain momentum from the mechanism which fired it, thus arriving at a crude idea of inertia.
**Palaeontology** was furthered in China in 527 with a book by **Li Tao Yuan** in which he described animal fossils.
**Indian decimal notation** began in the 6th century; on later inscriptions a dot signified zero.

**The Ma'daba mosaic**, the oldest-known map of the Holy Land, shows the area from ancient Byblos to Thebes and has a street plan of Jerusalem. It was made in Palestine *c.* 550.
**Silk production** was attempted at Byzantium in the 6th century after silkworm eggs had been smuggled out of China and taken there, reputedly by Nestorian monks.
**Abacus calculators** are described in a mathematical work thought to have been written by **Chen Luan** *c.* 570.

**The diagnosis of disease** in China in the 7th century was documented by **Chao Yuan Fang**, *c.* 610, who wrote a treatise listing 1,720 diseases classified into 67 groups.

**Chinese surgical treatment** in the 7th century included the removal of cataracts.
**Windmills**, probably invented in Persia in the 7th century, may have had their origin in wind-driven prayer wheels. Another theory, unproven, is that they were inspired by ships' sails. The axis of a wheel, driven by some 6 to 12 sails, was mounted on the first storey of a Persian windmill. Stone wheels used for grinding corn were located on the storey above.

**Greek fire**, used in the defence of the Byzantine Empire in the 7th century, was a highly inflammable substance of uncertain composition. Probably a mixture of pitch, naphtha and potash, it could be discharged from tubes in the prows of ships.
**Fine metalwork** including cloisonné, enamel and lathe turned jewellery was found at the Sutton Hoo ship burial dating *c.* 650, showing that metallurgy in the Dark Ages was not only used to make swords.

**Swords** were the most advanced product of Burgundian and Frankish metallurgy in the 7th and 8th centuries. Their blades were expertly forged, with strips of decorative metal running along the whole length. Handles and scabbards were inset with jewels and welded decorations.
**In northern England** the tides and moon were studied by the **Venerable Bede**, *c.* 673-735, who also wrote a treatise on finger reckoning.

# 700-1000 Islam reaches India and Spain

## Principal events

**Invasions from the Muslims in Spain, Vikings in the north and Magyars in the east destroyed much of Europe's culture and economic strength, though Charlemagne's conquests east of the Rhine brought Germany within the European orbit.**

**The Muslim world reached from Spain to Afghanistan by 736, and the papacy, although relatively isolated by Muslim control of the Mediterranean, used its new states for political ends, reviving the Roman ideal by crowning its main supporters Holy Roman Emperor. Royal authority in Europe at this time was often precarious, based only on the personal allegiance of a provincial nobility whose power was strengthened by the need to defend the kingdom's frontiers.**

**In China constant warfare weakened the T'ang armies and the Sung dynasty gained control, while in Japan the Heian period marked a moment of transition to a society run on feudal lines.**

### 700-30

**Pope Gregory II**, *r.* 715-31, appointed St Boniface, *c.* 680-754, to convert Germany.
**The Umayyad Arabs** took Spain in 715.
**Leo III**, *r.* 717-41, defeated the second Arab siege of Constantinople, 717-18, and began the iconoclastic controversy in 726 asserting the religious authority of the emperor and limiting the spread of monasticism.
**The Nara period in Japan** began with the establishment of a capital at Heijō in 710.

### 730-60

**Charles Martel**, *c.* 688-741, stopped the Muslim invasion of Europe at Poitiers, 732, and assisted Boniface in Germany. His son **Pepin**, *r.* 747-68, campaigning in Italy, established papal temporal power by a donation of land to the papacy, 756.
**Al Mansur**, *r.* 754-75, founded the **Abbasid Caliphate**, defeating the Umayyads in North Africa and the Near East, 750.
**The Gurjara-Pratihara** dynasty defended India against the Muslims after 740.

### 760-90

**Charlemagne**, *r.* 771-814, united France and conquered Italy in 774, northern Spain in 777, Saxony in 785 and Bavaria in 788.
**Baghdad** became the Abbasid capital in 762.
**An Umayyad dynasty** emerged at Cordoba in Spain, 756, tolerating Jews and Christians.
**Scandinavian trade** with Byzantium began *c.* 770.
**Turkish and Tibetan tribesmen** threatened western China *c.* 763.

### 790-820

**Charlemagne** was crowned Holy Roman Emperor, 800, reviving the idea of a Western Roman Empire. Byzantium recognized the title in 812.
**The Bulgar kingdom** reached its peak under **Krum**, *r.* 808-14.
**Ghana** was an important trading kingdom, bringing gold from southern Africa to the Sahara.
**Emperor Kammu**, *r.* 781-806, instituted the Heian period in Japan, 794-1185, in which indigenous feudalism superseded the Chinese-based social order.

## National events

**A single king emerged and ruled England until Viking invasions took over much of eastern England, where a Danish society developed. Although monastic culture declined, secular learning flourished under Alfred, 849-99, and town life with a money economy recovered in spite of the Vikings.**

**Ethelbald** of Mercia, *r.* 716-57, was overlord of all England, except Northumbria.

**Offa**, *r.* 757-96, brought Mercian power to its zenith and made the rulers of sub-kingdoms renounce their kingship.

**Offa** built a dyke between Mercia and Wales, and created a unified currency, bearing his picture, which was coined in many separate towns.

**The Vikings** sacked Lindisfarne, 793, and overran Ireland, 802-25. **Egbert of Wessex**, *r.* 802-39, inherited the Mercian supremacy.

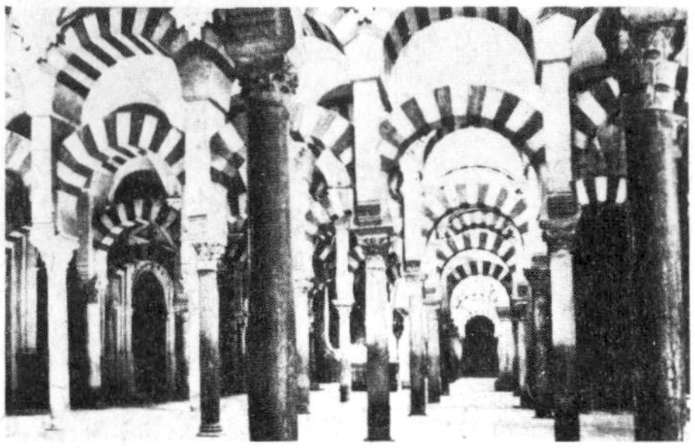

Islamic architecture: Mosque at Cordoba, 8thc. interior

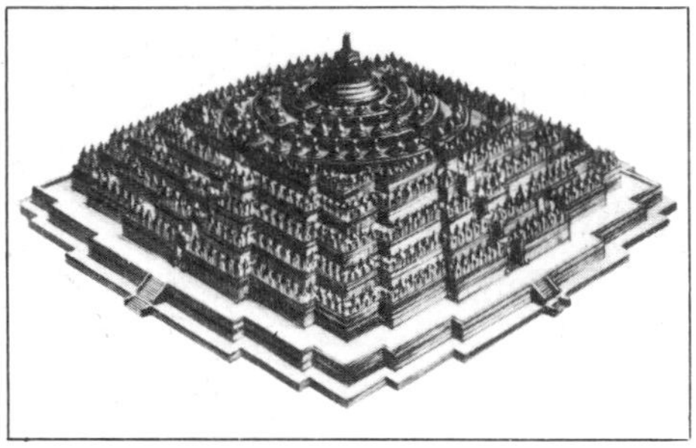

The stupa of Borobudur, Java, 8thc.–9thc.

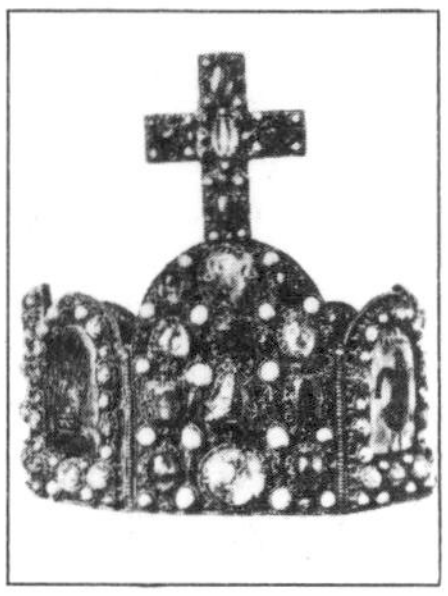

Crown of Charlemagne

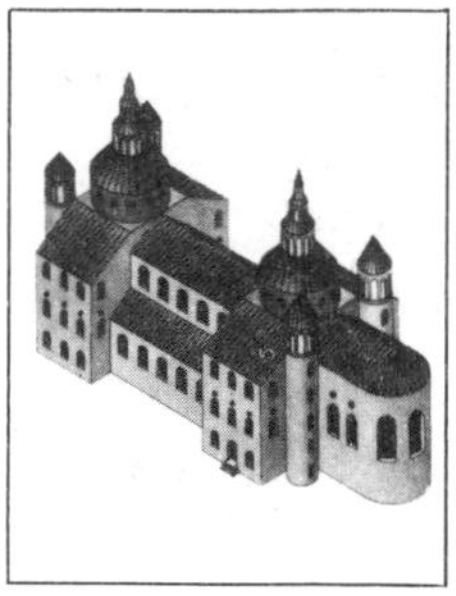

Carolingian church, *c.* 800

## Religion and philosophy

**The Christian Church continued the struggle to assert its authority over the secular powers of the Holy Roman and Byzantine empires while the assertion of the primacy of the Roman popes over the Eastern Church led to an increasing separation of Eastern and Western forms of Christianity. In the West, papal sanction of Charlemagne's empire brought the Church additional prestige. The practices of the clergy, however, were becoming increasingly lax, and would eventually prompt the Cluniac reform movement.**

**In the Islamic world, the Sufi movement was founded and grew, emphasizing an austere mysticism in response to the rational ideal and the reason of orthodox Islam.**

**The spread of Buddhism within Japan continued and won official support.**

**Mayan religion reached its most elaborate hierarchical form at the height of the empire's power in Central America.**

**Iconoclasm** as a movement began, 726, when the Byzantine emperor **Leo III** prohibited the use of icons as idolatrous, claiming the emperor was God's "vice-regent" on earth.
**A period of severe repression** and conflict between Church and state followed in which sacred images of Christ, the Virgin Mary and various saints were destroyed.
**The Islamic religion** reached India in 712 and Spain in 715.

**The Classical period in Mayan culture** in Central America reached its height. Mayan cosmology saw the earth as a crocodile and the Mayans placated their gods with sacrifices.
**Buddhism in Japan** became the state cult in the reign of **Shomu**, who built a magnificent Buddha (**Daibutsu**) and a temple (**Todaiji**) in Nara, in 743-52.

**The new Anglo-Saxon humanism** was introduced in France by the Northumbrian monk **Alcuin**, *c.* 732-804, who met **Emperor Charlemagne**, 781, and became an important figure in the **Carolingian Renaissance**. Alcuin encouraged the study of the liberal arts. His revision of the liturgy of the Frankish Church was carried throughout Charlemagne's empire and he created a new edition of the Vulgate.

**The Tendai and Shingon sects** were founded in Japan *c.* 805 by Buddhist monks returning from a visit to China.
**Sankara**, 780-820, the most important member of the new **Vedanta school of philosophy** in India, affirmed the one true reality (**Brahma**) as the source of all things. He also wrote commentaries on the *Upanishads* and *Brahma Sutra*.

## Literature

**Chinese literature of the T'ang dynasty reached its finest form in the evocative poetry of Li Po, Tu Fu and Wang Wei in the 8th century. With the later decline of the dynasty, social criticism and an elegiac mood appeared. Chinese influence on Japanese literature gave way to new vernacular forms of Japanese verse and prose.**

**The spread of Islam led to more sophisticated themes in Arabic poetry and to an extension of Arabic influence into Persian literature.**

**The epic saga took shape in Norway and Iceland. In England scholastic Latin developed and the growing power of Anglo-Saxon vernacular literature showed itself in the saga of *Beowulf*, in religious poetry and in the Anglo-Saxon Chronicle.**

**The Venerable Bede**, 673-735, wrote his *History of the English Church and People*, a major source of information on England between 597 and 731. He drew on wide sources in creating a work of literary and historical value. **In India, the Sanskrit dramatist Bhvabhutti**, *fl.* 730, wrote three outstanding plays, two of which tell the story of **Rama**.

**Nearly 49,000 poems** survive from China's golden age of poetry, the **T'ang dynasty**.
**Tu Fu**, 712-70, showed his mastery of imagery in such lines as "Blue is the smoke of war, white the bones of men". Equally famous is **Li Po**, 701-62, who wrote of wine and companionship. **Wang Wei**, 699-759, was a painter and poet of nature. The 8-line *shih* predominated.

***Beowulf***, the greatest surviving Anglo-Saxon epic poem, dates from the period between 700 and 1000. A vivid narrative of a warrior's struggles against dragons and monsters of the sea, it is based on northern European heroic legend, with elements of moral and religious significance probably added by Christian writers after the Angles brought it to England.

**A rebirth of European learning** took place under **Charlemagne**, *r.* 771-814, who encouraged the copying of old manuscripts. His biography was written by the German monk **Einhard**, 770-840, in personal and political terms. Charlemagne's court at Aachen attracted scholars such as **Alcuin**, *c.* 732-804, an Anglo-Latin writer and cleric with a humanistic outlook.

## Art and architecture

**After the period of confusion that followed the decline of the Roman Empire, European art again flourished. A Germanic decorative style subordinating realistic representation to stylized patterns is found in jewellery, Viking carving and Celtic manuscripts. In architecture, elements of the Romanesque developed, based on a combination of Roman, Byzantine and Carolingian art, replacing the utilitarian basilicas of the early northern churches with more complex structures using a system of bays, often with vaulted roofs.**

**Islamic art entered its classical age in the 9th century, the religious ban on figurative art producing a wealth of geometric designs in architectural detail, while Islamic and Christian styles mingled in Spain. Buddhist art flourished in the East, contributing to a mingling of cultural styles as Chinese influence reached Japan, while China itself felt the impact of Indian ideas.**

**Byzantine icons** have survived from Sinai, Constantinople and Rome. The early beginnings of defined painting schools can be seen in the life-size "Enthroned Virgin and Child", *c.* 705, commissioned by Pope John VII.
**Chinese Buddhist sculpture** combined the traditional linear delicacy with the Indian sense of form, resulting in such superb statues as the seated stone Buddha, 711.

**The Iconoclastic age** lasted in the Byzantine Empire from 726-843. In order to stop the cult of images and discourage monasticism, all figurative representations, except of the Cross, were either defaced or destroyed.
**The earliest Orissan-style temples** were built at Bhuvanesvar in east India, 700-800. A hollow terraced pyramid supported a conical beehive-shaped spire.

**The Great Mosque at Cordoba** was built by Spain's Arab conquerors, 785-990. The naves use elegant star vaulting and the whole was intricately decorated with coloured marbles and precious stones.
**The *Book of Kells*** was produced in Ireland at the end of the 8th century. It is the finest and most elaborate of early Western illuminated manuscripts.

**A Viking earth barrow**, *c.* 800, contained the Oseberg ship, as well as a cart, several sledges and numerous small decorated objects. The delicate interwoven wood carvings of figures and abstract motifs are typical of northern art.
**Charlemagne's Palace Chapel** at Aachen in Germany was consecrated in 805. Local Roman remains and the church of S. Vitale in Ravenna were used as models in an assertion of the continuity of the empire.

## Music

**The establishment of the Divine Office and Mass by the 9th century encouraged the development of chants more complex than Gregorian chant. At the same time, the Muslim invasions of Western Europe brought schools of singing, lute playing and musical theory which would have a lasting influence on European music over the next five hundred years.**

**The first compositions** by known European composers took the form of tropes, melodic passages added to the liturgy either as new music or as variations on the preceding plainsong melody.

**The Arabs** in conquering Spain brought with them **the lute** (the first fretted instrument to arrive in Europe), **the rebec** (an ancestor of the violin) and the violin type of bow.

**"Ut Queant Laxis"** – written *c.* 770 – was an early medieval hymn tune in the then unusual form of six separate phrases, each starting a step or half step higher than the previous one.

**Arab music** entered its golden age under **Harun ar-Rashid**, *c.* 764-809, whose musical tastes are revealed in *The Arabian Nights*. A style of romantic song flourished in the period.

## Science and technology

**The rise of Islam transformed the course of European science and philosophy. The Arabs were heirs to the Hellenic Greeks and acknowledged their role as custodians of that culture. Following the Athenian tradition they founded schools for wide-ranging, unprejudiced and objective study, most important of which was the Academy of Science at Baghdad. A great respect for Greek learning, and particularly for Aristotle, may have held them back from even greater discoveries, but some Arab scientists rejected Aristotle, arguing for a more experimental approach to science. With the spread of the Arab Empire, Arabic became the language of science outside the Far East, absorbing elements of Indian astronomy while benefiting to a lesser extent from achievements in China. Many Arabic texts on astronomy, chemistry and mathematics retained their influence until modern science began in Europe with the work of Galileo and Newton.**

**Mayan science**, with its detailed astronomical observations and advanced use of mathematics, reached its peak.

**Jabir** (Jabir ibn Hayyan) *c.* 720-815, called the "father of Arabic chemistry". He believed that the four elements (air, earth, fire and water) could be combined to make mercury and sulphur, and that these could then be combined to form gold. This theory greatly influenced early chemistry and eventually led to the phlogiston theory.
**Gunpowder**, probably invented in China in the 8th century, was used initially to make fireworks and only much later in weaponry.

**Printing** with blocks from which the letters stand out in relief was invented in Japan in or prior to the 8th century.
**Bells and organ pipes**, made at this time from bronze, indicate an advance in European metalworking.

**Arab paper** was made in Baghdad for the first time, 793, following the capture of Chinese papermakers during the battle for the city of Samarkand in 751.
**Viking ships** of the 9th century were clinker-built (using overlapping planks) with square sails, a single steering oar aft and many rowing oars. Their narrow hull shape made them faster than Mediterranean ships.
**The Baghdad Academy of Science** replaced Jundishapur, Persia, as the centre of scientific learning *c.* 800.

**820-50**

**The Carolingian Empire** was divided into three at the Treaty of Verdun in 843. **Scandinavians**, having founded Kiev and Novgorod, absorbed Byzantine culture and religion through trading contacts, *c.* 850. **Al-Mamun the Great**, *r.* 813-33, set up a House of Knowledge in Baghdad and encouraged the most glorious epoch of the Abbasid dynasty. **The Abbasid capital** moved to Samarra in 836.

**850-80**

**Frequent invasions** and the weakness of the monarchy gave new power to the provincial nobility in the Carolingian states and in Italy caused a decline in papal authority. **Roman and Byzantine** Christianity officially split in 867. **Basil I** of Byzantium, *r.* 867-86, attacked the Muslims in Mesopotamia and stimulated a revival of Byzantine civilization. **The Bulgarians** were converted to Christianity in 865.

**880-910**

**Urban development** in northern Europe, stimulated by long-distance overland trade, was disrupted by Norse raiders *c.* 900. **The Bulgarians** warred constantly with Byzantium under **Symeon I**, *r.* 893-927. **The Chola dynasty** displaced the Pallavas in India in 888. **The T'ang dynasty** in China fell in 907 and was followed by a period of weak imperial authority and constant barbarian invasions.

**910-40**

**Rollo**, *c.* 860-932, founded an independent dukedom of Normandy in 911 and was baptized in 912. **Henry I**, *r.* 919-36, became the first Saxon king to rule a unified Germany, whereas the French monarchy was weak. **Umayyad** culture reached its zenith in Spain under **Abd ar-Rahman III**, *r.* 912-61. **The rise of a military class** in Japan resulted in civil strife in the provinces, 935-41.

**940-70**

**Otto I**, *r.* 936-73, ended the recurrent Magyar invasions at the battle of Lechfeld in 955 and became the first Saxon Holy Roman Emperor in 962. **The Northern Sung dynasty**, founded in 960, brought a more modern humanism to Chinese government, social organization and thought. A Muslim **Ghaznavid** dynasty grew up in Afghanistan in 962.

**970-1000**

**Hugo Capet**, *r.* 987-96, became king of France and reasserted royal authority over the nobility, pope and emperor. **Venice** was given trading privileges in the Byzantine Empire in 992. **Viking invasions** of Europe reached their peak *c.* 1000, threatening southern France and Italy. **Basil II** of Byzantium, *r.* 976-1025, took Greece from the Bulgarians in 996.

**Egbert** became king of all England in 828. The Danes sacked London, a small market and trading town, in 836.

**Alfred of Wessex** organized English opposition to the Danes and won peace by ceding much of eastern England (the Danelaw) to the invaders.

**Alfred** stimulated the growth of learning and vernacular literature. His son **Edward**, *r.* 899-925, reconquered much of the Danelaw.

**Athelstan**, *r.* 925-39, completed the reconquest, but permitted the survival of Danish customs. **Local government** was organized in shires and hundreds.

**A monastic decline** had set in with the Viking raids but *c.* 940 a clerical revival occurred, providing a useful network for spreading royal authority.

**Danish attacks** overran much of England again in the reign of Ethelred II, 979-1016, but the monastic movement brought an artistic revival to Winchester.

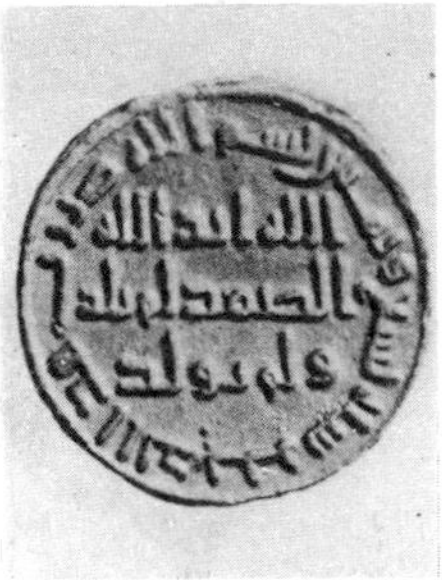

Arab gold dinar, 9th.–10thc.

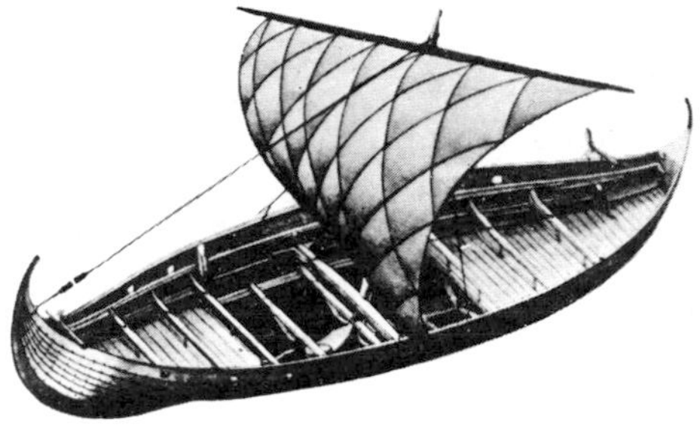

Viking ship

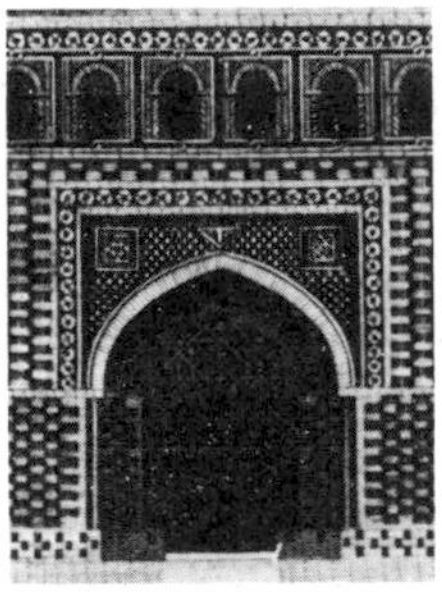

Islamic tomb façade, *c.* 900

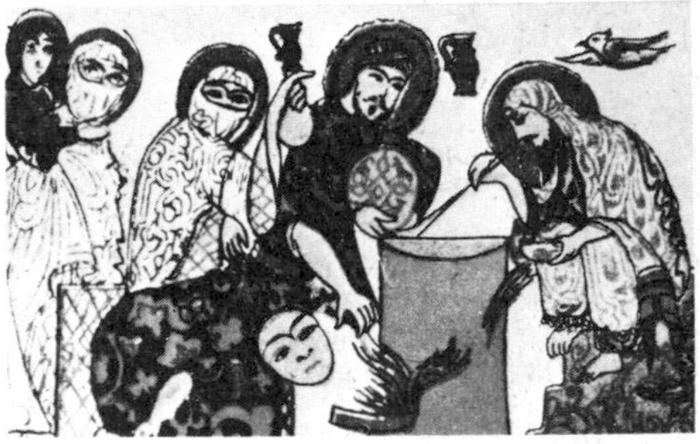

Arab manuscript showing preparation of perfumes

**Ahmad Ibn Hanbal**, 780-855, within the **Sunni branch of Islam**, founded the most orthodox of the four schools of Islamic law, which holds that the *Koran* as interpreted by the Islamic community contains the answers to all moral questions. In 833 **Hanbal** was imprisoned for refusing to accept **Mutazili** rationalist doctrines. **The Ch'an school**, the precursor of Japanese **Zen Buddhism** developed in China.

**The Fourth Council of Constantinople** was called in 869-70 **by Basil I**. It deposed Photius, patriach of Constantinople, who had challenged the Pope's authority in the East, and reinstated Ignatius, thus ending the schism with Rome.

**The Photian schism** ended in 880 and the Greek Church made peace with the pope. **The Abbey of Cluny** in France was founded, 910, marking a revival of the monastic movement. It was here that the **Cluniac reform movement** began, which introduced the notion that the Church hierarchy has a responsibility for clerical discipline and formed the basis of a widespread attack on abuses and corruption in the Church.

**Sufism**, a mystical literary and philosophical movement within Islam, stressed divine love through the immediate personal union of the soul with God. It developed a reaction against more orthodox interpretations of the *Koran*, and **Al Halláj** who was crucified in 922 for his teachings became revered as a Sufi martyr.

**Sa'adia ben Joseph**, head of the **Jewish academy in Babylon**, is known as the father of Jewish philosophy. He defended orthodox Judaism by reaffirming a belief in one God against gnostic dualism. He also repudiated the earlier **Koraite** rejection of the Talmud (the oral tradition of law) in favour of the Torah (the original scriptures that were given to Moses).

**The Vikings**, whose incursions into the Christian world reached a peak *c.* 1000, worshipped gods similar to those of the Germans. There were two tribes of gods, one of them (**the Aesir**) led by **Odin**, who lived in castle Valhalla where he was joined by heroes killed in battle and assisted by them in a perpetual fight against wolves.

**Arabic literature** had a strong tradition of lyrical desert poetry, which re-emerged at the peak of the **Abbasid Empire**, 786-861. The lyrics of **Abu Nuwas**, *c.* 762-815, reflected the town life of the caliphates, while Islam influenced the religious poetry of **Abu al-Atahiya**, 748-826. Another poet, **Abu Tamman**, *c.* 807-50, edited the fine Hamasu anthology.

**Vernacular literature** in both prose and verse was created in Germany and Britain, best shown in the plain narrative style of the *Anglo-Saxon Chronicle*, a history begun during the reign of **Alfred the Great** *c.* 871-99. The Welsh monk **Asser**, *d.* 909, wrote a biography of Alfred. The heroic ***Edda*** lays began to develop in Iceland after 860.

**Classical Japanese literature** emerged in the **Heian period**, 794-1192. The *Kokinshu*, 905, was an anthology of short poems with themes of love and nostalgia, showing the flexibility made possible by the phonetic *kana* script. Ladies of the Heian court wrote witty prose, notably the *Pillow Book of Sei Shonagon c.* 1000.

**Lyric and elegiac Anglo-Saxon poetry** survives in a manuscript known as the *Exeter Book*. This includes individualistic poems such as *The Seafarer* as well as work by an earlier poet, **Cynewulf**, *fl.* 850. *The Dream of the Rood* was a notable poem on the Crucifixion.

**A critical note had entered Chinese poetry** of the 9th century in the didactic verse of **Po-Chü-i**, 772-846. With the continuing decline of the T'ang dynasty and the unrest of the 10th century, nostalgia suffused the ***tzu*** **poetry** of **Li Yu**, 937-78. The *tzu* poets adapted the irregular structure and colloquial language of Chinese folk verse, usually sung to a tune.

**A revival of Persian poetry** using the Arabic alphabet produced the national epic *Shah-Nama* (Book of Kings) by **Firdausi**, 935-1020, who used legend and history in verse that became a model for Arab epics. **An Anglo-Saxon historical poem** with a central theme of feudal loyalty was *The Battle of Maldon c.* 995.

**The overwhelming size** and grandeur of **Mayan religious architecture** can be seen in the **Pyramid of the Sun** at San Juan Teotihuacan, which rose from a base of over 213m (700ft) in diameter to the height of 66m (216ft). **The constructional** and geometric skills of Islam are seen in the spiral-ramped minaret of the **Malwiyya Mosque**, begun at Samarra in 848.

**The Middle Byzantine age**, 867-1025, saw a second flowering of Byzantine art with the energetic redecoration of pre-Iconoclast churches. The mosaic of the "Madonna and Child" in the church of Hagia Sophia dates from 867. Figurative representation became increasingly stylized with the characteristic Byzantine distortion of a face – a small mouth, a long nose and huge, wide-open eyes. **The early German abbey** of Corvei was begun in 873.

**Phnom Bakheng** became the new administrative and religious centre of Cambodia during the Angkor period, 889-1434. The "mountain temple" design has a single base supporting six tower-like structures.

**During the Chola period**, 907-1053, in India, improved metal-casting techniques enabled notable achievements in figurative images, especially in portraying the complex and balanced poses of the dancing Shiva.

**An Imperial Academy** of painting was founded in western China during the Ten Kingdoms period, 907-80. **Ching Hao**, 900-60, wrote an essay on landscape painting which stressed the metaphysical implications of the art.

**Romanesque architecture** after 950 possessed a grandiose quality which derived partly from the use of stone vaults below the roofs and partly from a more unified concept of the church which developedin responseto theneeds of the clergy, monks and pilgrims who used them. Two main plans were adopted – that of an ambulatory with radiating chapels as at St Martin at Tours, 918, and the chapels on either side of the main apse at Cluny Abbey, 981.

**Plainsong notation**, which originated in Europe in the 9th century, first consisted of marks like accents over syllables to denote a rise and fall in pitch; they did not indicate by how much.

**Organum**, the practice of singing extra lines of music at intervals of a fourth or a fifth above or below plainsong, appeared in the 9th century. This was primitive polyphony.

**Pitch notation** was required to communicate to singers the relationship of two parts in an organum. A Flemish monk called **Hucbald**, 840-930, first used letters to denote pitch.

**Organs** were installed in abbeys and cathedrals of Europe by the 10th century. They were played to support parts of the organum sung by the choir, and followed the sung lines.

**The tambura**, a 4-stringed lute-shaped instrument, developed in India in the 10th century as a drone accompaniment to melodic instruments. The tambura gave a repeated chord below the melody.

**Chinese temple music** under the Northern Sung dynasty, 960-1279, involved huge choruses with orchestras of zithers and mouth organs in an organum style of complex sonority.

**Spanish metal mines** were taken over *c.* 850 by the Moors, who also prepared pure copper by reacting its salts with iron – a primitive forerunner of modern electroplating methods. **Al-Farghani**, or Alfraganus, *d.* 850, wrote the *Elements*, a summary of Ptolemaic astronomy studied in Europe until 1600. **Algebra**, as a word, first figures as al-jabr, meaning transposition, in a treatise by the Arab mathematician, **Al-Khwarizmi**, *d.c.* 850. The Arabs based their algebra on both Greek and Indian maths.

**Al-Rhazi**, a physician and encyclopedist, *d.* 920, and **Al-Khindi**, a scientist and philosopher, *d.* 873, were exceptional in objecting to alchemical and Aristotelian dogmas. They sought new concepts of the nature of motion and heat and encouraged the use of experiments to solve scientific problems. **Bardas** reorganized the University of Constantinople in 863 for the teaching of science. Soon afterwards the teaching was again suppressed by **Basil II**, *r.* 976-1025.

**Cotton and silk manufacture** was introduced into Spain and Sicily by the Moors in the 9th and 10th centuries. **Lateen sails**, triangular fore-and-aft sails which may have appeared in the eastern Mediterranean in the 2nd century, were brought to the West in the 9th century by the Arabs.

**Cordoba**, in Spain, reached its height as a centre of Islamic science in the 10th century under **Abd ar-Rahman III**, *r.* 912-61. **Optical lenses** of four kinds were described by **Than Chhiao** in China *c.* 940.

**The alembic**, an apparatus for distilling chemicals and perfumes, was illustrated in Arabic books of this time. The alembic played an important part in Arab chemistry and strongly influenced its development.

**The windmill** reached Muslim Spain from Persia in the 10th century. **Mining in Christian Europe** centred on the Harz Mountains in the 10th century, where the Saxons mined copper and iron. **Gerbert**, a French mathematician, 940-1003, who became Pope Sylvester II, is thought to have introduced the astrolabe and Arabic (Indian) numerals into Europe from Cordoba. He has also been credited with the invention of a mechanical clock in *c.* 996.

# 1000-1250 The Crusades

## Principal events

**Europe now began to take the offensive, expanding geographically and economically, her population rising. A new spirit of confidence, epitomized by the cosmopolitanism of Norman culture, brought a series of attacks on the Muslims in Spain and in Syria, where the Crusades provided an aggressive outlet for the military nobility of the flourishing feudal system. The papacy reached the height of its power during the reign of Innocent III, 1198-1216, in spite of continuing opposition to the gradual concentration of its power both from within the Church and from secular rulers.**

**In the 13th century Genghis Khan set up a Mongol Empire in China, swept across Asia and threatened Europe and North Africa, creating the largest empire ever known and bringing a new peace and unity to Asia in his wake. He did not, however, conquer India, where the various Muslim rulers built up their authority in the north.**

### 1000-25

**Basil II**, *r.* 976-1025, briefly restored Byzantine authority in Syria, Crete and south Italy and destroyed the Bulgarian army. **Canute**, 994-1035, built a unified Danish Empire comprising England, Norway and Denmark. **Mahmud**, the brilliant Muslim ruler of the Ghaznavid Empire in Afghanistan, 997-1030, plundered and annexed the Punjab. **The Chola dynasty** of Tamil kings unified southern India and took Ceylon and Bengal, 1001-24.

### 1025-50

**William I**, a vassal of the French king, became Duke of Normandy in 1035, organizing Normandy on full feudal and military lines. **The Umayyad dynasty** in Spain fell as a result of racial and religious pressures in 1031. The support of **Pope Leo IX**, *r.* 1049-54, for monastic reform stimulated the concept of papal supremacy over secular rulers. **Yaroslav**, *r.* 1019-54, brought Kievan Russia to its peak (promoting education and building.)

### 1050-75

**Ferdinand of Castile**, *r.* 1035-65, recovered Portugal from the Muslims in 1055. **William of Normandy** conquered England in 1066, while another Norman kingdom was established in southern Italy in 1068, finally ousting the Byzantines who also lost Georgia and Armenia to the Seljuk Turks, 1063-72. **The Berber dynasty of Almoravids** built a kingdom in Algeria and Morocco, 1054. **Asia Minor** fell to the Seljuks after the battle of Manzikert in 1071.

### 1075-1100

**Pope Gregory VII**, *r.* 1073-85, and Emperor Henry IV, *r.* 1056-1106, clashed on the investiture issue, over the respective rights of the Holy Roman Emperor and the papacy in appointing bishops. **The Almoravids** annexed Moorish Spain, 1086, but **Alfonso VI**, *r.* 1072-1109, retook Toledo. The First Crusade, 1096-9, captured Jerusalem and set up Frankish kingdoms in the Near East. **Alexius I**, Byzantine emperor, *r.* 1081-1118, recovered some territory in Asia Minor.

## National events

**Attracted by English wealth the Danes and Normans invaded, turning Anglo-Saxon society into a more flexible, feudal, system. Opposition to the king's authority grew among the barons and found expression in Magna Carta, while industry and town life prospered, offsetting the decline of Anglo-Saxon culture.**

**1000-25:** The English paid regular tribute to the Danes until **Canute** was generally accepted as king by the English in 1016 and appointed his leading supporters earls.

**1025-50:** **Edward the Confessor**, *r.* 1042-66, ruled England supported by the Danish earls and brought the Normans to the English court.

**1050-75:** **William I** of Normandy conquered England in 1066, bringing Cluniac reform with him and introducing a fully feudal society with grants of land for military service.

**1075-1100:** **The Domesday Book**, 1086, recorded land use and tenure in full for taxation purposes. **William I**, *r.* 1066-87, built stone castles and fostered the growth of towns.

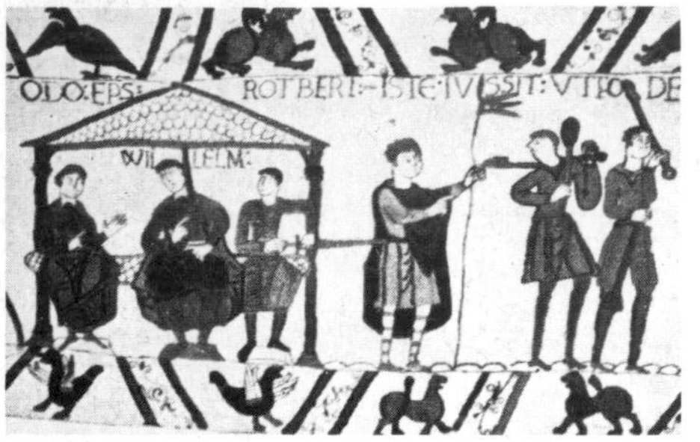


Bayeux tapestry: William the Conqueror and companions

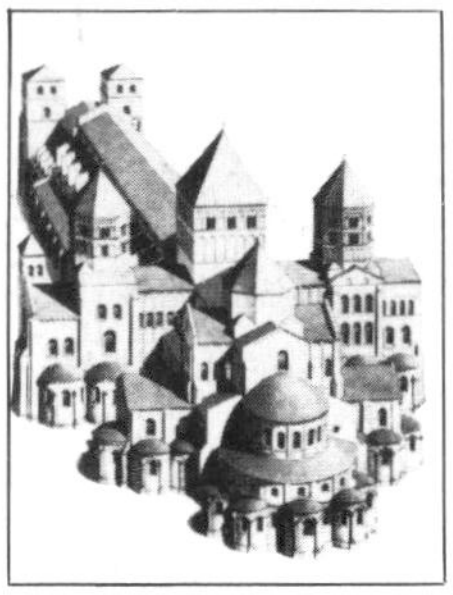

The Great Church at Cluny

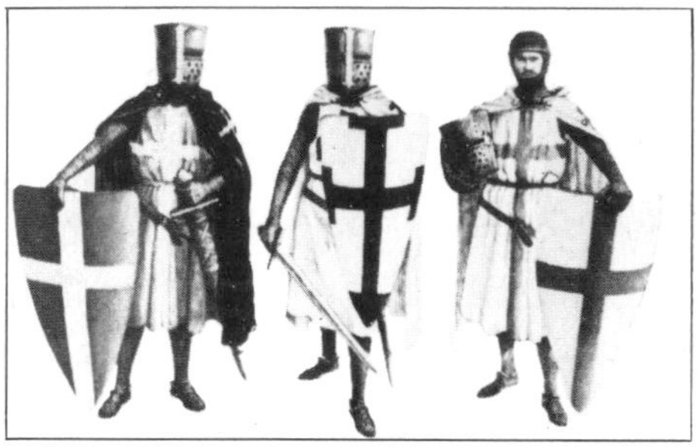

Crusading knights: Hospitaller, Teutonic Knight, Templar

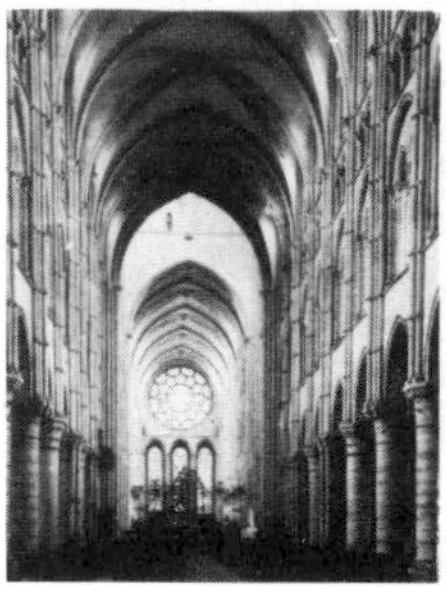

Early Gothic: Laon Cathedral

## Religion and philosophy

**In the emerging struggle for power between the Church and the rulers of the new European states, the papacy succeeded in asserting its right to judge the morality of secular political actions at the same time as it took the lead in the reform movements within the Church.**

**In both the Muslim and Christian world, there was a revival of philosophy and a return to the Greeks, especially Aristotle. This was essential to the rise of scholasticism, an important philosophical movement within the Catholic tradition, based on the notion that dialectical reasoning as well as faith and revelation could illuminate the mysteries of Christian belief.**

**The Mahayana form of Buddhism, which allowed lay salvation, spread from China to Japan. There it evolved into a popular devotional cult centred on ritual chanting, in sharp contrast to the elitist monasticism of Zen, which was also emerging within Japanese Buddhism at this time.**

**1000-25:** **Saint Symeon** (Simon), *c.* 949-1022, "The New Theologian", developed the orthodoxy within the Greek Church on meditation and revelation in a mystical direction. **Pope Benedict VIII**, *r.* 1012-24, promulgated a decree against clerical marriage and concubinage at the Council of Pavia in 1018.

**1025-50:** **Avicenna**, 980-1037, also known as Ibn Sina, was an eclectic Muslim thinker and physician. He wrote *The Book of Healing*, a monumental encyclopedia elaborating mainly Aristotelian theories of philosophy and medicine. **Buddhism** became firmly established in Tibet in 1038. **Pope Leo IX**, *r.* 1049-54, issued stern decrees against simony (the purchase of ecclesiastical office), thereby identifying the papacy with Cluniac reform.

**1050-75:** **The schism** between the papacy and the Greek Christian Church was fixed in 1054, when **Pope Leo IX** closed Greek churches in southern Italy for unorthodox practices, such as the use of leavened bread in the Mass. **Berengar of Tours**, 999-1088, argued that reason could justify the contravention of authority. He denied the doctrine later known as transubstantiation, but was finally forced to recant, 1059.

**1075-1100:** **The *Dictatus Papae*** of 1075 by **Pope Gregory VII** (Hildebrand), *r.* 1073-85, decreed that popes were able to depose emperors. **Roscelinus**, *c.* 1050-1120, was an early proponent of the scholastic tenet of nominalism, holding that the qualities we ascribe to objects, like colour, do not exist in reality but are just the product of thought or language. This led him to deny the unity of the Trinity, a position he was forced to recant at Rheims in 1092.

## Literature

**Of the European literatures, French was the most influential in the development of new literary forms in the 11th and 12th centuries, producing the *chanson de geste* in written form, the Arthurian romance tradition and the lyrical vernacular poetry of the troubadours, all of which soon became international. The common heritage of warfare against the Muslims in Spain was the subject of the French *Chanson de Roland* and also of the great Spanish epic *El Cid*.**

**In the Near East the solitary genius of Omar Khayyám flourished, while in Japan the late Heian period saw the emergence of underivative Japanese styles including the literary diary of which *The Tale of Genji*, written by a lady at court, is the best-known example.**

**1000-25:** **The greatest of all Japanese novels, *The Tale of Genji***, was written by the court lady **Murasaki Shikibu**, 978-*c.* 1031; it is an elaborate, realistic tale of court life.

**1025-50:** **The Sung period**, 960-1279, in China was mostly an age of prose. Its great writers were **Ou-Yang Hsiu**, 1007-72, and **Sung Chi**, 998-1061, who collaborated on a Confucian history, **Su Shih**, 1037-1101, widened the subject matter of tzu (song form) poetry and introduced vernacular words, thus contributing to Yan "drama", which resembled opera.

**1050-75:** **In Persia** the scientist, mathematician and poet **Omar Khayyám**, *c.* 1048-1122, wrote *The Rubaiyat* (quatrains), which expresses a rational, pessimistic and hedonistic philosophy – ideas then unacceptable to orthodox Islam. It is not certain how many of the almost 500 quatrains were written by him.

**1075-1100:** **The *chansons de geste***, epic poems consisting of a series of stanzas using a single rhyme and celebrating the history of the Age of Charlemagne, were sung by travelling musicians. The earliest written example, The *Song of Roland*, dates from *c.* 1100.

## Art and architecture

**The transition from Romanesque to Gothic architecture involved a structural and visual change in the aisled church, beginning in France and England. Separate inventions – stronger pointed arches at Cluny and rib vaults at Lessay – were then combined as in the vaults of Durham, which were supported by buttresses beneath the gallery roofs. External flying buttresses, first used at Notre Dame, allowed Gothic architecture to develop. With these the building became an independent frame in which larger windows were inserted.**

**Bar tracery produced the lovely patterns of French 13th-century architecture which spread swiftly across Europe, reaching Cologne in 1248 and England with the additions to Westminster Abbey in 1245.**

**Castles developed from the primitive motte-and-bailey to the sophisticated designs of Crusaders' permanent garrisons, such as the Krak des Chevaliers (first fortified 1110) in Syria.**

**1000-25:** **Ottonian architecture** in Germany took its cue from **St. Michael's Hildesheim** (designed apparently by Bishop Bernward) with its unvaulted double choirs and arcades of square piers alternating with round, short columns. **Dravidian architecture** reached a peak of sophistication under the Chola period in India. The great **Temple of Shiva** at Tanjore with its pyramid and dome-shaped finial profoundly influenced South-East Asian architecture.

**1025-50:** **The Muslims** raided west India between 1000 and 1026, defacing many of the temples. This led to the building of the most important **Gujarat temples** with characteristic colonnaded halls and "pyramids" of massed cupolas. **Wulfic's Rotunda of St. Augustine's Abbey**, Canterbury, 1049, marked the end of English architectural isolation, both this and Edward the Confessor's original **Westminster Abbey**, 1055-65, used Continental models.

**1050-75:** **The Byodo-in Temple**, 1053, in Japan has the brilliance and delicacy of ornament typical of the **Fujiwara** culture. The Phoenix Hall houses a wooden Amida Buddha by the contemporary sculptor **Yocho.**

**1075-1100:** **Durham Cathedral**, unlike all previous church architecture, was vaulted throughout. It used a new and more stable combination of round and pointed arches and had buttressed arches beneath the gallery roof. **The Bayeux tapestry**, *c.* 1080, whose continuous narrative describes the Norman victory over the English and the events preceding it, was sewn to adorn Bayeux Cathedral, though it was probably made in Canterbury.

## Music

**Polyphony developed further in both the religious and secular music of Europe in the Middle Ages, having long existed in folk music, particularly in Britain.**

**At the same time set musical forms, like the ballade, virelai and rondeau, evolved from songs and dances. Both developments reflected the medieval delight in uniting contrasting elements in a consistent whole.**

**1000-25:** **A cantus firmus** was used as a fixed melody about which a line of embellishment could be worked. In this could be seen the origins of counterpoint (two or more related tunes played together).

**1025-50:** **Guido d'Arezzo**, *c.* 997-*c.* 1050, advocated the use of the staff (a grid of horizontal lines) in notation and made simple rules for defining relative pitch of notes, later revived as the tonic solfa.

**1075-1100:** **Troubadours** appeared in Provence late in the 11th century, singing to their own harp accompaniment. They set stanzas of poems to music, producing complete compositions in new forms.

## Science and technology

**Arabic science and philosophy reached its height in the 11th century with the work of such major figures as Avicenna, al-Biruni and Alhazen in the Middle East and Averrhöes in Spain, but soon afterwards it declined.**

**It was at this time, in the early 12th century, that the influence of Arab science began to show in Europe with the introduction of Arabic numerals. These were used in the already powerful business world of Italy which, unlike China and the Arab lands, was to develop an economy based on money. Other signs of the power Europe was to achieve were rapid growth in the silk and glass industries in the south and the use of coal and the beginnings of cast iron manufacture in the north. This technology owed a heavy debt to Chinese expertise, brought to Europe at this stage via the Arab world but later derived directly from China, which would trade extensively with Italy after the visits of Marco Polo.**

**1000-25:** **Avicenna** (Ibn Sina), 980-1037, and al-Biruni, 943-1048, two of the greatest Arab encyclopedists of science, both lived in Persia in the early 11th century. **Avicenna** wrote on astronomy, physics and medicine, which he also practised, and his theory and methods were taught in Europe for the next 700 years. **Al-Biruni** wrote on mathematics, astronomy and astrology, geography and history, and was the first botanist to analyse the structure of flowers by methods important to plant classification.

**1025-50:** **Illustrated botanical texts** were published in China in the 11th century. These had medical as well as botanical importance since the pharmacology of drugs obtained from plants was a highly advanced science in China. **Alhazen**, or Ibn al-Haitam, *c.* 965-1038, wrote *Optical Thesaurus*, the first important work on dioptrics (the optics of the eye), which influenced the work of **Roger Bacon**, the 13th-century English scholar.

**1050-75:** **Mould boards**, curved boards on ploughs, which overturn the ploughed earth and thereby improve soil structure and aeration, came to be used in Europe from the 11th century onwards, although they had been known in China for 1,000 years. **Omar Khayyám**, *c.* 1048-*c.* 1122, a Persian poet and mathematician, solved cubic equations by geometric methods *c.* 1075, and worked at the sultan's court in Merv reforming the Muslim calendar.

**1075-1100:** **Chinese medical texts** written in the 11th century include one of a qualifying examination for doctors and enlarged editions of medical pharmacopoeias. **Alcohol** was probably first distilled from wine at Salerno in the 12th century. Although fully able to do so, the Arabs had not made alcohol because it was prohibited by the *Koran*. **Indian commentators on science** in the 11th and 12th centuries described the medical uses of yoga meditational techniques.

### 1100-25

**The Seljuk Empire** gradually split into separate regencies, 1100-25. **The Concordat of Worms**, 1122, brought a compromise to the investiture controversy. **Louis VI of France**, *r.* 1108-37, granted urban charters to many French towns, which like towns throughout Europe were growing. In **Manchuria** the Jurchen tribes overthrew the Khitai with Chinese assistance, 1116, and destroyed the Chinese Sung dynasty, 1136. **The Khmer Empire** in Cambodia reached its peak, *c.* 1100

### 1125-50

**Alfonso VII**, *r.* 1126-57, resumed the conquest of Spain while the Muslim dynasties of Spain and North Africa fought each other. After the fall of the **Frankish kingdom of Edessa** to the Seljuk Turks, 1144, the disorganized Second Crusade failed to halt the Turkish advance, 1147-9. **The communal movement** of north European towns claiming independence from royal authority reached Rouen, 1145. **Kiev** declined after the death of **Vladimir Monomach**, 1125.

### 1150-75

**Henry II of England**, *r.* 1154-89, added Aquitaine and Gascony to the Angevin Empire in France, and heightened the conflict of secular and papal authority by having **Becket**, Archbishop of Canterbury, murdered in 1170. **Saladin**, *r.* 1169-93, united the disparate Muslim tribes in Egypt and Syria under the Egyptian **Ayyubid dynasty**. **Civil war in Japan** between the local clans, 1156-81, accelerated the decline of imperial authority over the feudal magnates.

### 1175-1200

**The Seljuks** took Anatolia, 1176, and Saladin took Jerusalem, 1187, causing the Third Crusade, 1189-91, which rewon the city. **Muhammad of Ghur**, *r.* 1176-1206, took Delhi and Bihar in India. A Muslim kingdom was set up at Delhi on his death. **Yoritomo's** defeat of the Taira clan, 1185, in Japan inaugurated the Kamabura period. **Emperor Frederick I** (Barbarossa), *r.* 1152-90, was defeated by the league of Lombard towns in his invasion of Italy, 1176.

### 1200-25

**Venice**, which sought control of the eastern Mediterranean, persuaded the **Fourth Crusade**, 1202-4, to take Constantinople, after which the Latin Empire of the East was set up, 1204-61. **King John of England**, *r.* 1199-1216, lost his French lands, 1204. **Alfonso VIII**, *r.* 1170-1214, defeated the Almohads, 1212, who then declined in Africa and Spain. **The Mongols**, under **Genghis Khan**, *r.* 1206-27, had invaded China, Persia and southern Russia by 1225.

### 1225-50

**Assimilation of native ideas** by the ruling minority created a fusion of Muslim and Hindu cultures in northern India by 1230. **The Mongols** annexed the Chin Empire in China, 1234, overran eastern Europe and set up the Tatar state of the Golden Horde on the lower Volga in 1242. **Alexander Nevsky**, *r.* 1236-63, prince of Novgorod, defeated the Teutonic Knights, 1242. **Jerusalem** was finally lost to the Turks in 1244 and the Seventh Crusade, 1248-50, achieved little.

**Henry I**, *r.* 1100-35, stimulated economic development and created the first royal administration. Saxon and Norman integration was complete by 1125.

The civil war for the succession between **Stephen**, *r.* 1135-54, and **Matilda** reduced England to anarchy as the barons fought among themselves.

**Henry II**, *r.* 1154-89, reaffirmed royal authority over the barons by appointing lesser knights as sheriffs, 1170, but failed to assert his authority over the clergy.

**Henry II** reformed the common law, introducing the jury system, but **Richard I**, *r.* 1189-99, failed to develop Henry's policies.

**John**, *r.* 1199-1216, flagrantly ignored baronial interests and was forced to sign Magna Carta in 1215, subjecting the monarchy to the rule of law.

**National sentiment** developed among the nobility and townsmen in opposition to the pro-papal attitudes and expensive foreign policies of **Henry III**, *r.* 1216-72.

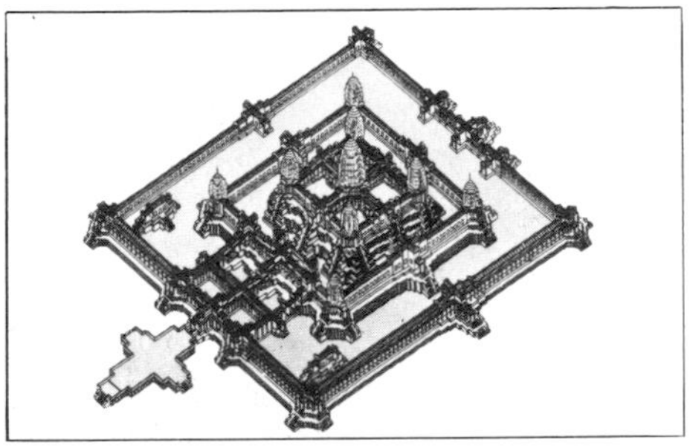

Classical Khmer architecture: temple at Angkor Wat

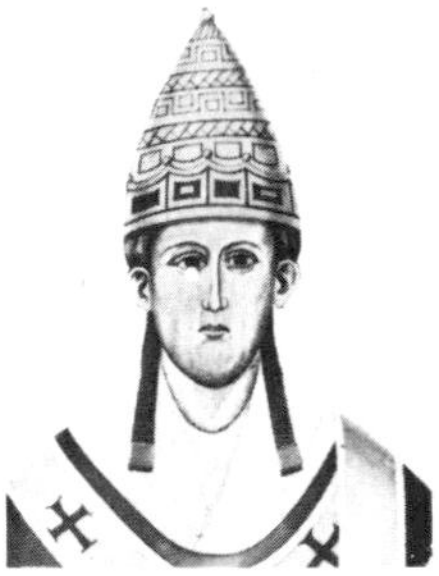

Pope Innocent III

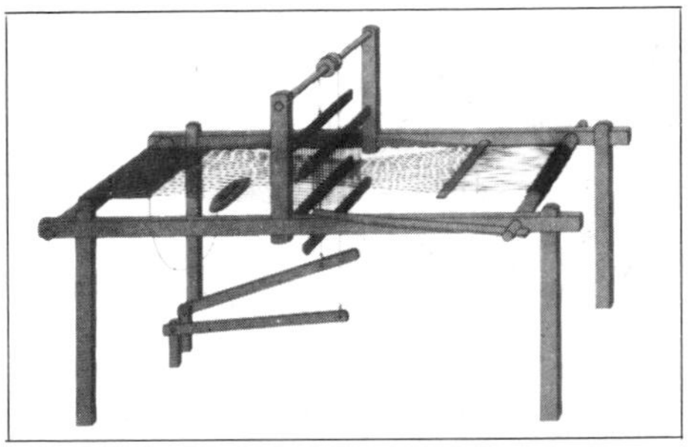

European treadle loom, 13thc.

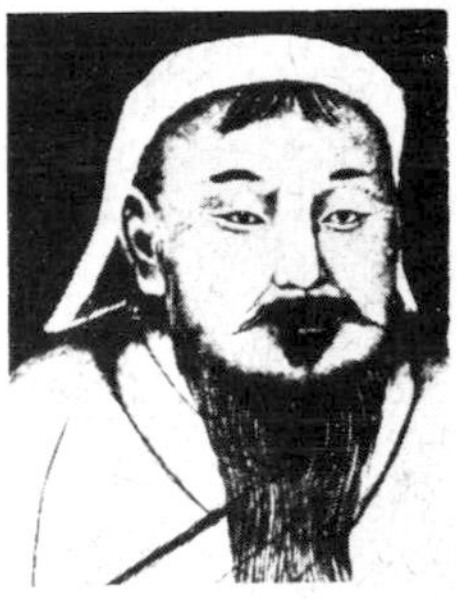

Genghis Khan

**St. Anselm**, Archbishop of Canterbury 1093-1109, one of the first scholastic philosophers, sought to establish the existence of God by reason, arguing that God must necessarily exist since He is perfect and it is more perfect to exist than not. **Peter Abelard**, 1079-1142, French theologian and philosopher, advocated reason as a source of truth. His nominalist ideas led to his condemnation at the Synod of Soissons in 1121 for his views on the Trinity.

**St. Bernard**, 1090-1153, Cistercian Abbot of Clairvaux in France, strongly encouraged mysticism and contemplation in opposition to the scholastic rationalism prevalent in Western Christendom. **Honen**, 1133-1212, founder of the Pure Land Sect in Japan, joined the **Tendai Sect** in 1148. He later proclaimed that the only way to salvation was **Nembutsu** (calling the name of the Amida Buddha). **Gratian**, a Benedictine monk, compiled the *Decretum Gratiani*, a collection of canon law *c.* 1140.

**Averrhöes**, 1126-98, the Islamic scholar, began writing his influential commentaries on Aristotle in 1169. He also argued that reason could serve to establish religious truths. **The Waldenses**, founded by **Peter Waldo** in 1170 in southern France, rejected the licence of the official Church and adopted a simple way of life, electing their own priests.

**Zen Buddhism** was introduced into Japan in 1191 by the monk **Eisai**, 1141-1215. Zen stressed personal instruction by a master, rather than the study of scriptures, as the way to enlightenment. His techniques included sudden physical shocks and meditation on paradoxical statements. **Neo-Confucianism** emerged in the 12th century in China. **Chu-Hsi**, 1130-1200, one of its most influential exponents, completed his commentaries, *The Four Books*, in 1189.

**Islam** became firmly entrenched in India with the establishment of the Delhi kingdom in 1206. **The True Pure Land Sect** (Jodo Shin) was founded in Japan in 1224 by **Shinran**, 1173-1262. For him, salvation came only through faith and the Buddha's grace. Because it rejected monasticism and ascetic practices, this became, and still is, the largest Buddhist sect in Japan.

**The Franciscan and Dominican orders of friars**, devoted to the care of the poor and the sick, spread quickly, 1225-30. **Nicherin**, 1222-82, a Japanese Buddhist monk, added a highly nationalist element to Japanese Buddhism. By 1250 he had proclaimed the *Lotus Sutra*, the central writing of the Mahayana tradition, as the supreme Buddhist scripture. He desired to end Buddhist sectarianism in order to regenerate and unify Japan against the threat of Chinese invasion.

**A miracle play was performed at Dunstable** *c.* 1100. In such Latin plays, performed in churches and drawing on both the scriptures and the lives of saints, lie the roots of the medieval drama as later practised.

**The first bardic period of Hindi literature** began in India. Among the important early epics is the *Prithvi Rah Raso.*

**The lyrical poetry of the troubadours** grew up in 12th century France. Written in a Provençal dialect and sung to music, it lauded a concept of love as a knightly duty then fashionable in the southern French courts. ***Mystère d'Adam*** *c.* 1175, marks a major development towards popular drama; it is in French, not Latin, uses the vernacular and was later played outdoors.

**The long Middle High German epic *Nibelungenlied***, which has survived in thirteenth-century manuscripts, was written by an unknown Austrian; its hero is Siegfried, it has connections with Scandinavian legends and has influenced many writers and composers, notably Wagner. **Chrétièn de Troyes**, *fl.* 1165-80, developed the prose romance in *Cliges and Lancelot.*

**The German minnesinger tradition**, parallel to the Provençal courtly poetry, is exemplified in the songs of **Walther von der Vogelweide**, *c.* 1170-1230, a wanderer and a beggar. He discarded the older strict form, as did his contemporary, **Wolfram von Eschenbach**, *c.* 1170–*c.* 1220, author of the great German romance, the grail-story *Parzival*, *c.* 1210.

**The Icelandic Classical period** culminated in the work of **Snorri Sturluson**, 1179-1241, who wrote the *Edda*, a handbook which set out the Icelandic myths and the types of poetic diction used in old Norse poetry. **Literature in Japan** declined with the Kamakura period, 1192-1333, but war tales, especially the *Heike monogatari*, *c.* 1215-50, became an established form.

**Chinese landscape painting** reached its zenith under the patronage of **Hui Tsung**, *r.* 1101-25. Great care was lavished on tiny details in an attempt to reveal the inner life of the objects shown. Li Chieh's treatise on **Sung architecture** is a blend of learning and practical instruction on survey geometry, uses of building materials and decorations, and includes recipes for coloured glazes for floor and roof tiles.

**At Autun Cathedral in France Gislebertus** sculpted all the nave capitals, *c.* 1125-35, the west door tympanum depicting the Apocalypse. **Abbot Suger** rebuilt the choir and westwork of **St. Denis**, near Paris, *c.* 1140-44. The first example of mature Gothic, its slender pillars and pointed arches allowed big lancet windows with stained glass in the apse chapels; statues adorned the porch.

**A change in the design of Cistercian monasteries** followed the death of **St Bernard of Clairvaux** in 1153. After the harsh simplicity of **Fontenay**, built in 1139, **Clairvaux III**, 1153, and **Pontigny** apse, *c.* 1185, are richer and more imposing. **External flying buttresses**, first used at Notre Dame, Paris, *c.* 1163, enabled clerestory as well as ground-floor windows to be treated as a frame, with a thin web of stone and glass between.

**In the second Angkor period** the Cambodian capital of **Angkor Thom** was rebuilt, 1181-95, followed by temples in **Angkor Wat**. The ashlar façades were deeply carved to resemble gigantic faces. **High Gothic architects** used the new construction techniques to varied aesthetic ends and made structure itself ornamental. Most important were **Chartres** and **Bourges**, 1195, **Canterbury** 1174, and **Lincoln**, 1192.

**The Chimu** subdued the Peruvian Tiahuanaco culture *c.* 1200. Adobe buildings at **Chan Chan**, the capital, have trapezoidal doors and intricate geometrical surface designs. Pottery played an important part in decoration. **An international style** known as **Rayonnant Gothic** was born in 1220 at Amiens Cathedral. **The massive "Black Pagoda"**, a Jain temple of the sun, was begun at Kanarak in Orissa *c.* 1200. Only the base, carved with erotic reliefs, survives.

**The Sainte Chapelle**, Paris, was built, 1240-8, as **St Louis'** palace chapel and to house the Crown of Thorns relic. The walls are like continuous sheets of glass and made the design a symbol of prestige.

**Three- and four-part polyphony** was composed round a *cantus firmus*, but early in the 12th century two parts were more usual. The harmony often used sounds dissonant to modern ears.

**Trouvères** in northern France developed on similar lines to the troubadours, producing *formes fixes* (set structures of contrasting phrases), among them the ballade, virelai and rondeau.

**The *conductus*** developed as processional music in a chordal style late in the 12th century. Composed for voices or instruments, it was based on original themes rather than plainsong.

**The minnesinger** created a tradition of German song inspired by the art of the troubadours. Notre Dame choir school in Paris flourished under the great masters Léonin and Pérotin.

**Muslim rule** in northern India after 1206, strengthened secular music and featured the use of the **sitar**. Southern Indian music remained restrained and classical, favouring the **vina.**

**"Sumer is icumen in"**, an English song of astonishing form, written *c.* 1240, was the first recorded canon. It is a four-part round over a two-part repeated pattern in the bass parts.

**Silk manufacture** began in south Italy in the 12th century as a result of Arab influence and by the 13th century water-powered silk mills were in operation. **Stained-glass windows** of the early 12th century demonstrate the high-level glass technology found in Europe. Glass was coloured by the addition of particular metal salts: those of copper for green; copper or gold chloride for red; iron or silver for yellow and cobalt for blue.

**Coal** was used at Liège for iron smelting after about 1150.

**Averrhöes**, or Ibn Rushd, 1120-98, the leader of Arabic science and the major encyclopedist of his day, worked in Cordoba. His scientific writings maintained the authority of Aristotle. **Maimonides**, 1135-1204, the greatest medieval Jewish thinker, worked at the court of Saladin and wrote on medicine, theology and philosophy. He described diseases and cures in a way which we now recognize as that of psychosomatic medicine.

**Stückofen**, the precursors of blast furnaces, operated in Styria, central Europe, as early as the 13th century. These furnaces, 3 or more metres high, burned charcoal, which produced a reducing atmosphere suitable for iron- and steel-making. **Cast iron**, made by melting and moulding the metal, was first produced in Europe in the 13th century. It was made possible by higher furnace temperatures. **Old London Bridge** and the Avignon bridge were built *c.* 1175.

**Leonardo Fibonacci**, the greatest medieval mathematician, wrote the first Western textbook on algebra in about 1200. **Universities** founded in Europe in the early 13th century included those of Paris and Oxford. **Roger Bacon**, *c.* 1214-92, was one of the few important experimenters in medieval English science. He had an extensive knowledge of astronomy and medicine and employed lenses to correct defective vision.

**Frederick II**, Holy Roman emperor, *r.* 1212-50, a serious student of natural science, wrote a treatise on falconry that is a model of natural history for its combined learning and observation. **Stern-mounted rudders** were first fitted to European ships at this time, although the Chinese had invented them centuries earlier. **Navigational charts** came to be first used by Western sailors in the 13th century.

# INDEX

# Bibliography

**Africa**
Fage, J. D.; *Cambridge History of Africa;* Cambridge U.P., 1978
Freeman-Grenville, G. S.; *Chronology of African History;* Oxford U.P., 1973
Shinnie, P. L.; *African Iron Age;* Oxford U.P., 1971
**Americas**
Lanning, E. P.; *Peru Before the Incas;* Prentice-Hall, 1968
Weaver, M. P.; *Aztecs, Maya and their Predecessors;* Seminar, 1972
**Asia**
  *General*
Reischauer, E. O. & J. K. Fairbank; *E. Asia; Great Tradition;* Allen & Unwin, 1961
Schumann, H. W.; *Buddhism;* Rider, 1973
Spuler, B.; *History of the Mongols;* Routledge, 1972
  *China*
Fitzgerald, P.; *Ancient China;* Elsevier, 1978
Fung Yu-Lan; *Short History of Chinese Philosophy;* Routledge, 1948
Liu Wu-Chi; *Confucius: His Life and Time;* Greenwood, 1972
Loewe, M.; *Everyday Life in Early Imperial China;* Transworld, 1973
Yap, Y. & A. B. Cottrell; *Early Civilization of China;* Weidenfeld & Nicolson, 1975
  *India*
Spear, P.; *History of India II;* Penguin, 1970
Thapar, R.; *History of India I;* Penguin, 1969
Watson, F.; *Concise History of India;* Thames & Hudson, 1975
Wheeler, Sir M.; *Indus Civilization;* Cambridge U.P., 1968
Woodruff, P.; *Men Who Ruled India: The Founders,* Cape, 1963
  *Islamic Empire*
Hayes, J. R. (Ed.); *Genius of Arab Civilization;* Phaidon, 1976
Holt, P. M. et al.; *Cambridge History of Islam;* Cambridge U.P., 1971 (2 vols)
  *Japan*
Morris, I.; *World of the Shining Prince;* Oxford U.P., 1964
**Europe**
  *General*
Bloch, M.; *Feudal Society;* Routledge, 1965 (2 vols)
Dodd, C. H.; *Founder of Christianity;* Collins, 1971
Hale, J. R. et al. (Eds.); *Europe in the Late Middle Ages;* Faber, 1970
Lach, D. F.; *Asia in the Making of Europe;* Univ. of Chicago Press, 1965–70 (2 vols)
McNeill, J. T.; *Celtic Churches: History 200–1200;* Univ. of Chicago Press, 1974
Mayer, H. E.; *Crusades;* Oxford U.P., 1972
Postan, M. M. (Ed.); *Cambridge Economic History of Europe;* Cambridge U.P., 1963–66 (2 vols)
Sawyer, P. H.; *Age of the Vikings;* E. Arnold, 1975
Wallace-Hadrill, J. M.; *Barbarian West;* Hutchinson, 1967
  *Britain*
Chadwick, N. K.; *Celts;* Penguin, 1971
Cunliffe, B.; *Iron Age Communities in Britain;* Routledge, 1974
Lennard, R.; *Rural England 1086–1135;* Oxford U.P., 1959
Loyn, H. R.; *Anglo-saxon England and the Norman Conquest;* Longman, 1970
Patourel, J. le; *Norman Empire;* Oxford U.P., 1977
Renfrew, C. (Ed.); *British Prehistory;* Duckworth, 1974
Richmond, Sir I.; *Roman Britain;* Penguin, 1970
Ross, A.; *Pagan Celtic Britain;* Cardinal, 1974

Wallace-Hadrill, J. M.; *Early Germanic Kingship;* Oxford U.P., 1971
Whitelock, D.; *Beginnings of English Society;* Penguin, 1971
Wilson, R. J. A.; *Guide to the Roman Remains in Britain;* Constable, 1975
  *Byzantine Empire*
Runciman, Sir S.; *Byzantine Civilization;* Methuen, 1975
  *France*
Evans. J.; *Life in Medieval France;* Phaidon, 1969
  *Greece*
Andrewes, A.; *Greek Society;* Penguin, 1971
Bowra, C. M.; *Periclean Athens;* Weidenfeld & Nicolson, 1971
Chadwick, J.; *Mycenaean World;* Cambridge U.P., 1976
Finley, M. I.; *Ancient Greeks: Life and Thought;* Penguin, 1971
Fox, R. L.; *Alexander the Great;* Futura, 1975
Hammond, N. G. L.; *History of Greece to 322BC;* Oxford U.P., 1967
Hood, S.; *Minoans;* Thames & Hudson, 1971
Lloyd, G. E. R.; *Early Greek Science;* Chatto, 1970
Lloyd, G. E. R.; *Greek Science after Aristotle;* Chatto, 1973
Meiggs, R.; *Athenian Empire;* Oxford U.P., 1972
Taylour, W.; *Mycenaeans;* Thames & Hudson, 1964
  *Rome*
Bloch, R.; *Origins of Rome;* Thames & Hudson, 1960
Brunt, P. A.; *Social Conflicts in the Roman Republic;* Chatto, 1971
Charlesworth, M. P.; *Roman Empire;* Oxford U.P., 1968
Heer, F.; *Charlemagne and his World;* Weidenfeld & Nicolson, 1975
Homo, L.; *Roman Political Institutions;* Paul, 1929
Keller, W.; *Etruscans;* Cape, 1975
Parker, H. M. D.; *History of the Roman World 138–337;* Methuen, 1958
Scullard, H. H.; *From the Gracchi to Nero;* Methuen, 1976
Stobart, J. C.; *Grandeur That Was Rome;* Sidgwick & Jackson, 1971
**Middle East**
  *General*
Bruce, F. F.; *Israel and the Nations;* Paternoster, 1973
Singh, P.; *Neolithic Cultures of Western Asia;* Seminar, 1974
  *Babylon and Assyria*
Jastrow, M.; *Civilization of Babylon and Assyria;* Arno, 1976
Laessoe, J.; *People of Ancient Assyria;* Routledge, 1963.
  *Egypt*
Aldred, C.; *Egyptians;* Thames & Hudson, 1961
Aldred, C.; *Egypt to the End of the Old Kingdom;* Thames & Hudson, 1965
Edwards, I. E. S. et al (Eds.); *Cambridge Ancient History I & II;* Cambridge U.P., 1971–75
Gardiner, A. H.; *Egypt of the Pharaohs;* Oxford U.P., 1961
  *Hittites*
Macqueen, J. G.; *Hittites and their Contemporaries in Asia Minor;* Thames & Hudson, 1975
  *Medes and Persia*
Olmstead, A. T.; *History of the Persian Empire;* Univ. of Chicago Press, 1958
  *Phoenicia*
Herm, G.; *Phoenicians;* Gollancz, 1975
  *Sumeria*
Kramer, S. N.; *Sumerians: History, Culture and Character;* Univ. of Chicago Press, 1971

## Major contributors and advisers to The Joy of Knowledge

Fabian Acker CEng, MIEE, MIMarE; Professor Leslie Alcock; Professor H. C. Allen MC; Leonard Amey OBE; Neil Ardley BSc; Professor H. R. V. Arnstein DSc, PhD, FIBiol; Russell Ash BA (Dunelm), FRAI; Norman Ashford PhD, CEng, MICE, MASCE, MCIT; Professor Robert Ashton; B. W. Atkinson BSc, PhD; Anthony Atmore BA; Professor Philip S. Bagwell BSc(Econ), PhD; Peter Ball MA; Edwin Banks MIOP; Professor Michael Banton; Dulan Barber; Harry Barrett; Professor J. P. Barron MA, DPhil, FSA; Professor W. G. Beasley FBA; Alan Bender PhD, MSc, DIC, ARCS; Lionel Bender BSc; Israel Berkovitch

PhD, FRIC, MIChemE; David Berry MA; M. L. Bierbrier PhD; A. T. E. Binsted FBBI (Dipl); David Black; Maurice E. F. Block BA, PhD(Cantab); Richard H. Bomback BSc (London) FRPS; Basil Booth BSc (Hons), PhD, FGS, FRGS; J. Harry Bowen MA(Cantab), PhD(London); Mary Briggs MPS, FLS; John Brodrick BSc(Econ); J. M. Bruce ISO, MA, FRHistS, MRAeS; Professor D. A Bullough MA, FSA, FRHistS; Tony Buzan BA(Hons) UBC; Dr Alan R. Cane; Dr J. G. de Casparis; Dr Jeremy Catto MA; Denis Chamberlain; E. W. Chanter MA; Professor Colin Cherry DSc(Eng), MIEE; A. H. Christie MA;

FRAI, FRAS; Dr Anthony W. Clare MPhil(London), MB, BCh, MRCPI, MRCPsych; Professor Aidan Clarke MA, PhD, FTCD; Sonia Cole; John R. Collis MA, PhD; Professor Gordon Connell-Smith BA, PhD, FRHistS; Dr A. H. Cook FRS; Professor A. H. Cook FRS; J. A. L. Cooke MA, DPhil; R. W. Cooke BSc, CEng, MICE; B. K. Cooper; Penelope J. Corfield MA; Robin Cormack MA, PhD, FSA; Nona Coxhead; Patricia Crone BA, PhD; Geoffrey P. Crow BSc(Eng), MICE, MIMunE, MInstHE, DIPTE; J. G. Crowther; Professor R. B. Cundall FRIC; Noel Currer-Briggs MA, FSG; Christopher Cviic BA(Zagreb),

BSc(Econ, London); Gordon Daniels BSc(Econ, London), DPhil(Oxon); George Darby BA; G. J. Darwin; Dr David Delvin; Robin Denselow BA; Professor Bernard L. Diamond; John Dickson; Paul Dinnage MA; M. L. Dockrill BSc(Econ), MA, PhD; Patricia Dodd BA; James Dowdall; Anne Dowson MA(Cantab); Peter M. Driver BSc, PhD, MIBiol; Rev Professor C. W. Dugmore DD; Herbert L. Edlin BSc, Dip in Forestry; Pamela Egan MA(Oxon); Major S. R. Elliot CD, BComm; Professor H. J. Eysenck PhD, DSc; Dr Peter Fenwick BA, MB, BChir, DPM, MRCPsych; Jim Flegg BSc, PhD, ARCS, MBOU; Andrew M.

Fleming MA; Professor Antony Flew MA(Oxon), DLitt (Keele); Wyn K. Ford FRHistS; Paul Freeman DSc(London); G. S. P. Freeman-Grenville DPhil, FSA, FRAS, G. E. Fussell DLitt, FRHistS; Kenneth W. Gatland FRAS, FBIS; Norman Gelb BA; John Gilbert BA(Hons, London); Professor A. C. Gimson; John Glaves-Smith BA; David Glen; Professor S. J. Goldsack BSc, PhD, FInstP, FBCS; Richard Gombrich MA, DPhil; A. F. Gomm; Professor A. Goodwin MA; William Gould BA(Wales); Professor J. R. Gray; Christopher Green PhD; Bill Gunston; Professor A. Rupert Hall DLitt; Richard Halsey BA(Hons, UEA); Lynette K. Hamblin BSc; Norman Hammond; Peter Harbison MA, DPhil; Professor Thomas G. Harding PhD; Professor D. W. Harkness; Richard Harris; Dr Randall P. Harrison; Cyril Hart MA, PhD, FRICS, FIFor; Anthony P. Harvey; Nigel Hawkes BA(Oxon); F. P. Heath; Peter Hebblethwaite MA (Oxon), LicTheol; Frances Mary Heidensohn BA; Dr Alan Hill MC, FRCP; Robert Hillenbrand MA, DPhil; Catherine Hills PhD; Professor F. H. Hinsley; Dr Richard Hitchcock; Dorothy Hollingsworth OBE, BSc, FRIC, FIBiol, FIFST, SRD; H. P. Hope BSc(Hons, Agric); Antony Hopkins CBE, FRCM, LRAM, FRSA; Brian Hook; Peter Howell BPhil, MA(Oxon); Brigadier K. Hunt; Peter Hurst BDS, FDS, LDS, RSCEd, MSc(London); Anthony Hyman MA, PhD; Professor R. S. Illingworth MD, FRCP, DPH, DCH; Oliver Impey MA, DPhil; D. E. G. Irvine PhD; L. M. Irvine BSc; E. W. Ives BA, PhD; Anne Jamieson cand mag(Copenhagen), MSc (London);

Michael A. Janson BSc; G. H. Jenkins PhD; Professor P. A. Jewell BSc (Agric), MA, PhD, FIBiol; Hugh Johnson; Commander I. E. Johnston RN; I. P. Jolliffe BSc, MSc, PhD, ComplCE, FGS; Dr D. E. H. Jones ARCS, FCS; R. H. Jones PhD, BSc, CEng, MICE, FGS, MASCE, Hugh Kay; Dr Janet Kear; Sam Keen; D. R. C. Kempe BSc, DPhil, FGS; Alan Kendall MA(Cantab); Michael Kenward; John R. King BSc(Eng), DIC, CEng, MIProdE; D. G. King-Hele FRS; Professor J. F. Kirkaldy DSc; Malcolm Kitch; Michael Kitson MA; B. C. Lamb BSc, PhD; Nick Landon; Major J. C. Larminie QDG, Retd; Diana Leat BSc(Econ), PhD; Roger Lewin BSc, PhD; Harold K. Lipset; Norman Longmate MA(Oxon). John Lowry; Kenneth E. Lowther MA; Diana Lucas BA(Hons); Keith Lye BA, FRGS; Dr Peter Lyon; Dr Martin McCauley; Sean McConville BSc; D. F. M. McGregor BSc, PhD(Edin); Jean Macqueen PhD; William Baird MacQuitty MA(Hons), FRGS, FRPS; Professor Rev F. X. Martin OSA; Jonathan Martin MA; Rev Cannon E. L. Mascall DD; Christopher Maynard MSc, DTh; Professor A. J. Meadows; Dr T. B. Millar; John Miller MA, PhD; J. S. G. Miller MA, DPhil, BM, BCh; Alaric Millington BSc, DipEd, FIMA; Rosalind Mitchison MA, FRHistS; Peter L. Moldon; Patrick Moore OBE; Robin Mowat MA, DPhil; J. Michael Mullin MA; Alistair Munroe BSc, ARCS; Professor Jacob Needleman, John Newman MA, FSA; Professor Donald M. Nicol MA PhD; Gerald Norris; Professor F. S. Northedge PhD; Caroline E. Oakman BA(Hons, Chinese); S. O'Connell MA(Cantab),

MInstP; Dr Robert Orr; Michael Overman BSc; A. R. D. Pagden MA, FRHistS; Professor E. J. Pagel PhD; Liam de Paor MA; Carol Parker BA(Econ), MA (Internat. Aff.); Derek Parker; Julia Parker DFAstrolS; Dr Stanley Parker; Dr Colin Murray Parkes MD, FRC(Psych), DPM; Professor Geoffrey Parrinder MA, PhD, DD(London), DLitt(Lancaster); Moira Paterson; Walter C. Patterson MSc; Sir John H. Peel KCVO, MA, DM, FRCP, FRCS, FRCOG; D. J. Penn; Basil Peters MA, MInstP, FBIS; D. L. Phillips FRCR, MRCOG; B. T. Pickering PhD, DSc; John Picton; Susan Pinkus; Dr C. S. Pitcher MA, DM, FRCPath; Alfred Plaut FRCPsych; A. S. Playfair MRCS, LRCP, DObst, RCOG; Dr Antony Polonsky; Joyce Pope BA; B. L. Potter NDA, MRAC, CertEd; Paulette Pratt; Antony Preston; Frank J. Pycroft; Margaret Quass; Dr John Reckless; Trevor Reese BA, PhD, FRHistS; M. M. Reese MA (Oxon); Derek A. Reid BSc, PhD; Clyde Reynolds BSc; John Rivers; Peter Roberts; Colin A. Ronan MSc, FRAS; Professor Richard Rose BA(Johns Hopkins), DPhil (Oxon); Harold Rosenthal; T. G. Rosenthal MA(Cantab); Anne Ross MA, MA(Hons, Celtic Studies), PhD, (Archaeol and Celtic Studies, Edin); Georgina Russell MA; Dr Charles Rycroft BA (Cantab), MB(London), FRCPsych; Susan Saunders MSc(Econ); Robert Schell PhD; Anil Seal MA, PhD(Cantab); Michael Sedgwick MA(Oxon); Martin Seymour-Smith MA(Oxon), MA(Oxon); Professor John Shearman; Dr Martin Sherwood; A. C. Simpson BSc; Nigel Sitwell; Dr Alan Sked; Julie and

Kenneth Slavin FRGS, FRAI; Professor T. C. Smout; Alec Xavier Snobel BSc(Econ); Terry Snow BA, ATCL; Rodney Steel; Charles S. Steinger MA, PhD; Geoffrey Stern BSc(Econ); Maryanne Stevens BA(Cantab), MA(London); John Stevenson DPhil, MA; J. Sidworthy MA; D. Michael Stoddart BSc, PhD; Bernard Stonehouse DPhil, MA, BSc, MInst Biol; Anthony Storr FRCP, FRCPsych; Richard Storry; Charles Stuart-Jervis; Professor John Taylor; John W. R. Taylor FRHistS, MRAeS, FSLAET; R. B. Taylor BSc(Hons, Microbiol); J. David Thomas MA, PhD; D. Thompson BSc(Econ); Harvey Tilker PhD; Don Tills PhD, MPhil, MIBiol, FIMLS; Jon Tinker; M. Tregear MA; R. W. Trender; David Trump MA, PhD, FSA; M. F. Tuke PhD; Christopher Tunney MA; Laurence Urdang Associates (authentication and fact check); Sally Walters BSc; Christopher Wardle; Dr D. Washbrook; David Watkins; George Watkins MSc; J. W. N. Watkins; Anthony J. Watts; Dr Geoff Watts; Melvyn Westlake; Anthony White MA(Oxon), MAPhil(Columbia); Dr Ruth D. Whitehouse; P. J. S. Whitmore MBE, PhD; Professor G. R. Wilkinson; Rev H. A. Williams CR; Christopher Wilson BA; Professor David M. Wilson; John B. Wilson BSc, PhD, FGS, FLS; Philip Windsor BA, DPhil(Oxon), Roy Wolfe BSc(Econ), MSc; Donald Wood MA PhD; Dr David Woodings MA, MRCP, MRCPath; Bernard Yallop PhD, BSc, ARCS, FRAS Professor John Yudkin MA, MD, PhD(Cantab), FRIC, FIBiol, FRCP.

170